L A

CULTURE A

LAOS
CULTURE AND SOCIETY

EDITED BY

GRANT EVANS

SILKWORM BOOKS

ISBN–10: 974-87090-4-3
ISBN–13: 978-974-87090-4-8

First published in 1999 by
Silkworm Books
6 Sukkasem Road, Suthep, Chiang Mai 50200, Thailand
E-mail: info@silkwormbooks.info
www.silkwormbooks.info

Cover photograph: Luang Prabang © 2001 by Vithi Panichpan
Set in 10 pt. Garamond

Printed by O. S. Printing House, Bangkok

10 9 8 7 6 5 4

CONTENTS

Religion & Ritual

Language & Literature

EDITOR'S FOREWORD

This is the first book in forty years which sets out to study the culture and society of Laos. *Présence au Royaume Lao* edited by René de Berval in 1956 as a special issue of *France-Asie*, was the last text that provided many and varied essays on Laos and its people.[1] In 1970 a group of intellectuals in Vientiane began the irregular publication of the *Bulletin des Amis du Royaume Lao* which lasted until the collapse of the Royal Lao Government in 1975. This journal contained many excellent essays on Laos, and its special issue on Lao Buddhism (no. 9, 1973) remains a benchmark for the study of Buddhism in Laos. The revolution, whose final *coup de grace* occurred on 2 December 1975, ruined this fledgling intelligentsia. More than twenty years on, intellectual life in Laos has still not recovered.

Much of what has been written on Laos has, understandably, focused on political developments, firstly as the Lao people were caught up in the maelstrom of the "Vietnam" war, in which Cambodia and Laos were unfortunate "sideshows." And then after 1975, all attention was on the political, economic and social changes introduced by the victorious communists throughout Indochina. The bamboo curtain descended and access to all of these countries by outside researchers became difficult, particularly for in-depth research of the sort that anthropologists like to do. Pure luck enabled me to slip under the bamboo curtain in the early 1980s and produce a case study of the failure of state-directed social and economic change among Lao peasants (Evans 1990). All other studies, however, such as the indispensable ones encouraged or executed by Martin Stuart-Fox were, of necessity, largely accomplished at a distance.

In the late 1980s the curtain began to lift, and aid workers, academics, and other outsiders began to gain unprecedented access to all regions of Laos. Having operated under the highly restrictive and controlled conditions of Laos during its period of "high communism" I was flabbergasted by the ease with which I was able to travel to Houaphan in 1988 to begin the research that is reported in chapter 6 of this book. Many other researchers have streamed into Laos since then and been able to conduct proper research on social and cultural changes taking place in the country. This book is the result.

Of course, the questions which interest academic enquiry move with the times, and the essays in this volume reflect a much greater circumspection vis-à-vis essentialist ideas of "culture" and "nation" compared with the 1950s volume, or even with writings produced ten years ago. My opening essay "What is Lao Culture and Society?" is indicative of this new mood, as are Søren Ivarsson's, Ing-Britt Trankell's, Peter Koret's, and Nick Enfield's essays stressing the way cultures are created and produced rather than existing as ahistorical essences. In a sense, these essays are "post-nationalist," something which makes me acutely aware of the fact that Laos has hardly even produced a coherent nationalist *ouevre*. Yet, the comfortable assumptions of such an *oeuvre* are already being taken apart by intellectual developments beyond Laos. But here, once again, the Lao are suffering the consequences of the repression of genuine intellectual life in the country during the past two decades.

None of the following chapters are complacent. How could they be, given the complex regional environment in which Laos finds itself, as shown by Jonathan Rigg and Randi Jerndal? Significantly, it is women traders who are engaged in these wider networks, as explored here by Andrew Walker, who challenges some conventional assumptions concerning gender relations in Laos.[2] A larger world is also the stage for Siambhaivan Sisombat Souvannavong's unique essay on Lao elites in exile, their return to Laos, and their engagement in a diasporic business culture. The essays on ethnic minorities by myself, and Khampheng Thipmuntali, raise perplexing questions about the nature of social and cultural change in "multiethnic" Laos, while my essay on Lao ethnography examines the ways minorities have been studied. Ing-Britt Trankell provides a fascinating account of the negotiation of old and new meanings in the rituals enacted in Louang Prabang, while Leedom Lefferts focuses on the ambiguous role of women in Lao Buddhist ritual. The essays on literature and language by Peter Koret and Nick Enfield are excellent studies of cultural change, but neither of them come to simple conclusions about the future of either the Lao language or its literature.

This book is the first crop of the new scholarship on Lao culture and society. We can only hope that political, social, and cultural change inside Laos itself will create an atmosphere that will produce more Lao intellectuals who can contribute to the second crop, and subsequent studies. Out of this a genuine dialogue may then occur between those born in Laos and those of us who are wedded to the place.

I would like to thank Craig Reynolds who scrutinized the text on behalf of the publisher and whose critical comments helped improve it. Finally, I would like to thank our publisher, Trasvin Jittidecharak, a Thai who is committed to promoting studies of Laos.

Grant Evans
Hong Kong
May 1998

1. This was later published in English as the *Kingdom of Laos* in 1959.
2. See also Ireson (1996).

CONTRIBUTORS

Nick Enfield is a Research Fellow in the Language and Cognition Group, Max Planck Institute for Psycholinguistics, The Netherlands. Contact: Nick.Enfield@mpi.nl

Grant Evans is reader in anthropology in the Department of Sociology, University of Hong Kong, PRC. He has written extensively on Laos, and on Southeast Asia. His latest book on Laos is *The Politics of Ritual and Remembrance: Laos since 1975* (Silkworm Books, 1998). Contact: hrnsgre@hkucc.hku.hk

Søren Ivarsson recently completed his doctoral research at the Nordic Institute of Asian Studies, Copenhagen, Denmark. He has authored several essays on Thai literature and history and an NIAS report on Laos. Contact: ivars@coco.ihi.ku.dk

Randi Jerndal is a lecturer in geography at the University of Götenborg, Sweden, through which she has published a monograph *Modernization Without Development? Implementing Market Economy in Laos* (1997). Contact: randi.jerndal@geography.gu.se

Peter Koret lectures in Thai and Lao language and literature at Arizona State University in Tempe, Arizona, USA. He has published several important essays on Lao and Thai literature, and currently he is working on an annotated translation of a Lao poem, *San Leup Phasun* and its interpretation in the twentieth century. Contact: borapet@imap2.asu.edu

H. Leedom Lefferts, Jr. is associate professor in anthropology at Drew University, New Jersey, USA. He is coauthor with Mattiabelle Gittinger of *Textiles and the Tai Experience in Southeast Asia* (Textile Museum, Washington, D.C., 1992). Contact: lleffert@drew.edu

Jonathan Rigg is senior lecturer in geography at the University of Durham, UK. He has written widely on Southeast Asia. His latest book is *Southeast Asia: The Human Landscape of Modernization and Development* (Routledge, 1997) Contact: j.d.rigg@durham.ac.uk

Si-ambhaivan Sisombat Souvannavong is a doctoral candidate in sociology at the University of Paris, and a director of Inside Asia, Vientiane, Lao PDR. Contact: inasia@loxinfo.co.th

Khampheng Thipmuntali is a researcher in the Institute of Culture, Vientiane, Lao PDR. Contact: P.O. Box 5246, Vientiane, Lao PDR.

Ing-Britt Trankell is associate professor in the Department of Cultural Anthropology at the University of Uppsala, Sweden. She has written *Cooking, Care, and Domestication: A Culinary Ethnography of the Tai Yong, Northern Thailand* (Uppsala University, 1995). More recently, she has published on Cambodia. Contact: Ing-Britt Trankell@antro.uu.se

Andrew Walker is a post-doctoral researcher in anthropology at the Research School of Pacific and Asian Studies, Australian National University. He has recently published *The Golden Boat* (Anthropology of Asia Series: Curzon, 1999). Contact: ajwalker@cres.anu.edu.au

INTRODUCTION:
WHAT IS LAO CULTURE AND SOCIETY?

1

GRANT EVANS

O NE of the paradoxes of studying Laos is that even those people most engaged in its affairs have questioned whether Laos exists as a "real" national entity. Veteran commentator on Lao politics, Arthur Dommen, says it is more a conglomeration of "tribes" than a people (1971: 17). One of the best writers on the "Vietnam" war, Bernard Fall, described Laos as "neither a geographical nor an ethnic or social entity, but merely a political convenience" (1969: 23). Arthur M. Schlesinger Jr., in *A Thousand Days* (1967: 302), his account of the Kennedy years, repeats this idea: "It [Laos] was a state by diplomatic courtesy." Jean Lateguy, in his novel *The Bronze Drums*, has one of his characters say: "The French are preventing them [the Vietnamese] from gobbling up Laos. Laos is a paradise, as I told you in Paris. Only, like Paradise, Laos doesn't exist; it's a figment of the imagination of a few French administrators" (1967: 147). Or a recent reviewer of several books on Laos writes: "Crafted out of an all-too-common colonial desire to geographically delineate what had previously been an ever-mutating group of petty Kingdoms and vassal states, Laos's borders enjoy scant congruence with the people it envelops, or in the many cases, divides" (Freeman 1996: 431). Journalistic commentary repeats these ideas *ad infinitum.*

Behind many of these statements lies the idea of "natural" nations rather than historical ones. This ideological view of the nation insists on a lineage that stretches far back into the mists of time instead of Laos's past discontinuity.

Martin Stuart-Fox has made a valiant attempt to confront these problems in an article which tries to establish the basis for writing a history of Laos. He recognizes the all too obvious political disunity of Laos over time, but he argues: "The discontinuity of central political structures was overcome by the continuity of political culture based firmly at the village level, anchored in the socio-religious Lao world-view" (Stuart-Fox 1993: 113). So, he argues, continuity is based in culture and society. Unfortunately, he never spells out what he means by a distinct Lao culture and society, and, as many of the essays in this volume argue, such an effort would face all sorts of problems.

One way some people have approached the issue is to ask about the origins of the term Lao. According to Lawrence Palmer Briggs (1949: 63), "Some writers maintain the Lao was the original generic name" for the Tai. This is based on various extrapolations from ancient Chinese texts where the terms Ngai-Lao and Ai-Lao can be found.[1] "The use of the term *Lao*, or *Laotian*, seems not to have generally extended, in early years, further than to the people of southern Nan Chao and northern Laos. The use of *Lao* is confusing because, while it is now specifically applied to a specific Tai people—called Laotians by the French—another branch, not especially close to the Laotian, has been called Ngai-lao, or Ai-lao; while the name has sometimes been used as synonymous with *Tai*. Recently, an attempt has been made to extend it to the Lawas, who are quite a different people" (1949: 63).[2] He further suggests: "The first definite appearance of the Laotians in history seems to be in the inscription of Rama Khamheng in 1292, when that king enumerated Louang Prabang and Vientian among his conquests" (1949: 65).

The attempts to connect Lao to the Lawa that Briggs mentions perhaps refers to the work of the Thai nationalist ideologue, Luang Vicit Vaathakaan, who in the early 1930s wrote:

> Lawa were called by various terms, such as *Lua* and *Lao*; but the Lao (Lawa) should not be confused with the people who are now called Lao at present. The Lao (Lawa) have been nearly lost, except those who are now living in the forest villages of Northern Thailand. Those whom we call Lao nowadays are in fact Thai, who have been genetically mixed with Lawa; that is why they are called *Lao*.[3]

The accuracy of this claim will have to be left to historians, but as shall be suggested further on in this chapter, such genetic mixing is common to all the Tai groups, not just the Lao. And we will see that this theme of racial purity/impurity plays a significant role in emerging French and Thai perceptions of the region.

For a nationalist historian like Maha Sila Viravong, whose *History of Laos* ([1959] 1964: 9) is one of the first major attempts to write a Lao history in the form that has become *de rigeur* for modern nations, his overriding concern was to place the Lao as far back in time as is possible:

> The word "Lao" has the following meanings:
>
> 1. An American professor [a missionary], Mr. Clifton Dodd said that the word Lao means big or a tall person, thus leading us to believe that the Lao race is a very large one and has had a great civilization with a high degree of moral virtue in ancient times.
>
> 2. His Highness Thammathira-Rajamahamuni has indicated in his monthly newspaper that the word Lao might have derived from the word Dao which means sky of the highest point because the Lao had the preference for the highlands in China to build their homes and considered themselves as highly civilized, drawing their roots from Then Thien, Thai etc., . . . which also means sky.
>
> 3. As far as I am concerned, the word Lao derived from the words Long, Lee, Lung or Lwang and the word Lwang itself could very well become Luang which, in turn, means big or civilized.
>
> In any case, our Lao race had come into existence in the universe at the same time as the Chinese and can be considered on this ground as one of the most ancient races of the world which had known a wide range of splendor and progress no less than any other races of the same era.

What is so striking about Maha Sila's text is the paucity of evidence used to back up his strong assertions about the Lao—but in this regard his book is typical of the genre. After all, this new style of historical record keeping was the way the modern world constructed its charter myths, and neither evidence nor interpretation could be allowed to get in the way of such mythmaking.

Houmphanh Rattanavong, the director of the Institute of Culture under the Ministry of Information and Culture in Vientiane, has argued in a like manner that the term Lao comes from the Ailao kingdom (circa 3 B.C.–2 B.C.) mentioned in Chinese chronicles and asserts that "Some people and Ailao sub-groups have kept their original and ethnic name" (1995: 267). Both the Thai and the Lao come from what he calls the "Ailao family group", and he goes on: "Therefore, although the people belonging to the ethno-linguistic Lao-Tai group have the same origin, they do not exactly have the same culture, traditions, and ways of life. Each people and sub-group has its own specific culture, way of life, and national identity. I speak of the "Siamese" people rather than the "Thai" people, to emphasize the fact that each culture has its own identity and characteristics" (1995: 266–7).[4] Unfortunately for Houmphanh, the so-called "Ai-lao family group" (as I have noted already) has a shadowy existence at best.

In the very influential *Ethnic Groups of Mainland Southeast Asia,* Le Bar et al. provide a few more cultural referents:

> **Lao:** This term is apparently of Siamese origin, referring to Tai speakers to the north and northeast of the central Chao Phraya plain, distinguished by their preference for glutinous rice; by certain differences in the style of their Buddhist architecture, religious script, and terminology; and by an historical tradition common to the various middle Mekong principalities which persisted up to the intervention of the French and Siamese Tai. When the French extended their control to the banks of the Mekong, they took over this Siamese term for the Tai-speaking inhabitants and adopted the term Laos for the protectorate they created. In this sense, the term Lao is practically synonymous with the Tai-speaking population of what was once the old kingdom of Lan Xang (Le Bar et al. 1964:188).

Georges Condominas in his insightful, influential surveys of Lao culture has also drawn attention to the fact that: "The movements of history have resulted in a double paradox on Laos as a state and on the Lao as an ethnic group . . . the Lao represent only one half of the population of the state which bears their name . . . *the independent Lao, even today, number less than a million while the Lao of Siam represent a mass of five million. . ."* (Condominas 1970: 9–10). But while Condominas in his work has provided insightful ethnographic accounts of the Lao, are they sufficient to provide the *differentia specifica* of a continuous Lao "nation" that Stuart-Fox, for example, is seeking for?

Perhaps we should turn briefly to the problem of the Thai northeast which, as we may deduce from Le Bar et al.'s reference to the extent of the kingdom of Lane Xang and Condominas's comments, forms the basis for Lao irredentist dreams. Again and again in academic and other commentary one will find references to the Lao-Thai border as being "artificial." For example, Le Bar et al. (1964: 215), write: "An artificial boundary between the Lao on the right and left banks of the Mekong was created by the French . . ." But, within a nationalist optic, the absurdity of the boundary was in the eye of the beholder—that is, it was just as artificial to the Thai as to the Lao, or even the French. As Keyes notes: "Many French officials agreed with the Siamese, albeit for different reasons, about the essential absurdity of the division of the Lao areas on ethnic grounds. Several of these officials argued strongly for French expansion into the Khorat Plateau since the people of this area were also "Lao." But the period of French expansion was over . . ." (Keyes 1967: 12). Keyes's study demonstrates how this region was gradually absorbed into the modern Thai state and how it came to be identified geographically as Isan, the Northeast, rather than ethnically.

Indeed, once the Thai state realized that they could not dislodge the French, state officials were encouraged, especially from the royalist-nationalist sixth reign onwards, to use the term Thai for all peoples in the kingdom and the term Lao was suppressed. In a recent collection of essays on regionalism in Thailand, Grabowsky (1995: 107) reluctantly admits that "although 'Isan' had originally been a Siamese invention in order to concede the non-Siamese identity of most of the region, it is nowadays used as a self-designation by the region's Lao and Khmer inhabitants who prefer to call themselves *khon Isan* ('people of the northeast')." Grabowsky who calls this a Siamese colonialist term, goes on: "Ethnic Lao count for almost 80% of the northeastern population. Yet, the Lao are not homogenous, but divided into several linguistic sub-groups. Apart from the Lao Wiang, significant numbers of Phuan, Phu Tai, Yo and various smaller groups live in the northeast" (1995: 108). But doesn't he open up a pandora's box of problems as soon as he admits that the "Lao are not homogenous"?

However, before we can deal with the problem of "who are the Lao?" and other associated problems like, "who are the Thai?" we first need to move into a more theoretical register.

CULTURE AND SOCIETY: THEORETICAL REFLECTIONS

IN the recent very productive debates on the nature of nationalism by historians, anthropologists, sociologists, and others, one thing has become very clear—we in the modern world are so steeped in the assumptions of nationalism that we find it very difficult to think outside its terms. Most probably the understanding of the title of this book by most of its readers is that it refers exclusively to the people of the nation-state called Laos. We unreflexively think in national units.

The general field of Tai studies is also dogged by the problem. This field is derived from an ethnolinguistic definition of a broader Tai "culture area" which encompasses groups in southern China, northern Vietnam, northern Burma, northern India, Laos, and Thailand. But an ambiguity at the center of this project is enacted every couple of years at the International Conference of Thai Studies at which papers on all Tai groups are given, but the name of the conference is derived from one nation-state—Thailand. Of course, the country changed its name from Siam to Thailand in 1939 at a time when the world was confronted with upsurges of megalomaniacal nationalisms, from Berlin to Tokyo, and the name Thailand was coined in an attempt to will into existence a nationalist dream of uniting all Tai under one state, thereby fulfilling at least one common nationalist credo that ethnic/racial groups should coincide with a state. This Pan-Thai reverie was not realized, but it continues to haunt Tai studies. Indeed, in the mid-1990s, Chatthip Nartsupa still felt compelled to explicitly distance his project on the "Comparative Study of Tai Societies and Cultures" from this early ogre: "We do not want to expand the Thai nation-state, with the implication of Pan-Thai-ism of which we have been accused. In fact, we oppose the state, all states in this region. We want to lay out a network of all Tai communities" (1996: 15).[5] Houmphanh Rattanavong gave vent to his unease at the Thai Studies Conference in Kunming:

> The term 'Thai', which itself constitutes a central theme of our conference, and which has served to designate all the members of the ethno-linguistic group of the 'Lao-tai', has undergone a slippage of meaning and displacement of role, since the word 'Thailand' has seen the light of day. And since this rather generic term is used to designate the citizens of Thailand instead of 'Siamese', one presently no longer knows when saying or writing 'Thai' which Thais are meant—whether Thais in general including Laos, or Thais, the inhabitants of Thailand? And when one says to us, 'The Laos are Thais', we have the impression that one accuses us of being Siamese, and are offended (1990: 162).

Thus Lao sensibilities, among others, continue to smart under Thai hegemony, and part of the "nationalist" purpose of Houmphanh's paper was to demonstrate that the word "Lao" predates the word "Thai" and is, he implies, generic.

But if Lao sensibilities are offended because an ethnic term is conflated with a nation-state name, they have not shown similar sensitivity internally where the use of the ethnic term Lao for the name of the state means that Hmong, for example, also have to call themselves Lao—Lao-Hmong or Lao Sung. In early February 1996 I monitored an e-mail billboard on precisely this matter among refugees from Laos which debated whether a pamphlet being produced in the US should use the term "Lao" or "Laotian" to refer to people from Laos. As one contributor tried to explain Lao would refer to the "ethnic majority of Laos" while Laotian "refers to all 'citizens' of Laos." For this he was swiftly attacked. "To me, calling Lao people "Laotian" is an insult . . . a term imposed on us in times of our subjugation; therefore if we continue to use that term, we're more or less intellectually enslaved." He went on to say that Laotian does not include other ethnic groups, and advises Hmong to "distinguish themselves" by using "Lao Hmong or Hmong Lao." He continues: "I painfully acknowledge that it is the fate of our country that she falls so low for the last two hundred years that other ethnic groups residing in Laos come to think of themselves differently" (3/2/96). This latter point was quickly confirmed in a reply from a Hmong who saw the idea of "Lao Hmong" as "insulting." "Hmong is Hmong always and forever . . . I will always be a Hmong wherever I live—in Laos, China, France, or Thailand. I cannot afford to be 'half' American or 'half' Lao and 'half' Hmong as the terms 'Hmong Lao' or 'Hmong American' suggests" (4/2/96). The conflation of an ethnic term with a nation is a problem common to Thailand, Laos, Vietnam, China, Cambodia, and Burma, among others, and minorities within them are always and inevitably reminded of their difference from the ethnic majority. Yet, the conflation of an ethnic designation with a state could be considered as part of the "natural" logic of nationalism. The multiethnic or multinational country of Laos has attempted to get around this by a tripartite definition of its population, roughly designating all ethnolinguistic Tai groups as "Lao Loum" (lowland Lao); Mon-Khmer and Austronesian groups as Lao Theung (midland Lao); and Tibeto-Burman and Hmong-Yao groups as Lao Soung (highland Lao). But the use of geographical terminology to register ethnic difference is already an important sign of a conceptual difficulty, while the Lao prefix only serves to entrench the centrality of the ethnic Lao to the definition of Laos. In Vietnam and China they attempt to get around the problem by designating the dominant ethnic group as Kinh in Vietnam, and as Han in China. Yet in both these cases the terms Vietnamese and Kinh, and Han and Chinese, are interchangeable for most people. In Thailand, however, officially one is only a Thai.

As Ernest Gellner (1983) among others has pointed out, it has been a common assumption of nationalism that nation and state should coincide. The fuzzy term "nation," of course, has bundled into it all sorts of assumptions about society and culture, especially the idea that they somehow are coterminus and have have clear boundaries. The fact that this is almost never so is surely one of the most intriguing paradoxes of nationalist ideology. But as both Anderson (1991) and Hobsbawm (1990) argue it is the role of nationalist movements to make people imagine that this is so, and for the states that they capture to try to make it so. This lack of coincidence between nation and state, of course, is a source of potentially endless disputes between neighboring states and a source of irredentist fantasies.

Wolf suggests that the very idea of a bounded society and culture was one advanced by the emerging modern state against the categories of premodern states and societies.[6] This created a situation where politicians and sociologists, for example, felt able to say that society is "a group of interacting individuals sharing the same territory and participating in the same culture"—a definition Wolf cites from a mid-1970s sociology textbook. In other words, it reproduced an idea very close to one of the central assumptions of nationalism.

Jack Goody has also sounded a note of caution over our common uses of the concept of culture. He asks: "Who is sharing what? At the abstract level of meanings and values I share with some, even well outside my own society, but not with others with whom I share a language and political allegiance" (1993: 18). He draws our attention to important differences in values between social groups in a society to the point where social interaction between them becomes quite uncomfortable. Elite classes from different societies may find themselves more at ease with one another than with their own lower classes, and vice versa—a situation which was certainly true in premodern times.

There is still a lot of conceptual slippage even in these critiques of preexisting uses of the idea of culture and society, not least in the ambiguities carried by the continued use of the terms themselves. This is because there is an awareness that there are significant variations in the way peoples in the world organize and conceptualize their lives both contemporarily and historically, and the concepts of society and culture have attempted to delineate these. Indeed, it is for this reason that I cannot think of any means by which we can do without them, but it is clear that the use of these concepts needs to be refigured and reoriented. In particular, they both need to be disengaged from any assumption that there is a simple homology between these concepts and the territorial state. Yet the latter has left its indelible imprint on the way we conceptualize cultural "boundaries," as if they are something like state boundaries, rather than perhaps the slow shading of one thing into another.

In the modern world only occasionally do we come across territorial borders that mark radical shifts between cultures and societies, and even then mixed populations almost always overlap such borders to a greater or lesser degree. One thinks of the northern frontiers of China where the historically very different ways of life of of nomadic herders, such as the Mongolians, and the settled way of life of the Han gave rise to distinct cultural complexes. Or, the border between Vietnam and Cambodia which, despite wet rice agriculture, involves a significant shift socially and culturally, compared with say the Cambodian and Thai border, or the Lao and Thai border.

CULTURE AREAS AND REGIONS

CONSEQUENTLY, the alternative I would propose as the overarching concept for "Tai Studies," and therefore for studies of Laos or Thailand, is the that of "culture area." Adam Kuper has written: "Culture areas are defined in part by historical relationships, and they may exhibit profound continuities despite superficial changes. Structural continuities within a region may signal shared roots, though local variants may be shaped by direct interactions, exchanges, even confrontations between communities . . ." (1992: 13). For a while the idea of culture areas fell into abeyance in anthropology partly because of confusions about how "coherent" such an area should be, and what "traits" to consider essential. One can see in this the problem of culture writ large. The greater interaction between history and anthropology in recent years has, however, historicized cultures and societies and made us aware of the problems associated with essentialist notions of culture that, as Goody remarks, "stripped societies down to supposedly continuing elements, to themes and patterns that persisted through all adversity, immaterial components that no bomb could destroy . . ." (1993: 17).

Sidney Mintz in a recent discussion of the Carribean has revived and reformulated Alfred Kroeber's concept of the *oikoumenê* (originally used by the Greeks to refer to the inhabited world). In Kroeber's view it constituted "a great historic unit . . . a frame within which a particular combination of processes happened to achieve certain unique results . . . an interwoven set of happenings and products which are significant equally for the culture historian and for the theoretical anthropologist." For Mintz (1995: 297) this idea is useful for understanding the creation of the initally diverse Carribean because, historically, "the imperial intentions of its rulers, even though those rulers taken together, represented different cultures with different ideologies" welded together the fates of these peoples. Perhaps it was something like this idea that Charles F. Keyes was striving towards when he produced his important work of synthesis *The Golden Peninsula: Culture and Adaptation in Mainland Southeast Asia* (1977), but which provides no theoretical basis for combining discussions of Vietnam with the "Theravada Buddhist Societies," besides their geographical location in mainland Southeast Asia. The perspective advanced by Mintz would suggest that at a certain level (to be established), particular regions make up congruous historical and conceptual units and any attempt to abstract from this discrete societies inevitably produces a distortion in our understanding. Not only do states and societies within such regions influence each other through a process of interaction, they exchange aspects of culture and indeed share aspects of culture across societal and political boundaries. For example, historically, Vietnamese interaction with the states of mainland Southeast Asia was more intense and sustained than China's, and as Woodside (1971) has shown, this interaction helped shape the Vietnamese state's view of itself. But the Vietnamese state was also more fundamentally linked into another *oikoumenê*, that dominated by the Chinese imperial state and was anchored in an East Asian culture area.[7]

As I intimated above, the idea of a culture area would appear to have the same problems as the idea of a culture, inasmuch as we need to be able to delimit it somehow. But if we are able to sufficiently de-link the concepts of society and culture from that of the state, an extremely difficult enterprise when the modern state is doing its utmost to tie them both more closely to it, then perhaps we may be able to develop a useable concept of culture area.

We can begin by first examining the underlying linguistic assumptions of Tai Studies. In this field we find a typical conceptual slide wherein the term "ethno" is hyphenated with "linguistic" to conjure into existence something like a Tai culture area, seen most clearly in "ethnolinguistic" maps. A map of "Thai Speaking Ethnic Groups" published in 1985, for example, tends to produce this illusion.[8] But can we conflate language with culture? Some people clearly think that you can. Recently Chatthip Nartsupha (1996: 15) has outlined such a framework as a basis for studying Thai cultural history and its relationship with other Tai groups. "The most obvious evidence of this relationship is language. The structure of language is the structure of thought, of the spiritual spirit which could link us back to various Tai communities even though they may reside outside Thailand." This statement, of course, is saturated with the assumptions of an older linguistic anthropology guided by the Sapir-Whorf hypothesis, which argued that the semantic structures of different languages carried with them a distinctive world view. In its most extreme formulations, these semantic structures were incommensurable. This whole approach was strongly challenged by the cognitive sciences in the 1960s and the universalistic theories of linguists like Noam Chomsky. More recent anthropological linguistics has tried to stake out an intermediate position which, while conceding that there are linguistic univerals, tries to inflect these by paying attention to linguistic and cultural difference. This research has drawn attention to the contextually sensitive nature of meaning, from which it "follows that we can't think of a 'world view' as inherent in a language, somehow detached from all the practices established for its use" (Gumperz and Levison 1991: 621). In other words language is considered first and foremost as an instrument of communication rather than an instrument of thought, and for this one needs communal "encyclopedias." As Clark (1996: 353) concludes: "Yes, people who speak differently think differently, but much of the correspondence comes from the common beliefs, assumptions, practices, and traditions in the communities to which they belong. There can be no communication without commonalities of thought. But there can be thought, even commonalities of thought, without communication." If we accept these achievements of modern linguistics then we have to reject Chatthip's strong assumption that linguistic affinity therefore implies a cultural affinity between various Tai speaking groups.[9] Indeed, some years ago, Wolters (1982: 4) warned students of Southeast Asian history that: "Linguistic similarities were not in themselves cultural bridges."

Of course, it may be a reasonable initial assumption to suppose that groups speaking a linguistically similar language have some affinity or had at least some contact in the past. Again it has been the work of historical linguists who have proposed hypotheses about the historic migrations of Tai groups out of what is now southern China, in particular the province of Guangxi, and into Vietnam, Laos, Thailand, and so on.[10] But these migrations took place a full millenium ago, and inbetween times many of the "original" Tai groups have been radically transformed by Chinese or Vietnamese culture, and are culturally Sinitic, and indeed reject claims that they are Tai.[11] Among the Zhuang, for example, religious orientation, family organization, and architectural styles and layout of villages have more in common with Han Chinese than with Lao. Indeed, as the modern Chinese state has strengthened its influence in these areas young people are becoming more fluent in Mandarin than in Zhuang.

The extent and process of the Tai migrations require much closer historical scrutiny than they have received to date. Leach in his Burma highlands study rejected ideas of "fabulous large-scale military conquest" by Tai groups. He writes: "Shan culture . . . is an indigenous growth resulting from the economic interaction of small-scale military colonies with an indigenous hill population over a long period . . . Large sections of the peoples we now know as Shans are descendants of hilltribesmen who have in the recent past been assimilated into the more sophisticated ways of Buddhist-Shan culture" (1970: 39). Writing of the Tai in Indochina, Condominas has argued: "where they succeeded in consolidating their power, the Thai were able to strengthen their position through a thorough policy of "Tai-ization" of the subjugated population . . ." (1990: 45). And Leach has argued elsewhere that the processes of linguistic dispersal have complex and diverse causes, and do not necessarily require mass migrations. Thus, for example, "the development of Romance languages was not a response to any movements of peoples. Romans from Italy did not move in large numbers to outer fringes of the empire. Trade and slavery and the administrative convenience of small numbers of bureaucrats had quite as much influence on who spoke what to whom as any form of migration" (Leach 1990: 231). Thus the evolution of Thai/Tai cultures across the region are best approached through their specific localized histories rather than by references to origins.

But just as linguists like to construct a proto-Tai language, so some ethnographers and historians have tried to conceive of an "original" Tai culture which could form the basic substratum of all Tai groups. Some hoped that the Black Tai would provide the royal road to such an original cultural complex, and they believed it was somehow located in beliefs in territorial spirits which predated the so-called "foreign" creed of Buddhism. On the other hand Maspero's (1981) work on Chinese religion used precisely these beliefs among the Black Tai to try to understand ancient Chinese culture![12] Obviously such an approach is seriously problematic; the Tai end up being a subcategory of the Han Chinese (or vice versa).[13]

The idea of protolanguages, especially those conceived of as somehow pristine, is challenged by Leach (1990), and more recently by Chris Hutton (1998). Hutton explores the development of linguistic theories that end with the "mother-tongue fascism" of the Nazi linguists, showing how the idea of some past linguistic unity produces as its corrollary theories of dialects and migrations by which this initial linguistic "purity" was diluted, dispersed, or lost altogether. Nationalism, and of course extreme nationalism, gave a special role to linguistics in tracing and accounting for deviations from a supposed pure linguistic source, and to charting the boundaries of a language family. The problem for ideas of protolanguages or mother tongues is that these boundaries are unclear and unstable, and they are not exclusive to one ethnic or racial group (Jews spoke German fluently, for example). As Hutton writes: "The notion of mother-tongue in combination with structuralist organicism implied that if one could not identify the boundary, one could not define a centre or origin either" (1998: 299). Some historical linguists place great faith in tracing phonetic shifts from an assumed protolanguage to give "histories" of migrations, mapped as branching family trees. The generalizing of this model and its appropriateness for specific linguistic situations has been challenged by Dixon (1997) who also points to the dependence of archaeologists and others on this model for historical reconstructions "without stopping to ask whether it is soundly based, and whether it is accepted by the majority of linguists" (Dixon 1997: 43). He points out that there can be no "pure" protolanguage, and further that linguistic diffusion across languages may be equally important for explaining linguistic change. The structuralist assumptions of historical linguistics have also been questioned by Thomason and Kaufman (1988) who, by insisting on locating languages in society and history, question abstract models of phonetic and other linguistic changes. As Dixon points out, assertions are often made where the historical record is scant, however the closer we come towards the present and the more we actually know about the linguistic practices of particular peoples, the more problematic assumptions about regular linguistic change become. People's actual use and pronunciation of languages is in fact much more complex than a number of historical linguists assume, some of whom claim to be able to tell us how a language was spoken thousands of years ago and by whom! Linguistics, however, cannot by itself provide some solid scientific base on which we can construct a mighty scaffold of cultural history.

Language exists in history, like culture, and does not stand above it as an ahistorical "proto" essence any more than an alleged Thai essence or Chinese essence. The picture of linguistic change or standardization is complex, even for China, with its long history of a self-concious literate bureaucracy. As John Ballard has argued: "the dialects of South China cannot be accounted for as mere dialectal variants of Mandarin (in some sense); rather they seem to represent linguistic traditions that have been more or less influenced by the standard language of the various capitals, that is, Mandarinized. Thus, Wu, Cantonese, Chu, and Min, traditionally regarded as being divergent dialects derived from Ancient Chinese (Archaic, in the case of Min), actually represent separate linguistic traditions that have incorporated much Chinese material" (1981: 167). And as a further note of caution for those who place their faith in the unidirectional assumptions of historical linguists, he argues that "the non-Chinese linguistic features incorporated into the Chinese spoken in this area would be regarded as Chinese . . . Moreover migrations would have kept the social situation in flux, so that linguistic influences would have constantly moved north and south" (1981: 170). In the much less self-consciously literate Thai/Tai areas, such an argument would apply even more forcefully.

Clearly, culture cannot be understood by isolating single traits or by hypothesizing supposed "original" features. What we require is both a more complex and a more dynamic conception of culture, but one nevertheless that deals with an identifiable field of research.

IS THERE A TAI CULTURE AND SOCIETY?

THE question becomes, therefore, is it possible to elaborate the main principles which order Tai societies? And do these principles undergo radical transformations over time? For example, Georges Condominas in his seminal essay on Tai political systems, describes how the *muang* as a political idea was a basic organizing principle of Tai communities as they migrated, conquered other groups, and organized occasional federations of *muang*. For some of these migrating groups this principle was later transformed by Hindu-Buddhist ideas of kingship into the "galactic polity" or "mandala" polity with the emergence of the Buddhist kingdoms which stretched from the Sipsong Panna down to the Chao Phraya delta.[14] Then with the growth of modern nationalism this principle became effective mainly as a religious or imaginary one. Whether one is looking back through time, or across certain groups of Tai today, this broad principle in its various mutations is recognizable. But, one might argue, similar principles were common to other Southeast Asian polities, such as Burma or Cambodia, or insular Southeast Asia (Errington 1989), and marked the region off from East Asia. Indeed, other cultural features are spread across this region, such as the various performances and artistic expressions derived from the Ramayana (Iyengar 1994), giving any traveler from Vientiane to Java or Bali a sense of cultural continuity, despite Islam in the former and Hinduism in the latter.

Of course, one might want to argue that this latter unity was a later "foreign" import from India and that an earlier period would have seen a clearer unity just among the Tai. But, how far back would such speculation have to go? Significant sections of Tai in what is now southern China were already in contact with Sinitic civilizations and partially Sinicized by the time Indian influence spread to Southeast Asia. Such problems of infinite regression, however, are built into the logic of theories of an original protoculture.

The bizareness of the suggestion that Buddhism is "foreign" in places like Laos or Thailand where emically it is almost universally considered fundamental to these peoples' identity, highlights the potential derangements possible within the logic of nationalism.[15] In real historical cultures as against imaginary pure cultures, borrowing and diffusion takes place continuously, although at different levels of intensity. What was once foreign becomes, over a few generations, hallowed custom. This is especially true if the foreign customs or creeds are adopted by state elites who then propagate them in their societies. This is what occurred with Theravada Buddhism in mainland Southeast Asia.

The influence of India on the evolution of several Tai societies has been, of course, fundamental. As has been pointed out by all major historians of the region, it was India which supplied them with their initial model of statecraft. Writing in the mid-1950s George Cœdès (1959: 20) while claiming that "the State of Laos" was founded by prince Fa Ngoum in 1353, argued that although Laos had taken various influences and blended them into a harmonious whole, what was crucial was that it had "inherited Indian culture in its various forms." Laos "has formed and still forms a march or out-post of Indian culture which the Laotians, who had become its champions, defended against the pressure of the Sino-Vietnamese populations. Laos has continued to carry out her mission as defender of Indian civilization and a rampart against Chinese invasion . . ." (1959: 23). Perala Ratnam (1982: 23) takes a similar view: "With Cambodia to its south, it rightly forms an important element of the 'Indo' part of Indo-China." The contrast with China, of course, draws an important line between those Tai who came under the sway of India, and those Tai who were increasingly encompassed by the Sinitic world, who were not Theravada Buddhists and for whom the cultural traditions of the Ramayana, for example, were foreign.

The formation of the Hindu states and the domestication of Theravada Buddhism was a fundamental watershed in the evolution of the Tai. By contrast, the Sinicized Tai only ever achieved loose confederations of *muang*, and any tendencies of these to evolve into states were quickly dashed by the Chinese or Vietnamese. From this time onwards, I would argue, the differences between the Tai in the Theravada Buddhist societies (the latter has become a commonly used category) and the Sinicized Tai are as significant culturally as those between, say, Lao and Khmer, and perhaps even more so. While the latter share a great number of cultural features one might also argue that the linguistic barriers between them are no greater than the linguistic barriers between a Lao and a Nung or a Zhuang.

It is also true, however, that Khmer populations shade off into Thai or Lao populations, and vice versa, and Lao shade off into Black or Red Tai, and beneath all of this there are even more ethnic overlays. As I suggested earlier, only occasionally do we find comparatively abrupt ethnic frontiers, such as with the Khmer and the Vietnamese, or the Lue in Sipsong Panna and the Chinese. The Sinicized Tai are something of a cultural buffer zone. Thus among the Black Tai we find houses raised on stilts and other features of material culture which overlap with the Lao, and we find a still basically bilateral system of kinship organization, and shared myths such as that of Khun Bulom, all of which facilitates two-way traffic between the groups. By the time we meet Tai groups who are even more Sinicized, however, the cultural dissimilarities begin to outweigh the similarities. Of course, on the ground, anthropologists have observed all sorts of individual compromises being made as people move between groups. But this is easier in some cases than in others. It is important to note that differences are not necessarily conceptualized as ethnic or racial, but simply practical. Thus Sinitic families which consider in-marrying women as potentially disruptive outsiders who need to be tamed by the mother-in-law are likely to repel young women who in Lao culture are fundamentally insiders, and so on.

Thus I would argue that the culture area which encompasses the Lao and the Thai is defined first and foremost by a common history as Hinduized states and Theravada Buddhism. Such a culture area, therefore, encompasses Thailand, Laos, the Shan, and the Tai Lue of Sipsong Panna, and also Cambodia, and Burma. (This, of course, displaces and perhaps even undermines the whole *raison d'être* of Thai/Tai Studies as it has been conceived to date). And, secondarily, this culture area is part of an *oikoumenê* which includes Vietnam and other parts of peninsula and insular Southeast Asia, and other Sinicized Tai groups.[16]

Such an argument has even further implications. It means that histories of nations have no meaning outside the modern context. One cannot write a history of Laos or a history of Thailand or Cambodia because these entities did not exist until the modern nationalist period. Their formation in the modern world landscape of nations was not the outcome of some inevitable historical (or cultural) teleology. Political centers and states waxed and waned and occasionally coalesced across of the whole of the terrain of the culture area I have identified. Their final confinement within the fixed borders of the modern nation state was wholly contingent on specific historical events and their consequences, as Thongchai (1994) has shown so eloquently for Thailand. National histories which do not acknowledge the fundamental contingency of the modern nation state are simply charter myths for those states.[17]

WHO ARE THE LAO?

IN contrast to the excerpts quoted in the opening pages of this chapter which spoke of the country of Laos as some kind of political fiction, I suggest that Laos is no more a political fiction than Thailand or any other modern state. Its borders and the state are internationally recognized. But, who are the Lao inside these borders? Like the previous question—is there a Tai culture and society?—this question is also a modern one.

David Streckfuss, in an expertly executed article, has shown how the Thai in the late nineteenth century began to slowly grasp the notions of race and identity being used by the encroaching European powers to identify nations, and then appropriated and applied them. The issue was less pressing for the Lao elite who had, by 1893, come under the French colonial umbrella, and it was the French who in international negotiations with the Thai (or others) decided who the Lao were. Streckfuss quite rightly stresses the centrality of an idea of race and racial purity to European colonialism—it is an idea which is implicated with those of proto languages and cultures that we discussed earlier. The Lao in the French racial index were equal, if not superior in their purity to the Siamese who were sometimes seen as "métissés de Chinois."[18] As Streckfuss writes: "By holding up the principles of race logic and identifying the Lao (or some other group) as a race oppressed by the minority Siamese, or by implying that the Siamese as a race were merely Chinese, the French were fashioning an ideological formulation that would prove to be both menacing and conceivably inescapable for the Siamese elite" (1993: 132). Such a logic was at first puzzling because the traditional polities of the region were well aware that they were "multiethnic," and kings were proud of the extent of their domain. But the Thai elite soon understood the logic of the new nation-state world and the word went out to the Siamese commissioners in the Lao areas that they were to impress on the local population and their leaders that "the Thai and Lao are of the same *chaat* [nation, lineage] and speak the same language within a single kingdom" (cited in Streckfuss 1993: 135), and as we remarked earlier the Thai reformulated the northeast, Isan, as a geographical rather than an ethnic region, otherwise the door would be left open to French claims. As Streckfuss shows through a detailed discussion of the Franco-Siamese Treaties between 1893 and 1907, the leaders in Bangkok learned how to advance their claims by demonstrating cultural similarity and claiming the Lao to be more or less a branch of Thai: "From 1900 onward, non-Thai groups, as separate peoples, seemingly disappeared from within the boundaries of the kingdom" (Streckfuss 1993: 142).

The debate over the relationship between the Lao and Thailand continued up until after World War II when negotiations were conducted between the Thai and the French about the return of the Lao provinces of Sayaboury and Champassak which the Thai had occupied during the war. During the negotiations in 1947 the Thai representative claimed, from the "'racial' point of view" (*Peninsule* 1988: 155), almost the whole of Laos. He argued that "most of the inhabitants of Lanchang belonged to the Thai race and could hardly be distinguished from their neighbours in the northeast of Siam and that their language and culture was similar" (158). But the French rejected these claims, saying: "As for the matter of ethnicity, there is no identity between the inhabitants of the two banks [of the Mekong], but only certain characteristics which they share in common, such as speaking languages which are of Thaï origin, and some of them belong to very different groups, such as the Moï [southern highlanders] groups" (162). As was true earlier in the century, it was French power which decided the argument, but it is interesting to note that the French "racial" argument had softened by 1947, while the Thai position on race had hardened.

In the meantime members of the Lao elite had begun to learn their nationalist lessons, and this saw its first coherent expression during World War II, as Søren Ivarsson's article shows in chapter 3, culminating in the Lao Issara independence movement in late 1945. A leading figure in that movement, Katay Don Sasorith, was one of the first to produce a coherent modern interpretation of Lao history.[19] Katay (1948), in exile in Thailand with the Lao Issara, attempted to intervene in the Franco-Siamese negotiations of 1947 to argue that neither had a right to decide Laos's future, and he rejects their claims to Lao territory which were based on

Laos's historical vassalage to Thailand, or in the case of France, its vassalage to the Vietnamese court.[20] His argument is that the tributary practices customary in the region before the French meant that a state could be subject to several centers at once and therefore no single state could claim clear sovereignty over another. Indeed, in several places, Katay clearly outlines a "galactic polity" model. There is certainly justice in Katay's critique of France and Thailand's spurious historical claims, but he himself proceeds by using the same logic to advance his own problematic historical claims. Indeed, it is interesting to see the extent to which Katay has learnt his arguments from the French in order to turn them against not only the Thai, but also French colonialism.

In an article first written in 1938[21] he draws attention to the anomalies inherent in the French usage of the terms "Laos français" and "Laos siamois," and thereby raises the Isan problem. He writes: "One should not forget that 'Siam' is a geographical expression which corresponds to no ethnographic reality and that the major part of the Siamese population is made up of Laotians" (1948: 2–3).[22] In a passage clearly penned after World War II, he claims that "The Laotian-Siamese on the right bank are becoming more and more conscious of their historical individuality and of their numerical superiority" (1949: 3), some of whom had even been bold enough to use Lao in the Thai national assembly. He cites the words of former members of the "Seri Thai" who had close relations with the "Lao Issara," to the effect: "'What is called Siam refers to us,' say the Laotians from the other side of the Mekong. 'Besides the real and the true "Siamese" who are our brothers and who form a tiny part of the population of the country, the others are foreigners, "métèques" [méstisses]. We, therefore, should have the power, the government, and not these "Siamese" pretenders who, mostly, have nothing in common with us'" (1948: 5). What is so striking about this passage is the way it reproduces the arguments the French colonialists used against the Thai earlier in the century. Katay would later reproduce similar views when he wrote: "the Siamese elite is made up almost totally of Thais of the capital and the big cities, of Thais it is better to say, who are *métissés* of Malay, Chinese and Khmer" (1953: 18).

But what is also interesting about Katay's argument (and which possibly reflects the greater impact of French left-liberalism on Lao intellectual thought, compared with Thailand), is that he does not allow himself to be drawn into a form of Lao irredentism. One might suggest that his caution came from the fact that he was in exile in Thailand, but a similar strain can be found in his later work. His main purpose is to argue for Lao independence and to this end he points to the anomaly of "the Lao" finding themselves caught under three different forms of rule: a protectorate in the north of Laos, a colony in the south, and under an independent state in

Thailand. What the Lao of Laos needed, he said, was an independent state. In a striking passage he writes:

> . . . although Lao and Thai are closely related, it is necessary however that each of us should live within our own natural limits [cadre naturel]. Politically, it must no more be a question of the Siamese "Siamising" the Lao than for the Lao to "Laoicise" the Siamese. Assimilation to the bitter end always provokes frictions and conflicts, and the best laws in the world cannot prevail over nature and inheritance [la nature et l'hérédité]. To form a single nation it is not absolutely necessary to speak the same language, to worship the same God or to practice the same religion, the same customs. The example of Switzerland and above all the United States of America clearly demonstrate this (1948: 4).

This outstanding passage with its apparently "republican" view of the nation as being made up of citizens without regard to ethnicity[23] makes it very different from nationalist discourses in Thailand. It is partly this consciousness which leads Katay in 1953 to recommend that Laos revert to its old name of Lane Xang "in order to avoid all ideas of racial particularism" (1953: 14). However there are deep confusions in Katay's discourse as we can see by his references to "natural" limits and groups, which appeals more to an "ethnic" conception of the nation. Katay, like many other Lao and foreign commentators on Laos since then, wavers back and forth between the two conceptions of the nation, thereby producing inevitable contradictions. Yet, it could be argued that what is uppermost in Katay's writings is an attempt to produce a political conception of the Lao nation.[24] This comes out most clearly in his discussion in *Le Laos* of "minorities" in the two countries.

In this text he is intent on distancing himself from any separatist tendencies among the Lao in Thailand, but he says any such movements are a direct outcome of the attempts by one racial or ethnic group to dominate another, such as is implied by the name Thailand (1953: 16; 20–21).[25] While not denying that the Thai and the Lao are of the same origin, the Lao branch is "numerically the most important without doubt" (1953: 17), and the "Lao-Siamese" in Thailand feel ostracized by the Thai. This, Katay suggests, had to be resolved by the Thai state. Obviously, one of the problems in the back of Katay's mind was that he did not want to give any succor to "pan-Thai" sentiments in Thailand by encouraging "pan-Lao" sentiments (after all Phibun Songkhram was back in power). And he was clearly aware that the princes of Ayutthaya, Lampang, Chiang Mai, and Bassac had all "disappeared successively, all to the profit of the Chakri dynasty" (1948: 63). But he also had an eye on ethnic problems in Laos as well. Considering the way Laos is seen these days, one may be surprised to read Katay's claim that: "Certainly, the ethnic problem in Laos will not be as complex as in Siam, because in Laos the Lao element predominates clearly and indisputably, as much by their numerical importance as by their degree of social and cultural development" (1953: 21).[26] This is because for Katay the "ethnic problem" in Thailand was a Lao problem. But he recognizes that there is some "disquiet" among the ethnic minorities in Laos, although some had shown their "patriotism" by wishing to be called "Lao Theung" (here he refers to the "Bolovens" and the "Mèos") while others still insist on their "racial particularism." Thus he concludes with a "manifesto" for assimilationist nationalism:

> We must therefore undertake from now on the long work of moral, if not racial, fusion necessary in order to bring together all of the different ethnic elements which make up Laos in order to make it a strong and unified nation. It is in order to begin this important work of national fusion that we wish to re-give to Laos, reduced to its present territorial limits, its ancient name of Lan-Xang (1953: 22).

By implication he is also suggesting that Thailand should change its name back to Siam.

Yet his vascillation between two different conceptions of the nation—a political and an ethnic one—continues to dog his understanding, and indeed, despite his best attempts he cannot escape from an ethnically based view of the nation which seeks its roots in antiquity:

> From oldest antiquity to the present day we have said in our everyday language:
> 　　*Sua Sat Lao,* meaning Laotian origin and race;
> 　　*Sat Lao,* meaning the Laotian Nation;
> 　　*Muong Lao,* meaning the Laotian country;
> 　　*Pathet Lao,* meaning the Laotian State.
> 　. . . It is clear, therefore, that even when *Muong* Luang Prabang, *Muong* Vientiane, and *Muong* Champassak had each a separate existence, *Muong* Lao nonetheless remained *Muong* Lao. For Lan-Xang, unlike many other empires past and present, but like present day Laos, lumped together within the limits of its territory a number of populations that were extremely homogenous. If we leave out a few ethnological Minorities (Khas, Meos, etc. . . .) that are scattered here and there, generally in the heights, the whole of *Muong* Lao spoke the same language, honoured the same genii, cultivated the same religion and had the same usages and customs. The same can not be said either of any of the ancient empires, nor of India or of the Great China of the present day (1959: 29–30).

He argues that the French should have restored "the Confederacy in favour of one of the ruling Laotian kings of the moment . . ." (1959: 31). Here we have a strong discourse on the ancient unity of the Lao—in the face of its obvious disunity. At one point he describes the traditional Lao polity as "polycephalous", much like anthropological descriptions of segmentary lineages, which under certain conditions come together and then dissolve into their constituent units again. In Katay's account, such a polity arises when "a great prince, of uncontested and incontestable merit, comes to rally around his name all the petit chiefs of rival states and regroup them again under his unique sceptre" (1953: 46). But the big problem for this perspective is the delimitation of the alleged "natural" units of such a state. Despite Katay's nationalist inspired interpretation that the various *muang* of Lane Xang form such a "natural" unit, there is not in fact in the traditional polities of mainland Southeast Asia any principle by which such units can be delimited.

No writer on Laos has surpassed Katay's justifications for the modern Lao state, and they have been largely content to repeat one or other of his arguments, or all of them. If anything, Katay's arguments have been among the most sophisticated and modern yet produced by any Lao intellectual. Indeed in 1947, having clearly asserted Laos's place in the international nation-state system independent from Thailand and France, he strikes a particularly modern note by suggesting that one "could dream of much later [creating], following the example of Switzerland and the United States of America [though one today would say Europe], a confederation of states of Southeast Asia (Siam, Burma, Malaysia, Cambodia, Laos, Vietnam, etc. . . .)" (1948: 64). With Laos as part of ASEAN this extraordinarily prescient idea has more or less found fulfillment.

THE CULTURE AND SOCIETY OF LAOS

ALTHOUGH it has always been a galling thought for Lao nationalists, it is I think incontestable that the modern state of Laos only exists because of French colonial occupation. Without this it is almost certain that at least the lowland areas of Laos would have become part of the Thai state, while upland areas such as Houaphan (which only became part of French Laos in the 1930s anyway) would probably have been absorbed by Vietnam. Furthermore we have to remember that the people of what is today northern Thailand were formerly known as Lao, and were only formally integrated politically into the Thai state a year before the French asserted their control over Laos in 1893.[27]

Since that time Laos's political, social, and cultural trajectory has been distinct because of the very nature of the modern state and its project of trying to create a congruent society and culture. The historical role of colonialism in the *longue durée*, I would argue, has been to spread capitalism, the principles of the modern state, and the ideology of nationalism into unconquered regions. Indeed, all colonial states one way or another made themselves obsolete. They virtually taught the indigenous nationalists their nationalism. Colonialism transformed some societies more profoundly than others, and this was true in Indochina. Often the French were accused of treating Laos as a "colonial backwater," or "colonial playground," while pouring all their energy into Vietnam. The critique of French colonialism in Laos often has the paradoxical quality of condemning the French for doing both too much and too little, e.g. of using "oppressive" corvée labor to build infrastructure, such as roads, and of not building enough schools and hospitals.[28]

The French set about creating the rudiments of a modern state apparatus which encompassed the whole of Laos, including the protectorate of Luang Prabang, and the administrative apparatus of the northern kingdom was adapted to this encompassing system. Through this system Lao began to learn the basics of modern statecraft, and indeed, the famous Prince Phetsarath was one who learned this lesson well. The colonial education system, however small in its beginnings, also began training Lao in the ways of thought of the modern world, and about their own history conceived of along the lines of a modern national history.[29] What is most intriguing about a short school history textbook produced in Lao in 1926 (Lê and Blanchard 1926) was how similar its themes were with ones written in the post-independence period (i.e. post-1954). But what is perhaps distinctive and unusual about the text is that it begins by discussing the southern minorities and their connection to the Cham kingdom, and by discussing Laos's traditional connections with the Khmer empire. In other words, it orients Lao history away from the Thai and towards Laos's Indochinese cultural connections. Something similar occurred a little later when the French established a Buddhist Institute in Phnom Penh in 1930 and in Vientiane in 1931 in order to counter Bangkok's influence on Lao and Khmer Buddhism.[30]

We still require detailed studies from social historians in order to understand the full implications of these state interventions into the reproduction of Lao culture, but there is no doubt that they began to impart a distinctiveness to Lao development. Similarly with language development, as discussed by Ivarsson below for the 1940s, and by Nick Enfield for the post independence period, the state has tried to intervene to standaridize the Lao language and after 1975 to clearly differentiate it from

Thai. Part of Peter Koret's purpose in his article is to show how Maha Sila Viravong attempted to develop a system for standardizing Lao literature by copying a Thai model, for the latter had set out on the path of standardization well before the Lao.

As they emerged into the modern world Lao and Thai society diverged because the latter made the transition first by constructing a form of absolutist state which then made the transition to a modern state with the fall of the absolute monarchy. In Laos this transition was overseen by colonialism. These two trajectories not only ensured certain cultural divergences, but they also meant that the military played a much greater role in Thailand than in Laos. Indeed for almost the whole period that Thailand was ruled by military dictatorships in the 1950s and 1960s Laos experimented with liberal democracy. It was the Vietnam War that destroyed this experiment and ushered one-party dictatorship into Laos, and saw the fleeing of a large part of the Lao elite and intelligentsia. And for a time, it saw the state set out on a radically revised Lao cultural program, which has veered back towards the path pioneered by the Royal Lao Government (RLG) during the 1990s. Thus the social structures in the two countries also have distinct modern histories which need further exploration. One obvious cultural and social differentiation which occurred with the 1975 revolution was the overthrow of the Lao monarchy and associated aristocracy, the consequences of which I have briefly explored elsewhere (Evans 1998).

The study of culture and society in Laos is, therefore, inevitably a study of the state's attempt to standardize features of Lao culture and society under several political regimes. Such studies will also document local resistance to such standardization. They must also be studies of the attempt by the state to educate non-ethnic Lao about this standard culture.

THE "MINORITIES"

THE current Lao government often speaks of the multiethnic Lao nation, and outside observers, as we have seen, also perceive Laos as being ethnically so diverse that they have been reluctant to concede that it is a "real" nation-state. This contrasts with Katay's perception in the 1950s of Laos as having less of a minority problem than Thailand because there was such a clear majority of one ethnic group in Laos, the Lao, compared with the Siamese whose numbers he claimed were inferior to the Lao in the northeast. The term "minorities" today, however, generally refers to the non-Thai/Lao groups. The Lao Peoples' Democratic Republic is usually considered to be more tolerant towards the minorities than the former Royal Lao

Government because it accords them appellations which acknowledge their Lao-ness. Thus in Laos one will commonly hear or read the generalization: "the Lao are divided into three groups, the Lao Loum (the lowland ethnic Lao), the Lao Theung (midland Lao), and the Lao Soung (highland Lao)." This tripartite categorization, which is often thought to be a communist innovation, in fact has an old pedigree.

In 1899 a long report on Laos in the *Revue Indo-Chinoise* provided the following description of the Lao population:

1. The Thays, made up of all the people who speak with slight differences of accent and slightly different vocabularies, the Thay language. The principal groups are: the Lao, the Phu-Thay, the white, black and red Thay, the Thay Neua, the Phuan, the Lue and the Yuan;
2. The Kha and the Khas on the way to being absorbed by the first category;
3. The inhabitants coming from neighbouring countries: China, Yunnan [?], Annam, Cambodia, Siam and Burma (1899: 12–13). [The discussion mainly focuses on the Hmong and Yao].

That the analysis of the ethnic situation in Laos has hardly changed in one hundred years is a clear sign of deep conceptual inertia.[31]

The most problematic category is the so-called Kha, a term which implies a slave-like, or inferior, status. One finds its use today as a pronoun in formal speech, *khaphachao*, i.e. slave of the Buddha, referring to oneself. As I have discussed elsewhere the meaning of the term Kha has changed over the past century from one which denoted inferior status in a formal system of hierarchy, to a pejorative one, as the nationalist state based on a concept of equal citizenship came into being (Evans 1998). Hence its continued use by many people in the pre-1975 regime was supposed to mark that regime as more prejudiced towards these people than the new one. In fact, as we have seen, the term "Lao Theung" was already current in the early 1950s and indeed Katay saw its use as a sign of "patriotism" on the part of the minority groups. Moreover, Katay also proposed the radical idea of renaming the country so that it would not be associated with a single ethnic group. Ideas of ethnicity were in a gradual social process of revision under the Royal Lao Government, and the shift to a mandatory tripartite terminology only came after 1975.[32]

The derivative category "Lao Theung," therefore, is also problematic.[33] As the report on the Kha in the *Revue Indo-Chinoise* already recognized, this "group" is extremely diverse: "The Khas represent in Laos at least a third of the population. They are found throughout the territory; they are divided into more than sixty families who speak different dialects" (1899: 90).

Their denomination as a "group" appears to have arisen out of two considerations: 1. They are considered indigenous to the region, unlike the Tai groups who "invaded" from the north; 2. In the racial logic associated with historical linguistics in the late nineteenth century they were considered to have been untouched by "Aryan" influence, unlike the "Thay," about whom it was said: "all can see their moral and intellectual life has been modified sensibly by the Aryans" (*Revue Indo-Chinoise* 1899: 12).[34] Hence the Thay were more "civilized" than the Kha. Thus did the French inject a racial logic into the traditional (non-racial) hierarchical schema in Laos.[35] The "coherence" of the tripartite schema, therefore, partly derives from the original racial logic set out in the late nineteenth century by the French.[36]

This kind of thinking can create all kinds of dilemmas in the field, because we find throughout Laos people who are bilingual, bicultural and "biracial" because of intermarriage between different groups. We have Chinese (Haw) who have married Lao whose offspring may grow up with the boys learning Chinese and indeed who later marry back into the Chinese community and become "pure" Chinese, while the girls grow up speaking Lao and marry into the Lao community. Or, as the 1899 article already realized, many Kha have become Tai, a phenomenon which has subsequently been documented again and again (Izikowitz 1951; Condominas 1990). Clearly many Lao or Tai have Kha "racial" ancestry. The extent of intermarriage between groups in Laos has received little attention, although I attempted to gain some understanding of intermarriage in a Black Tai area in Houaphan province (see chapter 6). Patterns of inter-marriage between groups seem to be determined by degrees of incompatibi-lity in marriage exchange patterns, the hierarchical relations between groups,[37] and so on, rather than ideas of "race," although one might argue that race has become increasingly salient over this century at least among urban-based educated groups. Much more research needs to be done on the whole issue of ethnic intermarriage in Laos.

Katay's assimilationist program outlined in 1953 was very radical and liberal for those days, suggesting as it did, "racial fusion." For real racists such miscegenation was an abomination.[38] Of course, Katay considered the Lao to have a higher "degree of social and cultural development," and that both because of the numerical superiority of the Lao and their cultural superiority the other groups would be assimilated "upwards." Such liberal ideas of superiority can, as we know, all too often give way to prejudice and mistreatment of minorities if there are no political checks on it. As we have already discussed, Katay's thinking wavered between an ethnic view of the nation and a political view of the nation. This remains true in the LPDR, whatever its rhetoric about multiethnicity, and in recent years a clearly assimilationist train of thought has become more apparent among the Lao elite.

The tripartite categorization was originally adopted by the Lao communists, in consultation with their Vietnamese advisers, as a political strategy designed to link all the ethnic groups in Laos through the use of the prefix "Lao." This use remained in force officially after 1975, and was propagated throughout the population. In the early 1980s, however, Kaysone Phomvihane called for more detailed categorizations of the ethnic groups in Laos. This task initially fell to the Lao Front for National Reconstruction and the Nationalities Committee, but was finally taken over by the Institute of Ethnography when it was established in 1988. Considerable confusion reigned about how many groups there were in Laos, but the institute finally settled on forty-seven, and this categorization was used in the 1995 census. The significance of this was that the disaggregation of the tripartite system into its constituent ethnic groups ensured that each of them appeared less significant in relation to the dominant ethnic Lao group, and therefore placed the latter at the cultural center and apex of the nation.[27]

As stressed earlier, the role of the nationalist state is cultural standardization, and the education system is one of the main instruments for teaching ethnic minorities in Laos about a Lao standard culture. In fact, in the current crop of textbooks for schools released in the 1990s, one finds fewer references to minorities than one did in those released immediately after 1975. In the history of the creation of modern nations there is nothing exceptional about the Lao state's attempt to promote such a standard culture. There are, however, some forces moderating this. First, ethnic diversity can be sold to international tourists, and to a degree this has created some sense of pride among the more "colorful" groups concerning their culture, thus off-setting their sense of inferiority in relation to the dominant culture.[40] Second, "ethnic identity" has become an almost sacred touchstone for many people in our globalized world by presuming to give people a sense of "roots." Generally, the world is more sensitive to ethnic issues than twenty years ago, and governments like the LPDR are aware of this (as the RLG would have been too had it survived). Many international aid organizations and non-governmental organizations (NGOs) in Laos now insist, often to the annoyance of their Lao counterparts, on paying attention to "ethnic minority needs" in their aid programs. Some Lao clearly feel that this attention to minorities creates national disunity, when in fact it provides a check on the power of the dominant group in the absence of democracy. But many of the confusions which occur in debates between Lao and foreigners about ethnic minority rights also arise from the fact that not only Lao, but foreigners themselves, often swing confusingly between ethnically based views of the nation and ones based on citizenship rights.

At a more general theoretical level it may be worth proposing that these confusions in the discourse of nationalism, which I have already noted several times, may in fact be inescapable. Anthropologists have remarked again and again on the general human propensity to "naturalize" culture. Or in Roland Barthes terms, to "mythologize" it. As he writes: "Myth hides nothing and flaunts nothing: it distorts; myth is neither lie nor a confession: it is an inflexion . . . the very principle of myth [is]: it transforms history into nature . . . [hence] it is not read as a motive, but as reason" (Barthes 1972: 129). Racial or ethnic ideas of the nation (and the slippage between these two notions) are attractive because they naturalize the nation, whereas the purely political idea of the nation as one composed of citizens, regardless of race/ethnicity, is too obviously a human cultural creation, and too "transient" to have deep claims on our allegiance. Thus even those who adhere to a political idea of the nation often find themselves, conciously or unconsciously, code-switching between the two competing ideas of the nation.

Culturally, the minorities in Laos would appear to fall outside the broad culture area based on Theravada Buddhism that I outlined earlier. This, however, is not strictly true because, and as I have argued elsewhere,[41] the minorities around Louang Prabang, for example, or in Champassak, played a central role in various state rituals presided over by a Theravada Buddhist king or prince. Indeed, it was these rituals, says Katay, that made the "Lao consider the Khas as being their brothers. Consequently in all the grand ritual ceremonies the Kha always occupied first place" (1953: 21). Beyond the groups immediately caught up in traditional Lao state ritual, recent research in Thailand has suggested that there may be important symbolic congruities between "galactic" polities and some of the upland societies. Thus Deborah Tooker's research on the Akha argues that because upland and lowland systems have historically interacted over a long time, they have developed "similarities in the *symbolics* of power" (Tooker 1996: 342). She sees in Akha practices similar ideas of potency radiating out from a sacred center, of spatial coding of hierarchy, and ideas of the purity of a ruler at the center of this space.[42] Otome Hutheesing has provided a similar view as a result of her observations of Lisu syncretism. "The merger of different religious traditions may also be viewed as a correspondence of similar basic structural ideas between Buddhist theology and village symbolic expressions; similarity is thus detected despite different levels of communication competencies" (1990: 135). Thus the symbolics of power between these particular upland systems and the lowland are coherent and translatable. This, of course, may not be true for other groups, such as the

Yao, for example. The overthrow of the monarchy in Laos has gutted the traditional symbolic forms of integration that existed, and as yet only less encompassing symbols of Lao nationalism have been substituted.

Here we appear to be on the boundary between the concepts of culture area and *oikoumenê*, a boundary which requires further exploration if we wish to understand cultural interaction inside Laos, and elsewhere in the region.

LAO CULTURE AND SOCIETY: A REPRISE

THE genius of Charles Archaimbault's detailed ethnographies of different regions of Laos (1971;1972;1973) is that they show how a "high" Buddhist court tradition was adapted in each case to local conditions, producing significantly different local religious and ritual traditions, but ones which were broadly recognizable over a wide culture area. In fact one could argue that similar processes occurred across the whole region. Lorraine Gesik's (1995) study of a ritual and textual tradition in southern Thailand is a lovely example of the process there. Indeed, it is precisely this localisation of ritual complexes, for example, that often marks something as Lao, or Thai, or Lue, or Yuan, or Phuan, etc. But Gesik's study also shows how the nationalist state appropriates a local tradition in order to weave it into a national story. This has occurred in Laos too.

As I have said several times, Lao culture and society is not coterminus with the geographical boundaries of Laos, and this is clear in several of the contributions below, such as Leedom Leffert's study of a Buddhist ritual in Xieng Khouang (chapter 10) where he continually makes comparisons with his fieldwork in Isan, and sometimes speaks even more broadly of "Southeast Asian Theravada Buddhist societies." Peter Koret's study of Lao literature (chapter 11) moves easily back and forth across the Lao-Thai border. Boundaries within this broad culture area are in fact difficult to demarcate, and are inevitably fuzzy. It is common for ordinary Lao, for Lao intellectuals, and foreigners to refer to the eating of sticky rice as a key marker of Lao-ness. A whole chapter is devoted to the issue in Mayoury and Pheuiphan Ngaosyvathn's book *Kith and Kin Politics: The Relationship Between Laos and Thailand* (1994), but this diacritica is not exclusively Lao. Black and Red Tai eat sticky rice, the Lue of Sipsong Panna eat sticky rice, and so do the northern Thai, as well as the people of Isan of course, as well as a number of non-Tai ethnic groups scattered throughout the region.

The need to codify and standardize culture is very much a preoccupation of the modern state. It is true that some institutions in premodern societies attempted to standardize aspects of culture (religious institutions, for example), and it is true that the premodern Sinitic states through their codifications of ritual went a long way towards the standardization of culture. However, this was not their *raison d'etre*, and it was a standardization that was oriented towards the apex of the state rather than the creation of a mass culture which is the aim of the modern state, especially through its system of universal education. Lao culture bleeds into a broader culture area, and engages in exchanges with adjacent groups. It has evolved and changed over time, and these changes are increasingly subject to an ongoing debate among the members of Lao culture, and increasingly outsiders, about what Lao culture is.

This cultural debate, however, takes place within certain recognizable cultural parameters. For example, to discuss what Lao culture is (or should be) a person does not refer to Confucian values as a Chinese might, even though the latter may never have studied Confucius. The venerable sage is, nevertheless, a symbol of Chineseness and the cultural debate defines in what way he is relevant to this identity. In Laos, on the other hand, one is likely to refer to Buddhism and Buddhist values as a way of articulating what are thought to be Lao values. Buddhism is a symbol of Lao-ness—but so is it a symbol of Thai-ness. Yet, a Lao would not speak in central Thai (although most of his listeners would understand) in order to advance an argument about Lao culture, even though there is a lot of overlap, and indeed increasing overlap, between the two languages (see Enfield, chapter 12). Here speaking Lao symbolizes Lao-ness.

In some respects the nation-state is being successful in making culture, and more particularly cultural identity, increasingly congruent with its borders. Thus, Lao in Isan, as Grabowsky (1995: 107) acknowledges, increasingly identify themselves as *khon Isan* within Thailand, and not as Lao. Khampheng Thipmuntali's study of the Lue in Muang Sing in northern Laos (see chapter 7) shows the multiple ways the Lue identify themselves, but their overarching identity is as Lao, compared to the Lue across the border in Burma, or in Yunnan. Cultural identity clearly can operate in several registers and there is no apriori reason for researchers to privilege some primordial Lao-ness over an Isan person's emic perception of themselves as Thai, or the primordial Lue-ness of a Lue in Muang Sing whose sees himself as Lao.

But in our increasingly globalized world there are also larger forces at work. A more powerful Thailand in every respect means that cultural developments there impact on Lao culture in profound ways, as Enfield's study of language in this volume shows. As I have argued elsewhere (1998), it is ironic that the Lao communists who wanted to reassert a "pure" Lao culture could only do so by retreating into isolation. Their destruction of Laos's pre-1975 fledgling intelligentsia and their enfeeblement of the school system in terms of qualified personnel and teaching materials, has meant that with the reopening of the country towards Thailand and the world most Lao are less able to manage the subsequent impact and less capable of comprehending it. But Thai culture also mediates "global" culture for the Lao, and furthermore, within Thailand itself there are anxieties about the Thai losing their traditional values in the face of foreign cultural influences. This type of anxiety seems to be universal now, and one product of this is a romanticization of tradition and the past. Thus, for Thai, the Lao are seen to embody "traditional values," and this is partly what Thai tourists go to see in Laos. At other times, however, these same Thai see Laos as "backward" and "underdeveloped." Similarly, the Lao sometimes like to project themselves as the protectors of real, traditional Buddhist values which the Thai have lost. But they also, in other moods, look up to Thai sophistication and development.

In a world preoccupied with "pure" cultures and clear cultural boundaries the borrowing of cultural traits from elsewhere is sometimes tinged with nationalist paranoia about cultural dilution. Yet, borrowing has always gone on between cultures, and as Michael Moerman wrote many years ago in an essay on Western influence on Thai culture, "it is unlikely for there to be anywhere a one-to-one correspondence between what is loaned and what is borrowed" (1969: 147). Indeed, how borrowing occurs can be a source of knowledge. "The ways in which Western culture is refined and reinterpreted, adapted and set in novel contexts can tell us about Thailand. Identifiable borrowed elements, by their very transformation, can help us delineate Thai culture and society . . ." (ibid). This argument applies equally to Lao culture and society, and to all other non-Western cultural practices and objects that are borrowed.

Alongside the modern state's attempts at cultural standardization now stands the increasingly important tourist industry, which has itself become a significant commercial force in the standardization of Lao culture, and minority cultures inside Laos. This industry is also involved in the invention of culture, and in this respect it has become a vital adjunct of the Lao state's current revival of "tradition." Ing-Britt Trankell (chapter 9) considers some of these issues in the context of Louang Prabang, and further studies are needed.

Laos's reopening to the wider world will have consequences for the cultural development of its peoples in ways difficult to forsee and in a world that is growing rapidly smaller. Not so long ago to be in the mountains of Laos, in Sam Neua or Udomxai, was to feel cut off from the world in ways increasingly unimaginable. Now Hmong walk into the post offices there and easily call their refugee relatives in Australia, France, or the US, and faxes pass from Hong Kong to Houaphan. In a short space of time video theaters opened up in the most remote market towns, showing television tapes of Bangkok fashion models dressed in ways scandalous for local women, kung fu movies, and films projecting the dream world of modern Asia and America. Satelite dishes now receive international news in Phonesavane in Xieng Khouang, and anywhere else that they can be shipped to and set up. Laos's delayed entry into the modern world, if I can express it that way, has meant the telescoping there of cultural and social developments seen elsewhere in Asia, which in itself will produce a unique outcome and ensure that Laos is different from its neighbors. It is this new complexity of social and cultural change that we anthropologists, linguists, sociologists, historians, and others must try to understand.

NOTES

1. These extrapolations are dubious inasmuch as we are unsure about the pronunciation of the characters representing a political unit called "Ai-Lao", and the historical material relating to this unit is extremely sketchy. The desire to connect this political unit with modern day Laos is driven more by current desires to make such a connection rather than established fact.

2. Adrian Room, in his *Place Names of the World*, writes: "Laos: Named after Thai people Lao (from Lava), with plural 's' added by Portuguese settlers" (1987: 135). There were never any Portuguese settlers in Laos, only a few French. It seems, however, that it was a very early Portuguese encyclopedia that first added the 's' to Lao, and this was later taken up by the French.

3. This text is translated in Choltira (1997: 14). After reading Choltira, Geoff Wade (University of Hong Kong) suggested to me that perhaps Lawa is the origin of the Mandarin pronunciation for Laos, roughly "Lao Woh".

4. Houmphanh gave a paper which was a variation on this theme at the Thai Studies Conference in Kunming in 1990. See Houmphanh (1990).

5. Indeed, in an attempt to escape these connotations this project launched its own *Tai* Studies Conference in mid-1998.

6. Wolf argues that if we look at the historical and ethnographic record, "social and cultural facts do not present themselves in units in which social and geographical space coincide, and in which constituent groups are arrayed and stratified in the tiers of a common, all-embracing architecture. On the contrary, we see various activities crosscutting one another in manifold intersects, yielding pluralistic patchworks rather than a bounded homogeneity of social warp and woof. Where these activities intersect they create nodes of nexuses of interaction, potential growth points of institutionalization, in the midst of overlapping relational fields. Such nodes formed by cultic affiliation, marriage alliances, polity-building, exchange or commerce may indeed become growth points of institution-building . . ." (1988: 757). Thus one could argue that because of their hierarchical nature and the personalized bonds between subordinates and superiors, the idea of a common society or culture was not salient in pre-modern societies. Even in the "culturalist" universe of pre-modern Confucian

states, one was either more or less cultured depending on one's proximity to an imperial high center, rather than there being a planar idea of a shared culture.

7. One of the most stimulating essays on Southeast Asian history which attempts to deal with some of these issues is Wolters (1982).

8. This map was published in the *Journal of the Siam Society* (vol. 76, 1988) and was produced by the CeDRASEMI, CRNS-EHESS in collaboration with the CEGET-CRNS, and Mahidol University.

9. Chatthip is not alone in this assumption which in fact is quite common. See, for example, a recent study of Zhuang by two Lao linguists Thongkien and Boualy (1990, in Lao) which suggests a "deep" cultural relationship between these groups.

10. Chamberlain's (1975) study is considered the key statement of this argument, continuing from the work of Benedict, Haudricourt, and Li.

11. For a further argument along these lines, see Evans (1997).

12. For an earlier attempt to try to deal with some of these issues, see Evans (1991).

13. This leads to peculiar attempts to assert that because one group is older than another it is therefore "superior." This logic can be seen in the title of Dodd's book *The Tai Race: Elder Brother of the Chinese* (1923), an inversion of received wisdom, as well as in Maha Sila's statement quoted earlier in this chapter that the Chinese and the Lao are as old as one another, and therefore (it is implied) of equal status. This latter reasoning is an interesting conflation of a traditional understanding of status as being determined by age, and a modern conception of nations as equal.

14. In this I follow Tambiah's use of "galactic polity." His elucidation of indigenous concepts gives the following definition: "The most central of these concepts is mandala (Thai: *monthon*), standing for an arrangement of a center and its surrounding satellites and employed in multiple contexts to describe, for example: the structure of a pantheon of gods; the deployment spatially of a capital region and its provinces; the arrangement socially of a ruler, princes, nobles, and their respective retinues; and the devolution of graduated power on a scale of decreasing autonomies" (Tambiah 1985: 258).

15. One can occasionally hear similar xenophobic claims about Buddhism in China.

16. One could assert, along with Foley (1997:391) that part of this region is a linguistic area. Of mainland Southeast Asian languages he writes: "In this region, languages of four different major language families are spoken: Sino-Tibetan, Thai, Mon-Khmer, and Austronesian. The ancestral languages and earlier stages of these languages from the four families were very different from each other, but centuries of mutual interference have reduced this diversity so that they now share many structural features."

17. For two intelligent accounts of the contingency of modern nations both of which look at the problem of "Indochina," see Henley (1995) and Goscha (1996).

18. This racial framework was remarkably persistent, and even as careful a scholar as the (non-French) Lawrence Palmer Briggs writes: "The most casual observer will be able to distinguish at a glance a Siamese of Bangkok, picked at random, from a Laotian of Vientian or Louang Prabang, chosen in the same manner. But this is because the Siamese of Bangkok shows his greater mixture with darker races, while the Laotian has remained of almost pure Tai stock" (1949:63). Like so many "racial" observations one is struck by the varying subjective perceptions of skin "color." Today the Lao (especially those from Isan) consider themelves the "darker race" compared with the Thai who have intermarried with the "lighter" Chinese. The popular "folksong" *Sao Isan* (Girl

from the Northeast), plays with this perception. Briggs, nevertheless, does repeat the idea of Lao "racial purity" compared with the Siamese.

19. Katay must be regarded as the most articulate and intelligent nationalist politician that Laos has produced. At times an idiosyncratic figure, his death in 1959 at a relatively young age deprived Laos of one of its key post-independence politicians. He deserves a political biography.

20. In a footnote to this text Katay, after noting the vagueness of some of the French delegation's formulations, speculates that "one should not think that the French Government had definitively given up its aims of expanding across to the right bank of the Mekong" (1948:53). This comment, no doubt spurred into consciousness by anti-colonial paranoia, nevertheless may contain an important kernel of truth and explain the puzzling delays of the French to legally formalize their presence in Laos. This is something for the historians.

21. This apparently previously unpublished article in his book on the Lao independence movement (1948) which is largely a collection of his own previously published articles, unfortunately had revisions added to it just before publication, and it is sometimes unclear whether the views Katay expresses are those of 1938 or 1947.

22. The term "Siam," he claims, is of Chinese origin.

23. For a very brief statement of the "two routes to nation formation," see Smith (1994: 717–721).

24. This wavering or confusion is very apparent in his search for a reason for the ease with which the French took over Laos, which is a potential source of shame for a committed nationalist. Thus he argues that politically in the past there was no concept of colonization and annexation of territories as one finds in the Occident. There was simply vassalage to multiple centers of power by (and here is the problem) "natural" political units. Thus when there were attempts by one of the centers to transgress this customary arrangement (though he does not seem to realize that such transgressions should not have been thinkable in his ideal customary world) then the "natural" units would fight back ferociously, as the people in Xieng Khouang did against the emperor of Annam or Chao Anou against the Siamese. Thus, he concludes, this latter Thai transgression against a "natural" Lao political unit caused deep resentment of the Thai and ensured Auguste Pavie's easy "conquest of the hearts" of the Lao (Katay 1948: 21–22).

25. Interestingly, this appears to contradict an earlier, more complacent attitude towards this name change in Katay (1948: 2–3): "In fact, the Siamese have always been designated by the term 'Thai'. The expression 'Thailand', officially adopted under the Government of Marshal Luang Phibuoul-Songkhram, was therefore more correct and meaningful. The opponents of racism have found in it dubious intentions, so that after their victory over the Axis countries the Allied powers, the guardians of peace, proscribed its use."

26 . This idea of the preponderance of the Lao was not new. Meyer (1930: 24) writes that of a population of 800,000, Lao and "Thai assimilated to Laotians" made up 600,000, while "Kha" made up 200,000, leaving the Hmong, Yao, Chinese, and others to make up a miniscule proportion. An ethnographic map conveys the same message.

27. As Rujaya and Wyatt (1995: 68) write: "The northern interior of what was to become Thailand was well-defined and in many ways culturally integrated by the middle of the nineteenth century. It was not, however, politically integrated."

28. In nationalist historiographies in Vietnam or Laos, especially communist ones, corvée is often cited as one of the horrors of colonialism. Western academics also have this tendency. Of course, when the nationalist state itself imposes corvée it is not referred to as such but is called instead something like "patriotic labor." This kind of labor is common in Stalinist systems (including large-scale prison "slave" labor). In 1997, for example, the new reform-oriented Vietnamese state decided to introduce a corvée of ten days labor every year for its citizens to build infrastructure, or pay a cash equivalent (*South China Morning Post* 14/3/97).

29. For a brief discussion of education in Laos, see the chapter "Rote Memories" in Evans (1998).

30. Again, for a brief discussion, see the chapter on Buddhism in Evans (1998).

31. Ing-Britt Trankel (1998) has explored some reasons why this schema is attractive.

32. As far as I can tell there was a great deal of terminological slippage in RLG days. So Hmong were generally referred to as Meo (a somewhat pejorative usage, derived from the term Miao in China which is not pejorative), Yao would be called Yao, while Goh (Ahka) would be called Kha, and sometimes all of them would fall under the term Kha, which often simply acted as a marker for non-ethnic Lao.

33. For an earlier attempt to deal with the problems of this category in the field, see Evans and Rattana (1990).

34. For a critique of intellectual myths associated with "Aryans," see Leach (1990). Interestingly, in India the "Aryans" are also thought to be invaders from the north.

35. Interestingly, it may have struck a chord in the traditional cognitive system because a cognate word for Aryan, *alinya*, exists in Lao and implies advanced, superior, true, pure, etc. I would like to thank Nick Enfield for drawing this to my attention.

36. It is significant that the current Lao immigration card is one of the few which asks visitors to specify their "race."

37. Thus in his study of the Kachin, Leach (1970: 219–222) draws attention to the potential contradictions inherent in marriage exchanges between Shan and Kachin, especially the different ideas of status given to wife-takers and wife-givers.

38. It is interesting that the one photo of Katay that appears in his 1948 book is of him with his arms around two Ta Oi women, with their large bamboo pipes, in Saravane province. For many Lao then, and today, this group is considered especially "primitive," one reason being the smoking of tobacco by women.

39. For a detailed presentation of this argument, see chapter 8 below.

40. Here less "colorful" groups, such as the Khmu for example, are at a disadvantage.

41. See the chapter "Minorities in State Ritual" in Evans (1998).

42. Tooker also wishes to contest the degree to which the Akha are "encompassed" by the dominant lowland systems and points to how the Akha also use their symbols to challenge dominant meanings.

FROM BUFFER STATE TO CROSSROADS STATE

2

SPACES OF HUMAN ACTIVITY AND INTEGRATION IN THE LAO PDR

RANDI JERNDAL AND JONATHAN RIGG

Like a wedge at the summit of an arch, Laos occupies a key position on the map of Indochina. From Burma and Thailand on the west to Vietnam on the east, with its foundations in the Malay peninsula and the Indonesian archipelago, the arch supports the weight of China and the mass of Central Asia, another world—an image evocative, perhaps, of an age of monument building long past. But like the keystone of an arch, Laos has the dual function of holding apart the other, larger stones so they do not tumble and fall and of tying all together so the structure thus created is solid. Throughout its history, Laos has had this dual role (Dommen 1985: 1).

SCHOLARS of Laos tend to be drawn in one of two apparently conflicting directions when it comes to depicting the country. On the one hand there are those who emphasize Laos's "marginal," "backward," and "peripheral" condition. Taillard goes so far as to write of Laos as "a dead angle" (Taillard 1989: 18), while Neher and Chi Do Pham both suggests that it is a "forgotten" country (Neher 1991, Chi Do Pham 1994). Other scholars, like Dommen in the quote above, stress the degree to which Laos is a "keystone," "crossroads," or "lynchpin" in the region. These constrasting perceptions of the country's place within the wider mainland Southeast Asian region reflect scholars' differing concerns and depend, crucially, on time and context. There are also studies which, depending on the lens being used, see Laos as both core and periphery at one and the same time.

How Laos "came to be" is not our concern here, although it is important to see the country's evolution within a wider context of evolving spatial relations in mainland Southeast Asia. Partly these evolving relations relate to processes of historical change. However the arrival of the British and French and their territorial struggle altered not just the balance of power in the region; it also, and perhaps even more fundamentally, constructed a new spatial "reality." For the first time geographical space, delineated by "lines" of control and ownership (international borders), became of overriding importance. Thus Toye, for example, finds that he is able to write: "It is a matter of land; the need for living space on the one hand and the fear of conquest and extermination on the other" (Toye 1968: xiii). Traditionally, space was conceived of in terms of cosmology rather than geography and control of physical space was not, in itself, significant.

This is clear in the Siamese royal court's insouciant response to the British envoy Captain Henry Burney's desire to negotiate the border between Tenasserim (south Burma) and western Siam in 1825. With Burney pressing the issue, the court, clearly somewhat exasperated at the Englishman's lack of understanding, replied:

"With respect to what is said about the boundaries, the Country of Mergui, Tavoy, and Tenasserim, no boundaries could ever be established between the Siamese and the Burmese. But the English desire to have these fixed. Let them enquire from the old inhabitants residing on the frontiers of Mergui, Tavoy, and Tenasserim, what they know respecting the contiguous territories, and let what they point out be the territories between the English and Siamese possessions" (quoted in Thongchai Winichakul 1994: 64).

Laos at this time became an object of dispute between Siam and France. Siam claimed suzerainty, and therefore historical rights over Laos, while the French disputed the claim. What is interesting is that neither France nor Siam considered Laos to have any claim to itself. French and Siamese troops marched into "Laos" in 1887–88 and occupied various areas and on this basis began to negotiate over ownership and control. As Thongchai Winichakul writes, "[t]he power of the new geographical knowledge exercised by both the Siamese and French forces prevailed and created a new kind of space" (1994: 111). It is clear that by the latter decades of the nineteenth century Siam's leaders at least had internalized Western concerns for geographical space. King Chulalongkorn (r. 1868–1910), for example, had begun to employ cartographers to delimit the extent of the Siamese kingdom. The Siamese were willing to negotiate with the French in Western terms and when this failed, to confront the French militarily (albeit unsuccessfully). To historians, Laos was a victim of competition between greater powers; to the colonial French, a resource-rich annex to Vietnam and a "back door" into China; and to the Siamese, the lost territories east of the Mekong. The people who lived within its boundaries were, in effect, being manipulated by and defined in terms of foreign economic and political needs. Neher takes this a further step to argue that "Laos might best be described as a quasi-nation, having emerged from maps drawn by European colonialists rather than from a sense of territory and nation hood among united people" (1991: 197).[1] The upshot of Laos's creation as a "quasi-nation," some scholars would contend, has been that "[t]he political history of Laos since 1945 has been dominated by the efforts of various Lao and foreign groups to construct a political entity named 'Laos' where none existed before" (Steinberg et al. 1987: 383).

During the civil war between 1954 and 1975 Laos was divided into two geographical entities, one controlled by the Pathet Lao and the other by the Royal Lao Government. The zone dividing these two units was a dynamic and flunctuating one, as each side in the conflict gained the upper hand, however temporarily.[2] In Toye's view, this surgery of Laos was an outcome of the country's role as a buffer state in the Indochina conflict and it delayed the construction of a unified Laos:

> At the heart of this confrontation [in Indochina] lay the kingdom of Laos, which the Geneva Agreement sought to establish as a neutral buffer state between pro-Western Siam and the Communist enemy to the north. But the Indo-China War had made Prince Souphanouvong and his Pathet Lao a force to be reckoned with. Laos had emerged from the war politically divided and deeply impressed by the new power of the Viet Minh. The French defeat at Dien Bien Phu left her exposed as never before. Whether the kingdom could ever become stable enough to act effectively as a buffer state was indeed the question (Toye 1968: 82–3).

The vision of Laos as neutral state, the modern analogy of "the nineteenth-century buffer zone" which was fundamental to the Geneva settlement of 1954 proved impossible to achieve (Toye 1968). Endless, and ultimately futile, international and regional negotiations were held and Laotian government coalitions created in order to avoid an extension of the Indochina conflict into Laos. Perhaps the only alternative to the temporary division of Laos would have been the incorporation or annexation of the country either by the Thai or Vietnamese. Thai fear of Vietnamese expansionism had already, in 1940, made her launch a campaign to "recover" the Laotian provinces on the west bank of the Mekong. Seen from the Thai point of view, the traditional geographical barrier was the Annamite chain.

Not all scholars agree with this interpretation of Laos as a product more of external feuding than internal coherence. Dommen, for example, writes that the territories unified by Fa Ngoum in 1353 and known as Lane Xang remained a powerful kingdom for 350 years, "a state in the true sense of the term, delineated by borders clearly defined and consecrated by treaty" (Dommen 1985: 18). He goes on:

> Lao historians see a positive proof of the existence of a distinct Lao race (*sua sat Lao*), a Lao nation (*sat Lao*), a Lao country (*muong Lao*), and a Lao state (*pathet Lao*). In view of these facts, we may safely reject the notion, fashionable among apologists for a colonial enterprise of a later day, that Laos was a creation of French colonial policy and administration (Dommen 1985: 19).

What is perhaps more interesting than this debate over the historical origins of a Lao identity, is that Laos has continued to find itself caught between competing powers. It is this which explains why the country has remained important—and thus a "keystone"—and yet has continued to be subservient to the interests of outsiders, and hence "marginal" or "peripheral." This is reflected, for example, in recent events. Since the late 1980s Laos has endeavored to build closer and more amicable relations with all of its neighbors, mirroring the process of reapproachment within the wider mainland Southeast Asian region. The country's future has once more become tied to that of its neighbors. Thailand has been Laos's largest foreign investor during the period 1988–1996, accounting for 38 percent of approved foreign investment (Lintner 1997: 32) and regional governments, along with the Asian Development Bank, have enthusiastically promoted the notion of a Greater Mekong Sub-region in which Laos would play a pivotal role—at least in geographical terms. But this has, in turn, led to concerns of overdependency, particularly with reference to Thailand. While it is too soon to speculate on the long-term implications of the economic and financial crisis which beset Thailand and other Asian economies in 1997, the immediate effect has been to heighten these concerns still further.

A FORGOTTEN COUNTRY AND A GOLDEN LAND

WITH the disintegration of the Soviet Union and rapprochement between the countries of Southeast Asia, reflected most clearly in the accession of Vietnam to the Association of Southeast Asian Nations (ASEAN) in mid-1995 so, it could be argued, Laos's strategic importance has been diminished. But while Laos may no longer be a (minor) player in the Cold War, economics and geography have created for it a new niche. Rich in land and natural resources, and strategically placed on a "crossroads" linking some of the fastest growing economies in the world, it has been suggested that Laos is a key node within mainland Southeast Asia (Stuart-Fox 1991, Lintner 1995). It has been argued that the countries surrounding Laos are bound by their dependence upon the Mekong River and Laos, lying at the heart of the Mekong, is in a position to play "a crucial role in the success of co-operative efforts in the subregion" (Pante 1994: 277).

The process of modernization, it seems, is regarded as an integrating force in the area. This was best exemplified by former Thai prime minister Chatchai Chunhawan's clarion call in 1988 to turn Indochina from "a battlefield into a marketplace." The priorities that underpin this new vision of cooperation within mainland Southeast Asia are reflected in the emergence of the Greater Mekong Sub-region, or GMS, comprising Laos, Cambodia, Vietnam, Thailand, Myanmar (Burma), and the Chinese province of Yunnan (map 1). Promoted by the Asian Development Bank, the rationale of the GMS rests on cooperative ventures in trade, investment, finance, technology, infrastructure, natural and human resource development, and in environmental protection (Pante 1994). For Laos, while during the period 1975–1989 landlockedness was perceived as a hindrance and constraint to national development, it is now being presented as an advantage within the context of the GMS. The GMS has, in short, become the vehicle by which landlockedness can be transformed from a national liability into a national asset.

INTEGRATION AND DISINTEGRATION OF NATIONAL SPACE

THE spatial organization of Laos is heavily concentrated on the western part of the country. The Mekong River forms the border between Laos and Thailand and much human and therefore economic activity is focused there. In the past the Mekong was a critical communication conduit and the alluvial lowlands of the Mekong Valley also permitted agricultural intensification to occur and, on that basis, a comparatively dense pattern of rural settlement to arise. Route no. 13, the main north-south highway, also follows the course of the Mekong for much of its length. Initially built by the French it is in the process of being upgraded and has reestablished itself as the main artery for transport in the country.[3] It is interesting to note the extent to which improvements to land transportation are undermining river transport. For example passenger vessels between Vientiane and Thakhek are reported to be less frequent now that the road has been surfaced and new (and much faster) bus services introduced. Nonetheless, the country's largest urban areas, notably Vientiane, Paksé, Savannakhet, and Louang

MAP 1

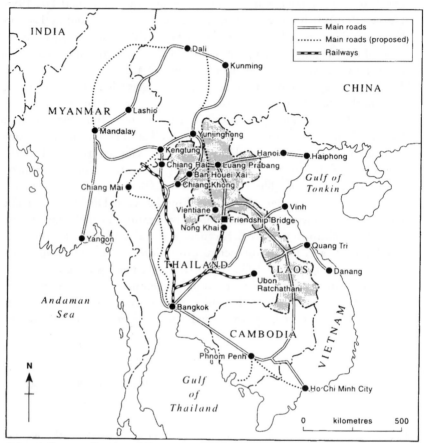

Map 1: Laos - Regional Integration

Prabang, are situated on the Mekong and only here is there the density of settlement to allow an integrated market and administrative system to evolve (table 1).

In addition to this east-west division there also exists a north-south dichotomy. The northern provinces, once again only at a general level, have less favorable conditions for agriculture with only small areas of lowland suitable for wet rice agriculture, meagre soils, and degraded forest resources which tend to be associated with problems of soil erosion and flooding. By contrast, Laos's southern provinces have abundant resources of alluvial lowlands which produce a surplus of rice. They also enjoy better access to markets, and have a high forest coverage allowing industrial activities based on forest exploitation to flourish.

TABLE 1   LAOS: POPULATION DENSITY

Province	Population	Area km² ('000s)	Population density
Attapeu	80	10,320	8
Bokeo	64	4,970	13
Bolikhamsai	145	16,470	9
Champassak	469	15,415	30
Houaphan	243	16,500	15
Khammouane	249	16,315	15
Louang Namtha	114	9,325	12
Louang Prabang	339	16,875	20
Udomxai	291	21,190	14
Phongsaly	142	16,270	9
Saravane	211	10,385	20
Savannakhet	640	22,080	29
Sayaboury	182	11,795	15
Sekong	58	7,665	8
Vientiane (municipality)	442	3,920	113
Vientiane (province)	312	19,990	16
Xieng Khouang	189	17,315	11

Source:Ministry of Agriculture and Forestry, quoted in Koninck 1994: 247.

With its history of spatial division, it might have been expected that the leaders of the newly created Lao People's Democratic Republic would set out to centralize power and reduce provincial autonomy. But instead the provinces were granted yet more autonomy.[4] From 1975, provincial agricultural self-sufficiency—irrespective of each province's natural endowment of resources—was highlighted as a key objective. Provinces were also expected to generate their own income, by collecting "internal" taxes. Stuart-Fox writes that "[w]hat was remarkable in a socialist state was the extent to which regional autonomy was given official recognition and even encouragement" (1996: 173). He continues:

> The central government was forced by lack of resources to make a virtue of necessity in encouraging regional self-sufficiency. This included not just the production of food crops and other basic necessities, but was extended to the financing and implementation of provincial development programmes (1996: 173).

After meeting their obligations to central government, the provinces were permitted to sell surplus production on their own account. The foreign exchange earned, after central government had extracted a percentage, could then be used as the provincial authorities saw fit (Stuart-Fox 1996: 173). In this way, provinces can be seen to have been operating like small, semi-autonomous "states," in the process working against the forces of national unity. Since all provinces have international borders, and since east-west communication links with neighboring countries are often better than north-south links with neighboring provinces, the autonomy granted to the provincial authorities tended to facilitate the growth of international, as opposed to national, economic relations.

But this view of Laos being comprised of numerous "mini-states" based on provincial units with considerable economic autonomy did not translate into political autonomy. Local party leaders were permitted latitude in their economic dealings, but they were still (central) party cadres who owed their positions to the leadership in Vientiane. The granting of considerable economic autonomy did not threaten the legitimacy of the Lao state; indeed, it was sanctioned by the centre. The different natural and human resource endowments of each province created the possibility for different economic activities to evolve and strong provincial leaders and entrepreneurs were permitted to exploit the comparative advantages of their fiefs. One such man was Khamphoui Keoboualapha, a southerner who became chairman of the Champassak administrative committee after the formation of the LPDR. He earned a reputation as an effective administrator working as the sectretary of the Lao People's Revolutionary Party in Saravane. "Under his direction," Stuart-Fox and Kooyman write, "Saravane was particularly successful in building trading links with Vietnam and Thailand" (1992: 64). But Khamphoui's skills brought him to Vientiane where he became deputy prime minister and where, it is said, he was the architect of many of Laos's economic reforms. He again used his close relations with Thai investors but this time at the national rather than the provincial level.[5]

The capital, Vientiane, and Laos's other major urban centres deserve special mention at this point. The communication system is best developed around Vientiane and the institutional superstructure favors the Vientiane region where political power and modern economic activity (banking, manufacturing and trading) all tend to be concentrated. In addition to Vientiane's population of around 250,000, the other major economic "nodes" are Savannakhet with a population of 109,000 and Paksé with 55,000 inhabitants. Louang Prabang with 20,000 inhabitants, can be regarded as a minor node (Lao PDR 1994: 6) (map 2). As one might expect, physical infrastruture is concentrated on these nodes. Taken together, Vientiane, Savannakhet and Paksé account for the great bulk of

Laos's small urban population and a large proportion of the country's domestic and international trade is channelled through these cities.

Although the tendency for political and economic activities to become centralised in the capital city is not unusual—Thailand's capital, Bangkok, is probably the world's finest example of a primate city—Laos's acute transportation difficulties makes this, potentially, far more of a hindrance because communication between the center and the periphery is that much more difficult. The Lao government has identified the upgrading of transport and communications to be possibly its most important task. Between 1986 and 1990 government expenditure on transport averaged 40 percent of total expenditure (Zasloff and Brown 1991: 149), while in the most recent Public Investment Program (1991/92–1995/96) 40 percent of total planned outlays were allocated to the transport sector (Nielsen 1994: 184). This was the highest allocation for any sector.

Even so, the task facing the government is immense: of the country's network of 13,300 kilometers of roads, just 20 percent are paved; 80 percent of the country is defined as mountainous; the average population density is just 17 per square kilometer making "the cost per capita of providing the necessary infrastructure . . . prohibitive" (Lao PDR 1989: 49); financial resources are limited;[6] and the legacy of the destruction wrought by the war in Indochina remains a serious obstacle. Even roads which have been relatively recently upgraded, like route no. 9 which was upgraded in 1988, are deteriorating because of lack of maintenance and the effects of the tropical climate.

ECONOMIC REFORM AND SPATIAL IMBALANCE

MOST studies of market reform emphasize that spatial imbalances become more acute as certain areas—under the effects of the forces of competition—benefit to a greater extent than others.[7] Thus, in the short-term at least, spatial inequalities are likely to widen. For Laos the available information on the equity effects of the NEM is thin, and often anecdotal. (But see the end of this section for a discussion of the results of the country's first expenditure and consumption survey.) However, for Vietnam, studies are more plentiful and these can be used as indicators of the likely pattern of spatial impacts in the Lao PDR. It should be emphasized, though, that while the emphasis here is on spatial inequalities (regional, core-periphery, and rural-urban), these are just spatial reflections of interpersonal inequalities.

A Living Standards Measurement Survey (LSMS) was undertaken by the Vietnamese government in 1993 to ascertain standards of living in

MAP 2

Map 2: Laos

Vietnam. This, as most prior observations had indicated, showed that while GDP per capita in the northern mountains and midlands, and in the north central coast region, averaged just US$75, in the Mekong Delta, as well as around Hanoi and Haiphong in the north it ranged between US$100 and US$275. Such data as are available all indicate that the south is growing faster than the north, and that the northern mountain provinces particularly are lagging behind the rest of the country. The emergence of such uneven spatial development was a particular topic of debate—and concern—at Vietnam's 7th Party Congress in 1992 (Beresford and McFarlane 1995: 60). However, although regional differentials exist, there is not the available statistical evidence to say for certain whether such differentials predate the reforms in Vietnam (see Fforde and Sénèque 1995: 116). Beresford and McFarlane quote figures to indicate that the North was highly egalitarian prior to reunification and the economic reforms. But "these figures probably indicate nothing more than what Vietnamese commentators have often pointed out . . . that equal incomes meant shared poverty" (Beresford and McFarlane 1995: 57). Vietnam, then, may be making the transition from shared poverty to unequal prosperity. "Official egalitarianism, in so far as it existed, has been abandoned . . ." (Bereford and McFarlane 1995: 58). In rural areas of Vietnam, the agricultural reforms have undermined the apparent uniformity of the past, contributing to a significant increase in inequality. The income spread in rural areas of Vietnam in 1990 was said to have widened to four to one and individual land holdings in some rice-growing areas had reached 100 hectares, and in upland areas over 500 hectares (Kerkvliet and Porter 1995: 16, Kerkvliet 1995: 73).[8]

A similar picture of widening spatial and interpersonal inequalities emerges in scholarship on Laos. In fertile areas, particularly those along the Mekong Valley where existing roads allow reasonable market integration, farmers are responding to and benefiting from the incentives enshrined in the New Economic Mechanism (NEM). But in peripheral highland areas the reforms are distant and often irrelevant. This emerging spatial dichotomy also has an ethnic dimension. The politically and economically dominant Lao Loum tend to populate the (accessible) lowlands while the minority Lao Soung and Lao Theung occupy the (inaccessible) uplands. There are reports of growing dissatisfaction among the Lao Theung and Lao Soung, many of whom supported the Pathet Lao during the revolution but now feel that another Lao Loum–dominated government in Vientiane is simply ignoring their particular plight. An aid worker quoted in the *Far Eastern Economic Review* in 1996 said that, "When [the Lao Theung and Lao Soung] come down to Vientiane, where the lowland Lao live, it's like Hong Kong to them. Here's money, here's development. In their own villages, there's nothing" (Lintner 1996: 26). But this is not to say that there is a

simple upland-lowland division in terms of prosperity, or a simple rural-
urban one for that matter. Within accessible lowland areas, the fruits of
reform are also unequally distributed.

Trankell, for example, reports that while villagers welcomed the
additional opportunities for economic enterprise created by the reforms,
they were at the same time quite aware "that the new system would
probably have at least as many losers as winners" (1993: 92). Håkangård's
study of route 13, the main north-south highway, notes that while for
richer households it had created numerous new moneymaking
opportunities, poorer households were too busy surviving to take advantage
of the reforms (Håkangård, 1992).

In 1990 Laos received assistance from the United Nations Development
Program to carry out the country's first expenditure and consumption
survey. The survey, undertaken between March 1992 and February 1993,
covered 2,937 households (19,574 people) drawn from a sample of 147
villages from every province of the country. The results of the Lao
Expenditure and Consumption Survey (LECS) were released in July 1995
(NSC 1995). They show, as one might have expected, a country where levels
of consumption are uniformly low. Of total consumption, 62 percent is
allocated to food, 13 percent to housing, and 5 percent to personal care and
recreation (figure 1). Average household consumption in 1992–3 was just
under 85,000 kip, or less than US$100. By some international standards, if
food accounts for 60 percent or more of total household consumption then
a household should be regarded as poor, and if it is above 80 percent then
its members should be designated as living in severe poverty. Using these
measures, the LECS revealed that 72 percent of households were poor, and
44 percent severely poor (figure 2).

However if we take poverty to be a function of inequality, then the
picture is rather different. Almost two-thirds of households fall around the
median level of consumption, defined as consumption within 50 percent of
the median (between 8,000 and 24,000 kip per "consumption unit," with a
median of 16,000 kip). One in four households have a consumption level
above 24,000 kip while less than one in ten have a level below 8,000 kip
(figure 3). The results of the LECS tend to confirm Laos as a country
displaying shared poverty while the experience in Vietnam would lead one
to expect inequalities to widen as incomes rise.

FIGURE 1

LEVEL AND STRUCTURE OF HOUSEHOLD CONSUMPTION, LAOS
(1992–93)

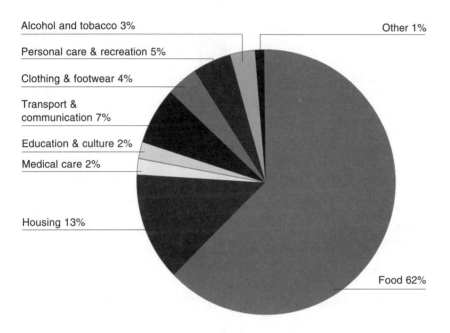

Alcohol and tobacco 3%

Personal care & recreation 5%

Clothing & footwear 4%

Transport & communication 7%

Education & culture 2%

Medical care 2%

Housing 13%

Other 1%

Food 62%

FIGURE 2

FOOD AS A PROPORTION OF TOTAL CONSUMPTION, LAOS (1992–93)

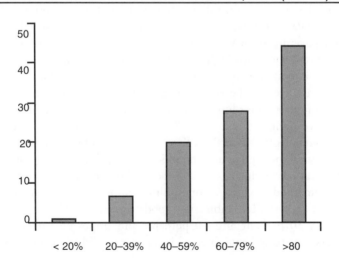

FIGURE 3

INEQUALITY IN CONSUMPTION, LAOS (1992–93)

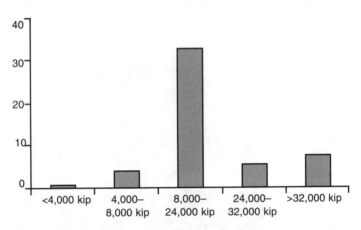

Note: The median consumption level is 16,000 kip per "consumption unit."
Source: NSC 1995

LAOS IN REGIONAL AND GLOBAL PERSPECTIVE

THE characterization of Laos as the "forgotten country" (see Neher 1991 and 1995, Sesser 1993, Chi Do Pham 1994) stems from its political isolation—especially between 1975 and 1989—and its economic marginality. In the context of the world system of relations, Laos virtually fell off the map after the full and final victory of the communist Pathet Lao in 1975. Partly this was a product of the quasi-isolationist policies pursued by the government in Vientiane. However it was also a result of Indochina's general isolation following the communist victories there.

Laos, in building physical, economic, and diplomatic links with Vietnam to the east, created the environment in which Thailand felt "impelled" to sever or restrict Laos's links to the west. During this period of confrontation —which culminated in a serious border conflict in 1987–88 over a series of contested villages at Ban Rom Klao—Thailand consistently used the border as a political tool and as an economic weapon, closing the border on at least four occasions, reducing the number of border posts, restricting trade in "strategic goods" which at one point numbered 363 products including bicycles and needles, subjecting goods for sale in Thailand to tariffs of between 30 percent and 60 percent, and imposing various non tariff barriers. Lee Yong Leng observed in a paper published during this period of confrontation that "Laos is a good example of a land-locked state at an ideological boundary suffering from the enmity of its neighbor [Thailand]" (Lee Yong Leng 1980: 47). It was, of course, partly a result of Bangkok's intransigent position that the Lao leadership embarked on a program of upgrading the French-built roads running eastwards over the Annamite chain and into Vietnam:

> Vietnamese leaders seem confident that history is with them. The refurbished road system, the new flow of commerce in Vietnam's direction, the emerging institutions of Indochina, the technical and political training of young Laotians will combine to give Vietnam an increasing role in shaping the destiny of Laos (Zasloff 1988: 58).

The leadership in Vientiane tried harder to maintain a semblance of balance in its relations with its two fellow communist neighbors to the north and east—China and Vietnam—during this period of confrontation with Thailand (1975–1989). Although many of the leading lights in the Lao People's Revolutionary Party (LPRP) felt they owed a debt to Vietnam, both national and personal, they tried hard to ensure that close relations with Hanoi did not lead to a deterioration in relations with Beijing. It is notable that only with the Chinese incursion into Vietnam in 1979 (following Vietnam's invasion of Kampuchea) did Laos come off the fence and criticize the Chinese as "international reactionaries." Even then, there is some evidence to indicate that signals were being sent to Beijing indicating that Vientiane had been forced into this position by the exigencies of *real politik*, rather than through choice. Stuart-Fox believes it is significant that the Chinese media was less savage in its denunciations of Vientiane than it was of Moscow and Hanoi, perhaps indicating that the Chinese accepted that Vientiane found itself in an almost impossible situation (1996: 147–157). Nonetheless, relations between Vientiane and Beijing remained antagonistic, if not overtly hostile, until the mid-1980s.

A marked improvement in relations between Laos and Thailand had to wait until the late-1980s. The continuing rapprochement between the two countries has been driven partly by global geopolitical developments, reinforced by Laos's economic reform program.

Trade restrictions between Thailand and Laos were lifted in November 1989 and, in April 1994, the first bridge over the lower reaches of the Mekong River was formally inaugurated. This concrete monument to the progress of rapprochement between the countries of Southeast Asia was unsurprisingly named the Mittaphap or "Friendship Bridge." Taken together, these economic and political changes have, it has been argued, transformed Laos—"one of the world's most isolated people's republics"

—to a virtual crossroads state (*FEER* 1996). With Vietnam joining the Association of Southeast Asian Nations (ASEAN) in 1995, Laos soon followed in 1997.

Economic reform and political rapprochement have allowed politicians, journalists and academics to talk of a Greater Mekong Sub-region (GMS) linking Laos with Cambodia, Myanmar, Thailand, Vietnam, and the Yunnan, China. The common denominator for all these countries is the Mekong River. But within the context of the GMS, Laos occupies a pivotal position, being the only country which shares borders with each of the other five Mekong states. Laos has been reported to be "an especially enthusiastic supporter of sub regional co-operation" (Stuart-Fox 1995: 179) and former Deputy Prime Minister Khampoui Keoboualapha stated in an interview: "We want to become the link between Vietnam, China, Thailand, Burma and Cambodia" (Lintner 1995: 19). The Asian Development Bank sees the GMS as a rational and pragmatic attempt to promote market integration among complementary economies to enable the efficient use of human, financial, and natural resources (ADB 1995).

> Given the globalization of the world economy, this [providing a receptive climate for domestic and international investment] can be significantly enhanced by facilitating economies of scale and specialisation, where sub regional co-operation can play an important role. In this context, there is a natural process of sub regional integration at work, spurred by the profit incentive of market forces, so that private sector developments often lead the process of co-operation (ADB 1995: 2).

Two main areas for GMS cooperation have been singled out: physical infrastructure—especially roads, but also rail—and energy. All the infrastructure projects have a core objective of facilitating trade and development among and between the countries of the GMS by reducing transport costs and increasing efficiency of movement. But the ADB goes further to include a whole raft of further desirable outcomes which, presumably, are expected to flow from this emerging, and vital, subregional grouping. It will support rural development, increase earnings of low-income groups by enhancing the mobility of rural communities, alleviate poverty and provide employment opportunities for women in areas along the route, and promote tourism (ADB 1995). Laos with its central location is involved in the majority of the planned projects (tables 2 and 3). All the potential hydropower projects are located in Laos and the country's strategic location for trade between the GMS countries is evident in the road projects of which five out of seven involve Laos.

In terms of energy resources, the countries of Indochina are relatively

TABLE 2 PROJECTS IN THE GMS			
Sector	Agency of projects	Total no.in Laos (%)	Projects
Transport			
Road	GMS	7	5 (71%)
	AIDAB	4	1 (25%)
Rail	GMS	3	2 (67%)
Water transport	GMS	9	2 (22%)
Air transport	GMS	3	1 (33%)
Institutional	GMS	2	2 (100%)
	Mekong	9	6 (66%)
	ESCAP	7	7 (100%)
Energy			
Hydropower	GMS	4	4 (100%)
	Mekong	4	2 (50%)
Transmission	GMS	4	4 (100%)
	Mekong	1	1 (100%)
Oil & natural gas	GMS	2	1 (50%)
Institutional	GMS	4	4 (100%)
	Mekong	1	1 (100%)
	ESCAP	1	0 (0%)
Total		65	43 (66%)

Source: ADB 1995.

well endowed, but their geographic distribution is uneven, indicating that comparative advantages exist in subregional cooperation.[9] Laos has been variously dubbed the "battery" of Southeast Asia (*Economist* 1993) and the "Kuwait of Indochina" (Lintner 1994). It has the largest hydropower potential—some 18,000MW according to a study undertaken by the Swedish International Development Agency (SIDA)—and, as yet, has only developed 1 percent of this potential (ADB 1995). Schemes can be divided into those based on the Mekong River and those located on tributaries of the Mekong. The plans include detailed provision for the transmission of energy between the countries of the region and *in toto* have been described as "the stuff of engineers' dreams and environmentalists' nightmares" (*Economist* 1993).

Laos may remain poor, but it is no longer isolated and inward-looking. The economic reforms have brought the possibility, indeed some would argue the inevitability, of greater economic integration. It is the nature of this integration which is the issue, and whether it can broadly be interpreted

TABLE 3 MAJOR GMS ROAD PROJECTS INVOLVING LAOS

Thai–Lao PDR–Vietnam East-West Corridor project. Twin corridors will improve transport between Laos, Vietnam and Thailand. One road corridor will connect the Khorat Plateau (northeast Thailand) with Thakhek (road no. 12) in Laos, pass through Mu Gia and terminate at the Vietnamese coast. A second corridor will link Mukdahan (northeast Thailand) with Savannakhet in Laos and then, using road no. 9), pass through the Annamite Mountains and terminate at Quang Tri in Vietnam. A second international crossing of the Mekong River will be considered as part of this project. The road investments will improve Laos's access to the sea.

Chiang Rai–Kunming Road Improvement Project via Myanmar and Lao PDR. The project will improve the international north-south road linking China's Yunnan province, Myanmar, Laos (road no. 1), and Thailand. The principal objective driving this project is the desire to improve and upgrade road transport links between Thailand and China. A parallel road runs from Phayao in northern Thailand, via Myanmar, to Yunnan.

Southern Lao PDR–Sihanoukville Road Improvement Project. This project will improve the links between Laos and the Cambodian port of Sihanoukville (Kompong Som). It will provide Laos with access to the sea through a third country and in the long term provide Cambodia with direct access to China through Laos.

Southern Yunnan Province–Northern Thailand–Northern Lao PDR–Northern Vietnam Road Improvement Project. This will provide an east-west link, connecting all the GMS countries.

Northeastern Thailand–Southern Lao PDR–Northeastern Cambodia-Central Vietnam Corridor Project. This project will link Ubon Ratchathani in northeast Thailand with Paksé, Strung Treng (Cambodia), Quy Nhon, and Da Nang (both in Vietnam). Thailand and Laos will be involved indirectly. According to Stuart-Fox it will "open up the Bolovens plateau" (Stuart-Fox 1995: 180).

Source: ADB 1995

as developmental or corrosive. It seems likely that Laos will be integrated into the regional economy in terms of the complementaries that exist between it and its neighbors, and especially Thailand. These complementaries would seem to rest upon the country's abundance of natural resources, its pivotal position within the context of mainland Southeast Asia and, though to a much lesser extent, cheap labor.[10]

In April 1995, the four co-riparian states on the Lower Mekong—Laos, Thailand, Cambodia, and Vietnam—signed an agreement in the northern Thai town of Chiang Rai on Cooperation for the Sustainable Development of the Mekong River Basin. The Mekong River Commission (MRC) was created to coordinate the project, replacing the Mekong Secretariat which was established in 1958. Laos successfully lobbied for the headquarters of the MRC to change its location from Bangkok to Vientiane on the basis that Laos as the natural—and "neutral"—keystone in the region is ideally suited to the function. Laotian diplomats pointed out that a third of the length of the Lower Mekong flows within its borders and 40 percent of its tributaries rise in Laos. Again, the Laotian leadership is identifying a role and a place for itself within mainland Southeast Asia on the basis of its geographical centrality.

ECONOMIC INTEGRATION, MODERNIZATION AND DEPENDENCY

THE view from the village: The key to economic integration, which is the touchstone of the GMS, is to develop Laos's physical infrastructure (see table 3). At present roads are so poor that the movement of people and goods is costly and slow. It has become usual, for example, for people traveling overland south from Vientiane to cross into Thailand to use the much faster Thai road network, and then to cross back into Laos either at Mukdahan (Savannakhet) or at Ubon Ratchathani/Chong Mek (Paksé). Table 4 shows travel times and average speeds of public transport links between major centers in the country.

Infrastructural improvements are seen by most politicians and officials as a self-evident "good." Former Deputy Prime Minister Khamphoui Keoboualapha was quoted in 1995 as remarking that "[n]ew roads will bring development to remote areas" (Lintner 1995: 19). However there are fears that they will also create new dependencies and inequalities. The improving road network is bringing many people into touch with the wider market economy for the first time. The ability to buy and sell with relative ease is making households dependent on the market. It is transforming relations between households, as farmers, for example, make the transition from traditional forms of reciprocal labor exchange to wage labor, and as agricultural systems increasingly rely on cash inputs. It is also transforming relations between the sexes as the unequal effects of modernization on men and women are brought to bear. Some studies elsewhere in the region show that the gender implications of technological change in agriculture have been to marginalize women. For example, the use of combine harvesters and mechanical hullers in rice cultivation and processing has tended to displace women from activities that were traditionally their preserve. Parnwell and Arghiros, with reference to the Thai experience, argue that mechanization has seen a decline in the importance of female labor in

TABLE 4 TRANSPORT TIMES IN LAOS (MAY 1996)

Route	Distance (km)	Time	Averagespeed	Road conditions
Roads north from Vientiane				
Vientiane to Van Vieng	160 km	3 hrs	53 km/hr	good, surfaced road
Van Vieng to Louang Prabang		13 hrs	-	undergoing upgrading, due
Roads south from Vientiane				
Vientiane to Pakxan	155 km	2–3 hrs	62 km/hr	good surfaced road with new bridges
Pakxan to Thakhek	190 km	5–6 hrs	35 km/hr	undergoing upgrading, due for completion by 1997
Thakhek to Savannakhet	139 km	3–4 hrs	40 km/hr	good, surfaced road
Vientiane to Savannakhet	484 km	10–13 hrs	44 km/hr	
Savannakhet to Vietnamese border	236 km	5 hrs	47 km/hr	rough road, partly sealed border
Savannakhet to Paksé	250 km	6–8 hrs	36 km/hr	poor road, unsurfaced, but being slowly upgraded
Paksé to Saravan	125 km	3–4 hrs	36 km/hr	new, surfaced road
Saravan to Sekong	98 km	4hrs	25 km/hr	dirt road undergoing improvement
Paksé to Don Khong	130 km	4–5 hrs	29 km/hr	unsurfaced, laterite

Note: These are approximate bus/truck times for the dry season as of May 1996. During the wet season road travel except on newly sealed roads is considerable slower and some routes are impassable. Laos's roads are being gradually upgraded and this, coupled with the arrival of new vehicles from Japan to replace aging Soviet-era trucks and buses, will increase average travel speeds.

agriculture as mechanical innovations have become monopolized by men. As a result, a process of "masculinization" of agriculture has occurred (Parnwell and Arghiros 1996: 21–22). In Laos it seems that the emerging sexual division of labor under the effects of mechanization is rather different—at least so far—and that it has selectively lessened the workload of men. Tractors and cultivators, particularly, have reduced the time involved in land preparation, a traditionally male-oriented task in Laos, as it is elsewhere in the region.[11] This has given men, but not women, the chance to look for work outside agriculture, leading to a "feminization of agriculture" and the subsidization of the reproduction of the non-farm workforce by women's subsistence production (Trankell 1993: 82). Taking a structural stance, it is possible to argue that in this way agriculture is providing a subsidy to industry.

Taking a class rather than a gender perspective, road improvements, in conjunction with the economic effects of the New Economic Mechanism, are also accentuating inequalities within villages. Håkangård's study of the effects of the upgrading of route 13 (the main north-south highway) suggests that while the road has brought cumulative gains to those households in a position to exploit the new opportunities it provides, for poorer households—as noted earlier—the need just to survive consumes all their time and energy (Håkangård 1992).

The role of road and transport improvements in the type of transformations outlined above are highly important, and often overlooked. Without the means to buy inputs at competitive prices, and to sell output at close to the market rate, farmers lack both the means and the incentive to enter into market transactions. Dick and Forbes on Indonesia write of the "silent revolution" or the "revolusi colt."[12] They argue that improved transport and communications does not just permit more efficient economic activity, they act as a catalyst for increased and different economic activities: ". . . in the late 20th century, preoccupied with production and figures on agriculture, industry and GDP, we risk becoming blasé about transport, sometimes perceiving it as an 'obstacle,' but seldom as a dynamic element in economic development" (Dick and Forbes 1992: 258).

But improvements in transport and communication do not just create new dependencies on the market and new patterns of relations between men and women. They may also widen spatial inequalities as the effects of road improvements bring some areas into contact with the market and leave others—comparatively—even more isolated. Gina Porter's work on Nigeria (1995) demonstrates that when a road is upgraded, businesses tend to gravitate towards the road. Shops, repair outlets, traders, local transport services, and marketing concerns congregate at the roadside, denuding offroad communities of services and, paradoxically, sometimes making it harder for people living offroad to gain access to these services. In Laos, road improvements are certainly leading to an explosion of roadside economic activity; whether, as in Porter's African study, it is simultaneously denuding offroad communities is hard to confirm. At a wider level it is possible to argue that the concentration of road improvement programs in lowland areas populated largely by Lao Loum (lowland Lao) is causing inequalities between the Lao Loum and Lao Theung (midland Lao) and Lao Soung (upland Lao) to widen.

The national perspective: The previous section focused on the likely effects of road improvements at the local level. However much of the recent discussion of the GMS and the infrastructural investments associated with it has emphasised the extent to which they will alter Laos's relations with neighboring countries and Laos's place within an emerging regional (mainland Southeast Asian) economy.

Already, improved access to—and through—Laos has markedly increased trade. Trade volumes across the Lao-China border have risen dramatically and so too has trade between Laos and Thailand. Plans to further upgrade and expand transport links—including a Thai-financed 250-kilometer tollway from the Thai border to Louang Nam Tha, and the extension of the Bangkok–Nong Khai railway line to Tha Deua and Vientiane and perhaps as far as Vang Vieng—will all drive the process of economic integration that is already well underway.

There are essentially two fears linked to the GMS. First is the fear that integration will bring few economic benefits to Laos. It will become a trucking stop, a transit country between more powerful economic players, in particular Thailand and China. The benefits that will accrue to Laos in such a scenario will be few. Towns on the main through roads may derive some benefit from increased economic activity, but it is likely that this will be narrowly focused from a spatial point of view. It might even have a negative economic effect in some areas. The plan to route a new highway linking Vientiane with China through the UNESCO World Heritage city of Louang Prabang has brought concerns that the increased traffic may undermine the city's tourist potential and also damage its incomparable architectural heritage.

The second fear is that neighboring countries' interest in Laos lies mainly in its abundant natural resources. "Slash and burn" capitalism of the type being pursued in the south where large-scale Thai-orchestrated logging is underway is regarded as bringing only short-term benefits, and long-term environmental costs (see Rigg and Jerndal 1996, Hirsch 1995). The tendency has been to see Thai commercial interests as the villains of the piece. And certainly, the manner in which Thailand's own natural resources have been plundered with apparently scarcely a care (until recently), and the shift of commercial attention to neighboring Laos, Cambodia, and Myanmar, does lend support to the view that having pillaged its own natural wealth, "Thailand" is doing the same to its neighbors. But it is important to remember that Lao actors are also involved—and with the government's express approval. Three military "development" companies have been awarded the rights to log and exploit the forest. The economic role of the army was spelled out ten years ago: "Our Army must continue boosting production of foodstuffs, essential goods, and goods for export; contributing to producing resources for society; building local logistics supply sources; and improving its own local conditions by itself. . . . It must try to participate in building the local economy and certain important state enterprises" (FBIS 11 February 185, quoted in Stuart-Fox 1986: 143).

The same criticisms have been leveled at the plans to develop Laos's hydropower potential. Not only are the dams environmentally destructive, but the power they will generate is largely destined for Thailand. The manner in which negotiations have been managed between the Lao government and the Electricity Generating Authority of Thailand (EGAT) has led critics to argue that Laos will become highly dependent on a single export to a single country, and that EGAT will be able to dictate terms. A document prepared by the Swedish International Development Agency (SIDA) suggests that the manner in which Laos's hydropower potential is being exploited—on a Build Operate Transfer (BOT) basis—raises "the imminent danger that the country [might lose] control over the exploitation over one of its major natural resources" (quoted in Lintner 1994: 70). Rigg argues that "plans to further develop the country's hydropower potential with a view to supplying the Thai market will only serve to further tie Laos into a dependent, and subordinate, relationship with Thailand" (Rigg 1995: 161). The irony which is not lost on all Lao is that while development of the country's hydropower potential for the benefit of Thailand is continuing apace, there are many regional centers which are without power or which have their electricity supplied for only part of the day by generators. Sekong just off the Bolovens Plateau and close to the site of a pump storage plant on the Houay Ho River is one. Even the proposal to extend the Bangkok-Nongkhai railway line as far as Vang Vieng, north of Vientiane, is motivated by the desire to exploit the iron ore deposits of the area.

The present situation in which Laos is dependent on a narrow range of exportable commodities can be compared to the French period when only coffee, cotton, and tin were extracted. In the period of confrontation between Laos and Thailand and China, Hans Luther suggested in the early 1980s that the country might become involved in a "new" structural kind of economic dependency. Luther envisaged Laos being integrated into a wider regional development scheme based on a division of labor between the countries of Indochina (Luther 1982). There is no reason why this notion should not apply in the current period of regional goodwill, except to point out that with a population of under 5 million Laos can hardly be viewed as a potential labor exporter on the scale of Myanmar. Unofficial estimates put the number of Myanmaris working in Thailand at close to 1 million (Silverman 1996). Moreover, estimating labor flows from Laos to Thailand is difficult because Laotians tend to merge with their brethren Lao in Thailand's Isan (northeastern) region.

CONCLUSION

THIS analysis has taken a rather pessimistic view of Laos's ability to enjoy the full benefits of GMS membership. It seems that while Laos is a critical component in the success of the GMS, its role will be largely as a supplier of natural resources and as a transport way-station linking, particularly, Thailand, China, and Vietnam. How Laos will benefit from closer economic ties—at least to the extent that the other members will benefit—is not clear. It is significant that Laos's integration into the region is seen almost exclusively in economic terms. Reports and papers by foreign advisors and funding agencies are almost wholly concerned with the economic aspects of integration; human resources, and the human implications of integration, are only briefly mentioned—and usually in terms of their being an "impediment." Perhaps this is why there seems to have been "no significant improvement [to] the quality of the primary and secondary educational system . . . since the start of the reform process in the mid-1980s" (Bourdet 1996: 10).[13]

The economic crisis that hit Thailand in mid-1997, and which then spread to other regional economies, has brought another dimension to this debate—although it is hard to gauge, at this stage, its longer-term implications. Dependency on Thailand when the Thai economy was healthy and growing at close to double-digit rates was all very well. But as Hans Luther put it, the result is that "when the Thai cough, the Lao catch pneumonia" (quoted in Lintner 1997: 60). The collapse of the Thai baht in July 1997 brought a corresponding collapse in the US$ value of the Lao kip. The prospect of a Thai economic recession highlighted the risks of integrating further into the Thai economic sphere of influence. Talk in Vientiane was of bolstering domestic industries and abandoning some of the grander industrialization projects which rely on further integration with Thailand.

Some scholars would take this pessimistic perspective further still and argue that development—or rather modernization—will bring positive harm to the country and its people. Recent post-developmental writing has emphasized the degree to which "development" has been a chimera concocted in the North and then imposed on an unsuspecting South. Escobar, for example, writes in his book on Third World development: "This book tells the story of this [development] dream and how it progressively turned into a nightmare. For instead of the kingdom of abundance promised by theorists and politicians in the 1950s, the discourse and strategy of development produced its opposite: massive under-development and impoverishment, untold exploitation and oppression" (1995: 4). Likewise, Sachs has argued that "[t]he idea of development stands like a ruin in the intellectual landscape. Delusion and disappoint-ment, failures and crimes have been the steady companions of development and they tell a common story: it did not work" (Sachs 1992: 1).

We do not subscribe to this view, although economic and social tensions are beginning to manifest themselves as economic reform and integration begin to bite. For those searching for a "culprit," the obvious place to look is across the Mekong to Thailand. An old proverb warns that "to listen to Thai ideas is to burn the grass in your yard" (Clutterbuck 1993: 33). Thailand is Laos's largest trading partner, its largest foreign investor, and the dominant economic power in the region. But while the environmental devastation of the forests of the south, the grand hydropower plans, and the insensitive approach that many Thai businessmen take towards Laos and the Lao can all be laid, largely, at Bangkok's door, it is all too easy to forget that Thailand's presence in the country has been sanctioned by the leadership in Vientiane. Behind every Thai venture in Laos there are influential Lao party functionaries who grease the wheels of business and conduct their partners through the red tape of the Lao bureaucracy. Admittedly, at times this may go too far. Commentators have, for example, explained Khamphoui's ejection from the politburo and central committee as a reaction against his close links with Thai investors. Yet though Bangkok may have to endure, from time to time, a certain amount of anti-Thai feeling in Vientiane, Thailand is also the country which holds the key to Laos's future development. Thailand is, at once, the cause of many of the problems that Laos faces and the solution to them. This is why managing economic and political relations between the two countries, within the context of the GMS, takes on such critical importance.

NOTES

1. More recently, Neher and Marlay have considered Laos "a satellite of Vietnam rather than a truly sovereign nation" (1995: 163).

2. It would be wrong to see Laos during this period as divided neatly into two. The Royal Lao Government managed to maintain its grip on urban areas more effectively than it did on rural areas. Thus "fingers" of Pathet Lao control extended into RLG territory, while urban "islands" where the RLG held sway existed in otherwise Pathet Lao-dominated areas.

3. As of April 1996 the road had been surfaced north from Vientiane as far as Vang Vieng and south from the capital as far as Savannakhet with some unsurfaced sections between Paksane and Thakhek (due for completion in 1997).

4. The thirty-year period of civil war and the spatial fragmentation and economic dislocations that this engendered had already given provinces a considerable degree of autonomy.

5. Khamphoui seems to have become too friendly with the Thais and in March 1996 he was ousted from the party's politburo and central committe after the Sixth Congress of the LPRP (Lintner 1996).

6. In the 1993/94 budget, out of total state investment of 122 billion kip (US$168 million), 57.6 billion kip (US$79 million) was allocated for "communications, transportation, postal services and construction" (Dommen 1994: 168). Although this is a large proportion of the budget, as a total figure for upgrading infrastructure in a country the size of Laos it is comparatively meager.

7. It is tempting to write that "certain areas benefit at the *expense* of others." This notion that the "Talents Effect" applies to market reforms is, in the most part, not borne out in the literature on economic reform in Vietnam. While it is clear that some groups are benefitting to a greater extent than others, the poor are generally not being further impoverished and livelihoods are improving, albeit to different degrees, on a broad front (see the discussion above). The Talents Effect is derived from the parable of the talents in the Bible: "For to every person who has something, even more will be given; but the person who has nothing, even the little that he has will be taken away from him" (Matthew 25:29)

8. Hoang Thi Thanh Nhan states that the income gap between rich and poor has widened from 1:2 in the early 1960s in Vietnam, to 1:3–4 in the 1970s and 1980s, and had reached 1:40–100 by the early 1990s (1995: 19–20).

9. Vietnam has abundant resources of coal and petroleum, while Cambodia has limited hydropower potential and promising prospects for off-shore gas and petroleum exploitation.

10. One of the reasons highlighted to explain the lack of growth in intra-Asean trade as a proportion of total trade is the lack of complementarities that exist between the economies of the association with the exception of Singapore. It is for this reason that having Vietnam, Laos, Cambodia, and Myanmar join ASEAN (Vietnam joined in 1995, Laos in 1997) is felt to be so attractive: it will create the economic complementarities that are felt at present to be absent (see Rigg 1995).

11. Trankell notes that few mechanical innovations, with the exception of the rice mill, have liberated women from the drudgery of manual farm work (1993).

12. "Colts" are the ubiquitous mini-vans used to transport people and goods.

13. It is estimated that 69 percent of children are enrolled in primary education which has a dropout rate of 60 percent (Lao PDR 1995: 7).

TOWARDS A NEW LAOS 3
LAO NHAY AND THE CAMPAIGN FOR
A NATIONAL "REAWAKENING" IN LAOS
1941–45

SØREN IVARSSON

IT is a commonly held view that the early beginnings of Lao nationalism can be traced to the Franco-Lao campaign for a so-called national renovation that took place in Laos during World War II. The study of Lao nationalism, however, has normally been linked with the struggle for national liberation, which leaves this French-sponsored campaign as something of a bizarre anomaly, and so far no study has been dedicated exclusively to this aspect of Lao nationalism.[1] With the development of alternative approaches to the study of nationalism epitomized by such keywords as "imagined communities" or "invented traditions," many scholars have focused on cultural matters to try to understand the way national consciousness and identity is formed. If we approach Lao nationalism from this perspective, the Franco-Lao campaign for a national renovation represents an attempt to build up a common and distinct Lao identity among the population. This campaign marks in fact the beginnings of a modern nationalist discourse on Laos and the Lao. Nowhere can we see this better than in the cultural policies set in motion during the Vichy period in Laos and in Laos's first newspaper, *Lao Nhay* (Great Laos), published in the same period.

Through an analysis primarily of *Lao Nhay*, I will try to outline some important aspects of the nationalist discourse of the 1941–45 period, namely, 1) the historical narrative advanced to legitimize the emergence of a united Laos; and 2) the attempts to standardize a "Lao" language in order to facilitate the national project. Before I turn to this analysis I will outline the background of the campaign and its general features.

THE CAMPAIGN AND ITS BACKGROUND

THE geographical shape of Laos can be traced back to the Siamese-French treaties from the turn of this century that marked the culmination of French colonial expansion into the Mekong region. In this west-bound movement the French had come into conflict with Siam, who, since the end of the eighteenth century, gradually had expanded its suzerainty over the small kingdoms and principalities found in the territory that later became Laos. The new possession of Laos was part of the overall colonial construction of French Indochina. In a recent fascinating study Christopher Goscha has illuminated how the French colonial project in French Indochina was guided by a vision to make this wider political space a reality (Goscha 1995a). The Vietnamese were supposed to form the indigenous backbone of this construction and from the beginning the Vietnamese were closely associated with this project. This pro-Vietnamese aspect of French colonial policies was tangibly expressed in the westward movement of Vietnamese that was encouraged by the French in order to staff the administrative apparatus in Cambodia and Laos with Vietnamese civil servants, and to exploit local resources by means of Vietnamese peasants and laborers.

This policy had wide implications for the demographic set-up of Laos. It has been estimated that Vietnamese accounted for about 60 percent of the total urban population in Laos in 1940 (Goscha 1995b: 429). Most French colonial administrators perceived Laos mainly as an administrative unit and no attempt was made to develop an indigenous political structure to unify Laos in the prewar period.[2] Of the traditional royal families that the French encountered in Louang Prabang, Xieng Khouang, and Champassak, the first was allowed to persist and a dual political structure was adopted, where the Louang Prabang kingdom in the north was regarded as a protectorate while the rest of Laos was regarded as a colony and administered directly by the French. As only limited investments and resources found their way to Laos, social and economic development lagged far behind that of other parts of French Indochina. Whereas the move towards an Indochina-wide political space had been set in motion, Laos and the Lao remained largely outside this structure up until the 1940s.

With the outbreak of World War II the French position in Indochina was challenged by Japanese occupation and Thai annexation of areas in Laos and Cambodia in 1940–41. In response, a Vichy-orchestrated campaign for national renovation within each separate domain of French Indochina was launched under the enthusiastic leadership of Admiral Decoux, governor general of Indochina from 1940 to 1945. Addressing the social, economic, and political spheres, the aim of this campaign was in broad terms to enroll the support of the local population, especially the local elites, to keep all of French Indochina under French suzerainty. In the case of Laos this campaign for a national renovation is of special importance as it implied a marked change in French policies with regard to this part of French Indochina. The overall emphasis was still on Indochina as a whole. However, the policies set in motion in Laos during this campaign aimed to make Laos a more viable part of the multilayered structure of French Indochina, with the individual *patries* at the bottom, the Indochinese federation in the middle, and the greater French empire at the pinnacle, uniting them all under its protective umbrella.

Already in the 1930s French policies in Laos had been subjected to public criticism. Advocating for political unification of Laos and regulation of Vietnamese immigration into Laos, Prince Phetsarath had called for a radical change in 1931.[3] As no such changes had been implemented the rise of Thai power had caused members of the Laotian elite to look favorably at Siamese control over Laos if this would grant Laos a form of independent status *vis-à-vis* Thailand. In dealings with the government in Bangkok in 1940, for example, Prince Phetsarath indicated that he would welcome Laos's return to Siam if the Lao and Thai kingdoms could coexist in a Thai-Lao confederation (Sila 1996: 61). Further, although the anti-French coup plotted by young Lao students at College Pavie in 1940 never took place, it indicated how the changing political situation nourished anti-French feelings among the Lao elite.[4] Consequently, French policies in Laos changed. An attempt was made to further integrate Laos into the Indochinese Federation in order to secure continued loyalty from the Lao elite by showing them that they had a future within the framework of French-Lao cooperation.

For Laos this change in French policies meant that more resources from the general budget were channeled into diverse sectors of society.[5] In order to better the standard of living various measures were taken in the economic sphere to boost Laos's economy and integrate it more firmly into the wider Indochinese economy. New roads were built, both roads linking different parts of Laos and roads linking Laos with other parts of Indochina. At the same time local agricultural production was to be stimulated. To this end the former Service Agricole was resurrected and put in charge of the agricultural extension on the Boloven plateau as well as the establishment of agricultural cooperatives. Likewise, the Service Forestier was reopened in order to improve the use of forest resources. In the social sphere the program aimed to improve the educational system by opening more village and temple schools. Similarly, the health situation was to be improved by establishing mobile medical units. In the administrative-political sphere several important issues were addressed. The Laotian elite was to be granted a greater role in the administration of their country. To achieve this the stream of Vietnamese immigrants into Laos was temporarily suspended and the École d'Administration in Vientiane was reformed to insure a steady flow of well-educated Laotian civil servants. Lao were also assigned to the newly instituted posts of provincial governor. Finally, the Louang Prabang kingdom, which had been forced to cede its territories on the right bank of the Mekong River to Thailand after the Thai attacks in 1940–41, was compensated for this territorial loss by being given suzerainty over all of northern Laos. At the same time the status of the kingdom was settled once and for all by designating it a protectorate *on a par* with Annam and Cambodia.

At the same time a politico-cultural campaign was launched under the auspices of the newly founded *Service de Propagande Lao* with the aim to "awaken among the Lao a national spirit (*âme nationale*) and progressively realize the moral unity (*l'unité morale*) of the country" (Pietrantoni 1943: 104). Laos no longer was to be perceived as a mere administrative unit, but as a *patrie* with a unified territory and a population possessing a unique and common identity. This campaign served two purposes. First, for Decoux and the French authorities to build up this specific Lao identity was not viewed as a goal in itself but as a means to integrate Laos further into the Indochinese Federation and make it a more viable member of this entity. Second, the French were up against a potent pan-Tai nationalist and anti-French campaign originating from Thailand which stressed the historical, racial, and cultural similarities between the Lao and the Thai. Following the 1932 coup in Siam, this pan-Tai nationalist ideology became a very important means whereby the new government in Bangkok sought to implant a growing sense of national unity among the population and secure political legitimacy.[6] Especially under the premiership of Phibun this ideology found powerful expression in an irredentist drive aiming at incorporating areas in Laos and Cambodia, among others, into a greater Siam. This irredentist cause was based on two assumptions: First, that these areas in French Indochina previously had been under the suzerainty of the Bangkok rulers and had been ceded to France under coercion when the traditional geopolitical map of mainland Southeast Asia had been redefined following the arrival of the European colonial powers; Second, that the population in these "lost provinces" were of the same "race" with the same way of life and culture as the population in Siam. Therefore, with reference to this internal logic of the irredentist drive the aim was to restore Siam to its "historical boundaries" and thereby revoke the injustice inflicted on Siam by France. In turn, this push was to pave the way for Thailand to gain a position as a "Greater Country" where the dispersed members of the "Thai race," liberated from the colonial yoke, were to be united.[7] It is generally acknowledged that the change of the foreign name of the country from "Siam" to "Thailand" was instituted in 1939 in support of this notion. Therefore, building up a specifically Laotian identity—distinct from the Thai—was an important strategy to counter Thai propaganda and rid the Lao patrie of Thai pretensions.

In building up this unprecedented sense of unified Laotian space and common Laotian identity among the population it would have been natural for the Louang Prabang king to unify Laos politically under his suzerainty. Actually, such a move had been proposed by the king himself as compensation for the territory the kingdom had ceded to Thailand (Pietrantoni 1943: 96). Even if this would have given the politico-cultural campaign an important unifying symbol, this suggestion was turned down by the French, as it was believed that this would cause problems due to loyalty to the former royal house of Champassak in southern Laos (Pietrantoni 1943: 96–97). Such local sympathies would have to be supplanted by a new consciousness that would pave the way for future political unification of the country. Thus the campaign stressed the oneness of the population from north to south with regard to history, race, language, and religion. At the same time a cultural renovation was carried out through which a specific Laotian cultural heritage was to be unearthed, reformed, and resurrected in order to communicate the common identity of the Laotian people as defined through a specific Lao cultural identity. That is, an identity defined in pure ethnic-Lao terms to which the other ethnic groups were to be assimilated (Pietrantoni 1943: 22).

As one of its most important means of propagating this new Lao identity and the vision of a unified space in the making, the Service de Propagande Lao launched Laos's first newspaper, *Lao Nhay*, in January 1941. At first it appeared as a handwritten journal but soon the handwritten characters were replaced by printed characters and *Lao Nhay* assumed a more professional appearance. In its pages readers could, among other things, read news from the diverse regions of their country (marriages, deaths, births, appointments, etc.), both modern and classical poems, information about agriculture, and practical information about the administration of the country. Originally, some of the articles also appeared in French, but this practice was brought to an end in 1943 as the French-oriented readers were directed towards a new newspaper, *Le Nouveau Laos*. *Lao Nhay* was published until the Japanese occupation in March 1945, making a total of ninety-seven issues.

Benedict Anderson has shown how a concept of simultaneity in homogenous and empty time is a prerequisite for the emergence of a national consciousness (Anderson 1991: 22–36). Anderson especially links this conception of time with two products of print capitalism—the novel and the newspaper. Through these the perception of imagined worlds where persons unaware of each other or unrelated events are linked together by calendrical coincidence was made possible. In turn, this consciousness created the possibility of the imagined community of the nation. In the same vein, *Lao Nhay* can be assigned a crucial role in the process Not that this newspaper was instrumental in creating a new national consciousness among the population in Laos at large; with a circulation of only about five thousand copies mostly in the urban areas this was not possible. But *Lao Nhay* indicates how a new nationalist discourse and a new unified space was in the making in Laos during the World War II. As the first nationwide newspaper to be published in Laos, *Lao Nhay* can as a phenomenon be regarded as a symbol of the new space. In the column News from Laos, the diverse regions of the country were linked together to make up Laos and through the local news Laos was filled up with people similar to the reader. A united Laos no longer remained an abstract space but was taking shape before the eyes of the reader.

Among the features that usually define a nation we find a shared history or a national history that forms the roots of the modern nation. In the next section I will discuss how in *Lao Nhay* we find the outline of a historical narrative which presents a unified Laos as the "reawakening" of a united Laos from the past.

THE HISTORICAL NARRATIVE

IN the columns of *Lao Nhay* we are presented not with detailed historical accounts but with valuable historical insights, which, when put together, serve to delineate the framework of a Lao historical narrative. In this historical narrative a unified Laos is not seen as something new and strange. On the contrary, it is presented as part of a continuous history and connected with the reawakening of an identity and sentiments that had always existed. In broad terms the proposed historical narrative is constituted by three periods: a golden age, a decline, and a reawakening, where the last stage refers to the developments set in motion by the campaign for a national renovation during World War II.

As the first major Lao kingdom of importance in the Mekong valley, the Lane Xang kingdom naturally occupies a central position in the history of Laos. Lane Xang stands at the beginning of the timescale in the historical narrative. In the newspaper, however, it was never deemed important to fix the proportions of this kingdom, either in terms of time or space, and Lane Xang becomes a kind of timeless entity of the past, synonymous with a distant golden age. First and foremost it was the period when King Fa

Ngoum in command of ten thousand soldiers brought unity to the country (*Lao Nhay*, 34, 1.7.42: 1). Later, during the reign of King Souligna Vongsa, the Lane Xang kingdom is presented as a prosperous Buddhist kingdom. Here religion thrived, and Vientiane formed an esteemed center for religious life, attracting monks from both Cambodia and Siam (Lao Nhay, 2, 1.3.41: 1). The same period was seen as the apogee of Lao craftsmanship (*Lao Nhay*, 35, 15.7.42: 1).

In the historical narrative, however, this unity that the Lao experienced during the Lane Xang period was lost as the golden age yielded to a period of decline when the country was brought to the brink of extinction. The onset of this period is marked by the breakup of the Lane Xang kingdom into two rival Lao kingdoms with centers in Louang Prabang and Vientiane respectively.[8] No longer did the kings possess the capacity to keep a well-trained army, and the martial abilities of the population deteriorated (*Lao Nhay*, 34, 1.7.42: 1). The sack of Vientiane in 1828 by the Siamese began a decline that ultimately could have led to a total extinction of Laos and the Lao. All that was left of the former Lane Xang empire was Louang Prabang, and that too could well have perished had it not been for French intervention (*Lao Nhay*, 2, 1.3.41: 4). Given the Franco-Lao nature of the nationalist project, it comes as no surprise that French colonialism appeared in so favorable a light. Further, Auguste Pavie was presented as the epitome of French colonialism and was treated as a genuine historical hero.[9] More importantly, in the historical narrative, the decline of this period also finds expression in changing states of mind.[10] First, as the political map of Laos was split into several kingdoms the unity of Lane Xang was lost. Political conflict emerged as rulers were guided more by "egoism" and "personal interests" than national interests. In this context the population lost the sense of belonging to a country:

> Clannishness took the place of what we term love of the nation or patriotism as the Lao of one *muong* seemed to be unaware that the Lao of another *muong* were their brothers. The horizon of our ancestors was quite narrow-minded (*Pathet Lao*, 1, 1941: 7).

Second, according to the historical narrative the origins of the so-called *su-su* nature of the Lao people can be traced to this period (*Pathet Lao*, 1, 1941: 7f). This is a Lao stereotype characterized by keywords such as "lazy," "indifferent," "ignorant," "uneducated," and "light-hearted." Rather than being a creation of the nationalist movement of the 1940s, this stereotype originated in early French descriptions of the Lao.[11] But it was resurrected as part of the historical narrative as the embodiment of this woeful period in

Laos's history that the campaign for a national renovation was to leave behind.

The campaign launched in the first half of the 1940s was related to these two major periods. It was perceived as the third period of the historical narrative, connected with the emergence of a united Laos awakened from sleep. Laos came into being at the turn of this century without connection to the former Lao kingdoms in the region. Thus, the period of decline makes it difficult to establish a direct link between Lane Xang (as a prominent Lao kingdom of the past in the Mekong region) and Laos (as a modern colonial formation). In the historical narrative, however, continuity is stressed and a close relationship between this golden age and modern Laos is explicitly established. The term for modern Laos (ປະເທສລາວ) and the historical kingdom (ປະເທສລ້ານຊ້າງ) are often used interchangably (e.g. *Lao Nhay*, 2, 1.3.41: 1 and 35, 15.7.42: 1). Similarly, in references to the population of modern Laos we find "Lao of Lan Sang" (ລາວລານຊ້າງ) (e.g. *Lao Nhay*, 8, 31.5.41: 1 and 20, 30.11.41: 9). In this way "Laos" emerges as an everlasting entity spanning the historical divide and the period of decline. Lane Xang is not just any Lao kingdom of the past but is *the* Laos of the past.[12] Through this historical projection, Laos was removed from the historical orbit of Siam and thereby from Thai claims on it. As expressed in one of the few articles dealing explicitly with the history of Laos:

> The Lao are different from the Siamese. Lan Sang has never been part of Siam. They possessed their own personality. As we go back to the most distant periods of our history we can record that our ancient state never has been vassal of another.
>
> Such an assertion is a historical fact. The Lao are quite distinct from their neighbours. It is only in vain that a deceitful propaganda attempts to distort the truth which the entire history proves: In heart, language, customs, as much as by their ancestors the Lao are Tai but they are first and above all Lao (*Lao Nhay*, 2, 1.3.41: 4).

The unity and distinct Lao-ness, which according to the historical narrative had once existed during the Lane Xang period, were lost under specific historical circumstances, to be "reawakened" by the Thai aggression of 1940–41. This event could have been interpreted as evidence for the inability of the French to defend Laos. But in the narrative it represented a necessary evil that violently shook the Lao out of their lethargy and made them conscious of their country and their unity (*Lao Nhay*, 2, 1.3.41: 1). As phrased, for example, in an editorial praising the achievements accomplished in the year that had passed since Decoux's first visit to Laos in March 1941:

What some claimed was impossible has been achieved: The Lao have gained
confidence in themselves, they have re-found their national spirit (*Lao
Nhay*, 27, 15.3.42: 1)

When the Vat Pha Kaew in Vientiane was inaugurated in 1942 after
having undergone a thorough restoration, this was hailed as a very
auspicious sign for the future of Laos. The fate of the temple was seen as so
closely related to the sorrows and happiness of the country that it was
characterized as the "national temple of Laos" (ວັດຂອງຊາດລາວ) (*Lao Nhay*, 26,
1.3.42: 10). In fact, the history of Vat Pha Kaew can be read as the essence
of the above mentioned historical narrative. Its creation dates back to the
Lane Xang kingdom and it is perceived as a unique symbol of that period.
Later it was raided by the Siamese invaders in 1828, the most auspicious
Buddha image of the kingdom was carried off to Bangkok, and the temple
was left in ruins. Following 150 years of devastation it was finally restored
and resurrected to its former glories under French tutelage in 1942. In the
same manner the historical narrative portrayed a new Laos in the making.
Although new and modern in its appearance it was formed from a specific
historical heritage.

TOWARDS A STANDARDIZATION OF THE LAO LANGUAGE

IN general, the notion of a national identity is closely linked with the
existence of a standardized national language. This section will discuss how
the campaign in Laos in the 1940s also reflects an ongoing attempt to
standardize and unify Lao language in order to establish a firm basis for a
Lao national language. As pointed out by Benedict Anderson, the existence
of the printing press both raises the need but also the means to standardize a
language, and in the case of Laos, *Lao Nhay* can be read as an open log of
this process. It will be argued that this process was guided by the need for a
consolidation of a specifically Lao, written language distinctly different
from the written language found in Thailand. In order to understand the
background for the discussions in the 1940s concerning Lao orthography, I
will first deal with the relationship between Lao and Siamese as presented in
some early studies of the Lao language.

The Lao and the Siamese languages are closely related. In their spoken
forms they only display minor variations with regard to tones and the
pronunciation of specific vocals and combinations of vocals. In the written
form, though, these languages have been subjected to different trends and
by the turn of this century they displayed different characteristics. Over a
long period the Siamese alphabet and orthography had gradually been

modified, and at the end of the nineteenth century the Siamese writing system appeared as quite a fixed system. Tone signs had been employed in order to indicate the five tones of the language, and through an enlargement of the alphabet and use of the *karan* ($\stackrel{<}{\cdot}$ indicating that the letter underneath (or several in connection with it) is left unpronounced) an etymological orthography had been established making it possible to distinguish between homonyms in writing.[13] This systematic nature of Siamese writing was stressed by the compilers of the first Lao word lists or dictionaries that appeared in the early period of the French colonial adventure in the Mekong region (see, for example, Taupin 1887/1893; Estrade 1895). In comparison, according to the same authors, the contemporary Lao writing system was far less complex because the orthography was related to the phonetic rendering of the word. While this orthographic principle made writing easy, it also made it impossible to distinguish between homonyms in writing, a tendency further aggrevated by the lack of tone signs in written Lao. Consequently, reading was made difficult and for many words it was not possible to determine the exact meaning when read out of context.

Although, the Siamese system of writing was seen as rather difficult, then, what followed implicitly from this comparison of the two languages was a hierarchical ordering in which Siamese represented a more developed and refined language in comparison to the more primitive and basic Lao (Estrade 1895: 10). This subordinate position of Lao in relation to Siamese was carried to the extreme in a dictionary published by the French missionary Cuaz in 1904 in which Lao was presented as a dialect of Siamese and thereby denied status as an independent language (Cuaz 1904). In agreement with this view Cuaz introduced the Lao-French dictionary as a "mere supplement" to his French-Siamese dictionary published earlier (Cuaz 1904: vi). Further, in cases where there existed a difference between the Lao and Siamese forms of a word, the Siamese form was given in order not to "confuse people" who already had studied this language (Cuaz 1904: xii–xiii).

In nationalist discourses language is generally perceived as the crucial criterion for nationality. Any discourse on the perception of Laos as a country independent of Siam with its own cultural identity had to reverse this relationship between Lao and Siamese and place the Lao language in a position on a par with Siamese. With regard to this process the Lao-French dictionary compiled by the French missionary Guignard represented an important break with the above mentioned hierarchical ordering of Siamese and Lao (Guignard 1912). Guignard placed the two languages side by side as different dialects within the overall "Thay" language family. In his introductory chapters we find a systematic presentation of the Lao language that was intended to parallel the French-produced dictionaries of the

Siamese language already in existence (e.g. Pallegoix 1854; Cuaz 1903). In this manner Lao was established on an independent basis and Guignard further drew a dividing line between the two languages as he identified a sixth tone in Lao whereas Siamese only had five tones (Guignard 1912: xx). To establish Lao as an independent language implies a process whereby the language is standardized and its structure codified with regard to its orthography and grammar. The existence of an officially sanctioned dictionary or grammar serving as an inventory of the language is the most tangible representation of language standardization. Guignard's dictionary, however, did not fulfill this role as it was intended for foreign students of the Lao language and never received official status. Furthermore, it did not solve the problem concerning the use of tone signs. In its own right, however, it can be seen as an important symbol of the liberation of Lao from its subordinate position in relation to Siamese.[14]

During the same period we find a consciousness in Laos of the need to stabilize the Lao language, and of the related politico-ideological aspects of this endeavor. This is evident, for example, from the reactions to a language reform of a rather radical nature suggested by M. Meillier, commisaire du gouvernement in Louang Prabang, in 1918. In short, Meillier proposed the use of Siamese letters to write Lao in order to facilitate the printing of books, particularly schoolbooks, in Lao ("M. Meillier à M le Résident Supérieur au Laos, Louang Pabang, le 10 Janvier 1918, No 93/5," c. 33, d. F4, AEFEO).[15] Not surprisingly, this proposal caused strong reactions from, among others, Prince Phetsarath, who stressed that such a proposal was to be resisted as it would lead to the disappearance of the Lao writing system and thus undermine Lao literature and language. Instead, the structures of the Lao language had to be standardized and codified ("Note sur la reforme de l'ecriture laotienne par Phetsarath, Vientiane, le 8 Février 1918," c. 33, d. F4, AEFEO). At stake was the survival of two of the most important cultural denominators that could serve to detach Laos from Siam. Were they to vanish this would seriously weaken any Laotian claim to be a country independent of Siam. It was obvious that any attempt to consolidate the Lao language as different from Siamese had important political implications for the Lao-Siamese nexus. This close connection between language engineering and national politics was also well-known to leading members of the École Française d'Extrême-Orient. In 1918 George Cœdès was asked to participate in the work to standardize Lao. At that time he acted as director of the Vajirayan library in Bangkok and he asked for certain precautions as he did not want letters to fall into the hands of the Siamese censors indicating his participation "in a project which had as its goal to defend Laos against Siamese political influence" ("Le Directeur de l'EFEO à M le Résident Supérieur au Laos, le 12 Septembre 1918, No 872", c. 33, d. F4, AEFEO).

The responsibility of carrying out the work necessary to standardize Lao was left in the hands of various committees appointed by the résident-supérieur in Laos in the first half of this century. None of these committees, though, was able to produce the needed key (that is an official grammar or dictionary) to standardize the language. Schoolbooks published in Lao and used during the 1920s and 1930s indicate how a process of standardization was going on and how, for example, the use of two tone signs and the *karan* had been institutionalized, marking a departure from the orthography referred to in the early Lao word lists and dictionaries (see, for example, Lê-Duy-Luong and Blanchard de la Brosse 1926 and Magniont 1932).

What none of the above-mentioned committees had been able to accomplish was carried out by the Buddhist Institute in Vientiane which published the first grammar of the Lao language in 1935 (Sila 1935).[16] This grammar was compiled by Maha Sila Viravong who had been one of the key figures in the Buddhist Institute in Vientiane since it was founded in 1931 by the École Française d'Extrême-Orient. Although never as successful as its counterpart in Phnom Penh, the institute can be associated with an attempt to resurrect Lao Buddhism. It was intended as a new center for religious education in Laos eliminating the need for Lao monks to go to Siam for higher education. Furthermore, under the authority of the institute an ambitious project was initiated to build up a tradition of religious texts in Lao translated from Pali. Given this emphasis on local tradition it can therefore come as no surprise that the first manual to codify the rules of the local language also should emanate from this institute. The first volume of the grammar presents a basic outline of some of the fundamentals of the Lao language: the alphabet, tone signs, and basic rules for their use, and some basic rules concerning spelling (e.g. the use of the *karan*, consonant clusters, and irregular Pali finals). It has to be noted that this grammar was not only intended as a guide to the contemporary language, but it also introduced important new elements. Formerly two alphabets had been in use in Laos. One was the ordinary alphabet used in secular texts. The other was the so-called Tham alphabet used to transcribe religious Pali texts. Through an enlargement of the "secular" alphabet with fourteen new letters (ຕົວລາວໃໝ່) Maha Sila's intention was to introduce the use of only one alphabet suited to render all the sounds of spoken Lao as well as the orthography of Pali-Sanskrit words. The motivation for this reform must be sought in the above-mentioned endeavor to establish a new religious textual tradition. Just as the religious texts were to be "localized," it was also the intention to make them more easy accessible by writing them with the same alphabet that was used in daily life. It was an attempt to "do as the Siamese but by means of what the Lao possess and have possessed" as it was put by Prince Phetsarath ("Proces-Verbal, le 3 Mars 1938," c. 33, d. F4, AEFEO).

Maha Sila's grammar was never granted official status, however, and consequently it never became the needed key to a standardization of the Lao language. The reason for this has to be sought in the fact that the undertaking to standardize Lao was caught in the crossfire between two contradictory approaches. On the one hand, we find the approach of the Buddhist Institute seeking to be able to produce Lao in a written form rendering the non-Lao words in conformity with the orthography of their Pali-Sanskrit origins. On the other hand, we also find an approach seeking to adopt a more simple and uncomplicated system of writing. These were the two positions that crystallized during the sessions undertaken by the Commission for the Fixation of Official Lao Writing and Orthography that went to work in 1938–39. Following intense discussions, the demand for simplicity became the victorious principle and consequently, with some minor modifications, the Lao alphabet already in existence was confirmed as the national alphabet ("Proces-Verbal, le 6 Juin 1938," c. 33, d. F4, AEFEO). From the proceedings it is clear that a spelling in conformity with some kind of phonetic principle was opted for, although no exact rules were laid out. Accordingly, the alphabet and grammar devised by Maha Sila was rejected though not totally discarded; his alphabet was used in religious texts published by the Buddhist Institute ("Arrête No 1021, résident supérieur au Laos, le 9 Août 1939," c. 33, d. F4, AEFEO). It must be noted that the model for the Lao language envisioned by Maha Sila was very close indeed to the spelling in use in Siam, and the later reform proposed by Maha Sila was interpreted as an outright attempt to adopt the Siamese etymological spelling system (Katay 1943: 3). Although it was never referred to in the proceedings of the commission, this view may also have been prevalent at the end of the 1930s and may possibly have contributed to the downfall of the Maha Sila model.[17]

Language standardization as discussed in Laos during World War II was thus certainly not a new issue. As the campaign for a national renovation propagated the vision of a unified Laos in the making, there arose a need to facilitate this project through a unification and standardization of the language. With regard to this problem the Lao Literary Committee, one of several committees emerging in the campaign for a cultural awareness in Laos, was especially concerned with language matters. Besides working for a renovation of Lao literature, the committee also had as one of its explicit aims to defend the Lao language (*Lao Nhay* 11, 15.7.41: 5). For the committee this endeavor was linked with a unification of Lao vocabulary and orthography and in *Lao Nhay* they found the medium through which this was to be achieved. As is evident from my presentation above, a standardization key had yet to be produced, and an analysis of the spelling employed in the columns of *Lao Nhay* indicates the difficulty of establishing a system of Lao spelling.

In the discussions concerning the Lao alphabet in 1938–39, the first line of approach was to use an orthography in accordance with the so-called phonetic principle. That is, in the early issues of *Lao Nhay* published in 1941, words are generally spelled according to the way they are pronounced (e.g. ລັກສະນະ, ລະຄວນ ທະຫານ, ທັມະດາ) and the *karan* figures only in very few words (e.g. royal names, ອງຄ໌, ອງຈັນທ໌). Systematic rules for spelling, however, were not laid out, and in the early issues we find variations in spelling, especially with regard to final consonants (e.g. ປະຫກ, ປະຫສ, ປະຫຍ; ຈິດທມານຍ, ຈິດທມານຣ; ອຣຸງຈັນ ອຣຸງຈັນທ໌; ໄທຣ, ໄທຍ). It was praised as a system that was easy to read and therefore suited to the educational level of the masses ("Vers la réforme de l'orthographe laotienne par Pierre Nginn, sd," c. 33, d. F4, AEFEO). But it is also important to notice that in this form the Lao written language was given a form radically different from that of contemporary Siamese.

This spelling system, however, was never given time to develop. Instead, from the beginning of 1942, a new principle for spelling was adopted. This change was motivated by a desire to enrich the Lao language through neologisms. Following long discussions by the Lao Literary Committee on this problem, it was decided to borrow words of Pali-Sanskrit origin from Siamese and write them in a Lao manner. Or, as Charles Rochet put it, to "Lao-ify" them ("Le Chef de la Section Laotienne d'Information à M Pierre Nginn, Vientiane, le 9 Octobre 1941, No 311/Inf," c. 33, d. F4, AEFEO). In praxis, this meant the overall implementation of what was called "simple etymological spelling" (ຕາມຄວາມຍ່າງງ່າຍ), which gradually superseded the original phonetic spelling. This resulted in widespread use of what Maha Sila earlier had termed irregular Pali final consonants (e.g. ລຄຣ, ຕເຍ, ກັມະກຣ, ລຸກສິສ, ບານສະງຸລ, ມຸລ, ທາທານ) and of the *karan* (e.g. ປະສງຄ໌, ກະສັຕຣ໌, ສັຕວ໌, ວິໄນຍ໌, ພິມພ໌, ອາໄສຍ). At the same time various measures were taken to codify this new way of spelling. First, as no dictionary was in existence, extracts from a new mini dictionary were published in the *Lao Nhay*. New words were explained and the spellings fixed (the first extract was printed in *Lao Nhay* 44, 1.12.42: 10). Second, a table laying out some basic spelling rules was printed out (ແກ້ໄຂວິທີສະກດຄຳລາວ *Lao Nhay* 44, 1.12.42: 9). Here we can observe an intriguing attempt to rehabilitate Lao from a historical perspective where the former widespread view of the hierarchical ordering of Lao and Siamese was turned upside down (Katay 1943).

One serious problem related to the new spelling principle devised in the *Lao Nhay* was that it moved the spelling of Lao dangerously close to that of

Siamese. Just as George Cœdès two decades earlier had stressed the close relationship between language engineering and politics, he highlighted the issue again in this case. Although he approved of the spelling employed in the newspaper, Cœdès raised the following issue in a letter to Pierre Nginn, the mastermind behind the reform and future editor of *Lao Nhay:*

> It is clear that Siamese orthography is much more conservative and accordingly more "etymological" than the Lao [orthography], and that all attempts to write Lao in conformity with its etymology will be inspired by the Siamese orthography. The only inconvenience (but I do not know how to avoid this unless the etymological principle is dropped for the phonetic principle) is that you certainly will be accused of Siam-ficating the Lao language at a moment where, in the political sphere, attempts are made to achieve just the opposite ("Le Directeur de l'École Française d'Extrême-Orient à M Pierre Nginn, le 23 Mai 1942, No 1074," d. F4, c. 33, AEFEO).

The initiators of the spelling reform were aware of this problem and on several occasions they were accused of using Siamese words and spelling like the Siamese which implied widespread use of what was called the Thai *karan* (e.g. *Lao Nhay*, 44, 1.12.42: 5; 45, 15.12.42: 9). In such instances the proponents of the semi-etymological principle vigorously argued that in no way did the new style imply the use of Siamese words. "Take the word ກິລາ (*kilaa*). It is a Pali word that both the Thais and we have borrowed" it was argued (*Lao Nhay* 45, 15.12.42: 9). So although the language engineers looked for inspiration in Siam they sought refuge in a distant origin of the words to argue that the reform of the language by no means implicated Siam-fication. Even if the simple etymological spelling at first sight moved written Lao closer to Siamese, the new system had been designed so that written Lao differed from Siamese in some fundamental ways, such as in the spelling of initial "pseudo-clusters" (e.g. ສຫວວງ, ສຫງງ, ຂວຣ, ສຫມ). A principle that already had been suggested by Maha Sila in his grammar from 1935 (Sila 1935: 29).[18]

Despite all the arguments and the fact that the proponents of the simple etymological spelling always had the upper hand in the articles published in *Lao Nhay*, this new spelling was stopped without further notice just as the publishing of Pierre Nginn's dictionary was terminated. The readers were informed of a return to the system of spelling without the *karan* (*Lao Nhay*, 69–70, 15.12.43: 5). A reading of *Lao Nhay* in the period following this announcement indicates how this resulted in a thorough return to an almost pure phonetic spelling system (e.g. ການ/ການ; ປະເທສ/ປະເທດ; ອຽງຈັນທ໌/ ອຽງຈັນ; ມູລ/ມູນ). Whereas the simple etymological spelling had been associated with an attempt to enrich the Lao language through recourse to foreign traditions, the new trend was associated with a rediscovery of local Lao traditions. Local manuscripts were to be consulted in order to sort out the words no longer in use to be incorporated into the modern language. This new strategy to reform the current language was outlined in an article quite suggestively titled, "The Original Lao Texts are the Most Precious Objects" (*Lao Nhay*, 87, 15.9.44: 1). In the same vein the new spelling system was characterized as a return to the "old accent" (ສຳນຽງເກ່ານ (*Lao Nhay*, 74, 1.3.44: 6). In order to move forward, it was deemed necessary to go back. In this way Lao writing was established as distinct from Siamese writing and the enrichment of the Lao language was removed from the Siamese orbit of influence.

This quest for standardization of the Lao written language in accordance with an orthographic principle requiring simplicity and distinctiveness from the language of neighboring Thailand has occurred not only in the first half of this century. As Nick Enfield shows in his chapter below, these principles also formed the basis for Phoumi Vongvichit's "revolutionary language reforms" that have had a major impact on language development in Laos since 1975. In recent years, however, Thai language has exerted an ever increasing influence on Lao language, and popular practice reflects both a tendency to use Central Thai words in daily use and a shift away from writing according to strict orthographic principles.

PERSPECTIVE

WHEREAS Laos was first unified only after World War II, developments during the war years contributed in an important way to this end. It is in this period that we can see the first serious attempt to create an unprecedented national space in Laos, and we can find the early beginnings of a modern nationalist discourse on Laos and the Lao. The purpose of this article has been to present some preliminary findings on two important aspects of this nationalist discourse, based on a reading of Laos's first Lao newspaper, *Lao Nhay*. The two aspects are the historical narrative brought forward to legitimize the nationalist project, and the attempts to standardize and distinguish the written language of Laos from the written language of Thailand. I have tried to indicate a new and different approach to the study of Lao nationalism from those previously used and thereby focus on a period neglected in the study of Laos's history. It would, however, be wrong to see the nationalist discourse set in motion by the Franco-Lao campaign for a national renovation in the first half of the 1940s as an isolated phenomenon. Endeavors to standardize the language during World War II must be linked with the long history of previous attempts to separate the Lao written language from Thai, a process that can be traced back to the beginning of this century. In the same vein, I believe that if we try to understand Lao nationalism from a cultural perspective, we must study how a distinct notion of Lao-ness, as opposed to Siamese-ness, was formed during the first half of this century with regard to other factors normally used to depict a national identity (such as history and customs). This will give us a better understanding of Lao nationalism and Lao national identity, as well as highlight the role played not only by the École Française d'Extrême-Orient but also by members of the Lao elite, a hitherto neglected aspect of French colonial and Lao intellectual history.

NOTES

This is a revised version of a paper presented at the 14th IAHA Conference in Bangkok, May 1996. I wish to thank Grant Evans, Martin Stuart-Fox, Scot Barmé, Chris Goscha, Stein Tønnesson, Jean Deuve, and Viggo Brun for valuable comments.

1. Valuable insights can be gained from Deuve 1992, Goscha 1995a, Gunn 1988, McCoy 1970, and Toye 1968. For contemporary accounts, see Decoux 1946, Pietrantoni 1943, and Rochet 1949.

2. In the early twentieth century, while Klobukowski acted as governor general of Indochina, it was suggested Laos should be split up, with different provinces placed under the administration of Tonkin, Annam, or Cambodia (Pietrantoni 1943: 20).

3. This criticism was raised in an interview with Prince Phetsarath concerning Vietnamese immigration into Laos (*France-Indochine*, 21 Mar 1931: 1). For a French voice raised in support of a change of French policies in Laos, see Bernard 1937.

4. Reference to this incident can be found in, for example, Langer and Zasloff 1970: 25.

5. A general outline of the program can be found in Pietrantoni 1943.

6. See Barmé 1993 for an analysis of this nationalist ideology of the 1930s.

7. See Wichit 1940 for a classic presentation of this theme.

8. In this connection no reference to the Champassak kingdom can be found.

9. This is evident from references throughout *Lao Nhay* and as a new series entitled "Great Men and their Everlasting Work" (ມະຫາບຸລຸດແລະການງານອັນຖາວອນ) introduced the first article was dedicated to the deeds of Pavie (*Lao Nhay*, 49, 15.2.43: 5). The protective aspect of France's relationship to Laos was also praised in the Lao national anthem from 1941 (ລາວຮັກຊາດ). Further, when it later was released on a record this was together with the French national anthem (*Lao Nhay*, 26, 1.3.42: 1).

10. This aspect of the historical narrative is clearly expressed in various articles published in *Pathet Lao* (a pamphlet published in French by *Lao Nhay*) under headlines such as "Les fautes des nos pères," "Appel aux jeunes Lao," and "Qui sommes nous?"

11. See for example Stuart-Fox 1994: 128–131.

12 . That the fate of modern Laos is related to the Lao kingdoms of the past was further expressed in symbolic terms as the classes graduating from the *College Pavie* in Vientiane were named after historical hero-kings of the past, such as Fa Ngoum, Souligna Vongsa, and Chao Anou (*Lao Nhay*, 83–84, 15.7.44: 2).

13. See Diller 1988 and 1991 for an analysis of various aspects of this process.

14. In a contemporary study by the French linguist M. Maspero, the same relationship between the two languages had been established (Maspero 1911).

15. AEFEO: Les Archives d'École Française d'Extrême-Orient, Paris. I wish to thank École Française d'Extrême-Orient for giving me access to their archive and Madame J. Filliozat for her support.

16. The grammar was divided into four parts of which only the first was published in 1935.

17. In his doctoral thesis on Lao literature, Peter Koret has stressed how Maha Sila in general relied heavily on Thai scholarship and patterns for Thai versification in his endeavor to establish an analytical framework for Lao versification. See Koret 1994: 99–108.

18. In the 1940s, however, the previous distinction that had existed between written Lao and Siamese was blurred by a reform of Siamese alphabet and spelling that was proposed in the middle of 1942 involving a simplification of the orthographic principle to be used. An outline of this reform can be found in various issues from June and July 1942 of the journal *Khao Khotsanakan,* the mouthpiece of the Department of Propaganda in Thailand.

WOMEN, SPACE, AND HISTORY

LONG-DISTANCE TRADING IN NORTHWESTERN LAOS

4

ANDREW WALKER

IN northwestern Laos, retail outlets in the provincial capitals and district centers are supplied by long-distance traders who make regular cross-border journeys to Thailand and China to buy manufactured goods and processed foodstuffs. A majority of these long-distance entrepreneurs are women (*mae kha*). Their distinctive appearance—makeup, nail polish, gold jewelry, hair pieces, fake leather handbags, and baseball caps—gives the rustic and muddy Lao trading system an unmistakably feminine character. The main trade route followed by these women runs down the Mekong River from the Thai border town of Chiang Khong to the river port of Pakbeng and, further on, to the northern "capital" of Louang Prabang (map 1). The northwestern trade route branches off at Pakbeng, along a rough road that runs north to Udomxai, where truck loads of Thai thongs, washing powder, and soft drinks are unloaded for local sale or distribution to surrounding provinces. Some traders continue on across the border to Mengla in southern China where they stock up with Chinese beer, cigarettes, and biscuits before heading south again to sell their latest load. From Chiang Khong to Mengla it is a little over four hundred kilometers by river and road but with the poor transport system and interminable administrative delays, a return journey along the full length of this route could easily take up to three weeks.

The literature on trade in southeast Asia suggests that women's involvement in such long-distance enterprise is very unusual. It is widely recognized that women dominate small-scale, local trade. "Markets," writes Jennifer Alexander (1987: 31) "are women's domains," a statement supported by studies in Indonesia (Alexander 1987; Dewey 1962), the Philippines (Szanton 1972), Malaysia (Firth 1966; Strange 1981); Vietnam

MAP 3

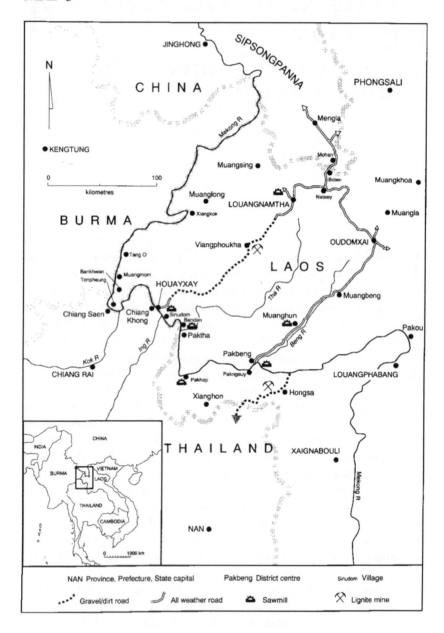

NAN Province, Prefecture, State capital   Pakbeng District centre   Sinudom Village

•••• Gravel/dirt road   All weather road   Sawmill   Lignite mine

(O'Harrow, 1995), Thailand (de Young 1966; Kirsch 1982), and Laos itself (Ireson 1992; Mayoury 1993). But, long-distance, large-scale, and wholesale trade in Southeast Asia seems to be usually the domain of men, typically Chinese men with interests in shopkeeping, transportation, and warehousing and an extensive network of contacts with suppliers and creditors in provincial towns and capital cities. A number of studies refer to the social and economic barriers between the two sectors, with market women rarely willing or able to make what Geertz calls the "'jump' from peddling to merchandising" (Geertz 1963: 31; see also de Young 1966: 105–8; Keyes 1984: 225; Preecha 1980; Szanton 1972). Even when long-distance trade is undertaken on a small scale it seems to be most commonly the domain of men (for example, Bowie 1992: 808–9; Chandler 1984: 105, 121, 125; de Young 1966: 105–6).

In Theravada Buddhist societies, such as Thailand and Laos, the non-participation of women in long-distance trade has been attributed to religious values. In an important paper on gender in Thailand, Kirsch (1982: 29) suggests that women's economic activity has remained "petty and localised" in part due to Buddhism's valorization of the roles of wife and mother. Keyes (1984: 229) explores the argument somewhat further suggesting that the role of *mae kha* is underpinned by the Buddhist image of the "nurturing mother" and that petty trading is a natural extension of the domestic economy. A woman provides for her family, he writes "through her productive activities in the fields and in craftwork at home, and it is but a small step to market the products of the family enterprise" (Keyes 1984: 229).

The views of Kirsch (1982, 1985) and Keyes (1984) resonate with reports of taboos and anxieties surrounding women's mobility in both Thailand and Laos, cultural forms which appear to stand in stark contrast to the celebration of the travels and adventures of men (Pasuk and Baker 1995: 69–70; Phillips 1965: 28; Singhanetra-Renard 1981: 151). In Laos, Trankell (1993: 22) reports that it was "often stated that women's life opportunities were hampered by the fact that rules of decorum restricted women's freedom of physical movement beyond what was recognized as the social space of the village." In a Lao village in northeast Thailand, Mills (1995: 257) has written vividly of potent "widow ghost" anxieties which she attributes to concerns about "the unnatural and dangerous consequences of allowing women to roam freely, their bodies and sexual powers unconstrained by the controls of society or of men." Keyes (1984: 235–6) shares some of these anxieties, writing of rural women's entry into prostitution when they are "unmoored" from Buddhist values and travel to the "hedonistic atmosphere" of Bangkok and the provincial capitals. More recently, the apparent hazards of trans-border feminine mobility have been highlighted with widespread media and academic discussion of trafficking in Burmese, Chinese, and Lao girls for the purposes of prostitution in Thai brothels (for example, Asia Watch 1993). All in all, it seems that women's mobility is a dangerous business, undermining masculinity as men don nail polish and makeup to avoid the predations of the "widow ghosts" (Mills 1995: 252–3) and corrupting "traditional" femininity as women abandon Buddhism and matrilineal spirits (Muecke 1984: 466) and are drawn into the brothels of Bangkok and Chiang Mai.

In this chapter my aim is to provide a case study of women's long-distance mobility that emphasizes its success, profitability, and enjoyment. The first part of the paper examines the long distance trading activities of women who buy goods in the Thai town of Chiang Khong and sell them mainly in Udomxai. The second part explores the historical development of women's role in this long-distance trading system. I suggest that the wartime era of the 1960s and early 1970s gave women unprecedented exposure to both mobility and trade and that this experience was put to good use in the restricted—but at the same time accessible—trading conditions that followed the communist victory in 1975. I conclude by suggesting that although mobile women face cultural barriers and tensions, there are also cultural spaces that they can occupy, paralleling their strategic use of geographic space in the rugged terrain of northwestern Laos. Positive, profitable, and rewarding "traveling identities" are not just the prerogative of men.

FROM CHIANG KHONG TO UDOMXAI

THE Thai trading town of Chiang Khong is the most popular point of supply for long distance traders throughout northern Laos. A large number of them come up river to Chiang Khong from Louang Prabang, returning with boatloads of cement, corrugated iron, condensed milk, and washing powder. Smaller-scale traders make the four-hour speedboat trip from Pakbeng, returning with stock for the retail shops that sprawl along the dusty road that climbs up from the port. Others come from Udomxai, Louang Namtha, Muang Sing, Muang Houn, and Hongsa, their vinyl handbags stuffed with thousand-baht[1] notes and crumpled orders from the shopkeepers in the markets that dominate the commercial lives of the towns. Less frequently, traders from as far afield as Phongsaly, Sam Neua, and Phonesavan make their way to Chiang Khong to buy direct, but more often they collect their orders from other traders in Pakbeng or Udomxai. Finally, there are the long-distance traders in Houayxay itself, strung out along the riverbank opposite Chiang Khong. Using and creating far flung connections, they have established a regular trade with the other towns of northern Laos, in particular the entrepot of Udomxai.

There is substantial variation in trading style and scale amongst those who visit Chiang Khong's crowded shops. The small-scale traders are most likely to come from towns and villages relatively close to Chiang Khong, typically riverside settlements downstream as far as Pakbeng. Their trading capital is limited—usually between ten and fifty thousand baht—but they attempt to maximize income by concentrating on high-profit items and making regular trading journeys, perhaps as many as two or three each month. Many of them are young, unmarried women or older women who are divorced or separated from their husbands. The larger-scale traders are much more likely to be married and often participate in trade with their husbands. While they may also have limited trading capital they have much better access to credit in Chiang Khong, a factor not unrelated to their more respectable married status. A "typical" trader in this category buys goods worth several hundred thousand baht, while some of the most successful are in the million-baht range. Most of the traders, small and large, work in informal trading groups of up to eight or ten friends, neighbors and relatives, sharing cargo boats for the downstream journey and assisting each other in supervising the loading and unloading of cargo.[2]

The wholesale shops in Chiang Khong—predominantly Chinese owned—sell an enormous range of manufactured goods, clothing, and processed foods (table 1). There are about ten general wholesale shops, together with several specialist hardware shops, and most of them report that the vast majority of their sales are shipped across the river to Laos. Most of the larger-scale traders spread their bulk purchases between four or five wholesale shops, even though each stocks a similar range of goods. The traders say that a single shop usually has insufficient stock, especially highly sought-after items such as good quality quilts during the cold season. Prices vary between shops. However, the main reason for spreading out purchases is to maximize access to credit with the large-scale traders typically buying more than half of their trading stock on short-term shopkeeper credit, usually for about a month. Some purchases, such as pharmaceuticals, electrical goods, and automotive products, are made at specialist shops more oriented to the local retail trade. Even the modern supermarket makes some bulk sales to the Lao traders. Finally, the large traveling market (*talat nat*) that visits Chiang Khong each Friday, is very popular amongst smaller-scale traders who can be seen crossing the Mekong on Friday afternoons, plastic bags laden with clothes, shoes, cosmetics, and plastic toys.

After making their purchases the traders spend hours, sometimes days, at the Chiang Khong port supervising the loading of the Lao cargo boats that head downriver to Pakbeng and Louang Prabang.[3] This is a stressful and

TABLE 1

MAIN PRODUCTS BOUGHT BY LAO TRADERS IN CHIANG KHONG

Wholesale shops		Specialist shops	Friday market
condensed milk	sugar	corrugated iron	clothing
orange juice	toilet paper	fibreboard roofing	cosmetics
soft drinks	sanitary pads	toilets	shoes
tonic drinks	thongs	charcoal stoves	plastic toys
Ovaltine	floor mats	motor oil	
instant coffee	mattresses	battery acid	
tinned fish	quilts	cement	Other
dried squid	washing powder	bricks	
biscuits	soap	fibro sheets	eggs
sweets	toothpaste	bicycles	coconuts
MSG	cloth	televisions	fruit
cooking oil	rope	pharmaceuticals	bottled water

Source: fieldwork, 1994–1995. Note: There is gender variation in the purchase of some of the products. Male traders are somewhat more likely to be involved in the purchase of construction materials, but certainly not exclusively so. By contrast, purchases from the Friday market are almost exclusively the domain of women traders, especially small-scale traders.

often unpleasant time. The port is hot and muddy and exposed and the women, fearful of losing their highly valued pale skin, squat in the shade of piles of boxes, fanning themselves with rough pieces of cardboard. The shopkeeper's pickups and trucks, which deliver the goods to the port, slip and slide on the steep concrete ramp and bog themselves in the mud beside the river. Accidents and near misses are common. The port laborers who load the cargo boats add to the stress, constantly increasing their charges and engaging the traders in muscular and sweaty negotiations. Inside the boats, the cargo is carefully stacked so as to minimize import duties on the other side of the river. Boxes of high-tax lemonade are loaded in inaccessible parts of the hull or concealed beneath low-tax biscuits and soap powder.[4] Bundles of thongs, which attract a 40-percent tax, are removed from their distinctive blue wrapping and repacked in the nondescript hessian sacks used for sweets and dried squid. No export taxes are collected by the Thai customs officers in Chiang Khong, but a range of service charges and administrative fees find their way into their tight back pockets.

Before heading downriver the traders and their laden boats must dock at the Houayxay cargo port where Lao import duty is assessed and paid. This too is a prolonged process and delays of two or three days are not uncommon. Though tedious and frustrating, this is the crucial period in the whole trading venture—Lao import taxes on many items are very high and minimization of tax is essential for trading success. Concealment of cargo in Chiang Khong is only a small part of the strategy of tax minimization. The Lao customs staff are fully aware of what the traders are doing on the other side of the river and, if they wished, could order thorough and enormously time-consuming inspections of the boats.[5] To avoid this, they negotiate. As Mali, a successful trader from Udomxai described it:

> "Say I have one hundred boxes of lemonade. I tell the customs officer that I have fifty boxes and he proposes that I pay tax on thirty. I protest that this is much too expensive and that it will eat up all my profit. I say that tax on five boxes would be much better. Eventually we agree on fifteen or twenty."

In return for accepting such blatant under-declaration the customs officers receive substantial personal payments.[6] While a certain amount of tax has to be collected to meet official expectations, it is in the interests of the local Customs staff to minimize the official tax paid by the trader. Traders have limited cash at this stage of the trading cycle and the more they pay in tax the less they will be able, or inclined, to pay as personal inducements. The level of tax and inducement paid by traders varies considerably according to the extent of cargo concealment, their persistence and negotiating skills, and the nature of their personal relationships with the customs officers. A total payment of about five percent of stock value is considered typical, though payments can range from 1 percent—almost unbelievably good—to over 10 percent, a level at which the venture starts to become unviable.

The cargo boats used for the downstream journey are privately operated by boat owners from Houayxay, Pakbeng, Louang Prabang and, occasionally, towns further downriver. They range in size from five to ninety tonnes, with most of the larger-scale traders using boats of at least twenty tonnes. If the boats leave Houayxay by mid-morning they can make the trip to Pakbeng in a single day, provided there are not excessive delays at the customs and police post at Paktha, where additional inducements have to be paid given that the customs paperwork does not tally with the cargo in the boat. Often, however, the final official inspections in Houayxay are delayed until later in the day, and a night must be spent moored at Paktha or one of the villages along the river. Most of the women seem to have overcome the fear that many Lao have of river travel, and the trip is often a lazy and restful time as the hours are whiled away with sleeping, cooking, eating and talking. Sometimes the women may join male traders and boat operators in games of cards or even whisky drinking sessions, though the women's drinking at this stage is usually restrained given that they need to keep a clear head for trading. If an unexpected stop is made for the night along the river, the traders may raid the cargo for quilts and mattresses if there are insufficient in the boat, carefully repacking them in their plastic wrapping in the morning.

At Pakbeng the cargo is loaded into waiting trucks—also privately operated—for the road journey north to Udomxai and Louangnamtha. The cargo of the various traders, piled in cardboard confusion in the hulls of the boats, has to be sorted into separate trucks and this too can be a time-consuming process, made more so by the regionally renowned lethargy of the port laborers. As the unloading proceeds, the traders are regularly approached by local shopkeepers (and sometimes traders from further afield who want to avoid traveling to Chiang Khong) who are keen to buy their goods. Many of the traders are reluctant to sell given their commitments to regular customers in Udomxai, though, if a high enough price is offered, or if there are goods left over that won't fit into a truck, a sale may be made. Several of the women who regularly travel to Udomxai have close friends and relatives in Pakbeng and they are often more willing to sell and may even have some stock specifically purchased for this purpose. Usually a night must be spent in Pakbeng and many of the women stay in a small ramshackle hotel located above the port, though some may sleep on the boats, sharing meals with the boat owners. Those who can, stay with friends or relatives. When the trucks are loaded the traders travel with them for the journey north. To Udomxai it is a bone-jarring six or eight hours, crammed into the improbably crowded and noisy cabins.

The large market in Udomxai is the most popular selling point for the long-distance traders in northwestern Laos. There are over two hundred shops in four large concrete sheds, constructed by provincial authorities in 1991 to stimulate commercial activity. The market has an array of small retail shops selling tinned foods, drinks, sweets, toiletries, beer, and cigarettes, and many specialist shops selling clothes, footwear, stationery, tools, and cassettes. The traders are rarely anxious about being able to sell their goods here, often joking that the shopkeepers fight amongst themselves to buy. On one of my first visits to the market a small crowd of shopkeepers stripped bare a truckload of goods that had arrived from Pakbeng, climbing up the back and sides, burrowing under the thick canvas tarpaulin and handing the truck's contents to their companions on the ground who stood on top of the goods to establish their ownership. There were many heated arguments as shopowners fought over cartons of lemonade and biscuits, trying to steal boxes from each other's piles in the confusion. The trader—a woman from Houayxay—was powerless to control the situation and could only wander around urging the shopkeepers to share. When the booty was organized into separate piles she went from one to the other writing down what each customer had taken from the truck. Many of them had actually placed orders on her previous trip to Udomxai or sent messages to her with other traders or travelers. In fact, she told me, she had orders that could fill five trucks, well beyond her financial or logistical capacity.

Marketplace bargaining is often portrayed as a central experience of women's involvement in trade, but in these transactions between long-distance wholesalers and local retailers it is relatively absent. Prices are only discussed in detail when the traders collect their payment from the shopkeepers, usually two or three days after the goods are stored away in the shops, if not already sold to the retail customers who frequent the market. The understanding is that prices will be the same as on the previous occasion and if there is any bargaining it is within a very narrow range and in a half-hearted manner.[7] The shopkeepers are advised of minor price rises when they collect the goods from the truck, not to initiate a process of bargaining, but to enable them to adjust their retail prices accordingly. If there are substantial price increases in Chiang Khong, the information may be telephoned through to large customers to give them the—rarely exercised—option of withdrawing their order. Moreover, the long-distance traders generally do not attempt to profit from excess demand by increasing their prices. Selling is easy for most of the year but there are times, especially in the wet season, when roads become impassable and energies are directed to rice planting, when good and regular relationships with customers are highly valued. Overstocking may be an infrequent risk, but with problems of storage at Udomxai and substantial debts that have to be promptly repaid in Chiang Khong, it could be catastrophic. Cautious pricing when demand is high is sound insurance (see Preecha 1980: 108).

Collection of payments is another time-consuming part of the trading journey. Huge bundles of small denomination notes are meticulously counted as the long-distance traders make their way through the market, gradually filling carry-bags with kip. Those who are going to Mengla in China use marketplace money changers to convert kip into Chinese yuan, or even repatriated American dollars which some insist are better value across the border. Others go to the bank to buy Thai baht, to repay their debts and fund their next venture in Chiang Khong. Others may have heard that exchange rates in Louang Prabang or Houayxay are better, and pack their kip away for the journey south. Traders who live in Udomxai may settle down at home for a week or so before their next venture, sitting up at night with calculators, reconciling receipts and tax forms and hurriedly written records of sale. Traders from other towns head down the road to Pakbeng in the passenger pickups that frequent the route. From there it is a few hours upstream to homes in Houayxay or downstream to homes in Louang Prabang. If all goes well the trip back from Udomxai can be made in a day.[8]

A SPACE OF OPPORTUNITY

FROM the fragmentary historical record it seems likely that the social organization of trade in Laos followed a typically southeast Asian pattern prior to the tumultuous events of the 1960s and 1970s. There was high participation of women in small-scale, localized market trade, whereas long-distance wholesale trade was dominated by Chinese men. There were some exceptions—Khmu women, for example, were active in long-distance exchanges of highland rice, forest products, and salt (Damrong 1994: 104–107)—but the overall pattern was clear.[9] Chinese dominance in long-distance distribution systems had thwarted early French colonial trading enterprises (Reinach 1911: chapter 10) and as trading and transport systems in neighboring Thailand developed the Chinese mercantile penetration of Laos increased.[10] In the 1950s Halpern (1961: 5–7) found that 80 percent of shops in the important northern trading town of Louang Prabang were controlled by Chinese and in the entrepot of Udomxai all of the shops were operated by Chinese families who had migrated from Thailand during the 1930s. Precise details are lacking but there were also Chinese commercial communities in Muang Sing, Louang Namtha, and Houayxay (Halpern 1961: 14; Izikowitz 1979: 312).[11] Chinese-owned shops in the northwest were supplied by wholesalers in Louang Prabang, Vientiane, and in the upper-Mekong Thai trading towns of Chiang Saen and Chiang Khong. Some of the wholesalers operated air services to the rough northwestern airstrips (Damrong 1994: 108–114), while others used riverboats to bring goods along the Mekong and packhorses and bullocks to carry them from small river ports into the hinterland (Halpern 1964: 96; Rowley 1960: 174).

Within the long-distance Chinese trading networks men predominated. Most of the merchants—especially those in the more remote areas—arrived as single men and there was a substantial gender imbalance in the Chinese community in northern Laos (Halpern 1961: 6–7). Many married locally, and while these marriages may have provided an avenue to commercial ventures for some Lao women, it seems probable that their activities remained localized—maintaining local commercial contacts, managing the day-to-day operations of retail outlets and, in some cases, providing a public Lao face for the enterprise when legislative restrictions were placed on Chinese involvement in some lines of commerce (Halpern 1961: 4–7; Purcell 1965: 179, 219). Long-distance commercial networks were probably maintained by Chinese men, given the importance of linguistic, social and cultural linkages with fellow Chinese suppliers and creditors in the major trading towns and further afield in Bangkok, Saigon, and even Hong Kong (Halpern 1961; LeBar and Suddard 1960: 219). Some of the more successful merchants maintained shops—and quite possibly wives and families—in more than one location (Halpern 1961: 5, 10; Mayoury 1993: 84). In summary it seems very likely that the situation in Laos was similar to the situation in Thailand where, in Kirsch's (1982: 29) words, "Private inter-regional trade tended to fall into non-Thai [Chinese] hands . . . No class of women traders arose to take control of the marketing system of the entire kingdom."

The tumultuous events of war and revolution in the 1960s and 1970s bought about fundamental changes in these regional trading systems, with important implications for women's involvement in trade. Large-scale refugee movement from the Pathet Lao zones (Muang Sing, Louang Namtha, Vieng Phukha, Udomxai, and later, Pakbeng) resulted in a massive bloating of the Royal Lao Government (RLG) outposts on the Mekong (Houayxay and Louang Prabang). In 1971 it was estimated that there were over twenty-eight thousand refugees receiving "food and rehabilitation" support around Houayxay alone (Whitaker et al. 1972: 26). The refugee movement gave many women an unprecedented experience of mobility, disrupting traditional occupational structures and drawing some women into the vibrant Mekong River commercial economies—fuelled by foreign aid, sawmilling, and drug money. In Houayxay there were numerous opportunities for cross-border commercial interaction with Thailand, many of them petty and localized but providing women with cross-border contacts and exposing them to a level of economic activity that they had never experienced before. One woman from Pakbeng, for example, made her first contacts in Thailand manufacturing and selling whisky to Chiang Khong's cross-river boat operators and traders who liked to spend clandestine evenings drinking with the Lao refugee girls. Some of her contacts, first made in the early 1970s, now provide a group of Pakbeng traders with accommodation on their regular trips to Chiang Khong. Other women worked as housekeepers for military officials, regularly flying to army bases elsewhere in the north and developing a taste for Heineken beer and sandwiches. And others worked on an island in the middle of the river (the island of "heaven and happiness") serving in restaurants and gambling houses and entertaining anticommunist troops on rest and recreation. The

1960s and early 1970s in Laos have been portrayed as a period of decadence, corruption, and prostitution—Mayoury (1993: 53) writes that "[w]omen were reduced to dull flesh"—but there is no doubt that new social and commercial opportunities also emerged.[12]

The large-scale refugee movements of the war years had a second important effect. Marriages, friendships and commercial contacts made in the crowded towns of Houayxay or Louang Prabang provided a wide range of options for postwar settlement decisions. In the domestic resettlement programs after 1975 some returned to their homes, some stayed in the Mekong river towns and others moved to new locations altogether. The overall effect was a geographic dispersal of family, kinship, and marriage links, a partial shift from the matrilocal tendency of Lao settlement patterns that provided some women with an unprecedented network of accommodation, information, and support throughout the region.[13] What Kirsch (1985: 313–4) refers to as the traditional "grounding . . . of women in their home locale" was somewhat disrupted. Som, for example, was born in Paktha. She spent the war in Louang Prabang where she worked with her mother as a petty trader in the market. After 1975 they moved to Udomxai, joining friends—originally from Pakbeng—who they had first met in Louang Prabang. With one of these friends she operated a restaurant near the market and, later, through contacts in the market they became involved in small-scale cross-border trade with China. Now, disillusioned with the China trade, she travels regularly to Chiang Khong staying with her friend's relatives in Houayxay who themselves moved there after the bombing of Pakbeng in the early 1970s. Spatially dispersed networks of contacts like these are common throughout northwestern Laos and, while they have proliferated in the modern trading system, many owe their origin to the confused demography of the war and of the postwar resettlement.

On the face of it, the period following the Pathet Lao victory in 1975 was not a promising time for new commercial opportunity. In the early years of socialist enthusiasm, a state monopoly was placed on external trade, restrictions were placed in internal trade, and price controls were put in place (Evans 1988). Attempts were also made to establish a network of state stores—with heavily subsidized stock—to supplant the independent trading system. Trading conditions were made worse by the Thai government's closure of the upper-Mekong border in 1976 (it remained closed until 1988) and the Chinese government's closure of their border a few years later (it remained closed until about 1991). Writing of this era, Ireson (1992: 8) has suggested that "[s]tate limitations on private commerce had the potential for destroying one of rural women's most important sources of power and autonomy." She writes, for example, that many village shopkeepers—"frequently Laotian women"—left Laos after 1975 or "quietly stashed their capital" until the situation improved (Ireson 1992: 14). The *Far Eastern Economic Review* (1977: 217) reported that "thousands of petty village merchants were coaxed . . . to return to rice production." In a similar vein (Evans 1993: 144) has argued that "the promotion of trading cooperatives . . . threatened the important role of women in trade." However, while the fortunes of rural traders and shopkeepers may have declined, there is some evidence that the restrictive trading conditions that followed 1975 facilitated the entry of some women into long-distance, wholesale trade. State actions on trade created opportunities for women that enabled them to build on their commercial and social experiences in the wartime era. There were a number of elements to this process.

First, restrictions on private trade, appropriation of property, and personal harassment resulted in a widespread exodus of the established trading class from Laos. This has not been well documented in the north but local recollection indicates that in Houayxay, for example, most of the established Chinese shopkeepers and entrepreneurs fled across the Mekong to Chiang Khong. Their commercial presence in Houayxay was replaced by sparsely stocked stores operated by the provincial authorities. In the major northern towns of Udomxai and Louang Namtha the Chinese merchants probably fled much earlier when the towns fell to communist forces in the late 1950s and early 1960s, and under the new administration there were no privately operated shops of any importance. With the removal of the established merchant class, the way was clear for others to take on new commercial roles, albeit initially at a relatively small scale given the restricted trading conditions. Preecha's study in northern Thailand suggests that the reluctance of successful market women to expand the scale or range of their operations arises in part from the presence of well established and well connected Chinese merchants (Preecha 1980; see also Geertz 1963; Szanton 1972). In Laos this important barrier to feminine ambition was removed.

Second, externally imposed restrictions created opportunities for windfall profits in what would normally be petty and localized trade. With the official closure of the border, women who were experienced as cross-border traders in vegetables, fish, or forest products could now make good profits by taking delivery of smuggled boxes of Aspirin, fish sauce, or salt. This was a risky business for Thai traders—a number were shot by Thai border police patroling the high riverbanks—but Lao provincial authorities took no action to prevent transactions on their side of the river. There was extraordinary demand in Laos for Thai consumer goods and by making shrewd purchases petty traders could quickly build up their stock of trading capital. Profits could be enhanced by transporting to towns and villages some distance from the border, supplying, for example, resettlement communities at Viengphukha who were still heavily dependant on imported goods. In a situation of very restricted supply, petty trade became a lucrative business. A similar process was observed on the Thai side of the border where smuggling "contributed to better distribution of income from established traders to small local inhabitants" (Bunyaraks et al. 1977: 2).

Third, the new government created new avenues of influence and petty patronage. Some of the early entrepreneurs were the wives, daughters, or relatives of provincial officials. These connections provided them with access to education, employment, or assets that could form the basis for trading careers. Air, the daughter of a well-connected official, explicitly linked her skill as a long-distance trader with her state-sponsored education in Hanoi and Moscow. Dam, after marrying into a powerful family in the new administration, left her noodle stall behind and became one of the largest wholesale traders in the northwest, eventually establishing a shop and small warehouse on government land. Other women who had acquired state jobs in the new administration used their non-traditional employment as a stepping stone into commercial enterprise (Ng 1991: 179). Indeed, Mayoury (1993: 133–4) has suggested that women were encouraged to resign from the state sector and pursue other careers as a result of fiscal constraints in the 1980s. Panh's employment in the post office provided her with the contacts and confidence to resign and pursue a wholesale trading career. When Noot was employed as a customs officer she saw that she could make much more money from trade and soon developed a lucrative business carrying goods from Chiang Khong to Udomxai. Her customs contacts were the envy of many. Other women were encouraged to become involved in trade by their husbands who sought to supplement meager state incomes with private economic activity (Evans 1995: xvi). A good number of the northwestern traders are the wives of petty bureaucrats, teachers, policeman, and soldiers and it is possible that the wives of local officials were more able to circumvent government restrictions on trade. Finally, some women were introduced to trade through connections with the state trading enterprises. Tan, for example, first got involved in trade by traveling with her husband who drove a state-owned cargo boat. There was often spare capacity in the boat and she and other private traders used it to carry their goods as far downstream as Pakbeng and Louang Prabang. Ireson (1992: 14) reports that some women were employed in state trading stores, another possible avenue of entry into independent trade.

By the early 1980s these intersecting socioeconomic developments had come together in the establishment of a border market on the Lao-Burma border, just north of the "Golden Triangle." Bypassing the closed Lao border, Thai shopkeepers from nearby Chiang Saen and Mae Sai travelled through Burma and across the Mekong to the small Lao village of Muang

Mom (map 1) where a twice-monthly border market was held. Soon after the market opened, authorities in Houayxay arranged for the extension of a rough riverside road to link the new market town with the provincial capital. State support for the market was probably motivated by the need to supply its trading stores in Houayxay and Louang Prabang, but the market also supported the newly emergent class of traders. Many women began their long-distance trading careers in the informal and opportunistic frontier atmosphere at Muang Mom. Early trading expeditions were financed with profits from smuggling, income from noodle stalls, the sale of gold jewelry, loans or gifts from relatives, or money they received upon marriage. "On market days Houayxay was very quiet" one recalled, "everyone went to Muangmom." They traveled in small boats, in old trucks abandoned by Thai sawmillers, by bicycle, on horseback and even on foot. Localized and small-scale cross-border trade was gradually transformed as distribution networks for the highly sought after Thai imports extended from Houayxay and Louang Prabang to Vieng Phukha and Hongsa and then to Louang Namtha and Udomxai. Despite official policies limiting trade, little attempt was made to restrict the new entrepreneurs. The taxes levied by the customs officers who camped at the market were heavy, but in the riverside atmosphere of sociality, whisky, and young women away from home, there was often room for compromise.

The border market at Muang Mom operated until the reopening of the upper-Mekong Thai-Lao border in 1988. In the intervening years many of the domestic restrictions had also been relaxed and those that remained— such as restrictions on interprovincial trade—continued to be loosely enforced in the northwest. With the reestablishment of a convenient, permanent, and well-supplied trade route through Chiang Khong, the overall level of trade increased dramatically. It was not uncommon for some of the more successful traders to increase the scale of their operations tenfold, in the space of only a few years. When the Chinese border reopened in the early 1990s there were even more opportunities. Suddenly petty traders living near the border were making day trips to Mengla to buy cartons of beer and tape recorders, and larger-scale traders supplying the markets in Udomxai and Louangnamtha could add a profitable Chinese side-trip to their trading itineraries. The level of trade has continued to increase until the present day but there is still substantial excess demand and opportunities for new entrants remain. With good contacts and shrewd buying, windfall profits are still possible. Long distance trading is now well recognized as an occupational option for women and new traders are still entering the market inspired, and in some cases assisted by friends and relatives. The widespread practice of trading in groups makes for relatively easy entry. An aspiring trader can travel with friends, buying very little and incurring few costs, while she makes contacts with suppliers and customers, increases her product and price knowledge and learns how to negotiate with port laborers, transport operators, and state officials. The emergence and consolidation of a class of Lao transport operators—not infrequently the husbands or relatives of traders—has also helped maintain accessibility for women in the long-distance trading system.[14] Alvarez and Collier (1994: 623), for example, have written of the role of local truckers in "expanding the territorial boundaries of 'community' within which . . . women can move about, seek redress for wrongs, and be reasonably assured of security and appropriate social and sexual conduct."

However, there is an important barrier that must be overcome in the transformation from small-scale to large-scale trade. Most of the larger traders are heavily dependent on credit provided by the shopkeepers in Chiang Khong. Generally credit is provided with considerable and understandable reluctance—the debts are unsecured and the shopkeepers have no legal redress in Laos. They have only a limited network of "enforcers" to call upon in the case of bad debts. The traders who have succeeded in gaining credit are those who have made regular trading trips to Chiang Khong and, more importantly, those who have been able to establish trusting and friendly relations with the shopkeepers. As with patron-client relations throughout the region, these relationships emphasize extra-economic sociality such as the sharing of meals and, less often, the provision of accommodation by the shopkeepers when the traders come to Chiang Khong. Some shopkeepers also make social visits to the traders' homes in Laos, especially those in Houayxay across the river, but occasionally also those in Louang Prabang. In establishing these relationships married women, especially those who trade with their husbands, appear to be at a substantial advantage. In Chiang Khong they seem to be perceived as more stable, reliable, and respectable credit risks than unmarried women, many of whom have difficulty getting credit despite a history of regular trading journeys to Chiang Khong. While unmarried women can demonstrate themselves to be good and reliable traders, they have difficulty establishing socially respectable relationships with the shopkeepers. Some of the male shopkeepers quietly entertain hopes of sexual access but the semiformal and domesticated relationships that surround the provision of substantial credit are highly problematic.

CONCLUSION: TRAVELING IDENTITIES

THE highly mobile and usually successful lives of long-distance traders in northwestern Laos suggest that there may be positive and valued "traveling

identities" available to women that are not constrained by the negative
stereotypes of feminine mobility referred to at the outset of this paper.
While further research is required—especially of traders "at home" rather
than "on the road"—I would like to suggest that there are cultural spaces,
within and between predominant cultural forms, that these women occupy
and exploit, paralleling their use of geographic space in the uneven terrain
of northwestern Laos. This is not done without some tension, pain, and
anguish, but it does suggest that gender identities may be more malleable
and problematic than some interpretations of supposedly "fundamental
ideas" (Keyes 1984: 223) may suggest.

Clearly, there are tensions between the roles of long-distance trader and
mother. It is not uncommon for traders to spend more time on trading
journeys than at home, forcing them to rely heavily on friends and relatives
for assistance in child rearing. Trading women often comment that the
regular absences from their children are one of the main difficulties of a
trading lifestyle and some of the women try to minimize their absences by,
for example, traveling in expensive speed boats rather than accompanying
the cargo boats for trips along the Mekong. Yet the role of mother is closely
intertwined with the role of nurturer and provider (Keyes 1984), and in this
respect most trading women are quite successful. Their houses are almost
universally modest, but increasingly their domestic lives are stocked with
washing machines, stereo systems, televisions, satellite dishes, battery-
operated toys, and glass-fronted cupboards displaying Chinese nick-nacks.
Most women traders probably contribute substantially more to household
finances than husbands who are in salaried employment, and a number of
men have joined their wives in trade in recognition of this. Moreover, when
both husband and wife are traders, there is often grudging masculine
recognition that the women are better operators because they are less likely
to be distracted, impoverished or, indeed, infected by whisky, gambling,
and girls along the way. The household finances are safer in feminine
hands. As Ng (1991: 179) wrote of Laos in 1991, "[s]ome women are
beginning to be aware of their economic edge over their husbands, and are
utilizing it subtly to improve their standing within the family." An identity
as long-distance trader is not, then, inconsistent with an identity of nurturer
and provider and, for some women, it reinforces a longstanding feminine
role of household economic manager (Muecke 1984: 464).

There are also cultural tensions and opportunities in the experience of
travel itself. Many of the women complain of the rigors of travel—sleeping
on boats, traveling all night crammed in the cabins of trucks with chain-
smoking truck drivers and spending days in the burning sun at the muddy
Mekong ports. Added to this is the stress of managing the transport of large
quantities of goods through difficult—and sometime treacherous—terrain.

The women rarely express concerns about their personal security, but the effects of this rugged lifestyle, stress, and sleep deprivation on their feminine beauty and charm are common preoccupations. "It's a bad life for a woman" one of the more successful traders told me. Yet, once again, there is a positive side. Many of the women value the adventure and excitement of travel very highly, especially when it is shared with their friends in trading groups. In Chiang Khong, for example, some of the women are literally wide-eyed with amazement when they observe extravagantly funded Thai public rituals. They enjoy browsing in Chiang Khong's well-stocked shops, buying clothes or occasionally a gold chain, eating in Chiang Khong's many restaurants, or just sitting around in the houses of friends eating one-baht *satay* sticks and watching television. In China there are even more shops and restaurants and electronic goods and cheap cosmetics and fake fur coats and hotels with televisions in the room. Even the stories of horrific experiences in Chinese toilets gain something in the telling. While it is masculine travel and adventure that is usually celebrated in Lao and Thai culture, it seems, as Kirsch has noted (1985: 313–4), that mobile women have been able to tap into a strong cultural valorization of travel itself, building a traveling identity that is more open and accessible to them. Moreover while the rigors of travel may undermine some aspects of femininity, the cosmetics, clothes and jewelry that are obtained in Chiang Khong and Mengla contribute to its distinctive refashioning.

Long distance trade and travel also create opportunities for sexual freedoms, though the traveling sexualities of women traders seem to be much more restrained that those of the men (Walker 1995). Some of the women traders have taken the opportunities of entering into sexual relationships with officials, boat operators, or even other (male) traders. For others, participation in trading groups, while providing a measure of respectability denied to women trading alone, also allows relaxed and relatively unsupervised interaction with male traders. Evening meals in boats and restaurants along the route are often accompanied by prolonged and ribald discussions of extramarital liaisons, prostitution, homosexuality, and the sexual desperation of some of their male companions. Some of the women are renowned for their whisky drinking in these sessions. Of course, this relative sexual freedom has its consequence, and amongst the trading and transport community I worked with, there was speculation about the promiscuity, willingness to engage in prostitution, or the AIDS status of some women traders. Others were more gentle in their criticisms, merely suggesting that some of the women were "not polite," "not respectful," or simply just "not good." But, once again, there are cultural opportunities here. Women's mobile sexuality may be dangerous, but it is also powerful, relatively disciplined, and, as longstanding cultural motifs recognize (Keyes

1984: 232–3), it can be deployed for material gain. While some trading women experience difficulties in obtaining credit, there is recognition that feminine sexuality can help negotiate passage and access in a trading system that is full of petty barriers and regulation. Nowhere is this more evident than in the negotiations between the traders and the tight-trousered officials at Houayxay's port. Here, customs officials are often locked in long, confidential conversations with young and attractive traders and it is not uncommon for traders to attribute their low rate of taxation to the charms of one member of their group. One woman was particularly successful: during the final inspection of the boat, her husband, also a trader, would always busy himself tying down the load while his wife talked (almost in whispers) with the customs officers and the immigration police in the crowded front cabin—standing just a little too close, making squeals of protest at the amounts they demanded, subtly drawing attention to the money tucked away in her brassiere and handing them little gifts of fruit or sweets as they left the boat. As Kirsch has indicated (1985: 313), longstanding sexualized practices can now be profitably deployed on a broader and more mobile stage.

How, then, are we to interpret the lives of these mobile women? Their experiences suggest that, in the right circumstances, there may be room for maneuver in Lao gender categories. Maneuver seems to be a more apt description of the social and cultural strategies of these mobile women than either the "unmoor[ing] from . . . Buddhist values" (Keyes, 1984: 236) that some seem to regret, or the "play[ing] havoc with gender ideologies" (Ong and Peletz 1995: 4) that others applaud. The long-distance trading women of northwestern Laos have created innovative traveling identities which resonate with—rather than abandon or subvert—some of the common cultural forms and practices in their communities. They have succeeded in a careful intertwining of motherhood, money, travel, and sex. While the emergence of women as long-distance traders is the product of very specific historical and geopolitical circumstances, their successful molding of gender categories suggests that there may have been other innovative opportunities in the past. And, in the future, if independent traders are sidelined by ten-wheel trucks, import-export companies, and supermarkets (see chapter 2 by Jerndal and Rigg), new cultural and geographic niches will probably emerge, allowing enterprising Lao women new opportunities for profit and pleasure.

NOTES

Research for this paper was undertaken during 1994 and 1995 as part of a broader study of trans-border trading and transport systems in northwestern Laos. Research in Laos was made possible by the Ministry of Communications, Transport, Post and Construction, and in Thailand by the National Research Council of Thailand. Research was funded by an Australian Post-Graduate Research Award and an Australian Award for Research in Asia. I would like to thank the traders and officials in Laos who tolerated my sometimes intrusive presence. Ian Faulkner and Neville Minch prepared the map.

1. All transactions in Chiang Khong are conducted in Thai baht. Lao kip are never accepted by the shopkeepers. During the period in which this fieldwork was undertaken the exchange rate was about 30 kip to the baht and about 25 baht to the American dollar.

2. The groups are relatively informal and group membership changes, though there are usually a few core members. Groups members rarely pool finances or trading stock, and often have separate regular customers. When group members come from different towns they provide accommodation for each other and also assist in maintaining contacts with suppliers and customers. Traders often say that trading in groups is much less convenient given that the larger volumes prolong every stage of the trading journey and it can become difficult to keep track of their own stock (boxes are usually marked with the trader's initials).

3. The smaller-scale traders use cross-river boats to carry their goods to small cargo and passenger boats moored at Houayxay's port. Small Lao cargo and passenger boats are not permitted to cross to Chiang Khong, while the large cargo boats are. For a detailed analysis of the operations of the cross-river boats at Chiang Khong, see Walker (1966).

4. In early 1995 Lao customs tried to crack down on these practices by refusing to allow any Lao cargo boats to cross to Chiang Khong to load. Rather they insisted that all cargo be brought across the river on the Thai cross-river boats and loaded, under their supervision, at the Houayxay port. They also limited the amounts that could be loaded onto the boats to reduce the chances of concealment. Nevertheless, amidst the confusion of traders, cross-river boats, and cargo boats at Houayxay, the practices continued.

5. In early 1995, customs officers at the inspection point just south of the Chinese border crossing near Louang Namtha started insisting that all the trucks be unloaded so that the cargo could be subjected to detailed scrutiny.

6. Of course, not all evasion is of this degree. Lemonade is a high-tax item and there is strong incentive to minimize tax. Evasion on lower-tax items is often much less substantial. Nevertheless substantial under-collection of customs revenue is widely recognized as a major fiscal problem in Laos.

7. Slightly lower prices may be offered to shopkeepers with whom the traders have a particularly close personal relationship.

8. By late 1996 some of the more affluent traders were taking advantage of the improved air services between Udomxai, Houayxay and Louang Prabang.

9. "Partly because of the long distances that must be traveled, men make up the

majority of the mountain groups that come to trade in the Lao village." (Roberts et al. 1967: 249)

10. Halpern (1961: 1) estimates that the official Chinese population in Laos increased from only 486 in 1911 to over 30,000 in 1955, though this probably understates the number of Chinese traders in Laos in the early years of the century. See also Purcell (1965: 170–2).

11. Chinese merchants in Laos came overland from Yunnan and overseas, usually via Thailand, from other southern Chinese provinces. The Yunnanese presence was strongest in the northern areas near the Chinese border. Generally it appears that the Yunnanese were involved in regional trade with hill-dwellers while other Chinese groups were involved in shopkeeping (Halpern 1961).

12. Kibria (1993: 57) has written of women's petty trading opportunities in wartime South Vietnam: "The peculiar qualities of the South Vietnamese urban economy—the abundance of luxury consumer items and foreign goods, combined with the plentiful discretionary income of certain segments of the population—often made such trading quite lucrative." Within Laos there is evidence that Lao traders made some headway against the Chinese in the localized economic booms of the war years (LeBar and Suddard 1960: 159; Purcell 1965: 219).

13. Mayoury (1993: 79–80) notes the increasing popularity of "neolocality." since the war.

14. For details on the long-distance transport industry, see Walker (1997), chapter 5.

ELITES IN EXILE
THE EMERGENCE OF A
TRANSNATIONAL LAO CULTURE

5

SI-AMBHAIVAN SISOMBAT
SOUVANNAVONG

I N the years immediately following the communist revolution in December 1975 about 400,000 Lao left their country as refugees or went into exile.[1] Those turbulent revolutionary times, however, have passed and Asia today is seen as an area of opportunity, not as one of wars and revolutions. Consequently some Lao exiles are returning to live in Laos once again, or are considering such a move, even though the country is still ruled by the Lao People's Revolutionary Party (LPRP). In France, some Lao are still willing to fight the LPRP government but a second generation has grown up with different ideas. They are not involved in Lao political or social life, and increasingly these youth foresee an opportunity to enter businesses as the former Indochina area embarks on economic development, whereas Europe has a two-digit unemployment rate.

The repatriation of many Lao from camps in Thailand beginning in the 1980s has shown the world, and Lao exiles in particular, that it is possible to live safely in Laos today.[2] Since 1991, this situation has been further confirmed for Lao exiles by various signs: the encouragement of foreign investment by the Lao government, urban development, infrastructure construction, increasing exchanges with neighboring countries, membership in ASEAN, development of tourism, favorable press articles, and enthusiasm of relatives who have visited Laos. France hosts 49,561 people from Laos, in comparison with 225,000 in the United States. Since 1991, the "Lao community" in France has debated the pros and cons of returning, in both conferences and in private gatherings.[3] Today some exiles proclaim that Laos living abroad should go back to Laos to help the country develop.

This essay is concerned with the question of why some exiles return, and the complex negotiations, personal and political, involved in this process.

We will see that it is not simply a product of macroeconomic calculations or political ideology, but is the outcome of one's life in the sense that motives for the return lie in a family's political economy, and involves all the tensions and mournings inherent in a cultural and social reconversion.

These Lao returnees are, however, exceptions to the rule. Out of all the Lao exiles, only 150 to 200 families have decided to go back and live in Laos, that is around 1,000 out of 400,000 people.[4] These people have spent twenty years in a host country and have built a new life. One does not live in a temporary spirit during twenty years—social networks are created, children given stability, and projects are planned for the future. One shifts from refugee status to being a citizen in a new society.

To illustrate the problem, we will study two families. They are not representative of ordinary Lao as they belong to "the Lao elite." The study of this social group, however, enables us to clearly show the two essential dimensions of the return project: the political stakes and the economic stakes. This chapter describes the life of this group of refugees, and its life in exile in France. We will see how the durability of exile causes the idea of return to fade, and we will see how their increasing distance from their culture of origin contributes to this. Then, we will analyze the factors that reverse this process and make the return a reality.

THE NOTION OF ELITE

THE pre-1975 elite, the *phou nyai*, "the men in high places," were mainly ethnic Lao. The elite lived in the urban areas and held the most important positions in the administration and in the economic sphere. Halpern (1963: 115) estimated that around two hundred families formed the Lao elite. Most of them were direct descendants from royal families of ancient principalities and from the officials who served in them, including military officers and high ranking servants. This social group of Lao notables is widely represented in France because of Laos's historic bonds with France from the colonial era. Hundreds of students, most of whom belonged to the grand families, were granted with scholarships from the Lao or the French government to pursue their studies in France. Familiar with French culture, the privileged of Laos naturally chose to flee to where they had already established some linkages whether it be in the academic, the professional, or the diplomatic fields. This was also the case for the well-off urban citizens, civil servants, officers, and businessmen.

An elite possesses some form of capital which enables it to hold a dominating position in social space. There are different forms of capital, but the three fundamental ones are economic capital, cultural capital, and social capital. Social space is structured by the distribution of material resources and the appropriation of socially scarce goods and values: ". . . the structure of social space as observed in differentiated societies is the product of two fundamental differentiating principles, that of economic capital and of cultural capital" (Bourdieu 1989: 13).

Both of the families in our study hold sizeable capital: the first family has built and holds social capital and the second one holds economic capital. Both of them share important cultural capital gained through an inherited and acquired level of education. This disposition enables them to make decisions, and to anticipate their country's or their life's destiny.

The Santiphab family is descended from a dignitary of the ancient principality of Vientiane.[5] As one historian puts it: "the Santiphabs have participated in the construction of modern Laos, and have held the reins of power." We will study the Pavatsad branch, which was most involved in Lao politics. The father of twelve children, Pavatsad held different positions in the royal government: president of the National Assembly, minister of culture, minister of education, and counselor to the king. Six children of Pavatsad have lived in France since 1975; the others stayed in Laos. The family based in France has been socially and politically involved in the Lao community and has tried to pass on the symbolic values of Lao culture through the perpetuation of religious, culinary, and housing practices. The family still holds a sizeable patrimony in Laos: properties, reputation, and a still active network of relationships.

The Setakit family, originally farmers in the south of the country, got out of poverty by trading with Cholon Chinese and Thai, and then were ennobled through marriage to a member of the Champassak royal family. Heng, the present patriarch of the Setakits, developed the family's capital by entering politics in the 1950s. He accumulated considerable wealth which later on enabled him to settle down in France and avoid the traumas of most refugees. In France the Setakit family have only focused on rebuilding their economic capital. They did not have any particular strategy to pass on Lao values.

Heng Setakit, seventy-two years old, had sent his ten children to study in France in the 1960s. In 1975, they were living in a spacious apartment in the 16th district of Paris, which is a well-off neighborhood, and they were attending the best private schools in town. Placed in boarding schools, they were taught Lao customs only on weekends by their aunts and uncles sent to France by Heng to supervise his children. Heng himself ran a company that imported luxury products (alcohol, cars) from France or Europe, which frequently brought him to Europe. When, he decided to leave for France in 1975, nine of his ten children were already living there and studying. They had only returned to Laos once or twice in their lives, during vacations.

Heng's wife's two brothers (who were also Heng's nephews) lived and worked alongside Heng: Toula, now sixty years old, a former director of a Lao Bank, is married to Mangkon, daughter of a diplomat, and has four children; the other brother, Meta, now fifty-six, is a former director of Heng's company and is married to Sati Santiphab (daughter of Pavatsad Santiphab), with three children.

Pavatsad Santiphab had also cultivated his connections in Europe, particularly in France, while attending international conferences or on assignments to find solutions to Laos's political problems. He had sent four of his children to study in France in the early sixties. One of them stayed there and married a French woman. In 1975, he sent his three daughters, still single, back to France in order to shield them from the country's uncertainties.

THE EXILE

THE Lao elite was the first group to leave the country, and they left in conditions different from ordinary Lao refugees: "the first people to leave, former civil servants and officers, businessmen, and well-off urbanites, have often benefited from connections in this country and did not have to ask for the UNHCR's shelter. They arrived directly in France, without having to transit in Thailand, and they could quickly integrate" (Choron-Baix 1990: 27). Heng, his wife, his elder daughter, and her husband left Laos in May 1975. Meta and his family joined them in June 1975. Pavatsad Santiphab accompanied his three children in July 1975. All these departures took place well before the official creation of the Lao People's Democratic Republic, on 2 December 1975. All of them simply bought a ticket to Paris, on one of the scheduled flights of Air France. This easy way of leaving, without suffering the difficult months or years in the camps, causes them to deny that they are refugees: "They did not flee! Uncle Heng did not flee, neither did Meta and his family, nobody! They came with their passports, everybody! Nobody went through the refugee [condition] . . . nobody crossed the Mekong . . . nobody has been a refugee!" (Melieng, 57, former nanny of the Setakit children). Pavatsad went back to Laos in August 1975, after having installed his daughters in a small, rented apartment located in the old district of Paris. Meanwhile, Heng settled down in his spacious Parisian flat bought some years before.

Like other Lao refugees, the newly arrived members of the Setakit and Santiphab families were confronted with the need for employment and immediately faced the prospect of downward mobility because their diplomas and work experience were not recognized. The three daughters of

Pavatsad carried on their studies and finished high school. They accepted the first jobs available—as cleaners, factory workers, and so on. As more Lao refugees flowed into France and established a social network, the daughters were able to find better jobs within two or three years—in an insurance company filing records. Thanks to the company's policy, they were later trained to become computer keyboard operators. The Setakits took a different route. Their economic capital enabled them to begin more ambitiously by setting up a family-run business. With the money he had transferred from Laos, Heng opened a grocery in the center of Paris selling Asian foodstuffs. In it he employed his relatives and five of his children.

THE NEVER-ENDING EXILE

WHEN they left their country, the Lao refugees did not view their journey as definitive. "I am accompanying you to give you roots . . . just a few years to bring you to adulthood . . . I will then go back to Laos," said Meta to his three children in 1975. However, the refugees soon settled into a long-term exile, as can be seen in every aspect of their lives: housing, change in citizenship, professional life, marriage strategies, establishment of a family, children's education, and daily routines. After twenty years of exile, return for most becomes materially impossible. So they eventually settle down in a country where they had only planned to stay a short while. "As one is only passing through, it is easy to settle down in temporary conditions, without any furniture or hardly any, and one accepts any job. Then one establishes social and sentimental relations while thinking that one day, one will leave and will not see anymore these new friends, that the new love affairs will last only the time of exile. Time passes and the hoped for insurrection in the country doesn't occur: the dictators remain in place and the exile lasts. It is almost incredible, as if it was someone else's story . . . Time passes by and the exile changes, events are understood differently, self perception and projects are modified as well. The exile eventually changes the exiles (Vasquez & Araujo 1988: 34–35).

Twenty years have passed and Pavatsad's daughters, single upon their arrival in France, have all started families. Two are married to Lao and have three children, from five to twenty years old. The third is alone, raising her two children. All of them worked for an insurance company as keyboard operators. Sati, the elder sister who worked as a keyboard operator for more than fifteen years has since joined the Setakits in their activities. They all explain their occupational immobility by financial necessity and "because we do not have the same education as the French . . . and it is too late, we were already adults when we arrived." They view their job as a means of survival: "it is just for living, to raise our children. It is risky to leave the company . . . maybe it would be worse in another one. And if we go back now, what would we do? When we quit Laos, we left everything behind us."

Heng and his elder son Sone, who graduated from the Institute of Political Studies and the Ecole des Hautes Etudes Commerciales,[6] had ambitious plans to develop their company selling Asian products, and they opened a big supermarket in the 13th district, the new Chinatown of Paris, followed by a subsidiary in Lyons, the second French capital. Chinese competition forced them into bankruptcy in the mid-eighties. They all suffered a long period of unemployment and downgrading, when they had to go work for French companies as watchman, pump attendant, or ordinary worker. The Setakits, especially the first generation, lived with difficulty during these somber years and experienced a loss of status. In 1987, after having repaid their debts and reconstituted their capital, Sone succeeded in gathering together the family to set up a few small Asian businesses (two restaurants, a gift shop, a grocery) located in a western suburb of Paris, at Velizy. The shops employed twenty people, among whom fifteen were relatives.

The Setakit children, who all grew up in France, were divided on whether to work with French companies in posts for which their studies had prepared them or to work with the family. Most of them had a good education, with twelve children out of seventeen completing a higher education. Among the graduates, four joined the family business, eight chose to work in foreign companies where they have careers comparable to their classmates. Sam, thirty-eight years old, graduated from a famous French business school and became a managing director of a multinational; Si, with a master's degree in computer science, became a senior manager of a big computer engineering company; Mesa graduated from a business school as well, and took a position as a marketing officer in an American firm.

INTEGRATION: PERMANENT OR IMPERMANENT?

INTEGRATION implies "making things complete, to achieve or restore the entirety," and is envisaged as a movement that brings a part into the whole, for example, an exile into the host country (Simon 1993: 25). Here, it is "to become French." Integration is the measure of how well a group or an individual conforms to a "normality" that is defined by the dominant group.

Yet, for the first-generation Lao (and for most of their children), the issue was not "to become French." They did not conceptualize their life in terms of *integration*. They simply thought of surviving (then, of living well), and of assuring their children's education, and rebuilding their social status, which they did through their social network of compatriots. The first generation of Lao refugees acted like other immigrants arriving in a new country: they created two parallel networks with different levels of relationships.

> The immigrants, specifically the first generation, use a strategy of material acculturation as a way of avoiding the dangers of assimilation and the pathology of de-culturation . . . He [the immigrant] confines his primary relations (feelings) to the circle of the family and the ethnic collectivity, and with the host community only develops secondary relations, and business relations. Thanks to this division, he is content to adopt the behaviour models required by the host country's public life while keeping intact the ways of thinking and feeling inherited from his original culture (Abou 1981: 57).

The Lao refugees managed the two relationships, as explained by Abou, without feeling uneasy or questioning themselves. "When we are with them [the French], we behave like them, we are in their world. But real life is with our friends, who understand us, who eat the same food as us . . . are Lao, just like us." Rather than Simon's (1993: 31) concept of integration as a form of social participation, of exercising one's "full citizenship," the concept of integration could be reformulated as being the constitution and maintenance of social networks. This will enable us to conceive of the existence of diverse forms of participation in modern life, without necessarily thinking in terms of "levels" of integration which suggest some kind of linear progression. We will use this conceptual approach to integration to understand Lao refugees in France.

Adjusting their relations into primary and secondary networks, our two families participated in French social life through their job, and through their understanding of institutions, organizations, and consumption patterns. As such, they could be considered integrated. Nevertheless, the two families had different strategies of integration: one corresponded to "avoidance," the other to "cultural assimilation."[7] The Santiphabs continued to think they were only in France temporarily. They lived in the hope of a possible return and mobilized themselves around a strong idea of Lao *identity*, what Hélène Bertheleu would call their *laocité* (Bertheleu 1994). Their children were socialized in a dense ethnic context but they gradually experienced *cultural adaptation*, and the permanency of their exile meant that gradually they no longer considered their stay as temporary. The Santiphabs were integrated into France mainly through their work. But their social status was achieved and confirmed through their participation in the Lao community. The children of the other family, the Setakits, assimilated. They arrived in France when they were very young, and they were not given a Lao *identity* by their parents. The Setakit children achieved a complete integration by adopting the values and practices of the dominant French society—their way of life, their language, their type of housing, their language, their personal and community relationships.

We shall now consider these various forms of integration through some of the practices and social relationships of the two families.

Living Space

The arrangement of the Setakit family's living spaces is strongly influenced by the French, especially in the houses of the children. At Heng's house, one can still find Lao decorative objects acquired before 1975, or in a final rush before departing that year. He decorated his 16th district flat with culturally (and financially) valuable objects: bronze drums, elephant tusks, Lao paintings, frescos, silverware, and china crockery engraved with his name. Heng's children, however, who are now all living independently, have laid out an utterly European interior. Depending on their revenue and their cultural capital, they have adopted the same style as French society. Sam, married to a French woman from the Parisian upper bourgeoisie, is living in an opulent house in Saint-Cloud, on the very smart outskirts of Paris. Wooden floor, discreet flowered curtains, antique furniture, modern sculptures and paintings, and books from the Pleiade collection constitute his everyday environment. At his brothers' house, one can find different styles from the very practical and neat "Ikea" style to a vaguely Asian mix of furniture coming from the family gift shop. The space is conceived in a European way which ignores the fact that the floor is a living space for Lao people.

Meta Setakit and the Santiphab sisters, however, who quit Laos and abandoned all their possessions, have reformed their environment with odds and ends rescued here and there. Like other refugees, it is the family and social networks which helped them equip their home at a moderate price or for free. Their living space is, typically, centered on the living room/dining room, with small and valueless ornamental objects of Lao or vaguely Asian origin (dolls wearing Lao costumes, small khènes or a calendar from a temple). They use a Western-style dinner table but continue to take off their shoes when entering the house.

Distance from the culture of origin can also be observed through eating practices. Due to their many years living abroad the Setakits have abandoned most of the Lao cuisine. Their taste has been modified (less spicy, less salty) and traditional courses using the pickled fish sauce *padek* have been discarded in favor of Euro-Asian foods: stews, curries, stuffed tomatoes, etc. The Santiphab sisters and Sati, though they never learned how to cook, have included Lao dishes in their cooking and will spend hours and hours during their weekends preparing traditional dishes. In their refrigerator and cupboards, one can easily find basic Lao ingredients and all kinds of sauces that can be kept for months.

The Childrens' Cultural Adaptation

In the arrangement of living spaces and in social and professional relationships, the children have generally adopted French cultural practices. The cultural adaptation is particularly visible in the relations between the children and the parents. Relations between Lao people are quite flexible, while respecting an elder-younger hierarchy. Parents therefore have some authority on most issues regarding their children. But in France, parental authority fades out in some domains, leaving the children to decide what is best, especially with regard to French institutions.

Cultural adaptation comes firstly with the language, and Lao has been abandoned for a long time by Heng's and Toula's children. Living abroad since their infancy, they have known only French or English languages which they have adopted "because we spoke in French all the time at the boarding school, with our friends . . . We spoke Lao only on weekends." When talking to their parents they use French. Should they have to answer in Lao, one hears pidgin Lao, a limited vocabulary and many syntactical and pronunciation mistakes: "*Bo, khoy yu alone . . . Sith pai see Grandma*" [No, I am alone, Sith went to see Grandma]. Meta and Sati have continued to talk in Lao to their children who have developed a wider Lao vocabulary thanks to their parents' social activities. The other Santiphab sisters, however, are experiencing the same problems with their children as Heng: born in France, they started talking Lao when they were very young, but once they started school they switched exclusively to French.

With regard to the choice of a husband or wife, which has always been fairly free in Laos, they have been given wide scope. Though the parents prefer an ethnically endogamous union, no splits occurred when the couples were mixed. In the three mixed marriages of Heng's children, the couples organized two religious ceremonies: the traditional baci and a celebration at the Catholic church. The French daughters-in-law, all belonging to the French bourgeoisie, attested to their integration and represented a form of social advancement. Meta's daughter, on the other hand, opted only for the Lao marriage ceremony with her fiancé, a Eurasian from the provincial bourgeoisie. Her more traditional parents encouraged their children to marry Lao people: "look for a Lao, he is like us, he will understand us and we will not have to adjust our behavior to his." Though they would also say "whether he is French or Lao, the most important thing is to marry someone who has goodness."

The few religious ceremonies organized by the family (only for big events such as marriage, birth, or death) show that religion has faded out of the lives of both families, with infrequent visits to the five temples in the Paris area. Difficulties with access to these places of worship partly explains this. Yet, every house holds an altar and some traditions are still kept alive. The Santiphab family remain closer to the Buddhism and animism which characterizes Lao beliefs. Without being fervent, they more regularly attend the temples, and continue the habit of praying to the spirits before a long journey, or of asking for their authorization to live in a new place, or of consulting a monk regarding a long-lasting illness.

The children are the ones who undertake any administrative formalities or arrangements for their parents. With regard to naturalization, Heng gave his children the freedom to decide, and when they reached their majority they became French citizens. Toula applied for French citizenship for all the members of his family the year of their arrival, and on acquiring their new status all the children changed their first names to French ones—Sebastien, Jean-Christophe, Philippe—demonstrating their desire to be fully integrated into French society. Sati, on the other hand, vetoed such a move by her own family: "as long as my parents are alive, I won't ask for another citizenship! My parents are Lao, I am Lao. Nobody will be French." After her parents died in the early eighties, she applied for French citizenship, mainly because administrative formalities do not make foreigners' lives easy in France. The Santiphab sisters will eventually abandon their refugee status as well, to live more quietly in France.

Social Relations

Heng and Toula continued to visit their former colleagues and Lao friends but the passing years have made these gatherings increasingly infrequent. Toula and Heng's children visit few Lao people, apart from the family "because, they are so weird these Lao . . . we do not understand each other, we do not share the same interests. They like going to parties, playing cards, going out always among themselves." Their social network includes "French people," high school or university classmates, and office colleagues. The main context in which they meet other Lao are events such as marriages, death ceremonies or community activities organized by their aunt Sati. This low level of contact does not bother them because "we are more French than Lao. We have always lived in France, we arrived very young. We have French friends, we feel French, and our parents did not push us to meet other Lao." Out of ten children, three married with French women, and five married Lao women (three of whom were their cousins).

Mixed marriages usually widen the gap with the "Lao community." Relations with other Lao only developed when the spouses themselves were involved in the Lao community, which was the case for two of them.

The Santiphabs, on the other hand, have few relations outside of the "Lao community." They never meet colleagues in circumstances other than work, and they avoid relations with their neighbors. Gatherings with other Lao are frequent: meetings on weekends, children's birthdays, card games, video shows of Thai TV series, improvised dinners to share a delicate Lao meal, and so on. On Sundays, they devote themselves to community activities: parents participate in organizing events, and their children attend Lao language or dancing lessons.

Community Relationships

In 1977, after the initial years of settling in, many refugee associations began simultaneously. These associations had either political or cultural objectives. Sati Santiphab and her husband Meta entered into one of these, the Samakhom, of which she held the presidency until 1992. The objectives of the Samakhom are to "support women and to help them; to strengthen links with other Lao refugees, to support mentally the newly arrived and the refugees in the camps; to safeguard Lao culture and customs; to help the refugees in their new life in France; the association will abstain from any political activities" (article 3 of the Samakhom statutes, 1977). During these years, around a hundred Lao associations were created in France (nowadays around eighty are more or less active).

These associations constitute a protected sphere within the host society where the Lao value system is able to be active again: the hierarchy between men and women, elder and younger, mandarin and ordinary people. They are instrumental in intensifying a Lao sense of identity, and in crystallizing energies to fight the LPRP. Those who actively participate in community activities are often exposed to "rituals which mark the belonging to a group in which one is registered, in a given class of human beings, opposed to others" (Sindzingre 1992: 900) and this dispels feelings of *anomie*. Community associations are a means for migrants to collectively endorse their native culture. Sati who arrived in France at the age of thirty-three had never really thought about cultural activities when in Laos, and like her other board members, " we spent our time having fun . . . the culture, the traditions, we never thought of! It was in the street everyday, everywhere." Through the association they claim their national identity, and ignore the ethnic and social differences that occurred in Laos. Lao costumes are often highlighted for women, and reinterpreted in fashion parades. The association undertakes ambitious projects focused on the safeguarding of Lao culture: Lao song contests, Lao dancing entertainment, lessons in traditional music, cultural exhibitions, New Year celebrations. When an entertainment is organized more than two hundred people will volunteer their time and talents to make the project a success. Each event attracts eight hundred to one thousand Lao.

Community activities enable elite Lao in particular to recover and revalidate the social status they held in Laos. As a representative of a grand family, Sati acquired in France social acknowledgment thanks to her community work. The other board members of the association also gain social status as well because of the visibility of the Samakhom's activities. There they find a new meaning to their lives: "we do our best, it is not easy everyday and all these sacrifices, all that time that we spend . . . but we do something for all the Lao, for the children who are growing up here so that they do not forget that they are Lao." At the head of Lao associations one often finds former *phagna* (honorary title), former ministers, descendants from grand families, and intellectuals. These positions are dissociated from the life they have in the French sphere. In the cultural and social parties, men and women are excessively elegant which often has little to do with their actual standard of living. Men wear ties and brandname suits, while women display traditional dresses in shimmering silk. Dresses costing from US$150 to US$800 are not unusual in a Lao refugee woman's wardrobe: appearance-conscious, she rarely wears the same dress in the same season and thus participates in an illusory, glittering world. There is a hierarchy in the parties which must be respected. The Samakhom's parties are attended by former personalities, the *phou nyai*, whereas others attract a younger set. And when one belongs to the elite, one cannot escape from some parties or marriage celebrations. The way tables are organized in these events, with special tables of honor, show the social stratification that existed in Laos before 1975, and this is reenacted in France, for an evening or a meeting.

From Community Activities to Politics

From the beginning, the border between a cultural association and a political one was blurred. "As everything is political anyway" (Sati), and anyway it is always the same people who attend the various meetings of the Lao community. After her arrival in France, Sati tried to resume the political activities of her father. She joined the Samakhom, and con-currently participated in the activities of many associations, some in the political domain. She was the only woman elected to the managing committee of the highly political foundation, of which 80 percent were former politicians: high officials, *phagna*, members of the royal family, army officers, and key figures of the Hmong resistance movement. She participated along with her husband in various prodemocracy and human rights demonstrations. In a more discreet way, the Samakhom was also a means for Sati to show her disapproval of the situation in Laos, for example, by using the theme of a dancing performance to send a message concerning the need for independence and democracy in Laos. "All this will lead me to be blacklisted but we have to continue to tell them that Laos needs freedom." In 1990, she finally got to work on her father's projects, with the support of her sisters. An association was created with the same objectives and name as the former political party of their father. Through her involvement in political and social life, she became the symbol of the "refugee militant." The Lao community considered her as its spokeswoman because of her status as a woman, her strong character, and her social background.

THE RETURN

SINCE 1992, two Santiphab sisters, eight Setakits (four of the first generation, and four children), as well as three close relatives, have "definitively" returned to Laos.[8] This trend is not finished as two other Setakit children are planning to go back and four more are studying the question. If the return of the older generation can be explained by nostalgia, even though they have a quiet life in France, the return of the younger generation is surprising because they have little or no knowledge of their native country and their education has prepared them to stay in France.

The process of return has been progressive and prepared by exploratory trips. Beginning in 1989 Tania Santiphab carried out three trips before her final move in 1994. A first visit by Sone, Heng's elder son, in 1991 was the starting point for the Setakits' return. Though he was struck by Laos's poverty, Sone realized that his father's fame had not vanished completely and that his name could still be capitalized on. Sone, an ambitious man with dynastic ambitions, then encouraged his father to return to Laos: "I really pushed him . . . rushed him off his feet. I wanted him to be back as from end of 1991. In France, he had become a weak man, almost a coward . . . I did not want him to be like that. I asked him to return, telling him that he still has business there . . ." Eventually in February 1992, Heng made the trip to Laos with his wife, and by December 1992, he was enrolled by the party in the first elections to the legislature![9] As Heng said: "as soon as I was back in my native country, the Central Committee gave me the great honor to participate in the electoral list . . . The electoral campaign is not very tough, as it is organized, everything is scheduled; we are altogether with the other candidates. Sometimes, we do the trips by helicopter, for distant muongs; we do speeches to make the population interested in their everyday life . . ." He was elected as a deputy in the southern province where he had held a similar position before 1975 and announced the news to all his friends and relatives in France with surprise and happiness: "what a delight and pleasure to announce to you that I have been elected as a deputy, after four months back on my native soil. It is done, we won! It is incredible but it's true! After seventeen years of absence from the country, I have been renewed with honor and pride by the people to be their leader on the political and economic scene. It is a truly unexpected event! This must be heaven-sent and I hope that it is God who supports me."

After his nomination as a president of one of the country's major institutions, he made a trip to France towards the end of summer 1993, completely transformed by this experience. He had regained the dynamism of a busy man. Sone seized this occasion to study with his father the opportunities coming up in Laos and in the region. "I would like so much to be an international regional businessman; in Kuala Lumpur, in Hanoi, in Kunming . . . but we need a foundation on which to expand, to be strong, to be somebody. For now, we are nothing. Why go back to Laos? It is always the same problem, to be a small fish in a big pond or to be a big fish in a small one. I would rather be a big fish in a small pond" (Sone). Sone traveled to Laos with his father in the autumn, followed by his brother Sam and his uncle Meta to deal with a coffee project. In 1996, the company employed in the high season from 150 to 250 employees and was growing more than one hundred hectares of coffee.

We have seen previously that the two families had settled satisfactorily in France. Why return to Laos then?

Existing Wealth in Laos

The families which left Laos relinquished all their possessions, in some cases to relatives for safekeeping, while others saw the new government seize them. Going back to Laos would mean starting a new life from scratch, though some of them still have some assets they could lean on to resettle. Almost all the members of the Setakit family left for France whereas the Santiphabs, an ancient Lao family, was still well represented numerically in Laos, as they had built extensive networks through marriages over generations. The Pavatsad family counts on Athit, the sixty-four-year-old elder son, who joined with the communists in his youth and who nowadays holds a senior position in the administration; Pavane, sixty years old, is the guardian of all the properties and the family rites; and two others, a sister and a brother. The Santiphabs have succeeded in keeping almost all the properties of their father Pavatsad, who had verbally divided them among all his children before he died.

The children who left Laos delegated the management of their shares to those who stayed, as the Lao law enables only Lao citizens living in Laos to own Lao soil. Since 1975, the legal owners of their properties are therefore their sisters and brothers who stayed in Laos. In downtown Vientiane, they own more than twenty properties which can be rented at a price of US$500 to US$1000 a month. In the provinces, they possess square kilometers of virgin lands as well. Today, disputes over inheritance are arising and becoming more and more tense as claimants return.

Elite returnees could also lean on another form of capital, their symbolic capital. But to what extent had their past achievements survived the passing of the years? The members of the grand families who stayed on in Laos usually experienced more harassment than the rest of the population: people were sent to seminars, were subject to strict police surveillance and some discrimination: "we did not dare bear our name. Some families, such as the S. have even changed their name. We only used our father's name, everywhere . . . If we used our mother's name, they refused to talk to us, because we were Santiphabs. We did not go out anymore." Today's elite is formed by the *nomenklatura* and no more by the former grand families. A whole generation has grown up learning a history revised by the new regime which presents the former regime, the *labob kao*, as an unegalitarian time ruled by imperialist powers. But the older leaders of the party and the government know well the achievements of these families, as they have fought them for more than thirty years. There are still marriage connections, former classmates, former colleagues who have never left and who now hold important positions, as department directors in the ministries. They have not forgotten the past and today it is easy to approach them and to reactivate former friendships. Meta, for example, contacted one of his former friends who holds a major position in the new regime. His old friend responded: "I was wondering why you took so much time before coming to see me . . . we sowed our wild oats together . . . we are *phi nong* (brothers), do not forget it; our parents were *phi nong*, we remain *phi nong*. We care about each other . . . keep this affection that we had for each other. You have to come back and live in our country . . . we will grow old together."

Threatened Wealth in France

Initially the Setakits had decided to build their life in France. How many compatriots had exclaimed "but the Setakits, they are not refugees!" They invested in France socially, economically and culturally. They created companies and made financial commitments. As for the younger Setakits, their capital was only constituted through their work in France, and they would only return to Laos if their capital in France weakened. For the Santiphab sisters the situations was different: "yes, we are thinking of it. I have been thinking for a long time that I would return when I retire, when the children are grown up. Life is difficult in France but we have a job, decent housing, loyal friends . . . In Laos, what are we going to do? We do not have any job, what are we going to live on, and where to live in? It is not possible to leave now to settle down there . . . Finally, we feel good here." Some years ago, Meta often repeated that "when my children treat me badly, don't respect me anymore, then I will go back to Laos . . . I would have no reason left to stay here. Why stay here and be unhappy when I can be far happier in my homeland, in Laos . . . I would even go into retreat as a monk."

The return stops being an imprecise matter, however, when unexpected pressures come into play. For example, economic destabilization. Sone, Heng's elder son, encountered difficulties with the businesses he started in 1989 in Velizy. None of the five shops achieved the targets set and the survival of the group was challenged in 1992. Sone had to progressively lay off his employees and family members. In 1994, two bankruptcies were declared. In 1996, the only business left was the grocery shop. The four brothers and three sisters-in-law ended up being jobless. The rising career of Heng's second son, Sam, in a multinational company stopped abruptly when he was dismissed from his position as chief operating officer in September 1993. Tania Santiphab at the same time had been unemployed for two years and could not find work despite retraining. Her husband, a forty-eight-year-old tennis teacher, had been progressively losing his trainees. For the first generation, this economic pressure also led to financial subordination to their children. Heng suffered from financial troubles since the first bankruptcy, and he and his wife were taken in charge by their ten children. He would present a monthly budget plan to them and every child would have to finance the expenses according to their capabilities. The situation became particularly painful when the new businesses, on which five children depended, went badly: "I have financially backed my parents to the limit . . . Phay kept telling me, 'You are taking away the food from our children's mouths to give to your parents . . .' The other brothers, they would say 'I give this' and they would give this amount. I was filling the gap, handing out what is necessary . . . Dad begging for money . . . Sometimes, he had tears in his eyes." (Sone)

> The point is that things were getting worse here. Either he would continue to be subordinated to the children and to ask for money every month, continuously or live there . . . You know our parents' life . . . what they have turned out to be . . . I think everybody understood what they wanted . . . They did not want to face these difficulties anymore, in terms of survival, I mean. Because to survive here, it is a real battle. Because, at the end of every month, he is not going to say to his children, "Hey, you did

not give me the money." I think that for parents, it would be quite gloomy
to end up in this situation . . . Then they decided to leave. (Tiet, thirty-four
years old, trained in accountancy, and manager of one of Sone's businesses,
married to a French woman).

Meta and Sati's children, who were still living with them, took charge of
many household expenses. Being unemployed, Meta felt guilty and became
an insomniac. He also knew that contrary to former unemployment
periods, he would encounter difficulties in finding another job because of
his age (fifty-five years old in 1994). Financial subordination is all the more
difficult for Lao men who have been inculcated with traditional values that
expect men to support the family, and to refrain from expressing their
feelings. Lao from this elite background have never had to deal with the
cooking, the washing, or the other housework, surrounded as they were by
servants twenty-four hours a day. In France these tasks made them feel
diminished. Heng and his wife had had to take care of themselves and the
housework since the first bankruptcy. They were also isolated in their house
at Velizy, which is far from Paris. But when meeting them in 1995 in Laos
Heng kept repeating boisterously: "Here, life is easy. *Sabaï!* No cleaning, no
meals to prepare! I am somebody here. All that is finished! We have servants
to serve us . . . Life is easy and anywhere we go, people know us, even in the
countryside!"

RETURNING TO REBUILD CAPITAL

THE return had come to stand more and more for a dream of being
acknowledged, and today Laos offers more hope than France. Heng's
children are completely assimilated in France, with few relatives in Laos and
no properties left, but the return of their father suddenly created a capital
that could be realized: "What an honor for me, and above all for the family
. . . I have found a new life here. With my deputy title, I think I can get
access to all positions, and with dignity. With this new station in life, I
possess more assets in every field: social, political and business" (Heng). We
can easily recognize here the notion of capital defined by Bourdieu. Heng's
return created two types of capital: an economic capital, that is the
appropriation of means of production and goods, and a social capital. These
forms of capital can also be symbolic, "which is the form that one or
another of these species takes when it is grasped through categories of
perception that *recognize* its specific logic or, if you prefer, misrecognize the
arbitrariness of its possession and accumulation. Social capital is the sum of
the resources, actual or virtual, that accrue to an individual or a group by

virtue of possessing a durable network of more or less institutionalized relationships of mutual acquaintance and recognition" (Bourdieu and Wacquant 1992: 119).

Heng came back to Laos to retire: "I left five months ago to have a quiet and peaceful life . . . but here is a new responsibility during my retirement." In France Heng totally withdrew from political affairs, avoiding the various opposition movements to the new regime. He kept his Lao citizenship and maintained regular links with the LPDR embassy. Already in 1986 he had been contacted personally and asked to return, as the new regime needed to advertise that it was really opening up. When finally back, he was therefore coopted: "I know that they are using me, that they are doing propaganda with my name . . . But I don't care, I am serving Laos and its people. And anyway, this position serves our interests too, doesn't it?" Thanks to his nomination, he was able to quickly set up his companies and to start his son's activities. Moreover, his properties were returned to him speedily: "Before being a candidate to the legislative elections, I was informed that our requests to have our properties back had received a favorable response." The rent from these properties secures him a comfortable income, and serves as a warranty for the bank loans required to develop his sons' business. Alliances, therefore, play a key role in the setting up of the Setakits' business. Athit Santiphab ensured all the paperwork was done in order for them to secure the bank loans essential to the financing of the coffee venture. The family network therefore contributed to the consolidation of this new capital: "The family spirit and even the affection which endows the family with its cohesion contributes therefore to ensure (obviously without pursuing it as such) one of the advantages specifically attached to belonging to a family group, namely participation in the capital whose integrity is guaranteed by the family, and which is the sum of the assets of all its members" (Bourdieu 1989: 416).

This return is motivated by its financial appeal: "You know that it is the economy that dictates everything . . . the way of life, the politics . . . there is the façade and one day it falls" (Sone). "I told Sone that it is his last chance here. After that, everything will be over! There is nothing left there [in France]. Everything has gone up in smoke" (Heng). "I could have kept moving on in the computer business . . . but it's now or never, at thirty-seven years old, to embark on my own business and to return to my country, Laos. If not now, I will never do it"(Sam, after being dismissed from his position as a chief operating officer). All of them think that there are more economic opportunities in Laos than in France: "We are all in the same situation; it is difficult here in Laos but we are all here because we think that we can earn more than in France. I am a businessman, I evaluate the risks, the opportunities . . . and here, the opportunities are tremendous"

(Sam). These kinds of expectations have nothing to do with those of a refugee. There is a clear lack of political thinking among the Setakit children. They go back because of the opportunities to make good money, and very quickly.

Social Reconquest

The return creates the possibility of setting up a new business and of finding a job that will enable one to have social status. It allows one to save face, not only with the children but also with the Lao in France as well. Sati and the Santiphabs, in contrast to the Setakits, possess, an important patrimony in Laos constituted not only by properties but also renown: "When I am thinking of all this, and of elder brother Athit, even if he is on the other side [the communists], I am, all the same, quite happy that he is still here. If he wasn't, there would be nothing left of the family [in the political field]" (Sati). She thinks that with some patience, she will be able to valorize her part of the inheritance. She knows that to be respected, one must have *dhana*. *Dhana* designates "the movables, the money, the property, the capital, the fortune, the treasure, the gift, the stake, the earnings" (Marc Reinhorm 1970). It is at once the dispositions (wisdom, intelligence, personal abilities, character) and the capital (studies, money, relations network, power) possessed by an individual and which determines the respect others owe him or her.

With the Setakits' project now in operation, Sati thinks that she may be able to use this new economic capital to reconquer her legitimacy in the Santiphab family and afterwards to use the family's heritage to reconquer a social place in Lao society: "Economic and symbolic capital are so inextricably intertwined that the display of material and symbolic strength represented by prestigious affairs is in itself likely to bring some material profits, in a good-faith economy in which good repute constitutes the best, if not the only economic guarantee . . ." (Bourdieu 1990: 119).

The Return: A Family Dynamic

The decision to return is encouraged by the ambitions of some family members and restrained by the fears of others. A priority is the children's education which is a major consideration for those who still have young children. The elder generation is generally not concerned by this question, easing therefore their choice to return: their children have grown up and are financially independent, some of whom have started their own families. The bachelors who decide to return do not carry such a responsibility either, even if they know that the issue remains open should they have children. "I am allowing myself two or three years. If I fail, I am young enough to start again in France" (Mesa, twenty-nine years old, a college graduate and marketing officer). The presence of children prevents most Lao from returning permanently to Laos, and those who do return will spend their time coming and going between Laos and France. It is difficult for them to opt for Laos where the education and health system is weak. "I can't leave— there is the shop and the house. And there is also Chouk. When he graduates the situation will be better; we would be able to go back to Laos then. We may sell the shop—they will be capable of managing on their own with the house" (Neung, forty-five years old, a college graduate and manager of the grocery shop, with two children, one twenty and one seventeen years old). We have seen that in some cases, children have become involved in the decisionmaking process, influencing their parents' choice: "You know what the situation is like here . . . and the children have pushed us" (Sati). What determines the weight given to the children's advice is *dhana*. In the two families we have been considering, the pressure to have the parents return to Laos is applied by only some of the children, with the others being informed later on. The ambitions of some their children, therefore, weighed heavily in their parents' choice: "If you do not go back, I won't be able to either! I need you to reactivate the kinship network. I need you to prepare the field, to start a business and to reintegrate us into the society!" (Mesa). These children only consider the economic factors, and do not realize the dilemmas confronting their parents. They are often oblivious to the social and political implications of a return. For Heng, who did not consider himself as a refugee, it was not a problem, but for Sati and Meta, on the other hand, it posed a dramatic choice because they had been involved for more than twenty years in political activities directed against the LPRP.

THE MEANING OF EXILE QUESTIONED

HOW can one justify one's exile and then return to a country that has become communist even when one disagrees with the present regime? How can one go back to a regime which has killed one's own father? How can one justify all the years of community and political activities? To Sati, the decision, ultimately, was a family priority as her husband's family had asked them to go back to Laos. She let herself be persuaded by the economic opportunities presented to her by all her relatives. But the Lao community did not see her decision in the same way. The Samakhom's board members, when informed about her decision, demanded that she justify herself at a plenary meeting. She was fiercely criticized for not consulting them and for not seeking their authorization for such a decision. During the fortnight preceding her departure, the Samakhom board members pressured her to hand in her resignation, as it was felt that her behavior could taint the association's image. A few days before leaving for Laos, she gave them satisfaction by resigning, conscious of the possibility that the Lao community may confuse her individual actions with those of the collective, and she wished to protect her twenty years of work and ensure a good working climate for her successors in the Samakhom.

She also handed in a report which assessed the work of the association during her fifteen years as a president, which was rejected because of the foreword she had written: "this document presents in a few pages the activities of the Samakhom, and the road it has taken over the fifteen years of my presidency, to gather together all Lao men and women. All was not perfect but if I look back, I can see the town that we have built and if I turn to the future, I see many roads to pave in order to build the future for our children. I am leaving today with sadness but full of hopes, as a forward scout" (Sati Setakit). This was how she justified to herself her departure from the Lao community. However, her community did not forgive her betrayal. The reactions were passionate, and the women she had been working with for more than fifteen years and who had become her closest and dearest friends, violently rejected her: bitter phone calls, demands to return the dance costumes and accessories which had been stocked for everybody's convenience in her garage, keeping her out of meetings and regular dinners. At the same time, Meta and Sati received warning letters from some Lao right-wing nationalists, accusing them of being long-time communists who had now been finally discovered. Sometimes they were met with public slurs, like, "I didn't know that communists were invited to this dinner . . . ," so they refrained from going out. Back from Laos a month later, they were still ignored by their former Samakhom friends, who during their absence elected a new president. They no longer received the dozens of daily phone calls which had punctuated their lives for twenty years, nor the invitations to informal meals, nor mail. All these reactions seemed all the more disproportionate in that her visit was only exploratory and lasted only three weeks.

Why this violent rejection of one who had been their companion for all these long years? The reason lies in the fact that Sati had been socially and politically involved for all this time and therefore her life came to belong to the public life of the Lao community, and in part had come to symbolize that community. Her peers could not accept that family decisions could be more important than community duty, although many would have recognized it privately. Thus, her return would appear to commit the whole community, and the community would then have betrayed its own convictions! In the refugees' eyes, to go back meant accepting that "the cause which made them flee does not exist anymore." To return to the country while the government that made them flee was still in power would mean accepting that government's legitimacy. Going back would mean admitting that the twenty-year fight had been in vain. For the leaders of the Lao community this was too traumatic; but perhaps the reaction to Sati's departure was also an unconscious recognition that the community had reached a crossroads. They had come to a time when they had to redefine the meaning of their exile, to conceive their journey in France as permanent and to abandon the idea of return as an overthrow of the ruling power.

> When I decided to go to Laos, I swallowed my pride (*kiet*) . . . Everything . . . I have accepted, to wipe away everything: the twenty years of exile, the work in the association, the criticisms I used to have of the present government, the seminar camps . . . I fled because of this regime. This regime is still in place and I am going back. One must be honest to oneself, and if we are, we cannot return. There is no valid reason to go back. I have sacrificed my honor . . . I had a lot of difficulties in making up my mind. How many tears, how many sleepless nights . . . But at the same time, I could see that things were changing. If we want to change things, we have to be on the spot. They are changing and they too have their pride. If everyone of us sticks to their line, we cannot move things. The question is who is going to make the first step forward. They have the power, we do not have anything. In exile we laid down some foundations to safeguard the culture . . . but Laos is there. This step forward, I would not have been able to do it if I hadn't been pushed. Something must happen to have things triggered off. Meta went to Laos, and I have chosen the family, the personal life. I have lost in the social field (sangkhom) but I have stayed together with my family (Sati).

Lao exiles in France rebuke those who are now taking a different path from the one they chose twenty years ago. It tries to maintain group cohesion by excluding those who are presenting different ideas. Sclerosed by its discourses, its annual rituals of parties and performances, it now has to face the mutations of the contemporary world, to redefine the meaning of its exile, and to define its place in the present changes. It is perhaps a tragic irony of exile that those most concerned with preserving Lao identity in order to return are now those least able to return, and are torn between their social commitments in France and adaptation to a changing Lao society. There is, of course, a price to pay when one returns—one's face, kiet, *vis-à-vis* those who stayed in Laos and those who were companions in exile. It is only a fringe of the elite who is going back, but it must pay a price to restore its position and to maintain it.

THE EMERGENCE OF A TRANSNATIONAL CULTURE

THE most well-assimilated of the Lao leave to return with ease for this faraway world which is virtually unknown to them, motivated simply by the economic opportunities that the new Laos offers to them—this ASEAN partner, this future crossroads of the Indochinese peninsula, which is passing from its landlocked status to its landlinked one, holding out the dream that all the businesses in the area will transit the country. They come, invest, take the money, and one day will go again: "It's not that things went wrong here [in France] . . . but we have to go forward. Asia is the future. Europe, it's over. Sone, he is always going forward. He thinks of creation, of doing business and it's there where he can do things. There are opportunities in Asia. The businessmen, they don't go backwards. Sone will never be an employee. It is natural to Asians to do business and we are lucky to have Laos, and relationships there. We have a way out, a path which leads us to Laos. After, I don't know . . . Vietnam, Malaysia" (Phay, thirty-four years old, a high school graduate, married to Sone). The return is not considered definite but simply as a business opportunity. This economic elite is the first to quit and the first to come back, but this time in an in-between position, all the while safeguarding their possibilities of leaving again anytime. They are not overburdened with issues of political consciousness, and Laos is not their world: they hardly speak Lao, do not know Lao customs, but they are the first to go back. "I have had all my education in France . . . What I wanted to do there, after having worked in an international company, is to create something which will allow me to return to my native country as much as I want, for me, for my wife, for my children. Therefore, I have set up an investment consulting firm, which has offices in Paris and Bangkok. The first thing I have done is to invest in my own country, in the coffee business. I came back for the first time in November 1993. In December, I set up a company in Laos. We started with 10 people and today, a year later, we are 253. We have a coffee plantation, a factory and the whole production is exported to France" (Sam).

Asia is now perceived as a region of promise, and Europe, which used to personify success, is now seen as the embodiment of the past. Laos is starting to enter the international scene. Concurrently one notices, perhaps for the first time in Lao history, the emergence of a transnational elite who, as the French anthropologist Catherine Choron-Baix (1990: 27–32) writes, operate in "an extensible social space. These migrants belong to a network of relations without frontiers, Australia, the United States . . . there is no longer a territorial anchorage . . ." The Lao living overseas are starting to operate in an Asian-style diaspora, which takes the whole world as a development base, and not a national territory. There is a mobility of people, mobility of capital, with the sky as its limit. As Phay expressed it: "I can go and live there [in Laos]. I will put my children in a boarding school, in the United States, in Singapore or in Australia. The elder will maybe go to Australia next year . . . For the little one, I will leave her in France, where my mother can take care of her over the weekend." In conceiving of its future in terms of this extensible social space, the small Lao elite is now behaving in a manner indistinguishable from the elites of other Asian countries today.

NOTES

1. The term "Lao" designates a person holding Lao citizenship (as distinct from the ethnic Lao, the most numerous group in Laos). In France, most Lao have acquired French citizenship. They are therefore French who originate from Laos. To facilitate reading, we will use the generic term "Lao" to designate people from Laos, whatever their present nationality may be. Likewise, we will use the generic expressions "Lao refugees" or "Lao exiles" to name those who left Laos for political reasons, although most of them have now lost their refugee status by becoming, for example, French citizens.

2. The United Nations High Commissioner for Refugees (UNHCR) convention sets out the status of refugees, defines their rights and binds member states to granting them political asylum. However it also has provisions for withdrawing refugee status when "the circumstances which led him to his being recognized as a refugee have ceased to exist" (Article 1C of the 1951 Convention). In the 1980s the UNHCR judged that these "circumstances had ceased" for the Lao, and a repatriation process was set in motion. Since then the UNHCR has encouraged the voluntary repatriation of Lao refugees living in Thai camps. By the end of 1988, however, only 3,453 people had agreed to return. It was only after 1989 that the plan speeded up, and 85 percent of all returnees have gone back since then. Under the program, 27,060 people have been reinstalled in the rural areas since 1980 (UNHCR, Vientiane, 30 June 1996) and have been learning to cultivate the land again after years in the camps. From 1975 to 1996, however, only 119 people returned "spontaneously" to Laos, that is outside the repatriation operation. These were people who were granted political asylum by countries such as France or the United States after 1975 but decided to return to Laos.

3. We are using here an indigenous expression used by Lao exiles to name themselves and we are not presuming the cohesion or the uniformity of the group. Lao refugees sometimes also use the term "diaspora" and to a lesser extent the expression "Lao expatriates."

4. These estimates are based upon data collected from embassies in Laos. We must stress that quite a number of native Lao returnees do not register themselves with their embassy in their adopted country, because of either a desire to be discreet, or negligence.

5. The names of people and the toponymy of places have been modified to preserve the private lives of respondents.

6. The Institute of Political Studies and the Ecole des Hautes Etudes Commerciales are vital institutions for the reproduction of the French elite. See Bourdieu (1989).

7. Typology as defined by Isabelle Leonetti-Taboada (1991: 55–73).

8. We will see later on that "permanency" is transformed for some of them into an in-between situation in which they come and go between the two countries.

9. The population elects its deputies from a shortlist of names preselected by the communist party.

ETHNIC CHANGE IN THE NORTHERN HIGHLANDS OF LAOS

6

GRANT EVANS

L AOS is one of the most ethnically diverse countries in mainland Southeast Asia. A quick look at the map tells us why. Laos lies in between the major states of the region: China on its northern border, Vietnam to the east, Cambodia to the far south, Thailand to the south and west, and Burma in the far northwest. Populations from all of these neighbors overlap into Laos. Unlike these other countries, the lowland, ethnic Lao after whom the country is named, do not constitute an overwhelming majority of the population. According to the latest figures, out of a total population of a little more than 4 million the Lao make up between 1.8 and 1.9 million—in other words, not quite half the population. If, however, an ethnolinguistic classification is used—in this case lumping together all speakers of Tai dialects, of which Lao is one—then the Tai-Lao group rises to between 2.3 and 2.4 million; that is, just over half of the population. By contrast, in all the neighboring countries the dominant ethnic group—Vietnamese, Chinese, Thai, Cambodian, Burmese—make up more than 80 percent of the population, sometimes even more than 90 percent.[1] The relative balance between the different ethnic groups in Laos is therefore unusual and one can see the political attractions of particular ways of drawing the ethnic map.

After their victory at the end of 1975 the communists carried into government with them a policy of categorizing the population into Lao Loum or lowland Lao, Lao Theung or midlands or uplands Lao, and Lao Soung, Lao of the highlands or mountain tops.[2] The first applied to ethnic Lao and Tai groups, the second applied to a range of Mon-Khmer and Austronesian groups scattered throughout the country, while the third was generally reserved for Tibeto-Burman, Hmong-Yao groups such as Hmong, Yao, Goh (Akha), Lolo and others in the far northwest.

The Tai in the upland valleys of Indochina have been referred to as "tribal" Tai, presumably because they have not formed separate states. The key groups are White Tai, Black Tai, and Red Tai who overlap into Laos, and the Tay (Tho) and Nung who overlap into China from Vietnam. In Vietnam these groups number over 2 million people. In Laos there are almost half a million Tai, while in Houaphan province, where the research for this paper has been concentrated, they number seventy-six thousand persons.[3]

In the following pages I hope to contribute to our understanding of the process of ethnic change in the northern upland valleys of Indochina through a study of the interaction between a Black Tai village and a village composed of Mon-Khmer Sing Moon people. This process which has been described as "Tai-ization" by Georges Condominas (1990) involves the ethnic conversion of people like the Sing Moon into Tai. The villages are in Muang Xieng Kho,[4] Houaphan province, Laos, and I have made field trips to the villages in 1988, 1990, and 1993. When I initially arrived in the *muang* and told officials there that I wanted to study a Black Tai village they sent me to Ban Sot which they assured me was "thoroughly Black Tai." The village in 1988 was composed of three hamlets—Ban Sot South, Ban Sot North, and just over the Nam Ma River, Ban Na Wan. One of my first surprises was to learn that Ban Na Wan was in fact composed of Sing Moon—something skated over, or unperceived, at the level of *muang* organization. In 1988 there were forty houses in Ban Sot, twenty-nine in Ban Sot North, and seventeen in Ban Na Wan. These figures have since fluctuated only slightly as some people have moved around within the village or migrated. The population, again in 1988, was Ban Sot South 265 persons (average of 6.6 persons per household), Ban Sot North 166 persons (average of 5.7 persons per household), and Ban Na Wan 77 persons (average of 4.5 persons per household), and this has risen since then. The village of Ban Sot was established some time in the 1930s by Black Tai settlers from neighboring Son La province in Vietnam. Over the years the population of the village has been augmented by further migrations from Vietnam, especially after 1954 as a result of disruptions caused by war with the French, and by marriage. Ban Sot North was begun in 1974 and Ban Na Wan joined the village after 1973.

ADMINISTRATIVE INTEGRATION OF BAN NA WAN

IN the traditional system the key social groups among Black Tai were the aristocrats who were privileged to receive certain gifts of forest products and labor; the next and majority group were ordinary Tai who worked their own land, and as "warriors" had rights in village decision making; the third group were Tai who had become debt "slaves" of the major households; and finally, there were non-Tai who had to perform labor on the aristocrats' fields but had no political rights. Sometimes they were house "slaves," *kon heun*, but it would appear that more often they lived in separate villages closeby (Dang Nghiem Van 1971: 182–3, uses the term "bonded peasants").[5] The latter were called *Xá* or *Sa'*, similar to the Lao word *kha* for "slave" commonly used in the not-so-distant past as a term for most hilltribes there.[6] The general term *Sa'*, is sometimes used by Sing Moon today to describe themselves or other similar groups, such as the Khmu. They have also been called *puok*, and also sometimes refer to themselves this way. The exact origins of this term are unclear to me; people often attribute it to the French, and it is quite possible that it came into general use among French colonial officials. Sing Moon in fact is a Lao rendering of K'tsing Mul, which is how the people themselves pronounce their name. They are also sometimes referred to as Lao May (new Lao).

Muang Xieng Kho is, apparently, the only place in Laos where these people are found. The majority (nine thousand persons) are in Vietnam, where they have been studied by Vietnamese ethnographers (Dang Nghiem Van et al. 1972; Dang Nghiem Van et al. 1984), and there are a few other scattered references to them (see Schrock 1972). According to the Lao Institute of Ethnography, in 1988 there were 2,164 Sing Moon people in Muang Xieng Kho (probably an underestimate); in 1993 I managed to construct a list of 33 villages in the Muang with villages ranging from 11 families up to 70. One *tasseng* (canton), Lao Houng, contained only Sing Moon villages, eleven of them. The most obvious distinguishing feature of this group today is their language which is different from the surrounding Tai, Lao and Vietnamese, although their language has borrowed heavily from all of them. In the past they were reliant on upland slash and burn agriculture. Their social organization is broadly egalitarian, and the kinship and marriage system reflects a stronger bilateral orientation than the neighboring Tai.

The Sing Moon in Ban Sot used to live up from the valley floor in a village known as Ban Houey Wan—that is a village situated up in the watershed rather than down alongside the river on the valley floor (*houey* means stream). The same background can be found among other Sing Moon in the area. In another joint Black Tai/Sing Moon village that I surveyed in 1990 the Sing Moon there originated from Ban Houey Loop. According to my informants after 1973 soldiers went up into the Sing Moon villages and instructed them to move down to the plains because they were allegedly "destroying the forest." This corresponded with the policy of the communists who were soon to come to power in Vientiane and attempt to put this policy into effect throughout the country.[7] The Sing Moon who were moved down to the valley floor were then administratively integrated into the neighboring Black Tai villages. One consequence of this, of course, was that they were also supposed to have access to paddy land. In fact, in Ban Houey Wan the Sing Moon had already cleared some paddy terraces which they combined with slash and burn, *hai*, cultivation. So, they were not pure slash-and-burn farmers as the government has often been inclined to say about upland minority groups in Laos, and in fact the move down to the valley initially disrupted their use of these upland paddy terraces (I shall come to the issue of access to land later). When the collectivization program was launched in Laos in 1979 the Sing Moon, now relocated to Ban Na Wan, were relocated yet again, this time to Ban Sot South. This also was in keeping with the intended political role of cooperatives which was to establish even tighter political control over the population (see Evans 1990, chapter 8). The cooperative in this village lasted until 1985 when it collapsed for many of the reasons I have also dealt with elsewhere (Evans 1990). The people in the village talk of the cumbersomeness of trying to do paddy and upland fields collectively, and of problems with "lazy" people. But even before the collapse of the cooperative, in 1983, the Sing Moon had left Ban Sot South and returned back over the river to the site of Ban Na Wan.

One could see this attempted integration as state sponsorship of "Tai-ization," with the Lao dominated government as the overall agent and their "cousins," the Black Tai, the immediate beneficiaries. But the picture is much more complex than this. The Black Tai of Ban Sot were not pleased about having the Sing Moon integrated into their village, even as a separate hamlet. Among themselves the Black Tai are quite contemptuous of the Sing Moon. When one mentions Sing Moon in any context Black Tai invariably chuckle and crack small jokes revolving around their assumed lower level of culture and intelligence. (Similar mirth is also reserved for the highland Hmong, but interestingly not for the similar Yao. One Yao man has married into the village, and while he has to deal with occasional patronizing remarks, the villagers here have given Yao "honorary" valley dweller status and deny that they are Lao Soung, a term used by the Lao government to group Hmong and Yao together).

CULTURAL DIACRITICA AND ETHOS

IN discussions of cultural differences local people invariably mention the language difference, and Black Tai joke about the funny sound of Sing Moon speech. Interestingly, one "upwardly mobile" Sing Moon (more about this later), said that the only difference between Black Tai and Sing Moon culture was that Sing Moon could speak not only their own language, but Black Tai as well. I found only one older Black Tai man who could speak reasonable Sing Moon, because in the early 1950s he had worked with the French and part of his job entailed working in Sing Moon villages in Vietnam. The Sing Moon in Ban Na Wan speak their own language at home and in the village, although the language is now heavily influenced by Black Tai and Lao vocabulary. The Black Tai also comment how the Sing Moon use Black Tai (and Lao) songs and dances and other elements of popular and material culture. It is not as marked as Condominas noted for the Laha, however: "Ethnographically speaking, evidence which is immediately visible when entering a Laha village is the extent of Tai-ization: clothes, houses, tools, are all the same as those used in a Black Tai village" (1990: 54), though it is partly true for Ban Na Wan. The women there, especially when they dress up, adopt traditional Black Tai costume—if they have one. Only six of the seventeen houses in the village are built in the large and sturdy Black Tai style, but none have the large stocks of timber one finds under the better-off Black Tai houses. The other houses are poorer, smaller, some very small, and less solidly built. In fact, the poverty of the village compared with Ban Sot South and North is striking. The Black Tai in Ban Sot say that the houses in Ban Na Wan are "not beautiful, and are like huts in the forest."

But the most strident charge the Black Tai level at the Sing Moon is that they are "lazy." They claim that they do not like to work paddy land and prefer to scavenge in the forest. This laziness, they say, led to a lot of ill-feeling when the Sing Moon were integrated into Ban Sot South between 1979 and 1983. They claimed the Black Tai would go off to work early in the morning and Sing Moon would simply stay at home. The ill-feeling caused the Sing Moon to move back over the river. One can guess that many of the problems associated with "lazy" people in the cooperatives, expressed widely throughout Laos at the time, here found a convenient ethnic scapegoat in the Sing Moon. Furthermore, the Black Tai are contemptuous of the Sing Moon because they are prepared to hire out their labor when they are short of money instead of trying to create wealth for themselves. In one discussion along these lines a *tasseng* official claimed that this was true with all "Lao Theung" groups throughout the Muang, and he singled out the Khmu. It was also said that if Black Tai marry into a Sing Moon village then they will become lazy, but if Sing Moon marry into a Black Tai village then they learn to work hard. The *tasseng* official, a politically astute man, was quick to point out, however, that not all Sing Moon were lazy. There were, he said, some households in Ban Na Wan who worked hard and had good houses and emulated Black Tai ways.

Finally, the presence of three opium addicts in the Sing Moon village was a further source of disdain, despite the fact that it was one of the Black Tai in Ban Sot with a sharp eye for trade who sold them their fix.

None of this overt hostility is reciprocated by the Sing Moon as far as I could tell—but then I cannot speak the Sing Moon language, and perhaps there is a vibrant "hidden transcript," typical of power-laden situations (Scott 1990), waiting to be discovered by outsiders. Perhaps one symptom of "resistance" was that none of the Sing Moon with whom I spoke would admit to having done wage labor for Black Tai in Ban Sot in the recent past. They normally traveled to the next Black Tai villages down or up the road to seek wage work, sometimes helping build houses, sometimes clearing land for hai. The Black Tai in Ban Sot were not so concerned about how recently the Sing Moon had done wage work for them, the simple fact of having done it in the past and the continued sale of their labor to others was enough to establish their lower status. One could, however, interpret the attempt by Sing Moon to seek work in villages other than Ban Sot as a way of asserting, however minimally, their independence from Ban Sot and thereby remove the relationship of dominance and subordination to more distant Tai. Furthermore, the reluctance to work for Ban Sot Tai is no doubt part of an ongoing dispute which I discuss below.

I would also like to raise the idea of a different "ethos" between the two groups. The idea of an "ethos" often seems to make intuitive sense, and the idea has been widely used in academic writing in the social sciences. But few ethnographies have documented the formation of an ethos—Bateson's *Naven* (1958), is probably the most famous exception. Compared with the Sing Moon one is struck by the personal self-confidence of most Black Tai, and by comparison, they are also much more competitive. This undoubtedly feeds into the high value they place on hard work, because hard work gives them the resources to compete for status in the village, manifest for example, in the ability to give lavish post-harvest parties and in the availability of homemade liquor to drink. Drinking itself is intensely competitive.

One important element of cultural organization of at least the White, Black, and Red Tai is the use of patronymics or *sing*. The élite are generally *sing Lo* or *Lo Gam* whose origin myth justifies their aristocratic status above the other *sing* (Lafont 1955). While these patronymics serve ritual purposes, discussed to briefly below, they are also associated with social status. *Sing Lo*, for example, is associated with the traditional elite, and while this elite no longer exists people are quick to inform others that they are *sing Lo* when the occasion arises because the origin myth for these people asserts that they are somehow intrinsically 'higher.' Although the wealth differentials in the village are relatively small to an outsider, they are enough to assert small status differences—so to be better-off and *sing Lo* certainly helps in status competition. Of course, some of the better-off members of the village are from commoner *sing*, and the claims to aristocratic lineage no longer play a key role in ordering the social structure. By contrast, Sing Moon who also have patronymics do not appear to use them in a competitive way, for the reason, I would suggest, that they do not have any ritual analogue (discussed below) and they are not as culturally deeply rooted among this group.

Generally, life in Ban Na Wan is more muted and the atmosphere is less competitive, and no doubt this is one of the sources of Black Tai charges of laziness. This also manifests itself in less intense drinking sessions, and slightly more egalitarian participation in them. This may seem paradoxical given that wealth differentials are much clearer in Ban Na Wan than in Ban Sot. That is between the six "upwardly mobile" households in their sturdy, large Black Tai style houses, and the other households, some of whom live in tiny ramshackle bamboo huts. But at parties held in these better-off households even the poorest members of the village participate and are not made to wait at the edge of the participating group until finally invited in, thus making his status clear, as I have seen done in Black Tai households. But it does seem to be broadly true that this culturally less pressing need to compete for status does mean that people are less anxious about working hard, and less thought appears to be given to long term planning. In this context Black Tai claims of laziness make sense. Only if Sing Moon want to be Black Tai do they have to work as hard as Black Tai. This involves an important shift in worldview or ethos, and a significant number of Sing Moon do not appear to be interested. As Lehman (1979: 247) has remarked:

> In interethnic systems where, by mutual agreement as well as objectively, the parties are of unequal status and have very unequal access to mutually desired economic resources and ecological "niches," ambivalence seems to be a function of the very fact of ethnic distinctiveness. That is, in many respects, the choice of a subordinate ethnic category is motivated by the perceived advantage of having alternate cultural standards as against competing with apparent promise of failure in the arena of someone else's cultural standards of achievement.

Some brief mention should be made, perhaps, of two poor Khmu households who are perched precariously at the edge of Ban Sot North. These two households live in the poorest houses in the village, engage in no paddy cultivation, and generally find themselves in a similar situation to the poorer Sing Moon and are treated with similar disdain. They work as blacksmiths and engage in occasional wage labor.

ACCESS TO RESOURCES

PADDY rice land in Black Tai villages today is mostly held in common. The land in the village is periodically redistributed to the households, theoretically according to their needs, calculated according to the number of workers they can put in the field and the number of mouths they have to feed. There is some privately held paddy land, and all slash and burn land, or hai, is also privately held and worked. The traditional system of holding paddy land is described by two Vietnamese writers:

> Collective ownership of the land and the ricefields is defined according to the following principle: the *peasant has only the right of occupation and exploitation of the land, but has absolutely no right to private ownership* . . . A peasant who has been exploiting a ricefield for such a long time that he does not even know any longer who used it before him, can still in no way take ownership of it. However, he is sure of one thing: this rice-field is the property of the *müöng* (a communal rice-field) which he or any other member of the community has the right to cultivate if it is allotted to him . . ." (Cited by Condominas 1990: 56).

So we can see that the traditional system is pretty much still intact in the villages I have studied. The main difference now is that village leaders, rather than aristocrats, have the right to allocate land, something which is done every year, although this in fact may mean no change for individual families from the year before. Where there are intractable disputes, then the *tasseng* is brought in, and then the *muang*.

Between Ban Sot South and Ban Sot North there is a small valley of collectively owned rice-fields. They are worked in both the wet and the dry season, and the size of the land able to be worked fluctuates a little according to whether there is enough water available, especially in the dry season. The area of land able to be worked in the wet season varies from around 11 hectares (ha) to 15 ha, depending on the availability of water, while in the dry season it varies between 5 and 7 ha. At Ban Na Wan there is around 3 ha of land, some of which is shared with families from Ban Sot South. During the dry season close to 2 ha of this land can be worked. If we take the year 1990 as an example, on average each household in Ban Sot South and North worked around 0.12 ha in the wet season and in the dry season 0.09 ha making an average of paddy worked for the year of 0.28 ha. The largest amount worked by any one household in that year was 0.55 ha of paddy and the smallest 0.048 ha. This last household quickly dissolved as it contained a single widowed woman who soon moved to live with relatives, whereas the households which worked close to half a hectare had between eight and eleven members in the household. The fluctuations around the average, however, are largely dictated by the number of workers available in the household. This is also true for Ban Na Wan. There the average worked by households in the wet season was 0.16 ha, and 0.12 ha in the dry season, giving an average for the year of 0.28 ha. The largest amount worked by one household was 0.39 ha and the lowest 0.14 ha. Once again this distribution roughly correlated with available labor in the households.

It is perhaps worth observing, in the light of comments that the Sing Moon are "lazy" and do not like to work paddy fields, that in 1990 they, on average, cultivated the same amount of paddy land per household as the Black Tai. This was also roughly the case in 1993.

But an absolutely fundamental part of the upland economic system are *hai*, the slash-and-burn fields. In Ban Sot South and North in 1990 these upland fields made up 36.8 ha, an average of 0.64 ha per household, and in Ban Na Wan it accounted for 10.4 ha, and 0.65 ha per household. In other words, combined paddy and *hai* meant that each household throughout the villages cultivated just under 1 ha of land per year. The largest amount of *hai* cultivated was 1.3 ha, and in general the families able to cultivate close to 1 ha of *hai* once again were the larger families who could field the workers to do the work. In 1993 the total amount cultivated by Ban Sot South and North had fallen to 30.7 ha, while in Ban Na Wan it had gone up slightly to 12.56 ha. In 1988 Ban Na Wan had cultivated 15.7 ha of *hai*, but in that year only the six "upwardly mobile" Sing Moon families worked on collective paddy land—one of the early signs of strain over the use of this land. The amount of *hai* worked by people in Ban Sot South and North in that year also seems to have been considerably higher, closer to 50 ha, but unfortunately I have never been able to quite clarify the figures for the amount of *hai* worked for this year.

Overall, however, what I would like to argue is that what we are seeing in the vicinity of Ban Sot (and I would suggest throughout the upland valleys of Laos and Vietnam) is a growing crisis in the upland system in several ways.[8] Population growth (approximately 2.9 percent)is a key factor, of course. Previously, limited amounts of paddy land resources could be offset by using larger amounts of *hai*. However, the availability of land for *hai* is now exhausted and intensified use of the land only brings lower yields. One consequence of extensive upland cultivation has also meant less water in the streams, and this has presented growing problems for the availability of water for paddy fields in the dry season. Small scale irrigation schemes, i.e. small dams are beginning to be put in place throughout Houaphan province and elsewhere by foreign aid organizations, but these will probably only just arrest a system on the verge of devolution. More recently other possibilities have also emerged to relieve some of the pressure on resources. Until government policy changed particularly since 1988, new mouths to feed had to be absorbed by the village economy. Now, however, there are possibilities of branching out into trading. Over 1991–93, with improved relations between China and Laos and Vietnam, one saw a stream of Vietnamese traders from Son-la on bicycles, motorbikes, or on the local bus (truck) that passes by the village, carrying Chinese and some Vietnamese manufactured goods. Some villagers have begun to take advantage of these opportunities. It has already led to a larger number of manufactured goods in the village. For example, in 1988 there were only one or two radios in the village. Now there are many, and this has increased the villagers' exposure to the outside world. The other important change in these two to three years was the growing migration of young people out of the village, to either the provincial centers or to Vientiane. Once established there they provide a basis for further chain migration. As one old man commented, once they go there is little for them to come back to.

Another response, however, has seen households begin the process of constructing terraced paddy fields further up the stream watersheds. One irony of this is that the Sing Moon in Ban Na Wan have been able to reactivate and extend the paddy fields which they were forced to leave in 1973 when marched down to the plains to "begin" paddy cultivation. In Ban Sot South and North a total of eighteen households had begun to build terraces over 1991–92 and through this process had added a further 6 ha of privately owned paddy land. A further eight households worked a small amount of private terraced paddy land inherited from their fathers amounting in total to 2.3 ha. Thus in dry season of 1993 many of these households chose to forego working on the collectively owned paddy and simply worked their own terraces. This had the important effect of releasing more land to other households, consequently the average size of a plot worked in dry season 1993 on collective fields was 0.16 ha compared with the 0.09 given above for 1990. The extension of terraced paddy usable in the dry season, however, is restricted by the availability of water in the streams and this has already been seriously affected by *hai* cultivation. In Ban Na Wan, as I have said, the old fields were reactivated and new fields cleared by what I am calling the six "upwardly mobile" families in the village. They were working 1.5 ha of upland terraces in the dry season of 1993, an average of 0.25 ha per household. Yet, they and the other families in Ban Na Wan also worked on the available 2 ha of collective land in this dry season, though a certain conflict of interest had emerged in that the terraces built in the watershed of the stream by both Ban Na Wan and Ban Sot farmers were diverting an already diminished water supply away from the collective fields at the base of the stream, in the valley alongside the river.

While the differences in the amount of paddy and *hai* cultivated by both the Black Tai and the Sing Moon are not great, the reality is that most Sing Moon villagers are poorer than Black Tai villagers. For example, at the end of the dry season of 1993, eleven households in Ban Na Wan had run out of rice. They lived by gathering or engaging in wage labor to buy rice, while some engaged in gold prospecting from the river (something they have been doing only since 1991). Their rice shortfall is a product of bad farming practices caused by a vicious circle of poverty. They are unable to enhance their yields on paddy land because they cannot afford fertilizer. As for *hai*, because they are among the least influential villagers they have been forced to farm the most marginal and distant upland plots. Distance leads to poor maintenance of the fields with regard to weeding, and so on. Some farmers opt for the immediate returns of wage labor closer to home. Consequently they also tend to get poorer yields from their upland plots as well.

Recently the crisis in the upland system has taken a more "political" form. In early 1991 Ban Na Wan approached the *tasseng* to request that they become a separate village. The administration agreed. Underlying this request is a dispute about paddy land. As pressure has increased on the overall system this has led to increasing arguments among Black Tai themselves about the distribution of paddy land. Given that many of the plots are small to start with the individual disputes seem like hair-splitting. But in another sense that is precisely what it is in a system with such a restricted supply of paddy land. Small shifts in proportions are significant, for the individual households at least. In deciding the amount of land two considerations are taken into account: the number of workers in the household and the ratio of non-workers to workers, and the quality of the land. As for the latter there are three qualities decided on for tax purposes. But not everyone is in agreement about the quality of their land. Thus, for example, when I was querying the fact that one household who fielded fewer workers had a plot larger than a household with more workers, I was told, well, that household is on better land so they do not need as much to get the same yield. The other household was present and they immediately objected that their land was just ordinary. The actual productivity of the land is something that can only be proven in retrospect, and there are all sorts of other things that can disrupt the potential yield, which means it can be an ongoing source of grumbling. There is also a fuzziness about when a young person becomes a worker and when an older person becomes a dependent. And so on. So there is much to argue and grumble about when it comes to access to communal resources, and it is up to the village leaders to distribute the land. They are generally from the stronger and better-off

families in the village and they look after themselves and their allies. Not
outrageously, and not in any way in the sense that they act like a class, as
with the former Black Tai aristocrats, but as a slowly shifting set of
household alliances in the village. This, of course, provides a source of
complaint for less well-off Black Tai villagers.

These complaints, however, also had an ethnic outlet and meant there
was opposition to the accommodation of the Sing Moon villagers on Ban
Sot paddy land. This had come to the surface once in 1988 when, as I
indicated above, only the six "Tai-ized" Sing Moon households cultivated
paddy. The Black Tai claimed that the Sing Moon did not want to do
paddy in that year, preferring instead to cultivate only hai. This is another
story I have never been able to clarify, but I certainly have the impression
that the poorer Sing Moon villagers were excluded from the paddy fields
that year by the Black Tai in collusion with the "Tai-ized" households who,
it should be remembered, were still part of Ban Sot village at that time. The
control of paddy land near Ban Na Wan in mid-1993 was in dispute and it
was up to the *tasseng* to decide on this matter. The *tasseng*, in the meantime,
persuaded Ban Sot to "loan" the land to Ban Na Wan because otherwise
they would have had "nothing to eat." This appeal to a moral economy is a
strong one and provides an interesting counterforce to the ethnic divide.
On the other hand, this same moral economy binds the upwardly mobile
Sing Moon to their poorer village members ensuring village solidarity in the
dispute with the Black Tai.

Consistent with the continuing claim of Ban Sot is the fact that the
village head of Ban Sot, in conjunction with the village head of Ban Na
Wan, has decided over these years who would work the collective plot of
paddy fields, and some Ban Sot households have continued to work in the
fields on the Ban Na Wan side of the river. Interestingly, most people in
Ban Na Wan and in Ban Sot claim they do not know who is the original
owner of this land. "No one knows," is a common response, except from
several old men of old established families in the village who claim to know
who cleared the land and established paddy fields on it. One thing which
appears to be at the bottom of these divergent claims is an anxiety about
future changes in policy (among the many that have already occurred)
which would allow the privatization of communal land. Acknowledgment
of exactly who was here first may give those older households prior claims.
The decision will have to be made by *tasseng* officials who are Black Tai,
some of whom expressed opinions to me about the laziness of Sing Moon
and their reluctance to cultivate paddy fields. But they are bound by a
government policy which still encourages the minorities to settle in the
valley floors. If the Sing Moon are excluded from the collective paddy
fields, then at least for the poorer families who have no terraced fields, there

is little incentive for them to stay where they are. Thus there is strong pressure from above for the *tasseng* to decide in favor of Ban Na Wan's collective control over that land. The decision for the "Tai-ized" Sing Moon was whether it would be better to make a play for the land as a separate village, or to take the risk of trying to operate as full Black Tai in the distribution game. They chose to go as a separate village. In some ways, for them, it does not affect the process of "Tai-ization." That is largely dependent on their relative affluence and ability to establish kinship links with Tai, and more secure access to resources helps them do that.

This dispute is not an isolated event. As far as I can tell, throughout Muang Xieng Kho similar forces have led to the exodus of Sing Moon villages from Black Tai villages into which they had been administratively integrated. Of the thirty-three Sing Moon villages in the *muang*, ten had been integrated into Black Tai villages. As I said earlier, one *tasseng* was occupied only by Sing Moon and thus there were no Tai villages close by into which they could have been integrated. The others, were either too high up in the mountains and escaped the relocations of the 1970s or were too remote from neighboring villages. But of the ten integrated at that time, nine of them have chosen to break away since 1990—all, I would argue, the political manifestation of a growing conflict over resources in the mountains.

The dilemma for the government administration bears some comparison with the traditional system. Thus to cite Vietnamese authors again:

> Once the administrative apparatus of the *chau* and the *müöng* has been firmly established, the *chau müöng* or *phia müöng* are acknowledged as chiefs of the *müöng* or chiefs of the rice-fields, who have the right to share out the communal rice-fields according to the law of the *müöng*. Collective ownership of the lands and rice-fields also appears as the right of ownership that the *ban* (village) has over the rice-fields. The *ban* is the supreme owner of its land and rice-fields. Consequently, the rice-fields of the *ban* can only be allotted to its members: neither *chau müöng* nor *phia müöng*, has the right to distribute the rice-fields of one *ban* to members of another (Condominas 1990: 57).

The laws of the *muang* in the upland areas of northern Indochina now have to be congruent with the laws and policies of the overarching states, and these do allow the overriding of the "supreme" rights of one ba*n* in favor of another. Thus throughout the *muang* the administration is charged with mediating disputes over rights to communal land between Black Tai villages and separating Sing Moon villages in accordance with larger national priorities. And the Lao state certainly appears to have established its right to do this as most of the villagers acknowledged the *tasseng*'s right to decide.

INTER-ETHNIC MARRIAGE IN THE UPLANDS

FINALLY, a brief look at rates of intermarriage in these villages can also give us some idea the relationship between the different groups in the highlands. The process of "Tai-ization" one would imagine should register itself here.

In general, the Black Tai of Ban Sot marry other Black Tai or Tai Wat (a group from Muang Wat in Vietnam who can be considered a localized group of Black Tai). Data gathered in 1988 showed that in Ban Sot South three daughters and two sons had married out of the village to Lao, two daughters and one son to White Tai, and one son to a Red Tai, while only one daughter had married out to a Khmu who was a soldier. Marrying into the village were three Red Tai women, and two Sing Moon women. In Ban Sot North two daughters had married out to Lao, two sons to Red Tai, and one daughter had married a Khmu. Marrying in were one Lao woman, two Red Tai women, one Yao man and one Sing Moon woman. In general, in Ban Na Wan, Sing Moon marry other Sing Moon. One daughter had married out to a Lao. On the other hand two Lao men had married into the village, and one Black Tai woman. (Since first gathering this data in 1988 three more Sing Moon women married into Ban Sot South). The picture that emerged of marriage patterns in a neighboring Black Tai village and its Sing Moon satellite in 1990 revealed a very similar picture. Overwhelmingly, Black Tai marry other Tai-related groups, and Sing Moon marry other Sing Moon. We can also observe that while women go from Ban Na Wan to the Black Tai of Ban Sot, no men do. Similarly, only one Ban Sot Black Tai woman had married into Ban Na Wan, no men. Generally, in these villages children are considered to belong to the ethnic group of their fathers and so the mobility of women does little to change group ethnicity.[9] There was only one exception to this. A poor Lao man who had no relatives elsewhere, and who had married into the village now considered himself Sing Moon and his children to be Sing Moon. The other Lao, whose father-in-law is one of the "upwardly mobile" Sing Moon, considers his children to be Lao. But the better-off members of the Sing Moon village are able to marry either Lao or Black Tai women and marry their daughters to Black Tai men. In this way they do establish kinship links with Black Tai, and given that the Black Tai are generally better off than the Sing Moon it provides a line of potential assistance if and when it is required. As such they are further able to develop their Black Tai lifestyle.

But with such relatively low rates of intermarriage between Tai and non-Tai we need to take a closer look at the arguments concerning "Tai-ization?"[10]

TAI-IZATION?

THERE is no question that Sing Moon are culturally subordinate to Lao-Tai culture, and Black Tai culture in particular. And Condominas is right to observe that "Tai-ization [is] born of the conquered peoples' hope of reaching a better status . . ." (1990: 71). As I have mentioned, and as was generally acknowledged, several of the Sing Moon were doing their best to acquire Black Tai status, and one of them had held the important position of *nai ban* (village head) from 1988 until 1991. But in the present, and perhaps also in the past, the process of conversion is voluntary and not coerced. Becoming "Tai" is a way of raising one's social status.

Among the Sing Moon one observes little cultural self-confidence and little pride in being Sing Moon.[11] They contrast with the Black Tai who are conscious that they possess a "great tradition." The Black Tai in Ban Sot were embarrassed when I first arrived there with books written in Black Tai which they could not read, and with questions about their history that they could not answer. They were embarrassed because they felt they should know. And the older men in the village more or less put their heads together to come up with accounts of their origin and so on. The anthropologist's presence, in a sense, caused a minor cultural revival (but this was at one point mocked by a slightly drunken younger man who danced around singing a ditty: "I'm a Tai Dam, I'm a Tai Dam" while laughing his head off). The fact that they know they have a great tradition and that they are surrounded by distinctively Black Tai material culture still gives the Black Tai a great deal of cultural confidence *vis-à-vis* surrounding groups, especially the Sing Moon. When that great tradition was actually maintained by a Black Tai elite then their general cultural confidence must have been that much stronger. By contrast the Sing Moon appear to possess no great tradition that they know of, and Black Tai material culture is acknowledged to be better than anything they have to offer and they adopt it when they can. Consequently they express no particular confidence about their culture, and in my initial enquiries they appeared to be a little embarrassed about discussing Sing Moon culture at all because they did not think there was much to discuss. Furthermore they had absorbed at least some shame from the Tai concerning their assumed cultural inferiority. The reconsolidation of the Sing Moon village of Ban Na Wan following its separation from Ban Sot has not caused any noticeable reassertion of Sing

Moon identity. The change has led to less cultural interaction between the two groups on a daily basis, but the long-term aim of at least the few better-off households in Ban Na Wan is to emulate the success of their Black Tai neighbors.

In the Indochinese highlands the notion of "Tai-ization" generally implies the adoption of Tai material culture, Tai ritual and cosmology, and Tai language. But it is worth considering to what extent there are cultural limits to this process and to what extent it is possible for these non-Tai groups to establish viable multiple identities. In an essay on funerals among upland Tai I charted one limit by pointing out that despite the extent to which Sing Moon now share Black Tai cosmology, they diverge from them in burial practices that encode their prior "ownership" of the land. I argued that despite the fact that some Sing Moon have aristocratic *sing* (patronymics) they do not follow the funeral practices of these *sing* by cremating their dead. They bury them. I also pointed out that this priority is acknowledged in Black Tai ritual: "the Black Tai each year pay ritual homage to the Lao Theung's prior dominion over the land. Until the coming of the Tai, one villager told me, 'the Lao Theung were in charge of the land . . . If we do not hold a ceremony for the phii of the Lao Theung before the harvest then the rice harvest will not be good.' Ritually this fundamental fact must be recognised, even in death. So there is cremation for the invaders from *Muang Fa* [heaven] and burial for the owners of the earth" (Evans 1991: 96). According to Vietnamese ethnographers there is a parallel Sing Moon ritual in some villages when offerings are made to the village protective spirit, the *sul col*. "In some places people believe that the 'mal te' ceremony must make offerings to the dead *phia tao* and *a-nha* of the Thai people in order to get their spiritual protection" (Dang Nghiem Van et al. 1972: 302). This was not the case in Ban Na Wan whose rituals for the village *sul col* were autonomous from the Black Tai. So ritual practices chart one ongoing boundary between Sing Moon and Tai, and because these rituals encode the Sing Moons' prior rights to the land they have good reason *as a group* to maintain them and therefore sustain Sing Moon identity.

Maintenance of Sing Moon language is a partial limit to ethnic interchange, especially in Sing Moon villages where it is used inside and outside the home. But Sing Moon also know Tai, and it has been up to them to cross the linguistic barrier. Their need to do this, both in the past and in the present, has been dictated by power relationships within the highlands. Tai power in the past, and Lao-Tai power in the present ensures that Sing Moon men and women know Lao-Tai. Of course, if they wish to raise their social status they need to know the dominant language.

The other main limit on ethnic change is not primarily cultural so much as an outcome of the social structure given that Sing Moon, and similar groups, have the lowest status in the society. Few Tai, for example, wish to marry down and those that do (though in my survey above I only observed Lao men intermarrying with Sing Moon) come from the poorer members of the dominant society. In a sense, ethnic endogamy tends to correspond with "class" endogamy. Only upwardly mobile Sing Moon can pursue more ambitious marriage strategies.

This is linked to the other systemic factor inhibiting ethnic conversion, that is the contingency of access to resources. We have seen that conflicts over access to resources in the uplands tend to be articulated along ethnic lines. Or at least this is one important fissure along which mobilization can occur. The conflict over resources was a dilemma primarily for the upwardly mobile Sing Moon who were divided about whether to play up their acquired Black Tai identity and throw in their lot with the Black Tai of Ban Sot against the other Sing Moon, or whether to act as members of the Sing Moon village. As we have seen, initially they tried the former approach but then they, and other Sing Moon villages in the *muang*, chose to go it alone. A key factor in this decision was one extraneous to the immediate environment of the highlands, that is, government policy on resettling people in the valleys. In this context, the upwardly mobile Sing Moon, by appealing beyond the social space dominated by Black Tai, can secure both their access to resources and remain the highest status families in the village, rather than attempting to be accepted as poorer members of a Black Tai village.

Their low status is certainly a factor inhibiting Sing Moon "Tai-ization," but these barriers are not the same as those found in societies with aristocratic, ranked lineages. Although traditional Black Tai society possessed "aristocratic" patronymics, *sing*, with their own separate myths, in fact these patronymics are distributed throughout highland ethnic groups and social strata in a rather puzzling way. Thus the Sing Moon possess *sing* including aristocratic *sing*. This puzzle cannot be fully explored here. One of the explanations given for their possession of these patronymics is that they acquired them from their overlords. So if a group of Sing Moon were subject to an aristocrat *Sing Lo* then they would acquire his *sing* as a mark of their subjection to that patronymic group. Vietnamese ethnographers have written: "Long ago Xinh mul people did not have family names, they only had an individual name. When the Thai came to the North-West, for various reasons Xinh mul people adopted Thai family names. For instance, the Vi family in Moc Chau is a Thai aristocratic family. Perhaps the Xinh mul people there . . . because they were under the "care" and "protection" of the Thai landlords, had to bear the family name Vi" (Dang Nghiem Van 1972 et al.: 280). This strikes me as a plausible explanation, and perhaps the adoption of patronymics by Sing Moon who were not directly subject to the Tai was for reasons of status, in which case it would also constitute an element of voluntary "Tai-ization." Diffusion of these patronymics through marriage is another way. In his study of the Khmu, Dang Nghiem Van notes that they have both a Khmu patronymic and a Thai patronymic (1973: 88). Significantly, Izikowitz in his study of the Lamet saw these patronymics as "clans" because they involved certain totemic restrictions. But as far as I can tell this is true for all the groups in the Indochina highlands who have patronymics, but it is not therefore evidence of actual "clan" organization. Izikowitz claims that the "most important task of the clans is to act as a regulator for marriage ties" (1951: 87). But evidence elsewhere in his book suggests that the fundamental exogamous unit is in fact the household (109). This is much more in line with practices throughout the highlands. Among the Black Tai and Sing Moon that I have investigated patronymics are not exogamous. Significantly, Izikowitz also seems dimly aware that the Lamet may have in fact acquired these "clans" from the Khmu who live all around them (85). The direction of cultural influence in regard to these patronymics remains problematic. One could argue that their existence among the upland Tai of Indochina (and then down through groups subordinate to the Tai) has its origins in Tai emulation of higher status Vietnamese/Chinese cultural practices (see, for example, Laufer 1917 and Evans 1997). Vietnamese ethnographers, on the other hand, whose political brief is to de-emphasize Chinese cultural influences in Vietnam, have chosen to see them as "survivals" of ancient exogamous clans. The former argument strikes me as most plausible, followed by Tai transmission of these patronymics to the various groups under them.

One important consequence of this culturally diffuse use of patronymics was that they were not a source of ethnic exclusivity. Furthermore, unlike the different and incompatible perceptions of rank and status between Shan and Kachin demonstrated by Leach (1970; also Lehman 1989), rank and/or status is perceived and understood in broadly the same way by Sing Moon (and Khmu and others) and the Tai thus allowing Sing Moon incorporation into Tai social structure if they choose to move in that direction.

Thus, while there are many factors favoring "Tai-ization" of subordinate ethnic groups in the highlands, there are also important cultural, social, and political factors which inhibit it and produce something much more like a dual identity among the Sing Moon. Today, however, the constitution of localized dual identities have been complicated by the expanding influence of the modern state.

NATIONALISM AND ETHNICITY

THE social space of the upland regions has changed dramatically from the traditional system which occupied the intermediate social spaces that Condominas set out to examine.[12] Perhaps when both Black Tai and Sing Moon lived in localized, intermediate social spaces the obvious source of cultural emulation for the Sing Moon was the dominant Black Tai. But as Condominas is aware these upland confederations were always constituted as elements of larger political entities, either the Chinese state or the Vietnamese state, and it should be pointed out immediately that the Tai emulated these systems. One only has to look at old photographs of Black Tai aristocrats to see that they are dressed as Vietnamese mandarins ("Vietnamization"), and they adopted and accepted titles from the Vietnamese state. Black Tai vocabulary is also studded with Vietnamese words. In the case of the White Tai, they adopted Vietnamese funeral practices, and among the Tho (Tay) the ritual incorporation of the elite was almost complete. And above I referred to the possibility of them adopting patronymics from these sources. Furthermore, the Vietnamese court firmed up its alliance with the Tho (Tay) élite, the Tho Thi, through the exchange of daughters in marriage.

So, the social space of at least the upland Tai elite was always larger than an intermediate localized space and the composition of that intermediate space was not only geographically determined, but also politically determined by relations with the lowland states. The Tai elite controlled access to a wider space because the source of their power was control over an intermediate space. In the traditional tributary structure they only needed to be partially "Vietnamized" in order to retain control of that space. Within that space was a Tai domain in which some peoples were becoming "Tai-ized" or partially "Tai-ized." On the other hand one can also say that the Tai elites at least also had dual identities, being, for example, more Vietnamese when dealing upwards in the political structure and more Tai when exercising power and influence downwards. This gradated, partial ethnic transformation was possible in traditional tributary state systems which were more tolerant than the modern nationalist state of semi-autonomous, intermediate social and cultural spaces.

It should also be noted, however, that throughout the whole region, ethnicity has been crucially influenced by policies of the colonial state. Leach recognized this in Burma: "The British prevented by force any further trend towards *gumlao* [egalitarian] organization; they encouraged existing *gumlao* headmen to behave as if they were *gumsa* [hierarchical] chiefs . . ." (Leach 1970: 258). Thus the British helped prepare the ground for the post-colonial ethnic revolts and separatist nationalist movements which have continued in Burma to this day. The Shan states were recognized as protectorates rather than as colonies, and so "Partly because of their separate administrative status, the Shan states were never affected by the pre-World War II nationalist movement to the same extent as Burma proper" (Lintner 1984: 405). In Indochina we can observe something similar. For example, French colonialism supported the upland Tai against Vietnamese encroachments and in 1948 attempted to establish a Tai federation in the same region as the old *Sip Song Chau Tai*. In contrast to Burma, however, and because of the historical peculiarities of the development of nationalism and communism in Vietnam and Laos, separatist nationalism failed for reasons which have been documented elsewhere (Fall 1962; McAlister 1967; Dassé 1976). And in further contrast to Burma, none of the other upland groups, except for the Hmong in Laos, became politically mobilized. Thus in northern Indochina we do not find, in the recent period, strong political movements which can give expression to more localized feelings of ethnic identity.[13]

The coming of the modern nation-state to Laos and Vietnam has also fundamentally altered ethnic relations within the uplands. The Lao state has never been very strong, but it has now penetrated the local level to an unprecedented degree (Evans 1990: chapter 8), and I think it is fair to say that these intermediate social spaces have effectively disappeared. The overthrow of the old Tai aristocracy by the communists saw the disappearance of religious rituals associated with the *lak muang* which defined these intermediate political spaces, and these rituals devolved to the *ban* level where only *phi ban* and *phi heun* rituals are now observed. Rituals which define the larger social spaces in which people move are now connected to the nation state, national days, etc.[14] In Laos there are some Buddhist rituals similar to those in Thailand and Burma reemerging parallel to these state occasions, and increasingly in conjunction with them. But unlike Thailand, and more like Burma, Buddhism covers perhaps only 50 percent of the Lao population. It is still not yet fully effective as a national ideology or as a vehicle for "Lao-ization." For example, in Muang Xieng Kho which is dominated by Tai peoples, only the occasional village has a v*at* because these upland Tai are generally non-Buddhist. From my observations, Lao who marry into a Black Tai village often drop all Buddhist rituals and *"tue phi seu seu"* ("simply worship spirits"), while Black Tai who marry into a Lao cultural universe begin to adopt Buddhism.[15]

In the modern context the direction of ethnic change at both the national level and at the local level has become more complex and problematic. For example, in the past the Black Tai may have had a direct economic interest in the incorporation of the Sing Moon into their village structures as a source of surplus labor. With the abolition of the traditional "feudal" system and the implementation of at least formal equality and citizenship of a nation-state, the Black Tai no longer have direct control over the Sing Moon, and in some ways the modern state increases the distance between them. The Sing Moon are able to become detached politically, economically, and ritually from the Black Tai.[16] It is in this context that we should view Ban Sot's reluctance to incorporate the Sing Moon after 1973. In fact incorporation took place under the direction of the communist modern state.

As explored by Anderson (1983), Gellner (1983), and Hobsbawm (1992), the aspiration, or fantasy, of modern nationalism is that within a delimited social space, the nation, people will be culturally of the same type. In other words, there is an assumed congruence between nation-state and culture. Unlike traditional tributary systems modern nationalism is generally intolerant towards semi-autonomous, intermediate social and cultural spaces and it is the modern state that sets out to systematically "Lao-ize" or "Vietnamize," for example, their populations in order to make them congruent with the legitimizing assumptions of modern nationalism, leaving aside other more pragmatic reasons.

In Laos lowland Lao culture is propagated through the education system, through the media and government propaganda, through government meetings and the high profile given to Buddhist rituals, and so on (Ireson and Ireson 1991). In this regard it is important to note that young Black Tai are becoming Lao, in their speech patterns, their dress, and their aspirations to a particular lifestyle which is Lao, a fact which partially facilitates emigration. If one takes a photo in a village the younger women race to put on their Lao style *sins* rather than traditional Black Tai dress. (One might add that something similar also happens in Sing Moon villages). Wedding dress for women also copies the lowland Lao style as does the ritual that accompanies it. Older people in the village comment on how the younger people are throwing away, *"tim ook,"* Black Tai traditions. But even these older Black Tai have made an earlier adaptation to broader Lao culture by using Lao names for themselves, just as Black Tai over the border in Vietnam use Vietnamese names. And to follow on from my earlier observation on housing styles, for example, perhaps one of the most striking changes in Ban Sot was the building of one house in a Laotian style, complete with a roof made of concrete sheeting (which saved it from a disastrous fire which destroyed thirteen houses two days before my 1993 visit to the village as each of the thatched roofs caught fire from its neighbor).

Anthropologists of ethnicity today are confronted with complex hierarchies of identification ranging from the most parochial to the global, and in a way that doubly reinforces Leach's (1970) early arguments against ethnic essentialism. The ethnic groups who have been at the center of this essay are still primarily subject to local social and cultural processes. But this is less and less true. Since my first visit I have been struck by the speed at which not only radios have proliferated in the villages with the accompanying thirst for pop music, but also the presence of small video shows in the smallest market towns showing everything from beauty pageants in far off Bangkok to gangster movies from Hong Kong. And from these wider cultural inputs cultural incongruities begin to proliferate, such as a young Black Tai farmer swaggering into the local small market town wearing his slightly battered dark glasses trying to look like some çcoolé Hong Kong thug. The consequences of these broader cultural changes are hard to predict in advance. But one thing is certain, the modern state will try its utmost to ensure that groups like the Sing Moon and the Black Tai will in the future be culturally closer to one another than in the past, because of their shared Lao-ness.

NOTES

1. As I have pointed out in chapter 1 of this book, many people have argued that the Lao ethnic group is the largest group in Thailand. Here, of course, we encounter the thorny problem of the emics and etics of ethnicity. A key general boundary for most people in Laos, however, is between the lowland Buddhist groups and the non-Buddhist groups.

2. For the problems contained in this typology, see chapter 1. There has also been a more conventional communist program of setting out to categorize all the ethnic groups in the country. Figures for the number of ethnic groups in Laos have swung between forty and sixty, sometimes going higher. For a detailed discussion, see chapter 8.

3. This figure was given to me by the Institute of Ethnography in Vientiane in 1988.

4. Here *muang* means district in the sense of an administrative space defined by the modern state. *Muang* or *müöng* (the latter being the Vietnamese spelling adopted by Condominas) can also indicate a variable political unit in the traditional Tai political system, each encompassing the other, with the pinnacle being a *chau muang*. While I do not write Muang Xieng Kho district, for example, I do write Ban Sot village, in spite of the fact that *ban* already means village. Why a redundant word is used in one context and not in another is simply a convention in writing about Laos.

5. For a brief look at anthropological discussions of the problematic nature of these categories, see Evans (1993b).

6. See the discussion on minorities in chapter 1.

7. In 1991 in the province of Attopeu in southern Laos we documented a similar situation among the "Lavae" as the Lao government calls them—in fact they are composed of Sedang and Brau—who were forced to move down from the mountains after 1975 (Evans and Boonmataya 1991).

8. In 1994 emergency rice relief had to be given to Muang Xieng Kho as a result of

the failure of the 1993 wet season harvest which caused a serious shortfall (*Kao San Pathet Lao*, June 11, 1994).

9. One can compare this with the observation of Dang Nghiem Van who claims that marriage to a Khmu invariably involved downward mobility for a Tai. "If ever a Thai married a Khmu the former would become a Khmu as a result of the marriage contracted and afterwards could set up house only in his or her spouse's hamlet" (1973: 79). My research revealed a less rigid set of social rules, suggesting that the movement of women did not affect status as much as it did for men. Also see the observations on Khmu marriage with other groups in Le Bar (1967) which shows a more diverse pattern. Clearly, more work is required in this area.

10. Izikowitz (1969: 139) also notes low rates of "intermarriage between Thai and Kha," although he says "there are exceptions." However, his observations are impressionistic.

11. In this regard we can compare them, for example, with the Karen who "usually attribute their relatively low position in the hierarchy to the foolishness or the laziness of the Karen . . ." (Kunstadter 1979: 153). Yet, compared to the Sing Moon, the Karen would appear to have more pride in their "Karenness."

12. For a full discussion of his concept of "espace social" see Condominas (1980: Introduction).

13. This was not true for the Central Highlands in the southern half of Vietnam where a separatist highland minorities movement came into being as result of the Vietnam War. This is discussed most thoroughly by Hickey (1982), and for the fate of these groups and this movement after 1975, see Evans (1992).

14. In this respect they are different from the Lue discussed by Khampheng Thipmuntali in chapter 7 whose *phi muang* rituals have been subsumed in Buddhist rituals which mediate their relationship with the larger Lao state.

15. To add a further cultural complication, I have also noticed that Lao marrying into Black Tai villages also have *sing*, something not present among lowland Lao, which suggests that these "Lao" were upland Tai in the past, although the people I have spoken with have no record of it. But it is another piece of evidence of long-term shifts backwards and forwards in ethnicity.

16. A similar situation for the Sing Moon has been documented in Vientam. See Dang Nghiem Van et al. (1972).

THE TAI LUE OF MUANG SING

7

KHAMPHENG THIPMUNTALI

AT the beginning of June 1995 I had the opportunity to visit the Sipsong Panna region in Yunnan province, China to study trade and cultural exchanges on the Lao-Chinese border.[1] On this very first visit I was struck by the similarities and the differences between the Tai Lue (or Dai) of Yunnan and the Tai Lue of Laos. The former have been influenced by the culture of the Chinese people, and the culture of the Tai Lue has slowly changed. In cities like Xieng Hung, Muang La, and Muang Mang we now mainly find Chinese who have built big shops and office buildings, and the Tai Lue live on the outskirts of these cities (Hsieh 1989: 275). Unfortunately, the time available to me was short so that I could not study the subject in depth, but subsequently I have read Hsieh Shih Chung's very interesting study on the Sip Song Panna Dai (1989) which describes the economic, cultural, and social changes among the Tai Lue in Sipsong Panna. But changes in the social life of the Tai Lue in Laos, both in the past and present, have not yet been studied in depth by researchers, and so this chapter is an attempt to contribute to our understanding of this area. In it I will focus on the Tai Lue of Muang Sing and will try to outline some of the cultural and social changes there caused by the development and expansion of Lao culture.

It is well known that the native homeland of the Tai Lue is the Sipsong Panna in China. Yet we now find Tai Lue in the east of Myanmar, in northern Thailand, in the northern part of Vietnam and in northern Laos. According to statistics released in 1995, more than six thousand Lue people live in twenty-six villages in Muang Sing, Louang Namtha province, Laos. Muang Sing township is a small town in the view of visitors, and today it has only just over four thousand houses, yet it is the biggest town in the northwestern-most part of Laos and is situated 12 km from the Lao-

Chinese border and about 30 km from the Mekong River. This location made Muang Sing an important town during the period of colonization. It was here that French colonialism and British colonialism came face to face, and therefore the traditional ruler of Muang Sing came under pressure from both of them, and control of the area itself was disputed for a while. Interestingly, on the road from China to Laos, we can see old guideboards which point to Muang Boten to the south and Muang Sing to west, but they do not mention Louang Namtha town (the provincial township today) which is also in the west and is only 60 km from Muang Sing. Here we can see the historical importance of Muang Sing in this region.

In the beginning, Chao Fa Soulinor had tried to build an autonomous region in Muang Sing, surrounded by satellites and brotherly towns.[2] But in 1895 Great Britain, which governed Myanmar at that time, pressured Chao Fa Soulinor to hand over Muang Sing to the colony of Great Britain. The Chao Fa met with the French representitive in Houai Xai to seek support, following which a dispute arose between Great Britain and France over Muang Sing. Great Britain, during negotiations in 1904, finally conceded that the part of Muang Sing located on the east bank of the Mekong River fell under French control. The towns located on the right bank of the Mekong River fell under British control and those in the north to China. Among the older generation bitter feelings are still expressed because of the divisions created between what were brotherly towns.

In 1907 Chao Fa Soulinor was succeeded by his son Ong Kham who did not share his father's preparedness to cooperate with the French. Finally he fled to Sipsong Panna in December 1914 and from there led an uprising against the French which went on for the next two years during which the Hor Kham (the Golden Palace) of the Chao Fa was destroyed. Geoffrey Gunn has written:

> The rebellion of the Lu probably commenced as an attempt by relatives of the Chao Fa to usurp power . . . With the flight of the Chao Fa to Muong La in Sip Song Panna, clan rivalry and court intrigue at Muong Sing became subordinated to the war of resistance mounted by the Lu people against the French (Gunn 1990: 144).

This revolt also expressed a desire of the Lue to rejoin the Sipsong Panna, but since then they have been progressively incorporated into firstly colonial French Laos, then the Kingdom of Laos after 1947, and since 1975 the Lao People's Democratic Republic.

WHO ARE THE LUE?

IF we rubbed out the line of demarcation between Laos, Myanmar, Thailand, and China and looked at the territory along the Mekong riverbank in history, we could see the deep relations between the peoples and rulers of this region. Muang Sing, Muang La, Muang Mang, Muang Nhong, and Muang Louang are Tai Lue towns which are related and whose people often visit each other or move to resettle. People use the river to make a living but not as a dividing line between each other. Muang Sing in the past was governed by a *chao fa*, and was surrounded by satellites and brotherly towns like: Muang Khan, Muang Lo, Muang Nhou, Muang Louai, Muang Ham, and Muang Oun. Most Lue people in Muang Sing were from Muang Xieng Hung, but many *chao fa* of Muang Sing came from Xieng Toung in Myanmar. This made Xieng Toung like an elder brother town and Muang Sing a younger brother town. Vat Houa Khoua temple is an important temple, built 150 years ago by Chao Fa Soulinor, a Tai Leu from Xieng Toung. Many people from Muang La, Muang Mang, Muang Louang, Muang Nhong, Vieng Phoukha, Ta Fa Muang Louai, Muang Len, and Muang Phayark also relocated to Lanna.

In 1960 Muang Sing received Tai Lue refugees from Sipsong Panna of China who sought political asylum after the Great Leap Forward, and then during the Cultural Revolution of the mid to late 1960s. Then, during the civil war in Laos many Tai Lue again relocated to Thailand.

As a result of war and revolution Lue are now scattered across several state borderlines, and within Laos we can find a similar dispersal of groups. Thus we can now find in the township and rural areas of Muang Sing a Lue group and a large Goh (Akha) group, while the remainder are Hmong, Tai Neua, Yao, Lao, Tai Dam, and Khmu. In Muang Sing we have seen, on the one hand, a change in the population following political change, and on the

TABLE 1   POPULATION BY ETHNIC GROUP IN MUANG SING

Ethnic Group	Villages	No. of houses	Population	Temples
Goh (Akha)	68	2351	11073	0
Lue	26	1199	6309	18
Tai Neua	5	327	1717	5
Black Tai	1	49	393	0
Khmu	1	19	81	0
Yao	6	137	894	0
Hmong	3	286	1875	0
Total	**110**	**4368**	**22238**	**23**

Source: Population census 1995.

other hand, a movement of highland people (Hmong, Yao, Goh) to the lowlands or plains. Hmong from Xieng Khouang, for example, have been migrating to Muang Sing in recent years in search of land.

The question "Who are the Lue?" was posed many years ago by Michael Moerman in his by now well-known and important paper, "Ethnic Identification in a Complex Civilization: who are the Lue?" In it he argued that anthropologists should not treat ethnic categories as natural, but as historical. Nevertheless, classification was difficult because:

> Ethnicity is impermanent in that individuals, communities and areas change their identification. If the origins of Thai tribes are political, one would expect these changes to be fairly common (Moerman 1965: 1222).

Thus in Muang Sing, according to the older generation, the Lue there previously were divided into two parts based on origin. The first group had moved from Xieng Toung, Myanmar over one hundred years ago, the second from Xieng Hung in Yunnan. So, while amongst themselves they would refer back to these places of origin, they also became Lue of Muang Sing.

The second argument advanced by Michael Moerman was:

> Various non-members may use ethnic terms differently. Burmese, Chinese, Siamese, and Northern Thai do not use the same labels. Moreover, translation of these labels is not always a matter of merely finding a convenient gloss, for not everyone recognizes the same categories (Moerman 1965: 1223).

The Tai Lue in the northern part of Laos are known by many names, and over the border in Sipsong Panna the Chinese people call them Dai (in the past they called them Bai-i or Shui-Bai-i). The Tai Dam in Louang Namtha call the Tai Lue in Louang Namtha "Kalom" or "Lue Kalom;" Lao people in Nambak district, Louang Prabang province, also call Tai Lue in Ban Nayang, Nambak district, "Kalom" or "Lue Kalom." Lao people in Ban Beng village, Udomxai province, call Tai Lue in Ban Beng village "Lao Lue."

The third aspect of ethnic identification mentioned by Michael Moerman was:

> Members may not always use the same term for themselves (Moerman 1965: 1223).

Tai Lue in the northern part of Laos accept other terms besides these

terms that other ethnic groups use for them. The Tai Lue in Muang Ou
Neua, Ou Tay, and Muang Boun Neua, Phongsaly province, accept that
they are Tai Lue-Sipsong Panna, because in the past Muang Ou Neua, Ou
Tay, and Muang Boun Neua were a *panna* of Sipsong Panna. Tai Lue in
Muang Sing accept that they are Lue Xieng Hung, Tai Lue who relocated
from Xieng Hung over a hundred years ago (like the Tai Lue in Houn, Tin
That, Nam Dai, Done Poi, and Ta Pao villages). Another group of Tai Lue
here accept that they are Tai Lue Xieng Toung (Tai Lue who came with
Chao Fa Soulinor, like the Tai Lue in Done Poi and Tap villages). Tai Lue
in Louang Namtha accept that they are Tai Lue Kalom and the Tai Lue in
Ban Beng village, Beng district, Udomxai province also accept themselves as
Lao Lue.

The following is a table of the terms which have been used for labeling
Tai Lue:

TABLE 2 TERMS USED FOR THE TAI LUE IN NORTHERN LAOS

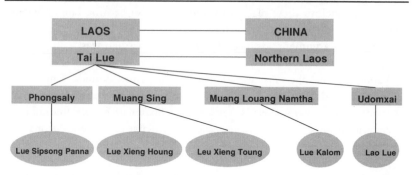

In fact for the Lue in Laos ethnic identification is not so difficult because
they always use the term "Lue" and then add some other qualification to it,
such as: Tai Lue Sipsong Panna, Tai Lue Xieng Hung, Tai Lue Xieng
Toung.

But among them, as Moerman points out in his article, there are
different levels of identification according to social context. For example,
Dai in Sipsong Panna will refer to themselves as Chinese, just as Lue in
Laos will refer to themselves as Lao, or those in Thailand as Thai. Those in
Laos will also identify themselves as being from northern Laos, that is a
kind of regional specification, to which they then may add that they are Lue
from Muang Sing. The other more detailed descriptions of their identity
seem to have purely local uses, i.e. Lue Kalom as both a self-appellation and
one used by others, or Lue Xieng Hung.

These localized uses, however, especially in Muang Sing, also contain a "memory" of the Lue's historical relationship with the Sipsong Panna, and so also refer the Lue to a larger remembered unit which is in fact now part of a special administrative region of the PRC. Ritual and kinship relations across the national border between Laos and China also keep this memory alive. Yet the Lue in Muang Sing in Laos are also becoming more Lao, especially the younger generation. Indeed, one of the most striking visual differences as one moves across the border from the direction of China is the way the grand Tai Lue houses of the Sipsong Panna give way to the Lao-style houses built by the Lue in Muang Sing. The other striking visual difference as one moves across the border is that the Lue women of Sipsong Panna dress in a way that marks them clearly as Tai Lue, whereas the women in Muang Sing dress like Lao.

The Lue in both areas, of course, enter very different education systems. In China Lue learn Chinese, in Laos they learn Lao and this has also meant that the Lue in Laos no longer learn Lue script.[3] Among the native villagers, Lue people will speak Lue. School children will speak Lao (the central language) with teachers at the school, but will speak Lue among themselves or mix the two.

Why do Lue on the Chinese side of the border appear to maintain at least the outward signs of Lue identity whereas in Laos they don't? In Yunnan and these days in Sipsong Panna the dominant ethnic group is Han Chinese whose culture and society is very different from that of the Tai Lue. Thus the Tai Lue through their housing styles and dress styles for their women clearly advertise this ethnic difference because it is a way that they preserve their ethnic identity in the face of a Han Chinese threat to it. This desire to preserve their ethnicity appears to have been one outcome of the destructive period of the Cultural Revolution when, as I mentioned above, Lue refugees fled to Muang Sing. As Heather Peters writes: "this period of repression and destruction of Tai traditional culture served to strengthen Tai ethnicity in opposition to the Han" (Peters 1990: 347), and indeed when the political situation in China relaxed in the 1980s this led the Tai Lue of Sipsong Panna to not only revive their relationships with the Shan in Myanmar, but also to look to Thailand for inspiration, especially in their revival of Buddhism.

For the Lue in Laos this sense of ethnic contrast is not great, nor do they feel any overt threat to their Lue identity. While there are distinctive features of Lue culture, language, and localized beliefs and practices, which we shall look at briefly below, there is in contrast to the Lue in China a certain similarity between Lao practices and Lue practices, and this facilitates their gradual absorption into a larger Lao culture.

LOCAL CULTS AND SACRIFICE

LIKE the Lao and Thai and other Tai groups the Lue believe in *phi* (spirits). They believe these ghosts and spirits have the power to determine their destiny. Therefore, it has been a popular tradition to make a sacrifice to the house, village, and town spirits. The *phi muang* (town spirit) in particular plays an important role in the living conditions of the people and the sustenance of the town. Town spirits include ancestors who built a Lue town and helped with its development in the past. After they died, these people became *phi muang* spirits of the town.

The Tai Lue believe that the *phi muang* will protect them. If the people do not pay their respects to the *phi muang* it will not protect them and the town will find itself without security and stability. Therefore, the Tai Lue of Muang Sing hold a ceremony where they make a sacrifice to the *phi muang* every year. Previously, the ceremony for the *phi muang* was organized by the Chao Fa Muang Sing. The ceremony usually took place in March, on the 13th day of the waxing moon, according to the Lue lunar calendar (January of the Lao lunar calendar and December of the international calendar). Tai Lue people used buffaloes to make a sacrifice to the *phi muang*. In Muang Sing, the Lue make the sacrifice with a black buffalo. In Muang Ou Neua, the Lue make a sacrifice to three *phi muang* with two buffaloes (one black and one white) and one cow. Each *phi muang* has its special *moh* (shaman). The cost of organizing the ceremony is borne by the people (including the people of other ethnic groups living in Muang Sing, who are not Tai Lue).

At a ceremony to worship the *phi muang*, the most important ritual was the "Teng Khouai" (spearing the buffalo). On the day of the ceremony the *moh teng* tied the buffalo to the town pillar. The *moh teng* dressed in a special costume: a long white shirt with long sleeves, with a red band around his head. A *moh louang* had the duty of preparing the water containing *bai som poy* (*Acacia cinchona*) flowers and five pairs of candles for the *moh teng*. The Teng Khouai ceremony was begun once the Chao Fa Muang Sing and other invited guests arrived. The *moh khab* (a man who had the responsibility of appeasing the spirits) invited all *phi muang* Sing to attend the ceremony (Muang Sing has thirty-two spirits). The *moh khab* also invited *phi* from Sipsong Panna and *phi* from Chiang Mai of Thailand to take part in the ceremony.

After the process of inviting *phi muang* ended, the *moh teng* brought with him the water and candles prepared by the *moh louang*, and went to pay homage to the buffalo and ask for forgiveness for taking its life. The *moh teng* walked around the city pillar three times in a clockwise direction, and speared the buffalo. When the buffalo fell down, Chao Fa Muang Sing and the heads of the local authority came to see in what direction the head of the buffalo was facing. The Lue believed that if the buffalo's head pointed in the direction of the city pillar it meant that the town would enjoy stability and security, and the people would be happy. But if the buffalo's head pointed in the opposite direction, that meant the town and the people would be unstable and unhappy. In 1969, the buffalo's head fell in the opposite direction from the city pillar, and in that year a lot of Lue people were forced to evacuate Muang Sing because of fighting (Nguyen Houai Nguyen 1970).

The *moh louang* cut some of the meat, liver, lung, tongue, the tip of the nails, mouth, horn, tail and ear and put it on a plate for worshiping the *phi muang*. Different kinds of food were also prepared from the buffalo's meat for worshiping the *phi muang*, and the leftover meat was distributed to the people and cooked, for the people who took part at the parties held on that day around the city pillar or in the house of the village head.

On the next day a Baci ceremony was held for *mae ti nang* represented by a *nang tiam* (a female shaman). The ceremony is attended by the *moh louang*, and *moh khab* (the *moh* who invited the *phi*), and the *moh phi* along with about one or two old people from each village. The ceremony was organized in the house of *mae ti nang (nang tiam)*. The people prepared a *pha khouan* with two boiled chickens (one hen and one cock) and sweet bananas, sugar cane, and 500 kip in cash. The *moh louang* tied the arms of *mae ti nang* with strings representing wishes for prosperity and good luck, and presented the *pha khouan* to *mae ti nang* when the ceremony ended. This signaled the end of the sacrifice to the *phi muang*.

A ceremony for making a sacrifice to the *phi muang* was held continuously until 1973. When the Neo Lao Hak Xat took control of Muang Sing at the end of 1972 they issued a policy aimed at liquidation of "superstitious" beliefs among the ethnic minority people, because these beliefs were considered to be factors obstructing improvements in the living conditions and agricultural production of the people. Thus since 1973, the Tai Lue of Muang Sing have given up the tradition of making a buffalo sacrifice to the *phi muang*. Even now, following the relaxation of religious policy in Laos, the Tai Lue of Muang Sing do not carry out the sacrifice to the *phi muang*. Buffalo sacrifices could be found throughout Laos in the past, for example in Vientiane and Louang Prabang, and in Chiang Mai (Levy 1959; Archaimbault 1959), but by the 1950s they had began to die out.

Nevertheless the belief in the *phi muang* still remains among the Tai Lue of Muang Sing, but that belief has slowly been incorporated into Buddhist rituals, with sacrifices now being made to Pha That Chiang Teum.

The Lue of Muang Sing say that in the distant past, the Buddha and Maha Ananta came to Muang Sing and had lunch on Phou That mountain (where Pha That Chieng Teum is located today). At that time, Muang Sing was called Muang Alavi. After lunch, and before going to Xieng Hung, Muang Mang, and Sipsong Panna, the Buddha asked Pha Ananta to bring one of his bones and his razor to this place after he died and to bury them in this mountain. Thus when the Buddha died, Maha Ananta took some parts of the Buddha's bones and put them in this mountain—Phou That Muang Sing. Some years later, Phagna Tan Hay (Than Hay) came to build a town on this mountain. While the construction work was underway a white crow flew over the site and flew down to snap at the heads of the servants while they were digging to construct a toilet for Phagna Tan Hay. The servants went to inform Phanga Tan Hay about the crow. Phanga Tan Hay told the servants to catch the crow by making a net and to keep it in a room with a child. Three years passed and the child learned to speak the crow's language. Phanga Tan Hay told the child to interrogate the crow. The crow answered that under the soil where the servants were digging the toilet were parts of the Buddha's bones. Then Phagna Tan Hay told the servants to dig deeper and they found the bones but could not remove them because the bones were deep in the soil. Therefore Phanga Tan Hay ordered his servants to build a stupa *(that)* there and named it That Chieng Teum. That Chieng Teum now also contains ancestral spirits such as Phanga Tan Hay, Thevaboud Louang, Phanga Nark, and Sa Boua Kham (Chao Fa Soulinor's wife).

As mentioned above, the Lue of Muang Sing also have a tradition of making a offerings to Pha That Chieng Teum every year. In fact, this tradition is a form of making a sacrifice both to the Buddha and to the ancestral spirits of the town *(phi muang)*. Every year in August on the eighth day of the waxing moon the Lue prepare food and sweet dishes and give it to a town elder who will use it for making offerings to the four spirits of the town, and to ask for rain.

Another ceremony for making offerings Pha That Chieng Teum is organized on 15 January, the day of the waxing of the moon in the Tai Lue lunar calendar. At the one-day ceremony, the monks will chant a prayer and all Lue people in Muang Sing and those Tai Lue who came from Muang Louang Namtha and Tai Lue from Sipsong Panna will jointly participate in the *tak bat* (merit making) ceremony and pour water on the soil and ask the Buddha and their ancestors to protect them from harm, and to bring them happiness.

All of these rituals have been basic elements of the Tai Lue community in the northern part of Laos, and contain local ritual practices that distinguish the Tai Lue from the Lao ethnic group. Nevertheless, buffalo sacrifices in the past and beliefs in a *phi muang*, and the Buddhist rituals associated with That Chieng Teum, are all structurally similar to practices found amongst the Lao and the Thai and other groups in the region.

BUDDHISM

TAI Lue Buddhism is the same as Lao Buddhism, that is, Hinayana (or Theravada) Buddhism. This religion originally came from India, Sri Lanka, and through Myanmar to northern Laos. The Lue in northern Laos have been strongly influenced by developments in Myanmar Buddhism.

Almost every Tai Lue village has a monastery. Before 1963, Muang Sing had twenty-four temples with about 300 monks and bonzes (Nguyen Houai Nguyen 1970). Today there are twenty-three with approximately 150–200 monks. One reason for the smaller number today is that state schools now provide education for the young, whereas in the past the temple was the key educational institution for young boys.When a man enters the monkhood it means he makes a spiritual act of merit for himself and for his family. Therefore every family, when their son gets to the ages of eight to ten, will send him to enter the temple as a novice, or when he gets to fifteen or sixteen, as a monk, or at twenty-two to twenty-five, as a *satu*. Most will leave the monkhood, but many men return when they get older. Old women can enter the temple as nuns, but most of them prefer to stay at home and go to the temples only for the religious ceremonies. Tai Lue people believe that by making spiritual acts of merit, after their death their souls will go to heaven.

Together with the belief in Buddhism, Lue society also, as we have seen, worships *phi* (spirits). If the people have done good things to the *phi* they will be protected And if the people have done something bad to the *phi*, then they will fall sick and the town will have bad fortune. Every family believes in *thevadha heun* (spirit of the house), *phi ban* (spirit of the village), and *phi muang* (spirit of the town).

As we have seen, Muang Sing is surrounded by a number of different ethnic groups, with Goh (Akha) in particular being the largest group in the *muang*, along with much smaller numbers of Hmong, Yao, Khmu, and also Tai Dam. In this respect Buddhism is something which differentiates the Lue, and as Moerman argued for the Lue of northern Thailand, "The villagers of Ban Ping see a fundamental division of humanity between 'people who have religion,' i.e. Buddhists, and those who do not. The historical superiority of lowland peoples is expressed in the superiority of those who have religion. When the villager is made to feel that he shares this precious superiority with all Thais, he identifies himself with the nation" (Moerman 1966: 167). This argument applies equally to the Lue of

Muang Sing and in this way Buddhism allows them to identify with the nation of Laos.

Before 1989, according to the policy of the Lao Buddhist Organization, Lao monks were not allowed to have contact with foreign monks. Since 1989 the Lao government has issued a policy on renovation for widening of all-round cooperation with other countries in the world, and this has provided the Lao monks with good opportunities to widen their cooperation and relations with the monks of neighboring countries like Thailand, Myanmar, and China. In particular it has allowed them to revive their historical relationship with Buddhism in Myanmar.

In January 1996, Pha Chao Bounsom (or Pha Chao Bounchom) who is a leading Tai Lue monk from Pangsa temple in Muang Phong Noy town of Myanmar came to Muang Sing for Thot Kathin (ceremony for presenting robes to the monks) at That Chieng Teum. On that day, besides Tai Lue living in Muang Sing and in Muang Louang Namtha, there were some Lue who came from Sipsong Panna to take part in the ceremony. During his stay for the Thot Kathin, Pha Chao Bounsom had a Hor Phakeo and a *Kesa Thanchay* stupa built in the area of That Chieng Teum stupa. Pha Chao Bounsom put under this stupa a carpet, his hat, and a mystic symbol which was written on a sheet of gold, stone, and brick. A Buddha image made of gold and 22 cm high was also put inside the stupa. Pha Chao Bounsom also built one stupa in the area of Xieng Chai temple, on his way from Muang Sing to that Chieng Teum stupa (about 9 km away). Like a modern *phu mi boun* Pha Chao Bounsom, while seated in his moving car, threw money (Thai baht) onto the street for his followers to gather in. After that he traveled by car to Sipsong Panna to Vat Louang in Muang Mang for Thot Kathin, and to Muang La, Muang Ven, Vat Pa Che, Xieng Hung. Then he returned via Muang Che, Muang La, Muang Yang, Chieng Toung, Muang Lien, and finally back to Vat Pangsa in Myanmar.

The monks in Muang Sing have often received invitations from the monks in Sipsong Panna to attend Buddhist ceremonies. In return, the monks in Muang Sing also invite the monks from Sipsong Panna to attend their religious ceremonies.

CONCLUSION

SINCE 1989 the Lao government has pursued an open-door policy and has opened its borders with China, Thailand, and Myanmar, thus providing opportunity for Tai Lue to widen their relations with the world. Some people in Muang Sing have gone to Xieng Khong, Thailand to find work, and some traders have become involved in cross-border business to China and Thailand.[4] Besides this, some villagers have also had the opportunity to visit their relatives in the United States of America and France, thus improving their knowledge of the world.

The northern border between Laos and China was closed in 1979 after tensions arose between Beijing and the governments of Vietnam and Laos over Cambodia. Thus, for some time relations between relatives on both sides of the border were disrupted. Since 1989, however, these relationships have been revived. For example, Tai Lue people in Nakham, Sor Houn, and Ta Pao villages of Muang Sing will now go to attend religious ceremonies when they are organized by their relatives in Sipsong Panna. And for their part Lue people in Sipsong Panna will also come to take part in such ceremonies when they are organized by their relatives in Muang Sing. Sometimes, even their relatives who are refugees living in the U.S. and France come, or send contributions for the ceremonies to their relatives.

In recent years, therefore, economic, social and religious ties between the Lue of Muang Sing and the Lue of Sipsong Panna have strengthened their sense of being Lue. On the other hand, because the Lue in Sipsong Panna are under increasing cultural pressure from the Chinese, they also look to Laos and Thailand as places where Tai people are in control of their own societies, and as places that they identify with culturally.[5] Thus besides the forces of education and so on mentioned above which are drawing the Lue of Muang Sing into the Lao mainstream, there is also the reality that there is no political unit to identify with in the Sipsong Panna. The Dai Autonomous Region is a small part of the Chinese state, and the ancient political unity of this northern region only finds its expression on ritual occasions, such as the sacrifices at That Chieng Teum.

In the near future, the development of the Golden Quadrangle between Laos, China, Thailand, and Myanmar with its massive plans for improved road and other communications between these countries, will bring not only increased intercourse between all of them, but also rapid social and cultural change. I fear that what will be left of Lue culture in Muang Sing will be an artificial culture created for business and for the needs of tourists who travel from far away in the hope of seeing an unfamiliar culture in the border areas of Laos. What they will not know, however, is that this culture has been restored according to the conception of tourist operators.

NOTES

1. I made this research trip along with Dr. Grant Evans of the University of Hong Kong and Brian Su of the Ethnobotany Institute in Kunming. I would like to thank Dr. Evans very much for his assistance in writing this paper. Sipsong Panna, usually

glossed in English as the twelve thousand rice fields, is the name for the old Lue kingdom.

2. "*Chao fa*" can be translated as "king," or simply as "prince." Principalities such as Muang Sing, however, were relatively small, yet they drew on the same political principles as the larger states in the region. Thus the appellation "Chao fa" technically applies in this case because Soulinor was at the apex of the structure. However, the smallness of the principality would make the terms "prince" or "lord" seem more appropriate in English.

3. This is also true in China where Lue are only able to learn their traditional script in the temples. Consequently, few young Lue in the Sipsong Panna can read Lue.

4. For more details of this trade, see Andrew Walker, chapter 4.

5. For details, see Hsieh (1989) and Peters (1990).

APPRENTICE ETHNOGRAPHERS

8

VIETNAM AND THE STUDY OF MINORITIES IN LAOS

GRANT EVANS

T HE Vietnamese communists have played a key role in the formation, development, and eventual success of the Lao communists.[1] Since the late 1940s they have provided such crucial material, military, and political-theoretical guidance to the Lao that many were inclined to see the Lao revolutionaries simply as "puppets" of the Vietnamese. Indeed, the antipathy of many Lao nationalists to the Vietnamese made this claim very plausible, as it did to many outsiders. The rarely analyzed term, "puppets," implies that the Lao revolutionaries had no autonomy, no interests of their own, and if they did have separate interests then these were always subordinate to the wishes of their puppet-master. Nationalist movements are never this docile, and as the Vietnamese discovered in the case of the Khmer Rouge, previous apparent harmony can rapidly degenerate into hostility.[2] It was two American political scientists who came up with the most apposite way of describing the Lao-Vietnamese relationship when they entitled their book on the Lao communist movement, *Apprentice Revolutionaries.*[3] The use of "apprentice" clearly acknowledged the asymmetrical nature of the relationship, but it does leave open the possibility of the apprentice achieving the status of a master craftsman sometime in the future. Indeed, following the rapid shifts in policy that have occurred in the economic and social spheres both in Vietnam and in Laos since the late 1980s, one can argue that the master-apprentice relationship between the two political movements has weakened considerably.

Nevertheless, many of the institutional structures and indeed patterns of thought found today in the Lao People's Democratic Republic are derived from Vietnam. As Langer and Zasloff (1970) argued in their early study of the relationship:

> Our investigation shows that in virtually every important field of Lao Communist development the North Vietnamese have played a critical role. They are largely responsible for selecting the Lao Communist leadership. . . The DRV also has provided facilities and guidance for the training and political indoctrination not only of the top leadership but almost the entire cadre structure of the Lao Communists. (Only a very small group, by contrast, has received training in the Soviet Union and Communist China). North Vietnamese have helped these cadres construct an army, a bureaucracy, a Marxist-Leninist party, and political and mass organizations, all based on the DRV model (1970: 173).

Analyses of Laos that were produced by Lao communists before the foundation of the LPDR were modeled on those produced by the Vietnamese.[4] After 1975 the Vietnamese not only continued to provide key advice on the structure of government, defence, education, and research, but Hanoi was a key destination for higher education, especially in the fields of social science and of ethnography.[5]

Nevertheless, there is one perplexing issue in this question of master-apprentice relationships within the communist movement, which is that the Vietnamese were in turn the apprentices of the Soviet Union, and to a lesser degree of China, just as the latter was to some extent an apprentice of the Soviet Union as well. As one Chinese ethnographer explained to Greg Guldin, "Soviet ethnography was 'swallowed whole'. . . because 'in the early 1950s we didn't know which road to follow, we followed the USSRs lead'" (Guldin 1992: 136). There is no equivalent study of the influence of Soviet ethnography in Vietnam, though it is clear that it played an important role in the training of ethnographers and in providing a theoretical framework. A key Vietnamese text, *What Is Ethnology?*, for example, contains "important articles from the Soviet Encyclopedia" (Le 1972: 10). The theoretical straightjacket of Marxist-Leninist theory as it had developed in the Soviet Union and the practice of the Stalinist state ensured that ethnographic theory and practice in all these societies was dogmatic and uninventive. The other straightjacket, of course, was nationalism, and it was this that inflected ethnography in either a Chinese or Vietnamese, or later Lao, direction.

Ethnographers in each of these countries were, of course, subject to the vicissitudes of politics,[6] but they all saw their work as subordinate to the developmental interests of the state and nationalism, and they all shared an evolutionist paradigm, and an interest in origins. Le Van Hao explains the role of Vietnamese ethnographers:

> To ethnology, an important branch of the social sciences, the task falls of studying the formation and development of ethnic groups and the characteristics of their material and cultural life in order to bring out their best traditions, reveal backward survivals so as to eliminate them step by step, contribute to the reformation and promotion of ethnic societies, strengthen union and solidarity between ethnic groups as well as national pride. (Le 1972: 9–10)

The stress on solidarity and national unity among minorities is a leitmotif of Vietnamese ethnography. Nationalism and a Marxist-inspired interest in evolutionism unleashed, however, a specifically Sinitic interest in lineage and a desire to locate the origins of the Vietnamese in deepest depths of historical time. Thus, in combination, the various social sciences in Vietnam concluded:

> The aboriginal Viet ethnic group was formed specifically in North Viet Nam . . . its presence on Indochinese soil did not result from any massive immigration. It may even take pride in the fact that its homeland was one of the cradles of mankind as evidenced by bones and other very ancient vestiges . . . (Le 1972: 24–5).

This conclusion was an outcome, no doubt, of Vietnam's perennial desire to differentiate itself from its northern neighbor, China, who also claims a "continuous history" stretching back thousands of years. Besides allowing the Vietnamese to differentiate themselves from the Chinese, this conclusion also ensured that none of the minorities could make a clear claim to predating the ethnic Vietnamese (dubbed Kinh by ethnographers) in the region. Similar imperatives among Lao ethnographers and historians have been dogged by the commonly held belief that the Tai-Lao migrated from the north and displaced the indigenous Austroasiatic groups. This was encoded, among other things, in the rituals of royalty in Laos (Evans 1998). The idea that the Lao are "invaders" produces a sort of frisson in discussion of these matters (much as discussion of the Cham does with the Vietnamese, or of the Tibetans among the Chinese), and consequently in recent years a counter-discourse which claims that the Lao were always there has emerged, although this is not yet well articulated.[7] On the other hand, the Lao also need to distinguish themselves from the Thai, but they do this more easily by asserting that they are the "older brother" of the Thai.[8] By comparison with the Lao, the overwhelming numerical dominance of the

ethnic Vietnamese in Vietnam, and their belief in their historical claim to
the territory, has imbued their ethnographers with a feeling of confidence in
the correctness of their research aims. This was further buttressed by a
Confucian scholastic tradition and a well-developed intelligentsia. By the
time the Lao revolutionaries came to power the Vietnamese had a well-
entrenched ethnographic establishment eager to impart its wisdom to its
one keen apprentice.

THE BEGINNINGS OF LAO COMMUNIST ETHNOGRAPHY

BEFORE 1975 there were no Lao communist ethnographies of minorities.
The only studies that existed were those done by Vietnamese who operated
in Laos during the war. The earliest of these dates from 1961 and is of the
striped Hmong of Sam Neua province (the base area of the Lao
Communists). Others were done, for example, on the Phu Tai, the Khmu,
the Loven, the Yao and so on, with at least fifty such studies of different
groups and areas being carried out by the Vietnamese up to 1975.[9] These
studies have later become a source of background information for young
Lao ethnographers.[10] These ethnographies were a kind of political
reconnaissance vital for the carrying out of guerrilla warfare, a lesson that
the Vietnamese learned in their early days (MacAlister 1967). The Lao
interest in minorities was primarily political too and the Neo Lao Hak Sat
(NLHS), the communist popular front organization, stressed the importance
of inter-ethnic solidarity in its propaganda and attempted to recruit
minority cadres. This, however, was not complemented by Lao studies of
minorities.

   After the revolution, a Committee for Nationalities headed by the
Hmong, Niahvu Lobliayao, was established in 1976 as part of the NLHS,
which became the Neo Lao Sang Sat (NLSS, Lao Front for National
Reconstruction) in 1979. However, the importance of studying minorities
was not clearly recognized until 1981 in an important speech by the Lao
party leader, Kaysone Phomvihane, which is presented and discussed in
another section below. This speech would provide Lao ethnographers with a
rationale for their métier and for the establishment of the Institute of
Ethnography in 1988 within the Committee for Social Sciences, which
began under the directorship of Sisana Sisane in 1985. In his speech
Kaysone says: "During the revolutionary process, the various minorities
who had chosen to come together with each of the other groups in the Lao
nation for political reasons had always been called the lowland Lao
nationality, Lao Loum (ຊົນຊາດລາວລຸ່ມ) the midlands nationality, Lao Theung
(ຊົນຊາດລາວເທິງ), and the highlands nationality, Lao Soung (ຊົນຊາດລາວສູງ).

Central Committee members should, however, come together with officials in various positions and with minority cadres so that they can together research and discover what is the proper way to call the various groups and to make a list of the various groups which make up the country" (1982: 47). This task finally fell to the Institute of Ethnography.

At the time of his speech several young Lao were in the process of studying ethnography in Hanoi. Many of them were refugees from the fighting and aerial bombing which had raged across Xieng Khouang and Sam Neua in the north, or Saravane in the south, during the war. They had been taken to Vietnam as young boys (around twelve years of age) and began their studies in Vietnamese schools.[11] They were drawn from the various ethnic groups, which made up those provinces and included Hmong, Black Tai, and so on. Having finished high school these young Lao nationals had to decide what to do next. It was not, however, for them to decide freely. One person who is today an ethnographer, wished to study to be a motor mechanic in the Soviet Union. However, trips to the Soviet Union were reserved for the well-connected offspring of the communist hierarchy, and so he was directed into ethnography because he was a "minority." He studied ethnography at Hanoi University, along with others who had been set on the same "career path," and then later did some post-graduate work under the tutelage of the Committee of the Social Sciences in Hanoi. Such committees had been modeled on similar bodies first established in the Soviet Union and then in China, and would be copied by Laos belatedly in 1985. (Such cloning is typical of Marxist-Leninist systems).[12] The committee grouped together institutes of history, geography, literature, linguistics, area studies, and ethnography, among others. Lao in Hanoi were allocated to these various institutes in order to become the cadre of a similarly structured institution in Laos.

One important figure in the development of Lao ethnography and linguistics was Professor Pham Duc Duong, director of the Institute for Southeast Asian Studies since the mid-1980s. Not suprisingly, he had been a soldier in Laos in the late 1950s and early 1960s, where he had learned Lao and developed an interest in linguistics. A perk of having served one's country was to gain access to higher education, which Pham Duc Duong did, and he went on to study linguistics, and in particular the place of Vietnamese within Southeast Asian linguistics (e.g. Pham 1991). His interest in Laos ensured that he would be the supervisor of several Lao graduates. Other key figures were Professor Dang Nghiem Van who had done studies of the Tai and Khmu in Vietnam, and Cam Trong who had worked on his own ethnic group, the Black Tai and also assisted Dang Nghiem Van with his research on Tai.

I have described the nature of Vietnamese anthropology in detail elsewhere (Evans 1985; Evans 1992). It is only important here to reiterate that Vietnamese ethnographers subscribed to a basically nineteenth-century Marxist evolutionary view of social structures which allowed them to align themselves with the evolutionary views of the state which was marching towards its endpoint, communism. This allowed these ethnographers, with a sense of rectitude, to define some social, economic, or cultural practices as "backward," or as "superstitious," and therefore reasonably (from the point of view of the state) suppressed.[13] It also provided simplistic class analyses of precapitalist social structures. But given the absence of room for theoretical innovation, a great deal of their effort went into categorizing and providing selective descriptive ethnographies of the various minority groups in Vietnam. The intellectually much less well-formed young Lao were in no position to contradict this approach, and they embraced it without modification.

The director of the Institute of Ethnography in Vientiane when it was established in 1988 was Khambay Nhoundalat, a Makong from central Laos. He studied ethnography in Hanoi from 1969–73, and was the first Lao national to graduate. He then went to the USSR for further studies, which he did not finish because of ill health. On his return he worked with the NLSS on minority issues. A further three students studied ethnography at Hanoi University between 1979–1983. They were, Somthone Lobliayao, a Hmong, Khampheng Thipmuntali, a White Tai, and Khamsao, a Hmong. Two Khmu, Souksavang Simana and Sinsay Keomanivong, both of whom had studied literature, one in Hanoi and the other in the USSR, and graduated in 1973, were recruited into the institute to study folklore and literature. A philologist and sociologist was also recruited, a Lao who had graduated in the USSR in 1986, Khambay Khamsy. Khamdeng Kommadam a Ta-Oi from southern Laos studied some ethnography in Vietnam, and then worked with the Nationalities Committee. In the institute he worked on an ethnolinguistic map based on the 1985 census. Not all the students who studied ethnography went into the institute. Others were recruited into the NLSS at the provincial level on their return, while one Hmong woman Viengmala, who completed her studies also in 1983, teaches history and ethnography at the National University in Vientiane.[14]

When the Lao students returned to Laos they took with them not only their educational formation, but also Vietnamese texts to guide them. After all, there were no such texts available in Laos,[15] and so these texts became the models from which the Lao worked when they began to construct an ethnic map of Laos or engage in fieldwork. I recall vividly a young returnee carrying out fieldwork among the Black Tai in Houaphan province working directly from a book on the Black Tai of Vietnam written by Cam Trong. Cam Trong's work is a rather idealized and schematized view of the Tai, mixed with some fairly dubious readings (or confusions) of myth and history. My Lao colleague could not fit his field subjects in Houaphan with the model and exposition he found in Cam Trong's book, which led him not to doubt the book but to declare that the Black Tai in Laos were "losing their culture." Of course, this latter statement may be true only in the sense that it indicates social and cultural change in these communities, but this was not something that interested him. Indeed, in the "Vietnamese ethnographic model" one is presented with generalized static and often idealized descriptions, of a particular ethnic group's traditional economy, society, religion, material culture, etc., and then often a brief section is added at the end which suddenly shifts its register to the present and claims are made that the best features of the culture in question are being preserved under socialism, now that feudal and imperialist shackles have been cast aside. This ending, however, has become less obligatory in the 1990s. The idea of writing detailed analyses of villages is eschewed in favor of a general, "synthesized" description of a particular group. These studies provide neither functionalist analyses or analyses of social or cultural change, although descriptions of historical change are sometimes given.

From 1985 to 1988 three Vietnamese ethnographers were assigned to Laos to help lay the groundwork for the Lao Institute of Ethnography. They were Dang Ta Ngiem, from the Vietnamese Communist Party's Minorities Committee who advised the Lao on minorities policy, along with Dang Nghiem Van and Le Cu Nam from the Institute of Ethnography. Nguyen Duy Thieu replaced them as an expert from 1989–1991, and in their time there these ethnographers carried out fieldwork in conjunction with the Lao, and wrote papers with the aim of producing a joint general survey of minorities in Laos. The demise of the Institute of Ethnography in 1993 along with the CSS ensured that this never occurred. Just before the demise of the institute, however, Khamdeng and Khampheng produced a survey of minorities called oddly, "Tourist of Ethnic Groups in Laos."[16] In their introduction they announced that the institute had decided that Laos had forty-seven different ethnic minorities, and the authors presented these minorities under six general ethnolinguistic headings: Tai-Lao, Mon-Khmer, Hmong-Yao, Tibeto-Burman, Viet-Muong, and Han (Haw). Beyond this the reader is simply given a thumbnail sketch of the various groups under these headings, their population, and a brief description of their economy and customs (in some cases hardly even that). Only a monograph by Nguyen Duy Thieu that appeared in 1996 in Vietnamese attempts a more comprehensive and theoretically coherent survey.[17]

Following the dissolution of the institute its members were directed to join the NLSS, but three members, Khampheng, Somthone, and Souksavang, petitioned their superiors to be allowed to join the Institute of Culture in the Ministry of Information and Culture, and this institute along with the NLSS has since then been one of the main centers for the ongoing study of minorities, although no substantial studies have been published.[18] A few students have continued to go to Vietnam to study ethnography, but although there is ongoing contact between Vietnamese ethnographers and the Lao, the relationship has weakened considerably. Lao researchers would prefer to study in Thailand or overseas, but often they cannot because their undergraduate qualifications are not recognized. Yet the inflow of foreign scholars since the late 1980s has at least made them aware of the practice of anthropology outside the communist world.

THE KAYSONE GUIDELINES

THE most important document produced by the Lao communists after 1975 was a speech given by Kaysone Phomvihane on 15 June 1981, at the end of a ten-day meeting called to discuss minority problems. Later published as a booklet (Kaysone 1982) this has formed the basis for discussion of minority problems up to the present, and elicited a commentary by a Hmong member of the People's Assembly as recently as 1995 (Yiabaoleu 1995). It was this document which provided the guidance for Lao ethnographers in their research when it began in the 1980s. Little attention, however, has been given to this document by foreign commentators on Lao minority questions. For this reason I will set out its main arguments at length below for it is crucial for understanding indigenous perceptions of the aims of their research and actions.

Perhaps what is most striking about this document for any reader of it in the 1990s is its tone and emphasis. Not only are listeners to the speech throughout referred to as "comrades," the speech is also studded with references to the building of socialism and communism, and the Soviet Union is lauded as a successful example of minority policies. By comparison, the 1995 commentary alluded to above makes reference to socialism only once, and communism not at all, although references to a Marxist-Leninist state and theory are common, as they are in the original Kaysone document. Of course, Kaysone's speech was given only six years after the revolution and not only had the country encountered severe economic problems but the "red brotherhood" of communist states were fighting one another: Vietnam had overthrown the Pol Pot regime in

Kampuchea in late 1978, and China had conducted an intense border war in 1979 with Vietnam, the LPDR's close ally.[19] Paranoia about "reactionary" China's intentions pervade the text (we shall return to this), and he bursts out in an extraordinary claim about Chinese settlers colonizing Kampuchea in order to attack Vietnam (Kaysone 1982: 71), an allegation bandied about in Vietnam at the time as well. Such rhetoric has disappeared from contemporary commentary in Laos. What is perhaps the most embarrassing feature of Kaysone's exposition for his fans these days is that he continually holds up the Soviet Union as a model of correct ethnic relations. The chaotic collapse of Soviet communism was still nine years away!

Insecurity and an intense concern with internal "solidarity" were pervasive at that time. Furthermore, since 1975 the LPDR had faced a serious internal rebellion by Hmong,[20] and therefore Kaysone's speech pays special attention to the Hmong. Besides all these regional and internal problems, Kaysone's text is intent on giving an outline of Marxist-Leninist theory on nations, ethnicity, and so on, to serve as a basis for the state's cadres when dealing with the minorities. It is worth providing a translation and summary of his argument on these issues in order to capture its true flavor.

After his political introduction Kaysone begins to outline the "theory": After humanity first appeared, he says, they

> came together to make their lives on the basis of sharing the same blood, and worked together . . . They established a clan (ຕິກ) and tribal society . . . From one clan another separates off into 2 clans, and then into 4 clans, and so on. Each clan has a person who is the head, and when they all come together into a larger grouping we call it a tribe (ເຜົ່າ). A tribe is when many clans of the same blood come together out of necessity for their livelihood and production. Some people call this a clan alliance. These tribes work common land in the area in which they live. A single council commands each of them, and the council is made up of the various clan leaders, while the oldest person in the council is the leader of the tribe. (This is like the commune (ໝູ່ບ້ານ) in Laos) . . . . when productivity begins to progress, society then divides into classes, and in general clans-tribes etc. go into decline, and people have wider and more complex relationships than before, . . .and a new group of people come into existence, an ethnic (ເຊື້ອ) group.[21] Each ethnicity has a separate spoken language, but in each area they are not yet totally separate, but they finally become separate, and this is also because there are many ethnicities who move into new areas and

they become mixed up. The economy of these ethnic groups right up to now is self-sufficient, involving simple exchanges, and along with their culture has not progressed greatly . . . Ethnic groups first appeared in slave societies and were constant up to feudal societies in the history of humankind. Each ethnicity is perhaps the basis for the appearance of a nationality (ຊາດ). This was true for Austria, Hungary, Russia, etc. . . . There may be cases where a specific ethnicity is slowly able to establish a harmonious relationship with other ethnic groups, and step by step are able to share language and thinking and economy, and they become a nationality. This is the case with various ethnic groups who have come together to progress towards the establishment of a nation, or through their collective resistance to foreign invaders during the feudal period, such as in Vietnam. This is also the case for the various ethnic groups in colonies who come together to fight imperialism . . . Thus, we can say that a nationality is a group of related people with continuous relations who have been created by history, according to their basic characteristics such as their spoken language family, their shared land area, their way of living, and their way of thinking which is shown in their ancestral culture . . . Ethnic groups also share these four aspects, but not as strongly. To strengthen the independence of a nationality one has to strengthen these four aspects . . . Race (ເຊື້ອຊາດ) is very different from nationality. A race shares general external characteristics (such as, hair, eyes, nose, lips, skin, etc.). The specific aspects of race are due to their developing in separate physical areas . . . Humanity is separated into three main races. [These, however, have become interbred over time]. Today in the world there are around 150 races. They may be gathered in one nation, or be a nation, but probably there are 2 or 3 different races in a nation. According to the views of a Marxist-Leninist state, the various external characteristics mentioned earlier have no importance for the people's level of competence. A nation (ປະຊາຊາດ) is very different from race and nationality. A nation is a gathering together of people of different ancestral origins but who have the same historical destiny. They have chosen to settle down in the same region, they have the same system of administration, have a constitution and laws, which are one. A nation may have only one nationality within it (such as Korea, the German Democratic Republic, Japan . . .); another nation may have many nationalities or many ethnicities (such as many countries in Asia and Africa). [A discussion of social class follows.] In every nation which has many nationalities the controlling class will come from the nationality which has progressed most quickly by oppressing the working people of all nationalities, the ethnicity that progresses slowly, which happens to all those developing small nationalities, have to struggle against the oppression of the larger ones . . . the real cause of nationality problems is social class . . . Each social class has their own aims and outlook and we need to realise this if we are to understand nationality problems . . . the capitalists have divided the world into two types of nationality, such as the ruling nationality and the slave nationality. They think that the ruling nationality is "precious and brilliant" (ປະຊົດເລີດລ້ຳ), and are the representatives of all that is "civilized," as for the slave nationalities they are "low and backward," and not able to be civilized . . .[22]

By contrast, he says, the socialist countries respect equality and unlike the imperialists and feudalists they promote solidarity rather than policies of divide and rule.

Moving to the difficult question of peoples who come from outside the current state borders, he argues that Russians who moved to Hungary, Poland, or other parts of Europe many years ago are no longer of Russian nationality.

In Asia we have Tai, Lue, Hmong, Yao . . . who have come to settle in Laos, Vietnam, Thailand and China. Or, we have Khmers in Kampuchea and in Vietnam but they are different ethnic and national groups. All of these ethnic groups and nationalities mentioned, although each formerly had a single common origin, since the time nations were created or after large migrations, have found themselves living in a given country and so they have a new history, and have become a separate ethnicity or nationality . . . (Kaysone 1982: 38–9).

The issue is, of course, how to create a sense of national unity. At the center of this must stand the ethnic Tai-Lao (ເຜົ່າໄທລາວ) because they are not only the largest group in the country and are found as a majority in almost every district, but they also have the "highest cultural development" (47). Therefore, "Lao culture must be the basic culture shared by all the ethnicities, and must be the one to provide the connections for the exchange of culture between all the ethnicities; spoken and written Lao is the common language and written Lao is the regular writing of all the ethnic groups;[23] nevertheless, each ethnic group should still preserve its spoken language, and their separate customs" (49). In what is perhaps his most radical suggestion in the whole speech, Kaysone recommends that cadres working in minority regions should try to learn the languages of the groups there (65). Needless to say, however, there is little evidence of this ever transpiring.

Kaysone's arguments are heavily indebted to both Soviet and Vietnamese theorizing, but there are significant shifts of emphasis and we shall now turn to one area in which the Lao chose not to be, or were not required to be, apprentices.

AUTONOMOUS ZONES

THE most obvious departure from Vietnamese, and indeed Soviet and Chinese practice, by the Lao communists is the absence of autonomous regions for minorities. In the nominally federalist structure of the Soviet Union the constituent states and minorities had a (theoretical) right to secede. Debates concerning federalism died an early death in the Chinese republican movement,[24] and lingered on briefly among the Chinese communists in the 1930s. In Vietnam it was part of the program of the Indochinese Communist Party. In 1935 the ICP stated that:

> each nationality will have the right to self-determination, i.e. to choose between adhering to the Union of Indochinese Soviet Republics [so-called French Indochina then comprised the 3 states of Vietnam, Cambodia, and Laos.[25]] and proclaiming itself an independent state . . . all nationalities will be free either to adhere to the Union of Soviet Republics or to leave it, and that the more important nationalities should not impose their will. Each nationality of the Union will enjoy, in addition, the right to autonomy, that is the right to solve local affairs, to use its mother tongue in its political, economic and cultural life, and to choose its own leaders in political and economic affairs. (cited in Viet 1968: 12)

The imprint of early Russian communism is stamped all over this programmatic statement.[26] The genesis of this policy lies in the weakness of the Bolshevik regime when it seized power in 1917. Faced by White forces who wanted to restore the unitary imperial Czarist state they proclaimed a policy of national self-determination which was aimed at neutralizing any support the Whites could gain from the minority areas in which they were operating. But important qualifications were immediately added, stressing the "class" nature of the policy. That is, only if the "toiling masses" (through the party which represented their interests best, of course) demanded separation would it be granted, leaving open a door for denouncing all forms of alleged "bourgeois nationalism." Furthermore, socialism was thought to transcend nationalism and therefore the latter was subordinate to the former. The Third International was supposedly an expression of this transcendence, but it too grew out of the weakness of the early, internationally isolated, Bolshevik regime. The latter called for the "self-determination" of all colonial peoples, and it was this cry which struck a chord among the likes of Ho Chi Minh, Mao Zedong, and many others. The "right to self-determination" became a centerpiece of communist propaganda and won support for Lenin and the USSR in the colonial world.

The very idea of self-determination for so-called national minorities always sat uneasily with the Chinese communists who held strongly to an idea of a unitary China. Early in the 1930s they were already attacking the Kuomintang (KMT) for their territorial concessions to the Japanese and failure to defend the imperial borders. Yet, they also had to raise support from the minorities because they often found themselves confined to these regions, and hence also proclaimed that they supported self-determination. In the face of a KMT opponent that was an unambiguous proponent of a unitary China, the ambiguity of communist pronouncements up until they seized power ensured them some minority support. They sustained the ambiguity in their own minds by saying that the minorities would "voluntarily" adhere to the Chinese state. But once they had taken power they made it clear that territories like Tibet or Inner Mongolia would not have the right to secede, although they claimed they would have "equality" and "regional autonomy."

The Vietnamese were no less troubled by the demands of communist orthodoxy concerning self-determination, and no less committed to the idea of a unitary state. The aim of an Indochina-wide republic faded away (Goscha 1995). The fact that the constitution proclaimed by the communists when they seized power for the first time in 1945 contained no provision for autonomous regions made apparent the fact that they had no clear place in Vietnamese communist thinking. Indeed, the regions that were established after 1954 were proclaimed by decree and did not gain a place in the constitution until 1961. The prominence given to minorities in Vietnamese propaganda, however, grew out of their need to gain their support in the mountainous base areas from which the communists operated.[27] After victory in the north, the establishment of autonomous regions was held out as a promise to the minorities of the central highlands in the south. This promise was quickly dashed in 1976 when, following the "unification" of the country, such zones were said to be no longer necessary and were, moreover, abolished in the north.

The idea of autonomous regions for minorities emerged as a reluctant concession to Marxist-Leninist nationalities theory in these states which were clearly dominated by one ethnic group—the Han in the case of China, the Kinh in the case of Vietnam. They were effectively abolished in China during the bout of Han national chauvinism that exploded during the

Cultural Revolution of the 1960s, only to be restored in the early 1980s (Hsieh 1989) because of the tremendous damage and division caused by the actions of the Red Guards during that time. Some minor concessions have been granted to these minority cultures, and they have often been spared from the full force of collectivization drives, or in the case of China, the one-child policy. Nevertheless, these autonomous areas remained in the firm grip of the communist party, and therefore under the clear control of the dominant ethnic group.

Kaysone and his comrades, on the other hand, are acutely aware that the ethnic Lao do not constitute such an overwhelming majority in Laos. Kaysone's sensitivity is seen by the fact that he quotes a foreign journalist (unidentified) who repeats an oft heard cliché about Laos that, because it has so many ethnic minorities it does not really constitute a proper nation (1982: 58). Kaysone sees this as imperialist propaganda aimed at undermining national solidarity in Laos. His is not a considered theoretical response to such claims because, of course, Kaysone the nationalist takes the naturalness of the Lao nation as an established fact. But what I think is also clear is that Kaysone and the LPRP were under no pressure from the Vietnamese to adopt a policy of autonomous regions. Indeed, given the ethnic distribution in Laos and the relative weakness of the state, they would have been seen as a potential source of weakness and division. The rapid abolition of these zones in Vietnam in 1976 thereby placed both parties back in step with one another again. Speaking directly to the problem of autonomous zones in his 1981 speech Kaysone says "the views of our party have been for a long time that it is not necessary to have these for minorities in our country" (1982: 69). Besides the reasons suggested above, the need for solidarity and fears of fragmentation, Kaysone had claimed several times in his speech that nowhere in Laos did any ethnic group have an area all to itself, and therefore it had no basis for autonomy. This claim, of course, sidesteps the fact that this was also true of the autonomous regions that were set up in Vietnam. He also refers to attempts by "reactionaries" to "encourage some ethnicities to create self-governing regions of ethnicities such as an autonomous region for the Lue, the Hmong . . . in order to break them away from the lineage of the Lao nation . . ." (1982: 60). Not only is he referring here to Lao and Hmong exile groups in Thailand, but in particular to China whose autonomous regions, he claims, "are merely pretentious hollow structures to show off to the outside, that's all" (1982: 71). Kaysone's special sensitivity to China at this time comes no doubt from his understanding of communist tactics *vis-à-vis* minorities in the Lao revolution whereby the Vietnamese often chose their advisers in Laos from among minorities who straddled their borders, such as the Black Tai or Hmong. Kaysone was acutely aware of Chinese attempts at the time to use minorities straddling their borders in order to foment unrest in Laos, or in Vietnam, and step by step undermine them. Of course, this was not successful, but his emphasis on this problem brings into an unusually sharp focus the communist political understanding of minorities and their role.

TRIBALISM, CULTURE, AND NATIONALISM

BENEDICT Anderson (1987) has written about how the colonial state was the first to carry out thoroughgoing censuses of the populations of Southeast Asia, systematizing ideas of ethnicity, and indeed creating such groups and politicizing them. His polemical zeal, however, identifies this with only the Western colonial state whereas I think it is historically more accurate to associate these characteristics with the modern nationalist state first and foremost, of which the European colonial state was one incarnation, carrying the practices of this modern form into areas where they previously did not exist. Communist states have embraced the panoptic categorizing zeal of the modern state and carried it to new heights. The intellectual framework generated by this zeal would inform Vietnamese and Lao practice, therefore we turn briefly to an examination of some of the background assumptions of ethnicity.

In discussions of the highland ethnic groups of Laos and Vietnam there is, in reality, a great deal of overlap and confusion between the concepts of tribe and the concept of ethnicity. Indeed, this confusion bleeds into discussions of ideas of the nation. Such confusion, however, is not exclusive to this region but is commonplace,[28] and is built into the parallel histories of nationalism and the concept of culture as shall be argued further on. When the French first started surveying the region they were still influenced by the nineteenth century evolutionist ideas of Morgan in which the tribe was thought to stand at one of humanity's earliest evolutionary stages. As such, tribes were believed to possess a common territory, a name, common language, common religious beliefs, and some kind of chiefly structure of government. This dogma later fed into communist ethnography generally, through the medium of Engels. The evolutionary theme informs Kaysone's exposition, and he basically adheres to the above criteria for a tribe as well. Interestingly, he claims that ethnic groups emerged under systems of slavery and feudalism (i.e. state systems) as a more general group consciousness emerges, and this later forms the basis of a national consciousness. It should also be said that the concept of the tribe has played an important role in Western anthropology as well, although its significance has declined in recent decades and been displaced by the notion of ethnicity. That is, people who formerly would have been called a tribe are now usually called an ethnic group. Whatever the shifts, however, underlying both the concept of the tribe and that of ethnicity is often a primordialist view of culture as a clearly bounded unit according to criteria similar to that outlined long ago by Morgan. The conceptual framework used to study highland minorities in both Laos and in Vietnam most closely approximates that of the tribe.[29]

Systematic critiques of this concept began to appear in the late 1960s (Helm 1968), and it was subject to a book-length critique by Fried (1975) whose basic thesis was:

> I regard the tribe mainly as a "secondary" phenomenon. While some of its manifestations go back five millenia or more to the appearance of the earliest states, the major locus of tribal formation has been in the period of European colonialism and imperialism. The process of creation of the tribe resembles that of the caste, the minority, and the ethnic group (Fried 1975: 10).

And further on: "Secondary tribalism is a political phenomenon bearing little or no resemblance to conventional notions of tribal behavior. It occurs, as already indicated, largely as a reaction to one or more states" (Fried 1975: 103).[30] As he indicates, the Chinese empire in order to control its frontier regions in the southwest would elevate individuals to positions as "tribal headmen" *tu-si*, a position not part of the preexisting structure. The Vietnamese court did this too, elevating *tho-thi* among the Tay groups on its northern frontier. More-or-less distant relationships between central courts and highland peoples, all modeled on an idea of tributary relations, can be found across mainland Southeast Asia, from the relations with the ethnic Jarai shamans, the "King of Fire" and the "King of Water," by the Cham kingdom and the Khmer kingdom, to those between the Champassak or Louang Prabang courts in Laos and the surrounding highland groups. These fairly fluid relationships were transformed by European colonialism, which brought with it foreign notions of nationalism and of fixed borders and allegiances, and officials who were armed with the anthropological idea of discrete cultures.[31] Indeed, the early practice of French ethnography would have a profound impact on the shape of Vietnamese ethnography.

But one can also see the influence on contemporary Vietnamese ethnographers of a prior tradition, inherited from the Confucian state, of describing barbarians on the periphery (see, for example, Voth 1971). The Confucian concern with rectification of names[32] (that is, the idea that a name somehow expresses an essence) is here boosted by the bureaucratic state's passion for naming and a positivist obsession with classification. This tendency was strong in Vietnamese publications, where the job of the ethnographer was to establish the "true" name and "true" characteristics of the various groups. The last official approved list of fifty-four names for ethnic groups was completed in 1979 and is used in official documents. By the mid-1980s, however, some ethnographers were able to pay attention to debates among anthropologists in liberal democracies and began to develop a more textured view. In an article on ethnonyms by Dang Nghiem Van (1991), we see him wrestling with the older idea of "true" names, while at the same time this article is an interesting survey of the many and various names by which different groups in Vietnam and in Laos have been known over time. On the one hand he wishes to argue that "everyone must agree that we should respect the self-called names of the ethnicities" ((3): 61). Yet, "we should motivate them and educate them to voluntarily accept the most correct name among the many names their ethnicity is having, in conformity with scientific research" ((3): 64). The need for the state to induce them to accept such a name is, however, not questioned.

The process of tribalization or ethnicization in Laos had its premodern precursors, as has already been suggested with reference to Champassak and Louang Prabang. More specifically, one can see it in the case of the Hmong who after they moved into the Tai Phuan principality in Xieng Khouang were integrated into it through the latter's appointment of Hmong Kaitong (canton chiefs), a system that was taken over by the French, while being centralized a little. A Hmong revolt which swept through northern Laos and Vietnam between 1919–21 alerted the French to the fact that they were imposing ethnic Lao laws and customs on the Hmong, and others, and therefore the administrateur des services civils en Indochine, Bathelemy, recommended a decentralization of administration to cater to these ethnic groups. As Savina wrote at the time: "The Government of the Protectorat has decided that the Miao (Hmong) race will no longer depend on any other race. The Miao will administer themselves in the future, like the Laotians, the Thô and the Annamites under the surveillance of the Government of the Protectorat. . ." (cited in Yang Dao 1972: 60). Called "divide and rule" by communist nationalists, such policies certainly heightened a sense of Hmong ethnic distinctiveness within a wider political universe. This is not the place to attempt a history of the process of ethnicization of the Hmong, or any other group in Laos. But it is certain that the prominence of Hmong leader Touby Ly Fong in the Royal Lao Government, and of the charismatic general Vang Pao, produced a growing sense of a distinct Hmong political identity.[33]

Prior to the revolution the NLHS used to claim that Laos had 68 ethnicities grouped under three broad "nationalities"—the Lao Loum, Lao Theung, and Lao Soung. Immediately after the revolution Lao researchers, with Vietnamese and Soviet assistance, attempted to gather information on minorities from every province and reported back to the central political department that there were 260 groups in Laos according to local names. The next systematic attempt by the LPDR to discover the ethnic makeup of the whole population was the census of 1983–85. This, however, produced the alarming result of 820 self-named ethnic groups. The results of this census have never been made public for analysis, but it was studied by the former Vietnamese expert in Laos, Le Cu Nam (1990). In a style similar to Dang Nghiem Van's, he notes the wide variety of names according to topography, place-names, mispronunciations of ethnonyms, color of costumes, the name of a patriarch of great prestige in an area, and so on. Such anarchy was unacceptable to the modern bureaucratic imagination, and so the Lao Institute of Ethnography was given the task of creating a more "rational" list, and they did this largely by accepting the broad ethnolinguistic categories used by the Vietnamese ethnographers:[34] Lao-Thai, Mon-Khmer, Hmong-Yao, Tibeto-Burman, Viet-Muong, and Han. In 1990 Khambay Nhoundalat, the director of the institute, came up with a list of thirty-eight groups, and it provides the basic categories for Nguyen Duy Thieu's (1996: 34–40) classification, where, alongside each "basic" category he lists a large number of so-called "localized" names. I have already referred to the publication by two members of the institute, Khamdeng and Khampheng (1992), which for the first time provides a list of forty-seven "basic" categories, and it is this "rationalized" list that provided the forty-seven ethnic categories for the 1995 census. (It is important to note that this list did not include other "minorities" who fall under the category of nationalities, such as Chinese, Vietnamese, Thai, or Indian).

An intriguing article in the LPRP's journal, *Aloun Mai*, by Daenjaleunsouk in 1993 provides perhaps the most intellectually challenging article in Lao concerning the problems of classification. He begins by noting that during the revolution the leadership, in conjunction with Vietnamese advisers, had divided the population into three large nationalities (ຊາວຊົນວຊາດໃຫຍ່) for the purposes of political mobilization. He then notes the various problems which have been encountered in developing an adequate system of categorization since 1975, and the ambiguities in the statements from the 4th and 5th Party Congresses (respectively 1986 and 1991) concerning the population being divided in three large ethnicities (ຊາວຊົນເຜົ່າໃຫຍ່). Why the change? he asks various "comrades," who respond: "To speak of three large ethnicities or three large nationalities is to mean the same thing . . ." (1993: 42). This, however, does not accord with the strict definitions provided by Marxist-Leninist theory, says the author. He then states the four conditions for a nationality: a common language, shared common territory, shared basic culture and personality, and a shared economy and market. He claims that these characteristics are only found in those countries which have been capitalist, not in countries like Laos which are "backward" and have been subject to "feudalism," and so the four requisite features are found in form only. He then tries to formulate the criteria for an ethnicity, and he comes up with three: shared language and culture (as for a nationality), and also a shared territory, but in this case he does not add in brackets as he does for nationality *Pathet Louam*, i.e. a shared country, but adds instead "this doesn't mean that an ethnicity must have an exclusive territory, but may share it with other ethnicities" (1993: 43). Interestingly, he also raises the problem of ethnically mixed marriages and says that a child may voluntarily adopt one or the other ethnicity. Equally interestingly, he engages in some quite atypical polemicizing with the Ministry of Education over their inaccurate use of ethnic categories in a geography text, and the inaccurate naming of ethnic groups contained in a book by an important monk, Bouakham Volaphet. He criticizes others for using pejorative names and still others for speaking loosely of "Lao Theung language, middle Lao language, Lao Soung language, etc" (1993: 45), none of which exist. Some cadres, he writes, have tried to propose using Khmu as a Lao Theung language, but he points out this language is unintelligible to so-called Lao Theung in the south, and so on. He argues that among neither the Lao Theung nor Lao Soung are there shared customs, or a shared language and that is why Tai-Lao has to be the common language. He concludes by saying that the idea of three large nationalities or three large ethnicities does not accord with "ethnographic science," and therefore in the "territory of the LPDR there is only one nationality, the Lao, as well as many ethnicities, and among each of these they have specific features, such as language and culture" (1993: 47). This conclusion is, I believe, the *de-facto* position of the LPRP and its functionaries. The collapsing of Lao as an ethnicity and Lao as a nationality naturally reinforces the cultural dominance of the Lao, as well as their social, economic and political dominance within Laos.

Ethnologists in these countries may have constructed an idea of Lao ethnicity as distinct from Lao nationality, just as the Vietnamese have with the ethnic concept of Kinh or the Chinese with the concept Han, but existentially and practically none of these majority groups separate the two ideas in their minds nor think of themselves as an ethnic group in the common use of the term which connotes minority, "backwardness," and so on. This is despite the fact that some publications on ethnicity include references to the dominant group, and despite the fact that the census has a category under ethnicity for Lao.[35] Consequently, discussions of ethnicity in Laos at the official level, while they often imply a Lao inclusion in the idea of ethnicity, invariably make it clear that it is the "ethnic minorities" who are being referred to. For example, a recent major restatement of party policies, in its section on ethnicity, refers to "supporting and developing the minority areas" (PCPC 1997: 251). Furthermore, as this publication demonstrates, the language of "three large nationalities" or "three large ethnicities," of Lao Loum, Lao Theung, Lao Soung, has dropped out of most official publications (e.g. it is not used in the new constitution proclaimed in 1991), and only the idea of Laos as a country with many ethnicities is underlined, with the Tai-Lao ethnicity remaining as its implicit or explicit core.[36]

However, as I argue in the introduction to this book, the category Tai-Lao often used in these contexts by either Kaysone or other officials in Laos, is a problematic ethno–linguistic category. Its origins in part lie in the fact that French ethnography worked its way across to Laos through the upland regions of the former Sipsong Chau Tai. And so, to give a somewhat extreme example, if one examines the *Cours d'ethnographie indochine* by Bonifacy (1919) the Lao are completely submerged among the Sinicized Tai. But from very early on the French had categorized the population in Laos into "the Thays," "the khas," and recent immigrants, such as the Hmong and Yao, a tripartite schema that found one expression in early Lao communist "nationalities" propaganda. Meyer in 1930 would describe the "Thaïs Laos" as "numerically the true masters of Laos" (1930: 24), and used the tripartite schema, but also adds a category for immigrants such as the Chinese, Siamese, Vietnamese, or Europeans. Interestingly, during roughly the same period the extraordinary missionary figure based in Kengtung, Burma, William Clifton Dodd, was carrying out his own research to prove that his mission stood at the door of a much larger Tai-speaking population (Swanson 1990). In what would become his very influential book, *The Tai Race* (1923), he used linguistic criteria to claim a cultural affinity across a diverse number of groups in Burma, Laos, China, and Vietnam. This would later provide fuel for the pan-Thai fantasies of the rightist regime in the Thailand in the late 1930s and early 1940s, but at a less spectacular level its basic premises were also asserted by the Lao communists, while making sure that the claim was not seen to encroach on the Tai of Vietnam—after all the French in the dying days of their colonial rule had attempted to set up a Tai federation in the parts of the old Sipsong Chau Tai which fell inside the Vietnamese border (Fall 1962; Connor 1984). The idea of a Tai-Lao cultural group would serve the Lao well as such a combination did indeed make them numerically superior in Laos. The political intent behind this seemingly neutral classification is, therefore, apparent.

Thus our attention is drawn back to the way these categories are constructed in the first place, and to what motivates their construction. What we find in the various discourses on ethnicity in the region are interpretations which wish to assert unity at one level (often a "deeper" one) and distinctiveness at another. Nowhere is this clearer than in Vietnamese ethnographic discourse. For example the last major compilation on minorities in Vietnam writes in its introduction:

> the cultural foundation of the different national elements on Vietnamese land, bears a deeper and deeper Vietnamese hallmark in the course of its development . . . It also reflects the most essential traits of the culture of each ethnicity . . . The manifestations of that cultural unity, which on the surface seem to be so different, are almost the same . . . Those "slight differences" only highlight the unified core, which serves as a basis on which the individual elements can develop" (Dang Nghiem Van et al. 1984: 12–13).

The so-called "unified core" is supplemented by a theory of a general "Austro-asian" culture spread across the Indochinese peninsula and Southeast Asia that is distinct from Han culture. In one move not only are the Vietnamese distinguished from the Han, but they are shown to share a deeper unity with all the minorities by virtue of their alleged participation in this "Austro-asian" culture, out of which is born the "community of the Vietnamese nation." The nationalist agenda that underpins all Vietnamese ethnography, therefore, could not be more transparent. Fundamental nationalist assertions such as these in both the Vietnamese and the Lao situations ensure that the dominant ethnic group is placed at the "unified core" around which more superficial ethnic variations revolve, for in the teleology of the nation they are imminently already *one* culture.

This further highlights an important peculiarity of communist nationalism in both Laos and in Vietnam (and one could add China). Smith in his various writings on nationalism has argued that there are two roads to nationalism: a civic nationalism which draws people together under one state as citizens regardless of ethnic affiliation, and an ethnic nationalism which mobilizes a heroic memory or myth of an ethnic group in order to elaborate its claim to nationhood.[37] I would like to argue that what we see in the case of nationalism in Laos, Vietnam, and China is a peculiar combination of both civic and ethnic nationalism. Due both to tactical constraints, and the demands of communist orthodoxy, they found themselves having to both elaborate and act on a version of civic nationalism (expressed as a "multinational" state), when in reality the fundamental motivation of nationalism in these countries was a form of ethnic nationalism, a fact which became increasingly apparent after their respective victories.

ANTHROPOLOGY IN LAOS

WHERE does this leave, firstly, the Lao anthropologist? Socialism as an economic system may have collapsed in Laos, but the same party and authoritarian political structure remains in place. This means that the published work of Lao ethnographers is subject to control and censorship by the party authorities and they are forced to conform to party dictates, which include the party's interpretation of what constitutes Lao nationalism. They are not free to take up the range of positions that one takes for granted within the world "community" of anthropologists.[38] I am not even certain that they would wish to, because much of this outside discourse takes place in terms that are unfamiliar, and with which they are only starting to become acquainted. By and large, they would be unsympathetic to current agnostic views towards nationalism found in anthropology elsewhere (views which inform this essay). Some align themselves more clearly with the developmentalist aims of the state than others, and therefore see their role in the party's terms as "making the life of the ethnic groups flourish, to create a life which is civilized, and to progress slowly towards doing away with customs which are backward" (PCPC 1997: 249), such as religious "superstitions," for example. A prevalent view is to see spirit worship among minorities as superstition, whereas similar practices among the Lao that are somehow incorporated under the umbrella of Buddhism are considered to be hallowed tradition. The less politicized individuals retreat into a form of simple descriptive ethnography of customs or material life, etc. While ethnographers in Laos and in Vietnam are looking for new directions,[39] it will be sometime before these feed through into practice and writing, and then they will still be confronted with restrictions on what they can say.

Among foreign anthropologists who have worked in the LPDR we find some who are closely aligned to the theoretical views which underlie the work of the Lao ethnographers to date. The study by Chamberlain et al. (1995), like the Lao researchers, adopts a grid of "ethnolinguistic superstocks" for purposes of classification. They write:

> This report will not engage in the current controversy being pursued by some anthropologists regarding the basis for classification. Our experience in Laos has been that wherever a group identifies itself as having a distinct ethnonym, there are always explicit linguistic features that accompany and

mark that distinction. Language, being an unconscious phenomenon, has internal consistencies in structure and the laws of sound change are regular and systematic. It is also the primary indicator of ethnic identity (as opposed to national identity with which it is sometimes confused). Hence the term "ethnolinguistic" which we feel provides the most reliable basis for identification and classification" (Chamberlain et al. 1995: 10).

The basic assumption of these writers is that culture and language are homologous. The very idea of "ethnolinguistic superstocks" (rather than, say, linguistic families) is most problematic, as it assumes cultural continuity across a whole linguistic family, whereas research done thirty years ago has already shown such an assumption to be very dubious (Hymes 1968), let alone more recent research (Hutton 1998; Enfield and Evans 1998). Despite the attractions of the hard edges of ethnolinguistic maps, they are cultural illusions.[40] Frank Proschan in a wonderfully textured article on ethnonyms among the Khmu has argued that because they designate "complex sociocultural situations, ethnic naming-systems are not likely to resemble the neat classificatory schemas that ethnoscientists and structural anthropologists have described for flora or fauna, kinship, color terms, or cultural artifacts . . . no classification of ethnic groups really satisfies such a definition, whether it be that of highland villagers or the census categories of modern nation-states or multilateral development agencies" (1997: 93). Through what is primarily a linguistic analysis he shows the highly contextual ways in which Khmu negotiate ethnic identity through their use of several cognitive models. His analysis demonstrates the barrenness of an older taxonomic imagination as represented by Chamberlain et al. and most Lao and Vietnamese communist ethnography to date.

But what are the attractions of this older taxonomic style of research? As has already been suggested, it has a history that is located in the positivistic worldview of colonialism and the emergent nationalist states. The likes of Chamberlain and others are enthralled by the scientistic claims of linguistics which assert not only an allegedly more scientific theoretical apparatus than the other social sciences, but that language is a more fundamental cultural reality than others—untenable propositions which cannot be argued here[41]—hence the importance of finding the "true" ethnonym. The similarity of this to the Confucian correction of names is not accidental, for the latter was crucially involved in the exercise of state power in the Chinese empire. It has continued in the PRC, and the "correction of names" in Laos or Vietnam is equally enmeshed in structures of power. Chamberlain and others would no doubt deny that their work directly contributes to the exercise of power because it is not their conscious intention. Nevertheless, the modern state's panoptic ambitions, and in its communist form its obligation to categorize its population according to ethnicity—to stamp it on an individual's identity card, and construct and carry out policies on this basis—make it clear that such categorization is not a politically neutral activity.

My argument here may seem to be at odds with what is occurring on the ground. That is, NGOs and foreign researchers appear to many Lao (officials in particular), to be too obsessed with minorities and their distinctiveness. Officials, especially those in charge of development projects, wish to stress the "unity" and "solidarity" of the Lao nation and that what is in the interests of one ethnic group is in the interests of all. The NGOs and others, however, are worried that the interests of the minorities are being overlooked in such projects. Therefore, in order to press their concerns, they often tend to essentialize ethnic identity (if not romanticize it).

Another outside source which has encouraged such ethnic essentialization has been UNESCO who, in 1993 sponsored a conference in Hanoi on the preservation of the "intangible cultural heritage" of the national minorities there, and two years later sponsored a similar conference in Vientiane on Lao ethnic groups. As Susan Wright has argued, "UNESCO, in its vision of a new ethical world order, maps out a world made of 'cultures' as discrete entities, without engaging with the issue of contestation over the power to define" (1998: 12). Indeed, at both of these conferences the UN officials "conspired" with the relevant ministries to ensure no discordant notes were struck at these conferences, and indeed the "programs for action" that emerged from them reinforced the Vietnamese and the Lao state's view of ethnicity.

But these examples simply demonstrate the degree to which ethnicity has become politicized—as if further illustrations were needed! Indeed, Fried many years ago, while arguing against naming as a "natural" guide to the existence of tribal or ethnic groups, sees the importance of this as political process. He writes: "This is not to question the use of names in the continual political process of affirmation and assertion of distinct character on the part of diverse population groups and aggregates at various levels of organizational complexity. The use of ancient names or the coining of new ones for this purpose is an aspect of the formation of tribes and ethnic groups as secondary phenomenon . . ." (Fried 1975: 38).[42] He devotes a whole chapter to the life-and-death importance of a codified tribal identity for American Indians making land claims before the US government's Indian Claims Commission (and the same is true for Australian aborigines).

Where, then, does that leave the study of ethnicity and of minorities?

Frank Proschan's study of the lability of ethnonyms[43] has provided one line
of march for future studies. In chapter 6 I try to capture the dynamics of
ethnic change in one part of the highlands, and there must be others now in
Laos working on such issues. Elsewhere this is certainly true. Nicholas
Tapp, with respect to the Hmong of China, has provided a compelling
argument against simplistic ideas of "Sinicization." He writes, for example,
of the practice of geomancy, *feng shui*, normally considered something that
the Hmong acquired from the Chinese. But for the Hmong it is "an
entirely Hmong practice, which just happens to be also practiced by the
Han Chinese and other neighbouring peoples . . ." (Tapp 1996: 83). He
continues:

> So the actual practice of *feng shui* by the Hmong demands an explanation of
> a completely different order to one merely couched in terms of
> "sinicization", the influence of one radically isolated cultural group upon
> another, or the influence of dominant literate models upon an oral
> tradition; an account which must be made in terms of local culture . . . Yet
> at the same time one must be aware of the way category of so-called "local
> beliefs" may actually be constructed by the terms of an official discourse, [a]
> kind of "folklorization" . . . An adequate account of cultural influences
> upon the Hmong must therefore recognize a wider Hmong ethnicity which
> extends into parts of Southeast Asia and at the same time fully take into
> account the context of "Chineseness" in which such processes of annotation
> and censorship might have happened in the Hmong use of "Chinese"
> geomancy (Tapp 1996: 83–4).

Thus Tapp highlights three coordinates: one localized, one located at the
level of the state ("Chineseness"), and another, "transnational," all of which
produce the complex outcome, Hmong ethnicity.[44] In a similar vein, one
may want to argue, in what sense is Buddhism or various Brahmanic
practices essentially Indian, rather than Thai or Lao or Khmer? Existentially
they are fundamental to these people's sense of ethnicity. If nothing else,
the sharedness of these cultural practices by all of these groups underlines
the fact that cultural boundaries are not necessarily linguistic ones.

As I have suggested in the introduction to this book, much theorizing to
date has been trapped, perhaps inevitably, in a web of nationalist
assumptions. And maybe we can only see this now that the "age of
nationalism" is on the wane (Hobsbawm 1992). The very concept of
culture, I suggest, arose in tandem with nationalist ideologies and they have
mutually influenced one another. From national context to national context
we find varying mixtures of assertions of both cultural primordialism and
constructivism in the creation of nationalist ideologies. Indeed, as Proschan

demonstrates, such a mixing of models can also be found in subnational
ethnic groups like the Khmu. In some cultures, however, such as those in
East Asia, strong primordialist "racial" sentiments are dominant, and this
sense of ethnicity feeds into their view of nationalism.[45] Anthropologists,
however, can only adopt a cultural constructivist view, and in doing so they
need to see beyond the modern state and its claim to be a bounded entity
and look at broader cultural unities and influences. In this respect some
Vietnamese attempts to unearth a broader culture area ("Austro-asian"), or
similar Lao attempts concerning the Tai (defined ethnolinguistically), are
flawed primarily by their nationalistic agenda. In the Vietnamese case it is
subordinate to the imperative of differentiating themselves from the
Chinese, and in the Lao case it arises from a deep-seated anxiety about
"national origins" and about the neighboring Thai.[46]

The way culture areas are defined is open to debate, but one thing has to
be clear: such definitions are provisional and primarily heuristic. By placing
particular ethnic groups within culture areas we are able to subvert or
qualify the hegemonic discourse of nationalism, just as a focus on locality or
context can do something similar. Through a combination of these levels of
analysis with the reality of the modern state we can hopefully achieve a
complex and dynamic understanding of ethnicity. Sensitivity to the
complexities of ethnic identity and to the different levels at which notions
of identity or matters of cultural similarity or difference are salient must
become the hallmark of future anthropological research in Laos, and in the
region generally.

The shape of Lao ethnography since 1975 has been determined by the
LPRP's alignment with Vietnamese communism. While this legacy
remains, today research is equally contrained by the concerted attempt by
the LPDR to cloak itself in "tradition" and nationalism instead of Marxism.
Any critical reflection on this invention of tradition is, for now, impossible
from within. So, for both political and cultural reasons it will probably be
sometime before Lao ethnographers begin to see eye to eye with some of
their foreign interlocutors.

NOTES

I would like to thank Frank Proschan and Nick Enfield for their comments on an early
draft of this chapter.

1. Initially the Lao communists were members of the Indochinese Communist
Party. After its dissolution in 1951 the Lao finally regrouped in the Lao People's Party
in 1955, which changed its name to the Lao People's Revolutionary Party in 1972.

2. Kelvin Rowley and I (Evans and Rowley 1983) attempted to analyze why the

apparently similar relationship between the Vietnamese and the Lao and Khmer communists worked smoothly in the former case but not in the latter. Our argument rested largely on how the geo-strategic interests between the Lao and the Vietnamese tended to converge in most cases over time, while in the Khmer case they often did not, and then began to diverge radically. We retained this analysis when we produced a revised edition of the book in 1990.

3. I have borrowed the idea for my title from Brown and Zasloff's book (1986).

4. Kaysone Phomvihane's (1975) book on the movement of Lao history was probably the first major statement by a communist leader, although it had been preceded by Phoumi Vongvichit's (1969) well known tract on "US Neo-Colonialism." Kaysone's book was later published in French and English (1981).

5. The terms ethnography and ethnology have been used in communist states to differentiate their studies from "bourgeois anthropology" and from the more theoretically inclusive tendencies of ethnology. Ethnography in Europe and the U.S. became associated with ahistorical studies of allegedly self-contained cultures and a lack of interest in problems of social and cultural change, or the linkages between local groups and larger regional, national, or international politico-economic structures. The latter typifies ethnographic practice in Laos and Vietnam. Anthropology in these countries has meant physical anthropology. However, today these views and attitudes are under revision in Vietnam and in Laos.

6. For the Soviet Union, see Gellner (1980), for China, see Guldin (1994), and for Vietnam, Evans (1985).

7. I have heard these views in seminars, and it is reflected in a recent statement of party policy which implies that all ethnic groups in Laos somehow had their "origins" there (PCPC 1997: 246).

8. Archaeological discoveries at Ban Chiang and Non Nok in northeastern Thailand showing evidence of an ancient civilization there also sparked off a debate in Thailand concerning the migration thesis versus the *in situ* thesis. My use of "older brother," of course, refers to Dodd (1923).

9. The most comprehensive list of Vietnamese studies can be found in the bibliography of Nguyen Duy Thieu (1996).

10. See, for example, Thipmuntali, chapter 6, who refers to a Vietnamese study from this period.

11. Jokingly, one of these young Lao, now grown to maturity and a father, said that if it was not for the bombing he would be an "ignorant" farmer and would never have received a higher education and be where he is now. Initially they were also taught Lao. Had they not been, he further joked, "I would be Vietnamese today!"

12. "The centralized academy of sciences system, with its satellite institutes, was imported directly from the Soviet Union into most of the satellite nations of the eastern bloc, even when it had to be imposed on an existing academy . . . Research suffered . . . from the fact that small, powerful administrative bodies were able to determine—without accountability—the topics to be researched in a given period, and the ones that would be funded" (Harlig 1995: 33). Harlig's book refers primarily linguistic research in eastern Europe, but the effects were similar in China, Vietnam, and in Laos.

13. The parallel with nineteenth-century views is made clear in the following passage from Sir Edward Tyler's *Primitive Culture*: "It is a harsher, and at times even painful,

office of ethnography to expose the remains of crude old cultures which have passed into harmful superstition, and to mark these out for destruction . . . Yet this work, if less genial, is not less urgently needful for the good of mankind. Thus, active at once in aiding progress and in removing hindrance, the science of culture is essentially a reformer's science" (Cited in Tambiah 1990: 44).

14. I would like to thank Nick Enfield for helping me to recheck and to gather some of this information.

15. None of these students knew either French or English, and so texts like that of Yang Dao (1972) on the Hmong were not accessible, let alone politically acceptable in these early years of the revolution. In more recent years some of these former students have put a great deal of effort into learning English.

16. The title in Lao was followed by this title in English. It would have been better translated "A Tour of Ethnic Groups in Laos" or "Touring Ethnic Groups in Laos." I think this title was designed to make a play for the new tourist market which had opened up in Laos. This purpose was defeated by the fact that the text was in Lao.

17. It is my impression that former members of the institute were not happy with the appearance of this text because it seems that the Vietnamese had agreed to produce jointly with the Lao a similar text.

18. The only monograph is a rather entertaining journalistic account by the head of the institute of his travels among the Lolo. See Houmphanh (1997).

19. For a discussion of the time, see Evans and Rowley (1990).

20. For an initial attempt to understand this revolt, see Evans (1982) chapters 2 and 3.

21. The French word "Peuplade" is inserted in brackets in the Lao text at this point. I will, however, translate it in English as ethnicity. The word "commune" above is also supplied in the original text.

22. The passages translated thus far come from pages 17–30 of Kaysone (1982). It is of interest to note that in this last section Kaysone also equates the Han leaders of Beijing with the capitalist countries.

23. Here one suspects that he has in mind the special writing system commonly used by Hmong which is based on the Roman alphabet, and therefore he insists that the ethnic minorities use written Lao for their own languages. At this time he may also be thinking of the Yao and others who use Chinese characters.

24. For the early debate among republicans, see Duara (1995), chapter 6.

25. The editor of Vietnamese Studies inserts this comment.

26. In 1931 the CCP expressed similar sentiments at its congress. Noting that the Soviet Union was the one place "where the national question has indeed been solved" it went on: "In the fundamental Law (Constitution) of the Chinese Soviet Republic it shall be clearly stated that *all national minorities within the confines of China shall have the right to national self-determination, including secession* from China and the formation of independent states . . ." (Cited in Connor 1984: 75).

27. For a more detailed discussion of Vietnamese policy, see Viet Chung (1968) and Connor (1984).

28. For example, one anthropological dictionary writes: "Ethnic group: a group belonging to a particular tribe or race." David Davies, *A Dictionary of Anthropology*, London: Frederick Muller Ltd., 1972.

29. I am uncertain whether the concept of "ethnos" as developed by Yu. Bromley had an impact in either Vietnam or Laos. As I mentioned earlier, there has been no

systematic study of the relationship between Soviet and Vietnamese ethnography. In a brief survey of the Vietnamese journal, *Ethnographical Studies*, I can only find one article by Yu. Bromley on "Lenin's heritage and Soviet Ethnography" (no.4, 1987), and an article by Be Viet Dang, the director of the institute at the time, "Concerning Iu. Bromley's work 'The Problems of Modern Ethnography'," (no.3, 1981). My reading of Bromley's concept places it very close to what I would call a primordialist approach to culture (see Bromley 1974). Recent interviews with Russian anthropologists indicate that "ethnos" has become a central concept in their discipline. One says: "Before 'ethnos' was invented, ethnographers were not allowed to address 'national question' issues, which were an exclusive domain of Marxist philosophers and scholars of scientific communism. . . Thus a certain change in the paradigm may be said to have occurred in the past 20 to 25 years" (Elfimov 1997: 777). For some sympathetic views of these developments see Dragadze (1980) and Shanin (1986). Two Russian anthropologists, Kossikov and Egorunin (1993), in a very critical paper on LPDR minorities policy, claim to use the concept of ethnos for classifying Lao ethnic groups. Its exact use is not clear from this paper, but perhaps it is clearer in their articles in Russian cited in their bibliography.

30. For an interesting correction to Fried's strong emphasis on the purely secondary nature of tribes, see Crone (1986).

31. Oscar Salemink has provided several insightful analyses of early French classificatory endeavors in the southern highlands of Vietnam, which also illustrate Fried's idea of secondary tribalism (Salemink 1994 and 1995). For an early argument along these lines in the context of Africa, see Colson (1968).

32. Significantly, the title page of Fried's (1975) book carries an epigram by Confucius on the rectification of names.

33. This was allayed by the allegiance of both of these men to the Lao kings, Sisavangvong and then Sisavang Vatthana. The importance of royalty in this regard is explored in a chapter on "Minorities in State Rituals" in Evans (1998).

34. Le Cu Nam (1990: 60–61) provides a list at the end of his article that matches Vietnamese names for particular groups with those from Laos. It is worth pointing out that these classifications are often based on very limited word lists (100–200 words), which are for various reasons considered enough to determine relatedness. Among the various criticisms that could be leveled at this approach which is based on lexical correspondence (sharing of certain basic words), is that it does not take into account ways of speaking, i.e. idioms and habits which make up language use and can produce a very different cultural picture.

35. I do not know whether the Vietnamese census includes the concept Kinh. See Khamdeng and Khampheng (1992) where a presentation of the Lao ethnic group begins the book; in Vietnam a book on the "multinational Vietnamese people" includes the Viet (Chu Thai Son 1991), yet generally books are reserved just for ethnic minorities, such as with Dang Nghiem Van et al. (1984).

36. Trankell (1998) correctly points out that the tripartite schema is still alive and well among many ordinary people and local officials (and one could add, foreign aid workers and consultants), and puts forward an interesting argument concerning the apparent "natural" attractiveness of the schema. Oddly, she leaves out its simplicity, compared with having to know the forty-seven officially recognized groups. Its persistence, of course, is also related to the fact that followers of the communists for many years had this essentially politically inspired schema drummed into them, and

then it was drummed into the whole population for many years after 1975. Whatever Kaysone or Lao ethnographers may think, the effects of this propaganda cannot be switched off overnight.

37. There are now numerous publications by Smith arguing his interpretation of nationalism. But for a good overview of his views, see Smith (1991).

38 . For example, during the disputes which have occurred in Laos between the Lao government and NGOs concerning the effects of building dams in some areas, Lao researchers who discovered evidence of offerings to a *lak muang* (territorial spirit) were told not to publish anything about this or to speak about it for fear that it would further fuel opposition to the project.

39. For example, an introductory book on anthropology I edited (Evans 1993) has been translated into Vietnamese.

40. This is especially true when such maps are reproduced within the national map as "icon." That is, floating free from any neighboring territories, thereby producing the illusion that the ethnolinguistic groups stop at the national borders. The most recently produced ethnolinguistic map of Laos is that of Chazee (1995). Chazee's study is rather savagely and arrogantly attacked by Chamberlain et al. (1995) because of his sometimes mistaken classifications, attributed to his lack of knowledge of Lao. In fact, however, both works share the same basic theoretical approach.

41. For a good recent presentation of anthropological linguistics, which deals with some of the exaggerated claims of linguists, see Foley (1997).

42. Hickey, as part of his general argument concerning the formation of a southern highlands ethnicity, provides an interesting account of their search for an appropriate name. At one point, for example, "Austrien" was proposed (1982: 114).

43. Ing-Britt Trankell (1998) also documents this lability.

44. Tapp's critique of "Sinicization" may seem to have implications for my argument about "Tai-ization" in chapter 6. In that essay, however, I have attempted to complicate the process by observing the role of the state in localized contexts, and the lability of ethnicity, including its reversibility.

45. For a discussion, see the various essays in Sautman (c.1995).

46. This is apparent in various articles that have appeared in the *Lanexang Heritage Journal*, produced by the Institute of Culture. For example, Amphay Dore, "Le Royaume historique des Ai Lao, une perspective geo-politique," (No.2, July–December 1996).

ROYAL RELICS

RITUAL AND SOCIAL MEMORY IN LOUANG PRABANG

9

ING-BRITT TRANKELL

T HE kingdom of Louang Prabang is not a direct predecessor of the contemporary Lao nation-state in the usual territorial understanding of the concept, but should rather be perceived of as a cosmological center and as a sacred space. The kingdom was allegedly founded in 1353 by the semi-legendary Fa Ngoum and his wife, a Khmer Princess called Nang Kheaw. They installed the golden Buddha statue—the Phra Bang, or "Prabang"—as a symbol of politico-religious power in Louang Prabang. The French established a protectorate over the kingdom of Louang Prabang, and as a result of further French colonial expansion, the former indigenous kingdoms of Vientiane and Champassak were eventually incorporated into the kingdom of Laos, with Louang Prabang as its royal capital. The Lao kingdom lasted until the communist revolution and the establishment of Lao People's Democratic Republic in December 1975, when King Sisavang Vatthana abdicated. In 1977 the king, Queen Khamphoui, and their eldest son, the Crown Prince Vongsavang, were taken to a reeducation camp in the northern province of Houaphan, where they eventually died. The fact that the fate of the royal family had never been officially disclosed in Laos at the time of my research, and that its members were never properly mourned in the course of funerary rituals, was conveyed to me as a source of chagrin in several private conversations with ordinary people.[1] Several informants mentioned the alleged suicide of the royal family. Nowadays, there are signs of an incipient cult of royalty in Louang Prabang. In 1997, amulets with a picture of the late monarch were being sold in local temples (Evans 1998b: 35–38).

In this chapter I will discuss some of the ritual and social features displayed during the state rituals in Louang Prabang.[2] The state rituals in post-revolutionary Laos consist of the That Luang festival of the twelfth month, celebrated in Vientiane in November, and the New Year's celebration and aspersion of the Prabang in Louang Prabang in April. Formerly both rituals took place in Louang Prabang. The contemporary division of the state rituals between Vientiane and Louang Prabang is a way to mark the political balance and relations between the two main centers of the post-revolutionary society. The New Year's celebration used to be a royal ceremony related to the fate of the kingdom, as demonstrated by the various practices of divination for the year to come. In spite of this historical reference to Louang Prabang in its more local and provincial meaning of the Muang Louang Prabang, it is now celebrated on behalf of the nation and has the Lao People's Revolutionary Party as its main instigator. It seems that in the case of the Louang Prabang ceremony the reference points of the *muang* may have been undergoing a process of official reinterpretation (which needed to be impressed upon the populace?) in which these points were being mapped onto the contours of a larger entity, an entity which we now know as the post-colonial nation-state of Laos. (Rajah 1990: 320)

The Indochina war seriously affected daily life in Louang Prabang. The fighting in the north caused an influx of refugees and internally displaced persons. Following the revolution in 1975, when not only the royal family but also key members of the royal staff and administration were taken to reeducation camps, the New Year's celebrations were temporarily discontinued. Related to this discontinuation, it is locally believed that the Prabang was removed from the city and brought to a secret place in Vientiane. Informants relate that a measure of continuity was provided by the cult of the Thevada Luang, the guardian spirits of the *muang*, the masks of which are brought out in annual processions to prevent the city from being struck by disasters.

RITUAL TRANSFORMATIONS, POLITICAL POWER, AND SOCIAL MEMORY

FOLLOWING the seminal work by Hobsbawm and Ranger (1983), the importance of parading and the display of public culture during festivals as expressions of social memory has been noted by anthropologists as well as by historians (Fentress and Wickham 1992).

In post-socialist Lao society, contesting views and versions of the social order are brought together within the ritual time and space of the New Year celebrations. The rituals serve to restructure the social experience and the social identity of the actors and participants and thus to frame social memory. Multivocal perceptions of the meaning of the rituals are sometimes difficult to grasp and not easily accommodated in the official view.

The celebration of the New Year in Louang Prabang is locally seen as part of the *moladok*, the cultural heritage, and therefore claimed to be faithful towards the past, even to the royal past, as an unbroken tradition brought down from the ancestors until present day. Such perceived continuity is in fact an important part of newly established so-called traditions. It is claimed that if changes were to be made, the rituals would no longer reflect and truly represent the authentic heritage. The present-day rituals are therefore perceived as static and unchangeable, although the king and the royal protection are now sadly missing and therefore commemorated. Nevertheless, the rituals can be shown to have changed substantially over the recent years and adjustments have been made to meet the demands of the current political situation. A number of functions have been abandoned, new elements introduced, and important characters and actors have been replaced by new ones. It is, however, important to distinguish between the performance of the ritual as a kind of social practice, and the ideological or cosmological meaning attached to it. Even if the actual performances and actors may have changed, it is not certain that the cosmology linked to the ritual has changed to the same extent. Rather, as mentioned by Hobsbawm, "new traditions" are to be seen as responses to novel situations which take the form of reference to old situations, or which establish their own past by quasi-obligatory repetition. It is the contrast between the constant change and innovation of the modern world and the attempt to structure at least some parts of social life within it as unchanging and invariant, that makes the "invention of tradition" so interesting for historians (Hobsbawm and Ranger 1983: 2)—and one might add, for anthropologists. The reason for this, as pointed out by Wright (1995: 243), is that anthropology has the additional interest to look into the symbolic production generated by public culture and its concomitant expression of identity and peoplehood. In Louang Prabang, elements of traditional local culture are transformed into rituals staged by the modern nation-state, but with all the royal regalia more or less intact. The state ritual is condoned and revered by the common people as well as by the communist party of the Lao People's Democratic Republic. Thus we are obliged to inquire about the links connecting the past with the present, ethnicity and local culture with the modern nation, and maintaining authenticity, while still claiming invariance and faithfulness to the irretrievable past (243).

One important feature in the ritual is the participation of ethnic groups. The New Year ceremonies were dedicated to the ritual confirmation of the political dominance by the Lao royalty over the aboriginal inhabitants of the surrounding areas, and issues of ethnicity were, and are still, therefore dramatically displayed during the ritual. But, although the parts played by the various ethnic groups are claimed to be invariant and ancient, they have in fact undergone important changes, reflecting the shift of power on the political arena. Related to this, there is now a growing emphasis on a common national identity.

Another such element, by which the post-revolutionary transformation of the former court rituals is brought about, is the substitution of the performance of the royal ballet by the beauty contest, which now marks the very start of the celebrations. The winner of the beauty contest represents the guardian spirit of the New Year, and she has many duties to fulfill that serve to bring about the collation of old and new histories, and to reconcile royal powers with the new powers of the modern nation.

LOUANG PRABANG COSMOLOGY

THE "tradition" on which the contemporary "traditional" New Year rituals rest relates to the political alliance between the Lao (Lao Loum) rulers of Louang Prabang, who were also the guarantors of the Buddhist state religion, and the aboriginal Mon-Khmer (Lao Theung) ethnic groups of the area. The latter were politically subordinate, but as "elder brothers" of the Lao they were in charge of the cult of the ancestral spirits of the place. The political and Buddhist supremacy of the Lao was ritually enacted through the annual cosmological journey, customarily performed by the king. In the old times it was the duty of the king to travel to the various mythological sites connected with the arrival of the Buddha and the construction of the World Pillars (Pinith 1987). This was to be done after the New Year in order for the king to receive the aspersion, in local English translated as "the bath for the king" (*song nam cau sivit*), from the people, before bringing out the Prabang in procession.

According to the royal protocols, now kept at the palace museum, the king started his cosmological journey, on the day after the reception of the New Year, at the religious center, the Vat Xieng Thong. There he was offered the purifying bath before entering the temple for worship, which included bathing the Buddha image. During the course of the following days, he first traveled south to the village of Sangalok, located at the mouth of the Nam Dong River, where, according to the legend, the "grandparents" (ancestors) died after killing a dragon monster that threatened the kingdom. Sangalok is also said to be the first stop of the Prabang upon arrival in the kingdom, as well as being, in more recent times, a Khmer village which supplied the royal guards and policemen. The following day the journey goes north, where the king should make a stop on Don Khun island outside the tributary of Nam Xeuan in order to receive the aspersion, and to enjoy a short rest, as an act of commemoration of the event when the Lord Buddha arrived at this place. The same day the journey continued north, up the river to the sacred caves of Vat Tham Thing just opposite the Pak Ou where the bathing ritual was repeated before the king returned to the city.

The important ritual elements in the king's cosmic journey include the traveling along the south/north axis and the offering of water of successively higher social and cosmological levels. The journey constitutes the symbolic recreation of the kingdom in connection with the Lao New Year. This symbolic recreation was performed by the king for the last time in April 1975. But it is significant that this ritual scheme is still adhered to, both in the contemporary New Year festival in the city, to which I shall return shortly, and in villages in the countryside.[3]

THE SPIRITS

IN Laos, the spirit cults are to a comparatively large degree incorporated into the official "religion," and they are highly relevant to issues of national and ethnic identity. In Louang Prabang, the cult centers on the Thevada Luang, the semi-human mythical ancestors who are believed to have once prepared the ground for the ancient kingdom. The Thevada Luang are represented by the three conspicuous masks personifying *phu ngyōe* and *ngya ngyōe* (grandfather and grandmother) and *sing khap sing khon* (the long-nosed lion). The *winyan*, "souls," of the Thevada Luang are regularly called and invited to listen to Buddhist sermons during the *wan sin*, the Buddhist holidays, and as we shall see, the masks play a prominent role in the New Year festival with its ritual reclaiming of the city's territory and cosmological space. As spirits of the place they serve the purpose of linking territorial units with social and cosmological elements.

The Thevada Luang preside over a pantheon populated mainly by ophidian water spirits, the nagas, that form their social and territorial entourage. The nagas are tutelary spirits residing in the hill of Phou Si, as well as in the caves, ponds, and springs within the city and in its hinterland. In order to control the waters, it was necessary for the king to mediate between the human beings and the cosmic nature represented by the nagas. The king's control also necessitated the keeping up of the alliance between the aboriginal inhabitants and owners of the land, the Mon-Khmer and their spirits. Each such alliance has its named personage, its shrine and commemoration. One such shrine is the city pillar, the foundations of which are still visible, located next to the big bo tree in the market place above the main ferry landing. The pillar is said to be animated by the human sacrifice of a Khmu woman, Nang Palasini, commonly referred to as *tu pa*, (elder sister). It is said that she voluntarily offered herself for the city pillar. Her *ho phi* (spirit shrine) is now located in the Vat Aram, in the same building as that of the Thevada Luang.

The human beings immediately in charge of the spirit cults are the caretakers of the Thevada Luang and the spirit mediums. The position is passed on along the male line, ideally from father to son. It is stated that this makes their office different from that of the mediums, who are chosen by the spirits themselves. The spirit mediums are in many ways important persons in the social environment of the city. They often work as herbalists, practice local medicine, and divine the causes of illness and social difficulties. This is usually done in the social setting of their own home, where they will receive their clients. The clients will pay a small fee for the services, part of which is for the medium and part for the spirit and the spirit house.

The mediums are supported by their allies in the cult, the *khwan cam*, a title that according the dictionary translates as "exorciser," but has the meaning of one who supports the medium during the trance and among other things invites the spirit to talk. The relation between the medium, *nang tiam*, and the *khwan cam* is important in several ways. The early stage of a medium's career typically feature an "illness" caused by a spirit possessing the medium and the unwillingness of the medium to accept this. The possession is diagnosed, and the possessing spirit identified, by the *khwan cam*, who will subsequently teach the medium and train her in the profession. The *khwan cam* is said to act like a bridge, *saphan*, between the medium and the clients. The *khwan cam* acts as an interpreter of the messages given by the spirit through the possessed medium. Once the possession is diagnosed and the spirit identified, it is considered dangerous and even immoral not to respond to the needs of the spirit.

In spirit possession, the mediums are often women and the possessing spirits are identified as male. This gendered relationship, however, is part of a ritual context that embodies a collective social memory about the condition and state of the society. Spiritual power and political power were never separate domains in the kingdom of Louang Prabang, and neither are they today. It is, therefore quite logical that mediums nowadays may be possessed by the naga spirits of powerful and nationally important political leaders, such as Prince Phetsarath who in the memory of ordinary people is primarily associated with the Lao Issara (Free Lao) and with efforts to promote socio-economic development and modernity. So in a sense it may be said that the mediums are possessed by the spirit of modernity.

THE NEW YEAR—ETHNOGRAPHIC NOTES

FOR the New Year festival in Louang Prabang in 1993, the official program listed four main events: 1) The morning market, 2) The construction of the sand stupa by the people, 3) The main New Year procession by the monks, novices, the *avosoh* (village elders), the Thevada Luang, and the Nang Sangkhan, 4) The return procession.

The program started as expected with the early morning market on the bank of the Mekong River on the day of sending off the spirit of the Old Year (*wan sangkhan pai*), which sets off a series of purification rituals and pilgrimages. In the afternoon the people of Louang Prabang cross the Mekong River in order to visit the temples and the caves on the opposite side, and fellow citizens will see to it that nobody disembarks at the *rive droite* without having received good showers of water. According to local myths, the Buddha crossed the Mekong from the west before climbing the Phou Si, the sacred mountain in Louang Prabang city. The main purpose of the people's visit to the right bank is twofold: the building of sand stupas, *(phasaat that saai)* which are constructed on the riverbank, and the visits to Vat Tham in order to fetch the water from the springs located in the caves under the temple, for the later aspersion of the Prabang.

The following day is called *sangkhan nau*, where nau means stop, marking liminal time. This is the day for receiving the New Year and for the visit of the ancestors, the mythical grandparents, Thevada Luang along with their adopted and only semi-domesticated child, the long-nosed lion. The masks of the Thevada Luang are brought in procession by their caretakers from Vat Aram, passing the Dala marketplace on the way to Vat Manoo, where the monks are waiting, and to Vat That Noi, from where they join in the main procession to Vat Xieng Thong. Actually the procession starts at Vat Vixoun from where the senior monks *(phra kaboen woo)* will be carried to Vat Aram to meet the monks and the Thevada Luang. It is not considered wise to depart from the procession route, since it would be like *lood pha sin nang ngak*, to tread on the skirt of the "female giant," and the temples that are part in the procession order are thus linked together, not only by the procession itself, but also by the participation in all the work and in the preparations by the inhabitants of the neighborhood.

The procession is headed by the monks and novices followed by the respected elders, the Khmu drummers, the Thevada Luang, the Khmu sword-dancers, the *nang sangkhan* (the winner of the annual beauty contest and personification of the New Year) seated on the animal of the year (that year the boar), her fellow beauty contestants, and finally the youths and musicians of the town, mingled with the rank and file of citizens, tourists and anthropologists, all suitably drenched in rice flour and water, liberally dispensed by the spectators along the route. On the arrival of the procession to Vat Xieng Thong, the *achan jai*, the senior abbot from Vat Saen receives the aspersion (*piti nam nam*) from the citizens as a purification before entering the temple.

The following day, which is the day of the arrival of the New Year, *wan sangkhan khün*, is also referred to as the day when the head of the Muang will thread on its own tail, *hae long, hai hoa muang pai jiab hang muang*. Some informants explained this in terms of space; the head (north) of the *muang* will go and visit the earlier part (south). On this day the Thevada Luang start out from Vat Aram alone, following the same route as the day before, but without stopping for the monks to join the procession. The monks from Vat Xieng Thong and the other temples in the northern part of the city wait at Vat Xieng Thong and will walk in procession to Vat That Noi, where they will be received by monks from the temples in the southern part of the city. After performing their dance, the masks will leave alone, and continue south to Vat That Luang in order "to let the head reach the tail" (*hai hua tüng lang*) which seems like going backwards until the territory closes in upon itself.

The parading of the Prabang after receiving the New Year is locally regarded as one of the main events of the festivities. Contrary to the parading of the New Year, the parading of the Prabang also includes representatives of the worldly powers and local officials walking in front of the Prabang. While the traditionally dressed Khmu surrounded the Thevada Luang with their drums and swords, the traditionally dressed palace guards protected the Prabang under the supervision of the director of the Royal Palace Museum, who himself carried the headdress and shoes of the Prabang. After the installment of the Prabang at Vat Mai, the Thevada Luang pay their respects, first to the Prabang and secondly to the king, whose position is nowadays taken by local government officials.

The composition of the parade, including both ethnic minorities and government officials, is an indication of the local importance of the Prabang in the conceptualization of the local social and cosmological order.

AMBIGUITIES OF REFORM AND TRADITION

WHEN having lived in Louang Prabang for some time, one inevitably becomes aware of certain incongruities between the official political ideology of the present regime and the equally official efforts to "preserve" the "ancient" traditions of the place. The introduction, in the late 1980s, of reform politics and the New Economic Mechanism also encouraged the marketing of "culture." In 1994, the entire city of Louang Prabang, with all its buildings, temples, and shrines, was declared a World Cultural Heritage site. This has influenced the state rituals, as part of the *moladok*, the heritage, and the display of the city's public culture.

Lao classical court dances, the performance of which was abolished in 1975, have recently been reintroduced, and episodes of the Pra Lak Pra Lam, "Beloved Lakshmana Beloved Rama," the Lao version of the Ramayana epos (Ratnam 1983), were performed, for instance, for the public in front of Vat Mai during the 1993 New Year celebrations. Three years later, the dilapidated building of the School of Fine Arts was undergoing repairs. Court dances are also performed by professional dancers in tourist establishments as entertainment for the guests, as are "folk" dances, where the dancers are dressed up in fancy ethnic dresses. However, while observing one of the dances describing an event in Sam Neua, where the plurality of the many peoples in Laos are joined together in dance, I was reminded that what was being performed was in some sense the politics of ethnicity. In this kind of staged authenticity there is a certain element of symbolic production of identity, which according to the official discourse is to be understood as expressions of national identity. So, while preserving the cultural heritage, the Lao national identity is at the same time being negotiated and put on stage for commercial purposes. Likewise, symbolic production of identity is being staged in the state rituals, now managed not by the king, but by the Lao People's Revolutionary Party.

The ambiguities inherent in the contemporary national political, and to some extent commercial, promotion of Lao culture are also apparent in the case of the former royal palace. The palace, which was built by the French in 1914–1920, has recently been restored in a project financed by the Swedish International Development Cooperation Agency, SIDA (Lind and Hagmüller 1991). After the king's abdication in 1976 the palace was turned into a museum, referred to as "The Royal Museum," in contrast to the Revolutionary Museum in Vientiane.[4] During the restoration, however, the name of the palace was changed a couple of times. During 1993 it was called the "Grand Palace Museum," but although the palace was undoubtedly royal, it was by no means grand. By 1996, however, it was referred to simply as the "Museum of Luang Prabang." In a pamphlet published by the authorities in Louang Prabang, the museum is said to be "the center of research and studies as well as a major source of income for the inhabitants in Luang Prabang." This is contrary to everyone's experience, since in reality the museum is locked up and not normally open to the public. Even officials complain that they are not allowed to have a look at the royal protocols, if they for some reason or other would like to check. Upon agreement and against payment, however, the museum does receive groups of visitors, mainly well-to-do tourists, for guided tours.

Although the building officially belongs to the nation, and thus to the people, the palace is not a public building in the usual sense of the word. The idea of a public building is created in modern societies and by modern nations. But, irrespective of the ideology of the political regime, the royal palace is in popular consciousness part of the Buddhist religion and worldview as a manifestation of royal and religious regalia, with all its symbolic load of power and potency; it is, among other things, a representation of the World Pillar. The royal palace is therefore not a public museum building in the modern sense, but is rather a representation of the royal sacred space, and of the royal power in the sense of spiritual power.

These differing conceptions regarding the nature of the royal palace were brought to the fore during the planning of the restoration work on the building, when the question of the bathroom was brought up. Since the bathroom had been installed in the 1930s in the gallery that was circumambulent of the living quarters, the architect wanted to remove it, as he felt it violated the original design of the living quarters and was to be seen as an "inauthentic" later addition. The problem was, however, that the Lao museum personnel resisted the idea of removing the bathroom. For them, it was an integral part of the palace, whether it was constructed in 1920 or 1930, and in any case the symbolic import of the palace was not bound to any particular decade or century. Moreover, as the king was never officially proclaimed dead, it was not for his subjects to take it upon themselves to change the design of his living quarters.

The conceptual anxiety that officials may have when trying to reconcile past royalty with present revolutionary ideology is less of a burden for the tourist industry. Louang Prabang is promoted on the tourist market as a place of romanticism and royal mystique. Thus, for instance, tourists and visitors are now invited to participate in the baçi ceremony, which is a meal where the spirits of life are being summoned. Performed on many occasions and at several levels of social integration, the *baçi* ceremony has been called a symbol of the Lao national identity (Ngaosyvathn 1990). A major instance was when the king performed the ceremony in the palace as part of the New Year celebrations, on behalf of the whole community (Doré 1987). Although tourists and travelers are not always aware of this, the *baçi* ceremony is now being traded and performed by the inhabitants of the Ban Pha Kham, i.e. the quarters surrounding the former palace, by people who "belong to the house" as the royal family's servants, officials, friends, or relatives.

In the February 1996 issue of *Le Journal Magazine*, a hotel advertises "Un demeure Royale centenaire dans un quartier historique de Luang

Prabang." The hotel in question is "Villa de la Princesse, maintenant appelée hotel Villa Santi." In an article in the same issue we are told that a good buy in Louang Prabang "is a picture, or postcard showing an officer wearing a peaked cap and a bitter smile. This is Somdeth Phetsarath, elder brother of the last king. He was removed from the throne and chose to die by making his soul leave his body. A nationalist and a follower of the Buddha, he commands great respect. He is a saint" [my translation from the French]. Today, his followers consider that his picture averts the evil eye.

The historical fact behind this tourist-exotic tale is that Prince Phetsarath, who died in 1959, was the leader of the independence movement Lao Issara after 1945, but before that he had been in charge of indigenous affairs during the French protectorate and prime minister (1941–45) of the kingdom of Louang Prabang (Deuve 1984; see also Evans 1998a). The ethnographic fact, as mentioned above, is that he is a naga spirit that possesses certain mediums in Louang Prabang.

Not only the royal past, but also the importance of the age-old and very contemporary spirit cults sits uneasily with the ideology of modernity, progress, and rationality adhered to by the party, as the following anecdote may illustrate. During the preparations for the 1993 New Year festival, there were rumors that this year the ancestral spirits, the masks of whom should to be "aired" once a year in connection with the festival, would not be allowed to figure in the processions, due to the trouble they had caused the local branch of the electricity company. Certain repairs of electricity poles and wires had been unsuccessful, and to succeed in their job workers had insisted on erecting the *ho phi* (spirit shrines) for the ancestors before carrying out further work. This done, the work continued without further mishaps, to the delight of the workers but to the dismay of influential officials who wanted to ban the cult of the ancestors and spirits. On the other hand, the masks are regarded as *vatthu boran*, "ancient material," and therefore, along with the cult, defined as part of the *moladok*, the cultural heritage.

SHIFTING CENTERS OF POWER

AS a state ritual, the celebration of the New Year can be expected to be a statement on the social and cosmological order of society, reflecting the status of social groups and their relations to authority and power. The annual state rituals are also statements about the territorial nature of the kingdom, where the Mekong River is extremely important. Thus the boat races in November were mainly dedicated to reclaiming the land from the nagas by chasing them out from the fields and streams and into the Mekong

River, at the time of the receding water. This was noted by Archaimbault (1972) in his now-classic analysis of the Lao state rituals which he observed in the early 1950s. Having witnessed the New Year festival in Louang Prabang in 1993, I was surprised that Archaimbault did not find the New Year rituals as elaborate or as important as the boat races. He justifies this as a conclusion (1972: 93–94) in noting that in Louang Prabang the New Year and the aspersion of the Prabang served as a purification, as an introduction to the ritual cycles which were to culminate in the That Luang festival and boat race in the twelfth-month rituals. In his structural analysis the rituals served the dual purposes of bringing about the migration of the aquatic elements, the ophidian nagas, and of an installation ritual, to confirm the socio-political situation and power relations.

The rituals for the twelfth month are nowadays performed in Vientiane. Since 1969–1970 they formed part of the That Luang festival centered on the Maha That, the national monument in Vientiane. The shift in the center of gravity of these rituals from Louang Prabang to Vientiane is related to the fact that the position of the king had become weaker. As a consequence of the events during the civil war, the king was no longer the single and undisputed leader of the nation but rather one among other national leaders, and eventually Vientiane rather than Louang Prabang came to be the national political center. Consequently the rituals for the twelfth month were discontinued in Louang Prabang sometime between 1971 and 1973. The reason for the continuation and elaboration of the celebration of the New Year in Louang Prabang, on the other hand, is the recognition of Louang Prabang as a center for the official Buddhist religion.

NANG SANGKHAN—FROM FOUNDING MOTHER TO REVOLUTIONARY DAUGHTERS

UNTIL 1975, the New Year celebrations in Louang Prabang included performances by the court ballet. The most important parts of the repertoire of the court ballet were episodes from the Lao version of the Ramayana, the Pra Lak Pra Lam. Perhaps more than other versions of this epic, the Lao one is a localization, true to particular Lao customs and traditions. Its author is believed to have been a court poet of Vientiane in the first half of the nineteenth century and the story "portrays Rama as a mighty king of Vientiane, exercising control over neighbouring territories" (Ratnam 1983: 234). In her study of the Pra Lak Pra Lam, Kamela Ratnam comments that

[T]he characters are extremely fresh· and novel... and bear little resemblance to their originals. . . . They move and behave exactly like Lao men and women and conform strictly to local customs and traditions. The social life, food and dress and other norms of general behaviour follow closely the Laotian pattern (235.)

Originally, the members of the court ballet were recruited from the Tai Lue village Ban Pha Nom, in the vicinity of the city. One of the favorite episodes from the Pra Lak Pra Lam to be performed at New Year was that about Nang Kheaw, where the Phra Lam transforms himself into the beautiful Nang Kheaw before Nandiyak, the monster that kills human beings with his index finger. While Nang Kheaw is usually regarded as the Mon-Khmer wife of the legendary founder of Louang Prabang, Fa Ngoum, the inhabitants of Ban Pha Nom claim her as their own. According to their version, she was a Tai Lue princess, who as the consort of Fa Ngoum brought the fine art as part of her dowry to be part of civilization. The Tai Lue ruler of Muang Xieng Hung in Sipsong Panna is said to have offered his beautiful daughter, a Tai Lue princess called Nang Kheaw Thida as second wife to Fa Ngoum as an act of alliance in the year of 1374. Ban Pha Nom, or as it is called in daily speech, Ban Nom, "Milk Village," was founded by the Lue entourage of various artisans and experts that were supposed to accompany the princess and to serve her in her new position as a royal mistress of Louang Prabang. The village traditionally paid tribute to the court by supplying dancers and musicians and by being silk weavers. After a change in the colonial and national law around 1960, this kind of tribute labor was prohibited. Instead, the School of Fine Arts was established. But most villagers say that they continued to serve the king even after the legislative changes relating to tribute labor. Informants told me that they did so out of loyalty and as long as there was a public appreciation and demand for their work, and individual dancers derived a feeling of personal satisfaction, stemming from their particular perception and interpretation of a certain character. An example of this is Lung Si Can, who received a medallion from the Khmer Prince Sihanouk for his strong casting of the character Totsakan in the Pra Lak Pra Lam. However, Lung Si Can was also the leader of those villagers who finally, in 1965, took the initiative to stop the performance of the temple dance and the Ramayana, as the court, according to the villagers' account, had abused the services of the dancers by asking them to pose for a French artist. After this, the members of the ballet came to be recruited from the School of Fine Arts. The Nang Kheaw episode—that of the founding mother of the kingdom—continued to be a favorite, and it was mentioned by elderly informants who had been related to the court. A news sheet from the Ministry of Information from 1969 displays a number of photos of the royal family in connection with that year's celebration of the New Year, and as a prominent item we see young girls of the Nang Kaew episode offering flowers while kneeling in front of the king and queen.

With the victory of the revolution in 1975, the Pra Lak Pra Lam was no longer felt suitable to figure in the state rituals of the New Year. This does not imply, however, that the Pra Lak Pra Lam has lost any of its local realism and political implications. As late as in 1979, the Culture Ministry of Laos presented the Ramayana ballet before foreign and Indian visitors, saying "we still draw inspiration form this epic. Ramayana is the symbol of the proletariat while Ravana speaks for the capitalist-colonialist powers. Rama and Hanuman are the creators of the guerrilla warfare, a strategy by which we have regained our independence" (Ratnam 1983: 248), and when episodes from the epic were reintroduced for the 1993 New Year celebrations, as a public performance on the night of the *wan hae prabang,* the aspersion of the Prabang, it had been preceded by discussions among officials as to which episodes should be chosen.

But already by the early 1970s, a substitute element had been introduced into the festival, namely the beauty contest. The winner of the contest (*nang sangkhan,* Miss New Year) represents the tutelary spirit of the New Year and is seen as the incarnation of the *sangkhan* (the horastic animal sign of the year). In the New Year procession, she performs in the main parades mounted on the animal of the year, surrounded by her fellow contestants. The beauty contest and the nomination of the *nang sangkhan* was introduced in 1973 by the *cau muang* (the mayor) of Louang Prabang, Tan Boonkong Pracitit. Although the tradition was inspired by beauty contests in Thailand, it became localized in the Lao context. I was told that while studying the history of Louang Prabang, Tan Boonkong came across a legend about a king called Kabinlaphom and his seven daughters (see appendix). Reading the legend about the seven daughters showing reverence for their father, he found the story fitting for the celebration of the New Year's water festival as a rite of purification. It was apparently felt that the nomination of Miss New Year better fitted the growing emphasis on a common national identity in Laos than did episodes from the classical Ramayana; and at the same time this new tradition was purportedly rooted in a still more local Lao legend.

In another geographical context, Pamela Wright (1995) has shown how the element of national identity may be introduced as a gendered feature in national holidays. In Louang Prabang we recognize such a gendered feature in the beauty contest and its public display of young women. The contest itself takes place in the People's House of Culture on the eve of the New Year celebrations. The winner is chosen by provincial and district officials, village leaders, and members of the Lao Women's Union. The jury reaches its verdict on the basis of the contestants' looks as well as their other qualifications and virtues as part of the modern society.[5] The winner thus represents "an idealized national femininity" (Cohen, Wilk, and Stoeltje 1996: 8–9), and the contest is an instance that shows the "link between women's productive and reproductive roles in society and official notions of beauty and femininity paraded in state-supported beauty contests" (8–9). According to informants among the jury, being a model for all the nation's young women, the successful candidate must demonstrate intelligence and a social attitude inclined towards progress and modernity. She should be reasonably educated in, for instance, mathematics and have basic computer skills (reflecting the needs of the sponsoring companies), and she should combine these modern attitudes and abilities with the traditional virtues of a good housewife, such as knowledge of traditional Lao recipes. Part of the emphasis is thus on how the candidate performs in her everyday duties as a young woman in a society that demands of women that they also be socially active outside the family, and work for the public in order to "construct the society." But moral standing is also important, and purity is emphasized; the candidates must be virgins, and their average age has thus been progressively lowered (in 1997 the winner was sixteen years old).

The choice of the winner of the contest was naturally subject to interest among the public, and people would ask me what I thought: was she beautiful? My fairly non-committal answer would be followed by complaints about her deficiencies and statements that next year, "they" must really try to find a prettier one. This, I think, may be taken as an indication that the official representation of the social order is still being contested. But as the tutelary spirit of the New Year the *nang sangkhan* is still an apt representation of progress and aspirations for the future. It seems that the great amount of attention paid to the *nang sangkhan* could be due to the fact that she performs duties formerly allotted to the king. The most important of these are the religious duties performed in the temple, such as the aspersion of the Prabang and other Buddha statues. The celebration of the founding mother of the kingdom has thus been replaced by that of the daughters of the Revolution.

These daughters of the Revolution also include representatives of the ethnic minority groups, who are welcomed as contestants. But as participants in the contest, even minority girls will perform as Lao, wearing Lao Loum dresses and dancing in the Lao style. Even if a minority girl should win the contest, which happened in 1989, when the winner was a young Hmong schoolgirl and thus officially not a Buddhist, she will perform the official duties, including pouring water onto the naga channel for the aspersion of the Prabang. In this context, at least, the emphasis seems to be on the outward practice of Buddhism for creating merit rather than the individual's personal beliefs in whatever spiritual beings. And since the emphasis is on the national rather than the ethnic nature of the ceremonies, as well as of the Revolution, the winner's performance should conform to the manifestation of Buddhism as the state religion, regardless of her inner religious conviction.

FROM ETHNIC VASSALS TO NATIONAL CITIZENS

JUST as the women have attained a different position in post-revolutionary Lao society, as "working daughters" who contribute to the development of the nation, so the perception of the role of the ethnic minorities has changed, from being one of royal serfs subject to paying tribute and contributing corvée labor to the court, to a position of national citizens (Trankell 1998). This change is reflected in the state rituals with regard to the role played by the Lao Theung ethnic minorities in the New Year festival. The nature and time frame of the changes in the participation of the minorities in the ceremonies is not entirely clear, however, and different informants have given varying accounts.

The disagreements concern the presence and participation of the Lao Theung, represented by the Kassak and the Khmu. According to certain officials, the participation of the Lao Theung in the royal processions at New Year is a traditional ("timeless") element in the rituals; "they are the ones who always walked in the front line," and since the official nomenclature does not make fine distinctions between different kinds of Lao Theung (Kassak and Khmu, respectively), the illusion of the timeless and unchanging ritual can be preserved. But more detailed conversations with Kassak and Khmu informants reveals a more complex picture. The participation of the Kassak in the royal New Year processions seems to have ended sometime during the 1960s, soon after the death of Sisavang Vong. A protocol drawn up and signed in 1966 by the provincial governor confirms indirectly the fact that the Kassak had not been participating in the New Year procession as it is being performed today. Rather it seems that they entered the city in their own procession. The protocol is a statement on "Objects Used at the Royal Ceremony of Longevity on the First Day of the New Year Before the Royal Baçi ceremony." The governor mentioned that four villages participated in the procession and the ceremony, including the Kassak lord's own village, Ban Hiacaluaong, as well as a Khmu village. When setting out from these villages, the members of procession are to sleep at Xieng Ngeun the first night, and the second night at Vat Vixoun, until the following day, that is, on the day of the New Year. The Kassak lord of Muang Khoon is to bring the longevity fruits to offer to the king in

the palace before the royal *baçi* ceremony. The document also specifies that
eighteen persons were needed to take care of the processional objects and
lists these objects as follows:

    1. Traditional gun   2
    2. Sword   2
    3. Spear   2
    4. Umbrella   2
    5. Flag   2
    6. Rattan   2
    7. Longevity Fruit   2
    8. Long Drum   1
    9. Cymbal   1 pair
    10. Gong   1

These processional objects must be complete from the house (village?).[6] In
return, the palace gives a sum of money to the Kassak leaders to purchase an
albino female buffalo as offering to their spirit house—while a black buffalo
is purchased from the contributions made by the population of the four
villages. As the longevity fruit is about to be offered, a Kassak leader says,
"These two rattan rounds and two melons are offered by the big brother to
the younger brother—Yes." After these offerings have been made, the
Kassak leader and his team leave the palace and return home.

    Other informants (members of the committee in charge of the ancestor
masks) told me, however, that the Kassak used to come down, not for the
New Year celebrations but for the twelfth-month rituals, dressed up in big
hats and in dresses with belts, in order to offer the *mak man mak ngyōn*, or
nam thaon pong, the pumpkin associated with the creation myth. This gift is
rather special, since this specimen is regarded as sacred and therefore subject
to rules of cultivation whereby only old people are permitted to plant the
pumpkin. This is further underlined by the statement that the plant is
supposed to yield only three fruits. The meaning of the offering of the
pumpkins, however, is given as the analogue of the offering of one's own
life for the king, or rather to offer and give to the king the time that remains
of one's life. Thus the aboriginal Mon-Khmer peoples, the Kassak and the
Khmu, paid ritual allegiance to the king, but not necessarily as part of the
New Year celebrations.

    In the reestablishment of the New Year procession in the post-
revolutionary society, however, the Lao Theung are represented by
members not of the Kassak but of the Khmu ethnic group, who comes from
a village south of the city. This new settlement is referred to as a *ban opajōb*,
indicating the internal migration of displaced persons due to wartime

conditions. Small groups of people related by kinship and family ties migrated down to Louang Prabang from the northern province of Phongsaly in 1968 as war activities had made their home area insecure. They received permission to establish their present village south of Louang Prabang. These people, who are thus not part of the aboriginal population of the area, make a living by the cultivation of bananas for the market. So in spite of the fact that they lack *na piang*, paddy fields, they do fairly well with the combination of cash-cropping and *hai*, swidden cultivation.

These Khmu villagers had opportunity to observe the ritual during their first years of residence in Louang Prabang, and claim that a group of (aboriginal) Khmu, employed as royal guards in the palace, carried the Prabang during the procession. In the procession they also observed the presence of soldiers and policemen, probably due to the insecurity and wartime conditions in the city. They further noted that the Kassak did not participate in the main New Year procession.

It was suggested to them by city authorities after 1975 that they participate in the New Year procession, which they have done since. Usually it is the village youths who use this as an opportunity to dress up in traditional Khmu costume and to celebrate. They had been used to celebrate New Year in Phong Saly together with other ethnic groups, such as the Phu Noi and the Tai Lue, so the participation in the rituals of other groups was nothing new to them. The New Year in itself is not important to them, since they celebrate their traditional New Year already in December/January as a post harvest celebration in the first month of the Laotian calendar and in a way they themselves think of as quite distinct and different from the traditional lowland Lao way of celebration. Rather, they participate for patriotic reasons, *phovaa hak saat*. The Khmu participation in the ritual is a way for them to confirm their attachment to the new society.

However, their patriotic efforts to form an integrated element in the nation by participating in the processions is not necessarily appreciated by the citizens of Louang Prabang. In 1997 when waiting for the New Year procession, I approached a couple of elderly gentlemen and asked if they knew where the *suan paw poak kha khmu*, the Khmu ethnic representatives, would be. The answer was,

"They do not belong here, they will not come."

"But I was told they will take part in the procession."

"No, it is not true, they never did."

"But I have seen them."

"When? In 1958? At that time we saw them too."

Later, when I spotted them in the procession, I pointed them out to the gentlemen.

"Oh, these ones? But they are not the true, original ones, they are only the refugees."

RITUAL AS SOCIAL MEMORY

DURING the New Year celebrations, the location of Louang Prabang is turned into a ritual space, with its own geo-cosmology, in which the particular points of orientation are expressed in terms of significant places in the city and through its relation to the rivers Mekong and Nam Khan. The ritual further serves to transport people out of time, into timelessness and liminality, and achieves a collation of past and present. It is an occasion where time, old and new, is fused with space in terms of universal forces of power, and royal power is joined and fused with modern forms of power, party, and the nation-state.

The state rituals, ancient as well as contemporary, thus have the twofold function of confirming the alliance between the aborigines, or ethnic minorities, and to mediate between nagas and human beings and thereby confirm as well as re-create the social order within the society and between humans and non-human powers.

By its fusion of past and present, the ritual will necessarily have some bearing on social memory. As Fentress and Wickham (1992: 45–47) have pointed out, for memory to be social, it must be transmitted, and to be transmitted it must be capable of being articulated. As for articulation, this does not necessarily depend on spoken or written language, but may be acted out, for instance in ritual. But articulation, in its turn, presupposes a link to a concept. As already indicated, I suggest that the concept in this case is the social order itself, and that this is what is being memorized and re-created by means of ritual.

In contrast to social memory as "pure" ritual, what makes the present case interesting is that we have a mixture of ritual memory and linguistically articulated memories in the form of informants' recollections of past ritual details and of more or less consciously invented traditions, as well as of written (historical) evidence such as protocols and news sheets. This makes it possible to unravel both actual historical changes in the "timeless" ritual, to point to contested and contesting versions of the ritual (and thereby social) order, and to demonstrate how the ritual succeeds in reconciling these differing versions and accomplish an illusion of unity and harmony in the face of officially and unofficially recognized historical discontinuity. In the words of Fentress and Wickham,

images of unbroken continuity are usually illusions. The transmission of social memory is a process of evolution and change. These changes may be hidden from the community itself, however; for to [its members] their stock of memories—their techniques, their stories, and their collective identities—seem to be things that have always remained the same (1992: 200).

Thus, informants might be quite conscious of the social changes brought about by the revolution, but they would insist that the ritual has remained unchanged. This illusion is promoted and reinforced, paradoxically, by the way in which the ritual achieves a perfect fit with contemporary social conditions, which makes it seem "natural" and therefore timeless and perdurable. Thus, for example, when the Khmu take part in the present-day procession, this is natural because they represent the aboriginal population that has been incorporated into the kingdom as vassals and serfs. In actual historical fact, the Khmu participants of today turn out to be recent immigrants who have taken over the position in relation to the revolutionary regime that was earlier filled by the Kassak in relation to the court. And when the beauty contest is introduced and given astrological significance, this is natural because the winner serves to physically embody the tutelary spirit of the New Year, and because she fills the same kind of role in relation to the present regime and its ideology as the legendary princess had in relation to the kingdom.

APPENDIX: LEGEND OF THE NEW YEAR

[A written version of this legend was given to the author by the Cultural Office in Louang Prabang. It was translated from Lao by a translation bureau in Vientiane, and it is here reproduced it in its "authentic" translation.]

A legend says there was once a rich man who had no children and whose house was located near the house of a drunken man. The drunken man had two cute children. One day, the drunken man entered the rich man's house and insulted the rich man, who said, "You are drunk. Why are you causing problems to the closest house which is mine, who has more assets than you. But you still slander me." The drunken man answered, "The fact that you have more assets than me is not important, since you don't have any children. When you die, you will not be able to take our assets with you, and you do not have anyone to inherit from you. As for me, I have children and I am more precious than you." As the rich man heard these words, he felt shame and despised and therefore prayed to the sun for three years, but he still had no child. Then one day, on the New Year day, the sun moved from the astrological fish sign to the sign of the horse, the rich man and his entourage went to a big *phosay* tree on the bank of a river where birds lived, then washed milled rice with water seven times, cooked the rice and offered it to the *phosay* tree spirit, while playing music in celebration of the *phosay* tree spirit's victory, and prayed to have a child. The fairy in the tree pitied him and flew to Indra. Indra then appointed Thammapala to be born from the rich man. As a boy was born, he was called "Thammapala Kumman." The boy was much loved by his father, the rich man, who built a seven-story temple near the *phosay* tree on the bank of the river to be near the birds seeking shelter in the *phosay* tree. Therefore, Thammapala learned the language of birds and at the age of seven even learnt the seven principles and taught ethics to the people.

In the world at that period of time, the famous Kabinlaphom was held as teacher. As he learnt that Thammapala Kumman was a scientist, he came to put questions to him. It was agreed between them that if Thammapala Kumman could give an answer to the questions, Kabinlaphom would allow him to cut his head off. Otherwise, Kabinlaphom would cut Thammapala Kumman's head off. There were three questions: (1) Where is the brightness in the morning? (2) Where is the brightness in the daytime? (3) Where is the brightness in the evening? Kabinlaphom gave him seven days to find an answer, but on the sixth day, Thammapala Kumman could not yet solve the problem and thought that if Kabinlaphom was allowed to cut his head off, it would be better. He then left the palace and lay down under two *tan* trees. On the *tan* tree was a pair of eagles, husband and wife, talking: "Tomorrow we will eat human flesh." The wife then became interested: "Whose flesh will we eat?" The husband said, "we will eat the flesh of the Thammapala Kumman, since he cannot find the answer to the questions of Kabinlaphom. Kabinlaphom will cut his head of tomorrow." The female eagle then asked, "What are the questions?" The male eagle answered that there were three questions: 1) Where is the brightness in the morning? 2) Where is the brightness in the daytime? 3) Where is the brightness in the evening? The female bird was very curious and asked further, "What is the answer?" Her husband said that in the morning the brightness is in the humans' face and that is why they wash their face. During daytime, the brightness is on the humans' chest, and that is why they splash their chest with water or perfume. In the evening, the brightness is on their feet and that is why they wash their feet before sleeping. As he heard the conversation between the eagles, Thammapala knew the answer, returned to the palace and in the following morning Kabinlaphom returned as agreed. Thammapala answered according to the conversation between the two birds, and Kabinlaphom agreed that the answer was correct. Before he was going to have his head cut of as an offering, he called his seven daughters and told them, "I will cut my head off and will offer it to Thammapala Kumman tomorrow. My head is sacred and powerful. If it is thrown in the water, the river will erupt throughout the land. If it is thrown in the air there will be no rain." He therefore ordered the seven daughters to place his head on a tray. The eldest daughter should catch my head and then all should start a procession with the head for a sixty minutes procession around the column and then return the head to its original place.

The daughters of Kabinlaphom are named:

The first one is called Thoongsawthy, ornate with *phila* flower and *pathamarat* precious stone and eats millet as food, holding in her right hand a wheel, in her left hand a conch and riding on Phaya Kut. The second is named Khorak. This daughter is ornate with *kang* flowers, *mukda* stones, eats sesame oil food, and holds in her right hand a bowl, in her left a cane, riding on a tiger. The third daughter is called Raksa. She is ornate with *luang* lotus flowers, *mora* stones, eats blood, and holds in her right hand a three-pointed spear, in the left hand an arrow, and rides on a pig. [The fourth one is missing in this version] The fifth one is called Kiriny, ornate with *champa* flowers and emeralds, eats peanuts as food, holds in her right hand a sickle, in the left hand, a gun, and rides on an elephant. The sixth daughter, who is called Kimitha, is ornate with *changkon* flowers, *bousalakham* stones, and eats *thany* bananas as food. She holds in her right hand a silver bowl, in her left hand poppy flowers, riding a buffalo. [The seventh daughter's name is also missing in this version.]

NOTES

1. During a visit to France in 1989, however, Kaysone Phomvihane, the leader of the Lao Peoples' Revolutionary Party, told journalists the king died in 1980. In December 1995, during the twentieth anniversary celebrations, Foreign Minister Lengsavat angrily admitted as much to journalists in Vientiane. This is the first mention of the king's death officially inside Laos to my knowledge.

2. The material for this paper was collected during anthropological fieldwork in Louang Prabang province of the Lao PDR from February to June 1993, February–March 1996, and April 1997. The fieldwork was financed by the Swedish Council for Research in the Humanities and Social Sciences. A first sketch of this paper was presented at the 5th International Conference on Thai Studies, London, July 1993. Since then my work has to some extent paralleled that of Grant Evans (see Evans 1998a), with whom I have enjoyed exchanges of ideas and opinions.

3. Thus, in 1993, I had occasion to witness the rituals that were carried out in a village in Muang Nan, Louang Prabang province, during the recitation of the *Vessantara Jakata*, the *boun pavet* in Lao parlance. As part of the ritual the senior monk,

the *satuu* of the village monastery was carried in procession as a representation of the *Pha Upakhoud* (the Buddha domesticating the Naga).

4. Memories of the Lao 'modern' recent history, especially photos and objects relevant to the independence movement are exhibited in Vientiane, an arrangement which is at the same time a statement of how the relation between Louang Prabang, as power center of *l'ancien Regime* and Vientiane as the capital of an independent nation, is supposed to be perceived. A suggested exhibition on culture in Louang Prabang, to be arranged for the inauguration of the restored Palace Museum in Louang Prabang, was for instance turned down by the Ministry of Information and Culture in Vientiane.

5. As for beauty standards, the following stipulations are employed: Candidates should be pretty and have a beautiful face with black eyes and arched eyebrows; the hair should be worn in the Lao bun *(kaw phom)* which is related to religious and moral standing (and said to be a sign of Lao lineage); the height should be about 160 cm, the hips and bust should be rounded in soft lines and not protruding; arms and bust should be proportionately placed in relation to the neck.

6. The document mentions, however, that for that year the participants had failed to supply items 8 and 9, the long drum and the pair of cymbals.

WOMEN'S POWER AND THERAVADA BUDDHISM

A PARADOX FROM XIENG KHOUANG

10

H. LEEDOM LEFFERTS, JR.

MONG the complexities of Lao culture and society, the relationship of Theravada Buddhism to the state plays a significant role. In these discussions, however, concerns about the relation of gender to religion—and thus to the state—tend not to be addressed. By highlighting women's roles in Theravada Buddhism, this paper hopes to encourage future discussions concerning the relationship of religion to the nation, and of the nation to the household and the individual.

As with any human social organization, a complex series of exchanges gives rise to and perpetuates Theravada Buddhism. Theravada Buddhism's continued strength, as a formal religion among many Lao today is an outcome of these exchanges. This paper proposes that these exchanges include, first and foremost, women as mothers and their relations to their sons as monks. These relations are relatively unvoiced in Lao culture, yet they are apparent in the uses and meanings of textiles, a product of Lao women and a requisite for monkhood established by the Enlightened One. The mute nature of the relationship between mother/woman and son/monk has led to its neglect by textual scholars. The behavior that forms the paradox of this article is contrary to text-based interpretations of Theravada Buddhist precepts and offers an alternative method for interpreting an important dimension of Lao culture.

This paper emerges from a paradox observed on the morning of 7 March 1991 in the compound of a newly established *vat* near Baan Naa Nuu, a village not far from Phonesavane, the capital of Xieng Khouang province. The occasion was a ceremony termed by the Lao Phuan celebrants, "Bun Khong Haut."[1] This ceremony revolved around the raising in rank of two monks, an elderly one and one who looked to be in his late twenties or early thirties. The paradox observed is of the mother of the youngest monk holding onto the robe of her son, and it was noted during the procession around the main structure of the *vat*—a combined *kuti* (monk's quarters) which also served as an enclosed meeting hall, or *sala*. This procession immediately preceded the ritual washing of the main participants by means of water poured down a trough made in the form of a serpent (*naak*), and then the movement of these monks to their new statuses.[2] This paper does not present a full description of the ceremony, but rather deals with the action of the mother and the implications to be derived from it.

SOME ASPECTS OF THE BUN KHONG HAUT

WHAT I observed was the monk's white-haired mother holding onto the robe of her son with her left hand. How is it permissible for a woman to touch—let alone hold onto—the robes worn by a Theravada Buddhist monk? My studies in Thailand over the twenty years preceding this ceremony had confirmed the rule that women and monks must not touch. Rules in the Vinaya explicitly ban women and monks from associating without chaperones, sitting on the same bench, or touching one another (Vajirananavarorasa 2512: 55–81). Once a woman, usually the mother of an ordinand and her husband, has donated robes or the cloth to make a monk's robes, she cannot touch them again. Only after these robes have been discarded can they be used in otherwise "profane" activities, such as cleaning rags for the *sala*, etc.

These impressions had been reinforced by my many observations of women's presentations of gifts to monks. These gifts either traveled by way of the hands of men, who could deliver them directly into a monk's hands, or were placed on a cloth held by a monk. In no case had the woman held the cloth at the same time as the monk had held his end.

I am confident, however, that the incident in I observed was no accident. The end of the monk's robe was draped (deliberately?) so that the woman could hold it while walking in the center of the procession. The men carrying the monk's palanquin were not uncomfortable with her presence; they did not try to force her away. The woman did not look as if she were being dragged along; she walked comfortably in the midst of the hubbub that characterizes a joyous Lao or northeast Thai Theravada Buddhist procession.[3]

My occasion for visiting Xieng Khouang province on those cold days of early March was to conduct research on Lao textiles in preparation for a forthcoming exhibition which would survey Tai textile production and meanings in mainland Southeast Asia and southern China (see Gittinger and Lefferts 1992). Attendance at this ceremony assisted, in unexpected ways, in fulfilling my research goals.

Other than the event observed, I saw magnificent displays of cloth as offerings and for use. This visit took place sixteen years after the end of the war and in one of its most battle scarred areas. Phonesavane was a ramshackle town of wooden one-story stores and residences; because of the danger of unexploded "bombies," walking randomly across the landscape was to court death or dismemberment. Thus, this magnificent display of cloth and the holding of such a ceremony were significant indicators of the reflorescence of Theravada Buddhism among Lao.

Toward the beginning of the ceremony both of the monks who were to be elevated in status were presented with several raised bed-like platforms (*meng*) covered with paper roofs constructed in the triply layered fashion of Theravada Buddhist architecture. These *meng* were grouped under a large, but congested, temporary bamboo thatch-roofed structure erected on the *vat* grounds. The paper on the *meng* roofs bore painted color outlines representing, on the lowest tier, tiles; on the middle tier an alms bowl out of which lotuses sprouted profusely; and, on the uppermost tier, an inscription which defined the occasion for this ceremony and named the donors of the *meng*. Many objects were displayed on and around the beds, including the eight requisites for a newly ordained monk, large numbers of factory woven textiles tailored into men's clothing, and handwoven textiles that could be used for *phaa thung*, women's skirts, and *phaa hom*, blankets. Garlands of Lao paper money in small denominations hung around each *meng*. A small bamboo *prasat*, monument, covered with white cloth and containing a pillow, accompanied each *meng*. I was told the *prasat* were given in memory of the fathers of the monks who were to be raised in status. Following the washing of the monks, the sets of requisites placed in the *meng* were used to reequip the monks for their new status.

This cloth and clothing were donated by laypeople to make merit. For weeks after the ceremony the receiving monk would distribute the cloth and clothing to visitors, thus permitting other laypeople to gain merit in a widening circle of redistribution. Laity also used cloth to save merit: each monk, after washing under water poured through the trough and donning new robes, walked over the backs of a line of prostrate men. Over the men's backs women had placed either plain white scarves or checked *phaa kamaa*. After the monks had walked over the men covered with these scarves, the women picked up the shawls and placed them over their own heads or around their necks.

THE PROCESSION

THE crux of this paper concerns behavior, which took place during the procession that circumambulated the *vat* prior to the reanointment.

A number of monks, mostly from other *vat*, walked at the front of the procession. Following the walking monks adult men and women, not rigorously separated, carried on palanquins covered by blankets the two monks who formed the focus of the procession. Each monk sat cross-legged, holding a long, burning, yellow wax taper between hands raised in a prayerful attitude. At the rear of the procession young men, enjoying themselves and somewhat drunk and making a display of their masculinity, held aloft three tall, pyramidal bamboo scaffolds supporting homemade rockets in the form of serpents, *naak*, colorfully decorated in paper with flamboyantly extended bodies. A Lao musical ensemble composed of kaen, drums, and cymbals, all making joyful noises accompanied these carousing young men and their high structures. In the center of the middle group of adult men and women, the monk's elderly mother held on to the robe of her son with her left hand.

UNRAVELING THE PARADOX

WHILE I had never before seen a monk and woman touching, I had heard it said that a mother may "hold on to her son's robes" so that she will be dragged into a higher rebirth as he attains merit through his ordination. Because of the textual prohibitions, I had never taken the expression literally. An assumption behind this expression is that a mother obtains merit through her son, that she is a passive object in need of the merit of son as monk to improve her status in later lives through better rebirths.

Tannenbaum, in a recent volume, quotes Shan Theravada Buddhist monks in Mae Hong Son province, northwestern Thailand, who directly connect a monk's robes and the improvement in merit of a mother who thinks of them. These citations occurred in ordination sermons, such as the following, in which "a monk told the story of a woman who had sponsored her son's ordination as a novice." Directly quoting the sermon:

She had made a lot of merit but also some demerit.

> She died; her bad deeds stuck with her, so she was stuck in hell. She fell into hell. In her heart she put aside the reddish orange flames and her thoughts came to the robes, the robes of her son. She thought the robes and the flames were the same. The fires of hell were extinguished. The fires of hell disappeared. Those who were the monsters that guard hell, all became

beautiful people. Those who were birds with small and crooked mouths [hungry ghosts] all changed into *hangsa* [Brahma] birds and all of them ascended straight away into heaven. (Abbot, Wat Pha Nawn; Maehongson Town; February 2, 1985; ordination sermon); (Tannenbaum 1995: 113–4, see also p. 120).

Keyes (1984: 227–8) cites a variation of this story from the North Thai *Anisong Buat*, in which the relation between a mother's action and salvation is somewhat less distinct. In this, as a mother sees the flames of hell, she describes them as "the most beautiful yellow, truly just like the yellow robes of her son just after he had been ordained." However, this does not result in her salvation. Lord Yama, the God of the Underworld, persists in throwing her into hell. Then, a "huge golden lotus, the size of an ox-cart wheel" rises up to save her. The story does not state a causal connection between the mother's recollection of the color of her son's robes and her salvation.

In these instances we see a close association between women, especially mothers, and monks' robes. However, simply positing that thinking or speaking about robes leads to the expiation of bad karma and rebirth to higher heavens does not adequately explore the paradox in the Xieng Khouang event. While the Tannenbaum and Keyes citations direct attention to the relationship of mother, robe, and son/monk, they do not state the close connection I observed. In the Xieng Khouang scene, the mother holds the robe; she does not just walk at a respectful distance thinking about its color.

APPROACHES FROM MATERIAL CULTURE

IN undertaking further analysis in order to comprehend this event, I have come to see that the incident involves more than a woman dreaming or speaking about salvation through a connection with her son's robes. The central image is the robe connecting the monk to his mother. In other contexts I have written of the meanings of Thai and Lao things, especially textiles, which are not celebrated in words (cf. Lefferts 1992a, 1994). Anthropologists recognize the existence of symbolic systems other than those which are captured in or represented by words (Tambiah 1981; Turner 1980). I submit that the relationship I observed, while only hinted at in Lao and Thai texts, may be most adequately understood in terms of symbolic manipulation almost entirely contained in a domain of material culture.

The incident observed concerns three related themes, which are important in understanding and translating Southeast Asian Theravada Buddhist material cultural systems. These themes are:

1. The display of power through action, largely without benefit of verbal expression,
2. Gender in a system having as its foundation a textual tradition controlled by and oriented towards men, and
3. Ultimate possession.

I will discuss these in order and then conclude with a summary of the role of cloth in defining social and religious organization in Lao and northeast Thai Theravada Buddhist cultures.

The Display of Power through Action

A cultural anthropologist posits that thought occurs not only in the mind of a person, hidden from the eyes and ears of others, but also in the open; it is made manifest through a number of channels, one of which might be verbal. The methods used by individuals to communicate their thoughts are chosen from the repertory of expressive systems available in that culture. These are more or less mutually agreed upon and are subject to clarification and expansion through the concerns of people in daily interaction.[4] Clifford Geertz (1973: 360) states:

> Human thought is consummately social: social in its functions, social in its forms, social in its applications. At base, thinking is a public activity—its natural habitat is the houseyard, the marketplace, and the town square.

Regarding what I observed, Geertz's approach suggests that what we may be concerned with is not so much what we have been told about the separation of women and monks, as with what we see, the arrangement of people and things. I my case we see a woman—the mother of the monk—walking behind her son, elevated on his palanquin, and holding onto a portion of his robe.

Describing the event in this manner brings to the fore several interpretative levels. First, the mother is below and behind her son. She is not only behind him in terms of distance, but she is also below him in terms of height; both dimensions are of special importance for connoting distance in Lao and Thai culture (Formoso 1990). Detailing these dimensions enforces the recognition that, without doubt, this is a ceremony focused on monks; the mother's role is secondary.

Second, the mother does have a right to a direct connection with her son;

she is not severed from him, but does have a link. This is connoted through her grasp of the cloth.

Presented in this manner, the kind of public statement that accompanies this event, while paradoxical, is direct. The ceremony memorializes monks; it positions these monks hierarchically with respect to one another. The monks at the front of the procession walk. Because of their robes they are of the same category as the monks on the palanquins. Their position, while at the front, shows hierarchical importance, which is comparable to the importance of vertical elevation. These walking monks precede the lay participants and, in that sense, are "above" them. However, they move themselves in this ceremony, while the two monks who are its focus sit and are carried.

The lay congregation that celebrates them, though elevated, surrounds the monks who form the focus of the ceremony. Thus, while the lay people celebrate and raise these monks, they contain them. This containment is intentional; other methods of moving these monks to the ceremony are available, such as having them walk themselves, having other monks carry them, etc. Tambiah (1970: 110), quoting a former abbot of a northeast Thai-Lao village, remarks that raising in rank comes about because "the villagers judge that he is fit to be made *somdet*." Carrying a monk above the crowd shows his elevated status *vis-à-vis* the laity, at the same time his containment by them shows that this celebration occurs because they deem it appropriate.

The monk whose mother follows him is also above her. Just as every person must be born of a woman, this monk precedes and is elevated above the woman who bore him. He moves along at one level on a path while she moves along at another level. Although behind him, his mother remains with him, exercising a connection to him. Contained in this event, then, are the open expressions of two kinds of power. On the one hand, there is the power that comes through the teachings of the Buddha, which are perpetuated through the line of members of the *sangha*. On the other hand, there is the power of origin and lineal descent, codified through the presence of a monk's mother, without whom he could not be where he is.

This paper thus specifically addresses the literature on the complicated relationship between Buddhist monks and their mothers (cf. Keyes 1984, 1986; Kirsch 1982, 1985). The intricate linkages that we see in this event give a fair approximation of the depth of issues that we are dealing with and present it to us in open discourse, confirming the thrust of Geertz's statement.

Gender in a System Controlled by Men

Theravada Buddhism as practiced in Laos and Thailand can be characterized as a philosophical-religious textual system heavily weighted towards male hegemony. Males as monks control the progression of ceremonies and the verbal and written texts by which these ceremonies are made manifest. In addition, many outside observers (most of whom, including myself, are males) and most members of the Sangha (all of whom are male) state that women have little or no role in Theravada Buddhism as currently conceived and are, at best, its supporters and nurturers.

However, an undercurrent of disagreement as to the total power of men and monks in religious systems generally and in Theravada Buddhism in particular has begun to be expressed. Cort's recent article (1996), exploring the role of material culture in Jain religion as a mechanism for understanding something about that religion other than that available through (male) texts, bears on this point. He concludes:

> Jainism, as with any religious tradition, is in part a vast historical enterprise of trying to find, realize, and express the values and meanings of human life. The study of texts alone is insufficient for an adequate understanding of that enterprise. To the extent that human life is by its very nature embodied, physical, and material, the study of religion therefore must involve itself with the study of the material expressions of religion (Cort 1996: 631).

My studies (Lefferts 1992a, 1992b, 1992c, 1994) show that Tai textiles present, in an nonverbal, unwritten manner, women as active agents in Theravada Buddhism.[5] These items of material culture offer ways to understand the daily and annual re-creations and perpetuations of this philosophical system that differ from those usually presented through text and sermon. Material culture, as text and sermon, requires interpretation and contextualization. As Cort (1996: 614) points out, however, partly because of "the nature of the Euro-American academy itself," oriented as it is to written text, we tend not to see the expressiveness of non-textual items of material culture.

In Lao and northeast Thai Theravada Buddhism, women produce and weave textiles. Even as factory woven, dyed, and sewn robes have become increasingly available, textiles remain nominally presented by women, through men, to monks. During Lao and northeast Thai-Lao ordination ceremonies, *Bun Buat Naak*, women, usually mothers, present new robes to ordinands. These presentations come after the *naak* (serpent) dons liminal cloth to set him apart from both lay and monk. Donning these "serpent" clothes deepens a son's alignment with women, specifically the women of his household, just as he is about to sever his ties to the household (Lefferts 1994). Thus, women control men's (sons') access to the monkhood, even as, through the presentations of robes, they renounce these sons in order to gain merit.[6].

This event provides a non-textual, albeit textile, entry into understanding relationships in Theravada Buddhism. Specifically, it shows a connection between a mother and her son, a monk. It shows the ambiguities in that link in terms of subject positioning and resultant subject hierarchy. However, it also shows, in terms of both monks' positioning within, yet above, the crowd of celebrants, that such a link is possible, recognized, and accepted.

Ultimate Possession

This event also hints, however, at a deeper connection between a mother and the monk who is her son. It shows that this mother has not and perhaps cannot totally renounce the robes that she "made" and presented or, by extension, the residual rights she possesses in her son. It also shows that her son, even as a monk, cannot totally renounce his relationship to his mother, to whom he owes his embodiment.

These assertions, which present a central paradox in Buddhist thought, would not have been possible without the recent works of Weiner (1992) and Hendry (1993), stemming from Mauss (1954). The paradox is that Buddhism uses physical objects, including people, to communicate and carry out its goals. The resolution of this paradox is that a dynamic tension exists between the two—a recognition of embodiment as appropriate, not as something evil to be discarded.[7]

Recognition of the close and cooperative relationship between materiality and the attainment of enlightenment permits us to see that it is appropriate for a mother to hold onto her son's robes. This mother gave birth to and, in some ultimate sense, is responsible for this man who is being raised in rank; she is also responsible for the robes which he wears. Just as a gift carries with it the obligation for a return (Mauss 1954), so the (re)presentations of son and robes require a (re)presentation of the embodiment that made this ceremony possible. Following Weiner, I suggest that these robes and this son can never be totally alienated from the person who (re)produced them.

This son/monk—as a physical body—could not exist without this mother. The robes, which connote his movement from "sonhood" to monkhood, also came from her or her representative. Buddhism in no way denies their physical existence; Buddhist philosophy depends and capitalizes upon the existence of both son and robes to sustain its goal of the continuing possibility of enlightenment through observation of the precepts of The Way.

Finally, we note that son becomes monk through donning the robes. The son moved through his life before monkhood in the company of his mother; it is often stated that young men become monks for their parents, in particular their mothers (Tambiah 1970). The son's mother nourished him; it is through an acknowledgment of this debt and its continuing repayment (*bunkhun*, cf. Mills, n.d.; Mills1990; Mulder 1990) that a son becomes a monk.

The robes signify the attainment of this new status. These robes are the product of the mother's work; just as she (re)produced her son, both in body and in mind, so that he would undertake appropriate actions, so she has (re)produced the means to actualize the movement to monkhood. Through wrapping himself in robes at ordination, a son wraps himself in his mother's work (Hendry 1993). As he has now become the embodiment of his mother's work, so this event demonstrates the link of ultimate possession between monk and mother. The power of embodiment and wrapping makes the mother's presence in this ceremony as palpable and contingent as the monk—her son—and his robes.

This monk's mother has a recognized and respected place in this procession, holding on to the robes she made and, in an ultimate sense, continues to possess, just as she also continues to possess, again in an ultimate sense, her son.

CONCLUSION

THERE has been a great deal of discussion about the role of women in Theravada Buddhism in Laos, Thailand, and elsewhere in mainland Southeast Asia. That discussion tends to treat culture as if it were a single unit. It also tends to state that, if women cannot be nuns, they cannot have power equivalent to a monk. This paper, arising from the visual paradox of a mother holding a portion of her monk son's robes while he is in a procession to reordination at a higher level, takes a contrary tack. It suggests that an analysis of material culture shows women legitimately occupying recognized, central, and active locations in this Theravada Buddhist system.

The action of holding onto the robe asserts a particular relationship, that of mother to son. This is not any woman accidentally holding onto this robe, it is the one to whom the weaver is especially and uniquely related.[8] Moreover, this relationship is an active one; a mother is not simply any person who nourishes a baby who becomes a young man. A mother is actively engaged in forming a son of the proper maturity and disposition to engage in appropriate actions on his own behalf as well as hers. The production and gifting of cloth, especially the production of white cloth (Lefferts 1996), initiates a movement—acts as a trigger—to move the young man towards undertaking these actions. The photograph shows that these actions are initiated, carried out, and recognized through a "conversation" of items of material culture, specifically cloth. Textiles signify the power of Lao and northeast Thai women; women produce and reproduce a tradition, which assigns them a formative role in the continuity of Lao and Thai social systems. Women also (re)produce the means by which all Lao and Thai Buddhist laypeople—men as well as women—obtain salvation.

Gifts of people and their statuses—which identify them and license their actions—are gifts of the highest order; such gifts can never be totally alienated from the producer/giver. The producers and givers of these gifts in Lao and Thai Theravada Buddhism are women, specifically mothers.

This paradoxical action of a mother and son observed in March 1991, records a fragment of behavior by which we can make sense of a larger humanity. Paying attention to the messages contained in material culture enables us to see behavior to which we might otherwise be insensitive.

NOTES

The research on which this paper is based was conducted over an extensive period; the specific example which forms its focus was observed while I was sponsored by the Lao Committee of Social Sciences, with the financial assistance of the Social Science Research Council, New York, holding a Southeast Asia Regional Research Fellowship. I thank Mr. Houmphanh Rattanavong for his assistance in approving and expediting this project. This work was part of research undertaken for the Tai Textile project, under the overall sponsorship of the Textile Museum, Washington, D.C. Acknowledgments are due to the several venues in which earlier editions of this paper were presented, initially as part of a symposium on "Gender and Buddhist Traditions of Thought" at West Chester University, Pennsylvania, USA, in 1992, followed by talks given at the Asian Art Museum, San Francisco; the Los Angeles County Museum of Art; the Siam Society; and, finally, at Drew University. I appreciate the astute comments of many commentators, inluding Grant Evans, Louise Cort, and an anonymous reviewer, in refining this paper.

1. Tambiah (1970: 109–115) uses the spelling "hot" for this ceremony.

2. Summary descriptions of this ceremony appear in Levy (1968: 33–37) and Tambiah (1970: 109–115); it is also reported by Condominas (1968: 105–6) and in an early report by a Thai monk sent as an ethnographer to Thailand's Northeast, Phra Yanrakkhit (R.S. 119 [1900/01]). I am indebted to Prof. Richard O'Connor for the Condominas and Phra Yanrakkhit references.

3. This was the second time I witnessed a ceremony to raise monks in status; the first was in Baan Chaan Laan, Amphur Panna, Ubon Ratchathani province, northeast Thailand. The observation of the mother holding on to her son's robes was not made there; however, at that ceremony, where twenty-eight monks were ordained, the raising in rank of the one monk was not a prominent event. At the Bun Khong Haut in Xieng Khouang, the raising in rank of these two monks was the only event.

4. This issue is perhaps most cogently captured in the works of Edward T. Hall

(1959, 1982, 1983), although it forms the basis of much anthropological thought (cf. Turner 1980). It might be said that, in some respects, this paper is an expansion of ideas laid down decades ago that have not been adequately treated by ethnographic writing in Theravada Buddhist Southeast Asian cultures.

5. This parallels the exposition by March (1983) concerning the roles of cloth and writing among the Temang of Nepal.

6. Extensions of this thought provide ways to see how women, in presenting robes, participate in fundamental ways with the "symbol of transmission" represented by robes in Buddhism. Faure (1995: 350) points out that the focus in Mahayana sects has generally been on the transmission of robes as the "conferring of automatic deliverance." While it would be inappropriate to generalize this meaning into the Lao Theravada Buddhist context, it is certainly permissible to say that the gifting of robes and, thus, their ultimate control by women is an important mechanism by which women become and remain active participants in Buddhism's central ceremony.

7. The implications of this striving for balance between the material world and non-existence have occupied much of Buddhist art and thought. Perhaps its most well known resolution in Southeast Asian Theravada Buddhism is the sculptural form of the *naga* Muchalinda surrounding and protecting The Buddha during meditation. The same point is made in the paintings and sculptures of Nang Thoranee, sometimes called the "Earth Goddess," wringing her hair in order to subdue the forces of Mara as the Buddha obtains Enlightenment. The point of these representations is that the forces of this world work in conjunction with, not in opposition to, Buddhist doctrine at the moment of salvation

8. In *The Entrance to the Vinaya* (*Vinayamukha*) (Vajirananavarorasa 2512: II, 92–101 et passim), in the chapter on rules requiring forfeiture or abandonment (*Nissaggiya Pacittiya*) of material items, namely, the first section on cloths (*Civara-vagga*), and many others relating to various uses of cloth, the fourth through the tenth rules, *sikkhapada*, note that men or women related to a bhikkhu have opportunities for giving and processing cloth not available to non-relatives. Here is written recognition of different categories of laypeople with respect to monks, with relatives having a privileged status. I suggest that this privileged status comes through the primary relationship of mother and son/monk.

BOOKS OF SEARCH
THE INVENTION OF TRADITIONAL LAO LITERATURE AS A SUBJECT OF STUDY

11

PETER KORET

W ORKS of Lao literature have traditionally been referred to as ຫນັງສືທນັງຫາ "Books of Search." A commonly given explanation of this title is that one cannot expect to immediately understand what one reads in a Lao manuscript, but should be prepared to "search" for its meaning (Koret 1994). People who traditionally had an active involvement in the composition, transcription, and performance of the literature had to rely on their overall knowledge of the literary tradition in order to interpret individual works. It is not surprising, therefore, that they have been compared by a major contemporary scholar of Lao literature to modern-day intellectuals (Jaruwan 1979). There is, however, a significant difference between the concept of "search" in traditional Lao understanding, and "research" as conceived by contemporary literary scholars.

Traditional Lao literary "searchers" of meaning were different from modern scholars in that the literary tradition was an integral part of their daily lives, and that was the reason why it was studied. They examined the literature in order to understand more deeply the lessons it taught and the way in which its teachings could be more effectively communicated. The purpose of their search was therefore to assist the literature's fulfillment of its social function in Lao society.[1] In contrast, modern Lao literary scholarship by Lao and Thai scholars has developed in proportion to the decline of literature's role in society.

This work is a short study of the transition from search to research in Lao literature. As we will see, before the second quarter of this century, when Lao people were still actively writing or copying Lao stories, analyzing the literature would have been thought of as inappropriate and unnecessary. In more recent years, when the literature has stopped being actively copied and has begun to be analyzed, the appropriate questions, by and large, have not been asked. The answers that have been given have not merely been unfaithful to their topic but have unintentionally changed it. Rather than adapting the analysis to better conform to the subject, the subject has been restructured to prove its worthiness according to the rules set forth in the analysis. To understand why and how this has happened, one must first consider how modernization in general, and modern technology in particular, has effected not only the evolution of Lao literature but also the evolution of Lao people's thoughts about their own past. Whereas a longer work would give proper attention to several important literary scholars, this study focuses primarily on the work of Sila Viravong. Sila Viravong pioneered the study of Lao literature, and his works continue to have great influence on contemporary literary scholarship. Sila Viravong's career is of particular interest in that it marks the halfway point between the "search" of Lao literature, where the searcher is actively involved in the literary tradition and studies the literature in order to make it better fulfill its social role, and the researcher, to whom the major role of the literature is to serve as the subject of his study.

TRADITIONAL LAO LITERATURE AND ITS ROLE IN LAO SOCIETY

LAO literature was the major intellectual and artistic tradition of the Lao from at least the sixteenth century through the first half of the twentieth century. It was the primary means by which traditional wisdom was preserved from one generation to the next. As in ancient societies throughout Southeast Asia, the link between art and religion in Laos was inseparable. In Lao society, the cultural center has traditionally been the Buddhist temple. In the past, the majority of Lao men spent a considerable amount of their teenage years as temple novices, where they gained literacy and received their general education. The ability to read, perform, and compose literature was entirely based upon skills that were learned in the temple. In the eyes of the Lao, both literature and the process of learning itself are intimately associated with the Buddhist religion. With few exceptions, works of traditional Lao literature are presented as life stories of the Bodhisattva taken from the Buddhist scriptures regardless of their content or origin.[2] This both legitimizes the works in the eyes of their sponsors and affords them the high respect with which the Lao public views them, not merely as entertainment but also as teachings of the Buddha. At the same time, the popularity of the stories makes them a useful vehicle with which to spread Buddhist teachings among the Lao. Traditional Lao literature developed under the patronage of the royal court of the kingdom of Lane Xang. It was influenced both by the literary tradition of the neighboring kingdom of Lanna and an earlier and probably oral Lao tradition of poetry and storytelling.[3] At the end of the seventeenth century, the kingdom of Lane Xang split into three separate entities, followed by a long period of political turmoil and foreign domination. Lao literature rather than ceasing to exist, became a product of village culture and in this way survived.[4] There is evidence that a large percentage of literary works and the majority of poetic literature were composed after the disintegration of Lane Xang. To understand the body of works that comprises "traditional Lao literature" as it appears to us today, therefore, it is essential to take into account that a) much of the existing literature was not produced by the royal court of Lane Xang, but rather more recently on a village level, and b) even the works that were originally composed during the period of Lane Xang have been influenced by the centuries in which they have been transcribed to serve the needs of village society.

KNOWLEDGE OF LAO VERSIFICATION PRIOR TO THE MID-TWENTIETH CENTURY

DEFINING the fundamentals of Lao versification has been a central concern in the twentieth century study of Lao literature. A major achievement in the career of Sila Viravong was his identification of the rules that make Lao poetry "poetry."[5] To give perspective to his work and the role that it has played in the standardization of traditional literature, one must ask the question: Prior to the literary research of Sila, how did people who were actively involved in the creation, performance, and consumption of poetry perceive Lao verse and the components of its composition?

During my three and a half years of research in Laos and northeast Thailand, I have asked many people and searched through many manuscripts, but have found no evidence for the existence of a text of Lao versification that is of earlier origin than the work of Sila. I have asked at many temples and have similarly never heard of the rules of poetry being taught. I have talked to many people who have transcribed and composed Lao literature. I have found that frequently they themselves could not tell me the rules of the poetry that they were engaged in writing.

There is a simple reason why the rules of literary composition were not taught inside of Lao temples. They were not taught because the Lao did not consider that literature was being written there. The great majority of Lao stories, whatever their origin, were composed in the form of Jataka tales, life stories of the Bodhisattva. Lao people commonly believe that what modern scholars refer to as Lao literature are merely translations or at best adaptations of such texts. Whereas stories are thus afforded a sacred status that literature in and of itself would not be given, the question of literary art is viewed as an irrelevant and even sacrilegious one. To whom does one teach poetic rules? The origin of most Lao works is impossible to pinpoint. Few of the stories include the name of a composer and most if not all originated beyond the memory of any living Lao. These facts reinforce the commonly held Lao belief that works of such sacredness could not be traceable to an author of mere flesh and blood. Khamphaeng Kettavong, a French-educated Lao scholar, explained to me the resistance that he faced from Lao monks when he discussed the artistic as opposed to religious merit of individual Lao stories. His analytical approach to the literature was viewed suspiciously as if he were violating sacred texts.

The monks at the temples are not expected to write literature but they are expected to copy it. Classes are taught in the religious script that is used to record the stories. The process of transcribing is learned by observing one who is experienced in the skill. It is in the transcribing, where the only preparation deemed necessary is to learn how to write the alphabet and hold the stylus, that the creative process goes on. My research has revealed that the transcribers, in their revision of manuscripts, show an astute awareness of the skills and the rules of Lao poetry in which they have neither been formally trained nor express any knowledge. This knowledge is the result not of a classroom education in poetic rules but rather years of exposure to poetry, which has played an integral role in their everyday lives.

THE MODERNIZATION OF LAOS AND NORTHEAST THAILAND AND THE TRANSFORMATION AND DECLINE OF TRADITIONAL LITERATURE

DURING the twentieth century traditional literature has become increasingly marginalized in Laos and northeastern Thailand. A major factor in the decline of the literature is the decrease in the cultural and political authority of the Buddhist temple as a result of the political manipulation of the monkhood by a) the Thai government in Isan for the purpose of integrating the region into the Thai state, and b) the revolutionary movement of the Lao Patriotic Front (Neo Lao Hak Sat) and subsequently the communist government in Laos to align religious practices to fit the aims of the revolution.

The state institutionalization of secular education in the twentieth century has marginalized the role of the Buddhist temple as religious education has been replaced by modern schooling with a western oriented curriculum. As a result, fundamental skills necessary for literary preservation, performance, and appreciation, including a knowledge of traditional scripts, methods of transcription, etc., were neglected, and the literature grew increasingly distant from people's daily lives. In place of the Lao literary epics of the past, students in the twentieth century were taught to emulate literary compositions of Thai and western origin. The imitation of western cultural traits became a source of status in modern society, whereas acknowledgment of interest in traditional culture came to be viewed contemptuously as a sign of one's poor education and low class.

Literature in northeast Thailand has undergone a greater degree of marginalization than in Laos as a result of the government policy of assimilating the region into the Thai state. The Thai government initially faced the threat of French claims to Isan based upon the Lao ethnicity of the majority of its population, followed by challenge of instilling a Thai identity in the region's inhabitants. As a result, there was a suppression of literature and other cultural practices that the people of Isan share with the neighboring Lao. The curriculum of compulsory education further alienated the people from their traditional customs, teaching exclusively the history, language, and culture of the central Thai. As contact has grown between the people of Isan and other parts of the country, Thai cultural practices have increasingly been adopted as a necessary prerequisite for individuals wishing to become successful and respected members of modern Thai society.

Modern technology has also played a role in reducing the relevance of traditional literature. Modern forms of mass communications such as radio, film, and television spread Thai and western culture and replaced the role of Lao poetic epics as a source of entertainment. Lao literature, never a static tradition, evolved to meet the changing demands of its audience. The musical entertainment form known today as *mau lam* was largely developed during the twentieth century.[6] *Mau lam* originally consisted of works of Lao literature performed to musical accompaniment with melodies based on traditional chanting styles. Throughout the years, *mau lam* has increasingly been influenced by Thai mass media, particularly the popular form of country music known as *luk thung*. In *mau lam* performances of the past few decades, traditional works of literature have largely been replaced by tales of modern origin, in which the use of Thai vocabulary has steadily increased.

With the establishment of publishing houses in Laos and northeast Thailand, the transcription of information onto palm leaves became obsolete. Printing, with its effect on how information was stored, distributed, and consumed, came to have a major impact on both the literature's content and social use. The conventions by which literature was composed were very much a product of the medium in which it was recorded, and when the medium no longer had a practical application in Lao society, the literature was forced to adapt to meet the changing demands of its audience.

PRINTING TECHNOLOGY AND ITS EFFECT ON TRADITIONAL LAO LITERATURE

TO place in perspective modern conceptions of traditional literature, it is necessary to look in some detail at the development of printing technology among the Lao. Whereas publishing was initially intended to increase the effectiveness of literature's traditional role, it gradually transformed the literature and its content. In the following section we will divide the influence of the print media on literature into three categories: the adaptation of the literature in order to preserve its traditional role in a rapidly changing society, the preservation of the literature for future generations, and the transformation of the literature into an academic subject of study.

The earliest publications of Lao literature largely fit into the first category. Dating from the late 1930s, publishing houses in northeast Thailand and Bangkok produced and distributed cheaply priced editions of Lao stories. The height of their popularity was from the 1940s through the early 1960s. These publishing houses served an important purpose in that they could distribute the literature in a more convenient way than in the past. By recording the stories in the Thai script, they made traditional literature accessible to the Lao speaking people of Isan who were educated in government schools where traditional scripts were not taught. Despite their difference in packaging, printed works of literature were intended to play a role in society similar to poetry recorded on palm leaves. Like traditional works of literature, publications of verse were generally not meant to be read silently, but rather performed before an audience. They were intended to serve as aids for the performers of *mau lam*, and for monks to use in their sermons.

An examination of one of the major writers for these publishing houses, Nauy Phiwphin, reveals many similarities to traditional transcribers of Lao literature. He was educated at a temple, where he gained his knowledge and appreciation of the Lao literary tradition. The ideas expressed in his writing are similar to those of previous generations of Lao transcribers. In traditional Lao literature (as in many oral poetic traditions), there is no concept of individual authorship of a given story. Similarly, from the contents of Nauy Phiwphin's introductions and his writing itself, one can see that he had no intention of writing or claiming to write "original" tales himself but rather took pride in his knowledge of traditional sacred works and his ability to improve on them. The extent and type of changes that he makes in his stories appear consistent with traditional transcription practices. In traditional literature, the author of a work would typically ask readers to add to his composition to the best of their ability. Whereas this type of request serves a practical purpose in a literature that it is continually transcribed and revised, it makes far less sense when the story is in a fixed form on a printed page. Nauy Phiwphin, however, not wishing to abandon this convention, includes a lengthy passage (one of the longest passages that is obviously of his own creation) exhorting his readers to improve on his composition. He attempts to adapt the convention to the new medium by asking his readers to send in their corrections by mail.

Printing technology has also served to maintain the relevance of literature in its religious context. A company in Bangkok currently prints traditional Lao stories in the Thai script on palm leaves, advertising the works as suitable for religious offerings. One temple in the Lao province of Savannakhet exchanged most of its considerable collection of old manuscripts for these modern reproductions. For the monks in the temple, who made regular use of Lao apocryphal Jataka tales in their sermons, the new technology was beneficial in that it increased the efficiency with which the literature fulfilled its traditional role. The Thai people who traded the manuscripts, however, were not interested in convenience in use as they came from a generation in which the literature was no longer performed. The old works were of value as collector's items.

During the mid-twentieth century, the spread of technology in Laos lagged behind neighboring northeast Thailand. Although there are publications in Laos dating from the 1920s, the first Lao language newspaper to be issued on a regular basis did not appear until shortly before the Second World War. Throughout the 1940s, printing in Laos remained very basic. The transcription of literature onto palm leaves, therefore, remained widespread long after it had disappeared from northeast Thailand. In the 1930s and 1940s, it was common practice for monks in Vientiane to obtain published versions of Lao poetic tales from neighboring Thailand and recopy them onto palm leaves for the purpose of circulation.[7] In one palm leaf version of *Nang Auraphim,* for example, failing to take into account the change in medium, the transcriber advertises the exciting qualities of the story that follows and asks the reader to purchase a copy.[8]

The second major use of the printing press is in the preservation of literature for future generations. The publication of works in this category marked a major departure from the past. From its origin, Lao literature was produced to meet the needs of an existing audience. A major incentive in the early publications of Lao literary works in Thailand was economic, and a publisher's success was measured by the extent to which literature could be adapted in order to maintain its popularity. The motivation behind preservation, in contrast, was the belief that that the social function of the literature was rapidly declining to the point that the literature would disappear if special efforts were not made to preserve it. Therefore, rather than creating the literature because it played a role in society, it was produced precisely because it did not, but was "worthy" to be saved. Two major figures in the preservation of traditional Lao literature are Phra Ariyanuwat and Pricha Phinthaung, both of Isan origin. Similar to the people involved in publishing, both men gained their knowledge of the literary tradition from their religious education. Whereas some of their transcriptions were produced as early as the 1950s, the majority of their work dates from the late 1960s through the 1980s. As the demands of the market were not criteria in their work, their projects have had to rely on private funding largely from sources outside of Isan and Thailand itself.

The third major consequence of print technology was the establishment of literature as an academic subject of study. The print media, with the efficiency that it provided in the storage and dissemination of information, paved the way for studies of an analytical nature that would not have been possible when knowledge was collectable at best on hand-copied manuscripts scattered over a wide geographical region. Similar to the people involved in the publishing of Lao literature in the previous two categories, the earliest literary scholars were males who had ties to the temple. The majority was skilled at the performance and composition of Lao poetry. In contrast, academics who presently study and write about the subject are largely removed from both the literary tradition and the environment in which it was produced. This is observable, for example, in the prevalence of women as literary scholars. In the past, Lao literature was generally composed, transcribed, and performed exclusively by males, as a literary education was attainable only inside of the temple. It was often considered improper for women even to handle such texts or to play any role other than that of a respectful audience. It is noteworthy that among the academics in Thailand and Laos that have made studies of Lao literature, it is almost exclusively the males who are knowledgeable in traditional scripts, and base their research on literature recorded in manuscript form. In contrast, the majority of female academics use as their sources printed transliterations.

The difference in perspective between academic scholars and the more traditional "searchers" of the literature can be seen in the type of criticisms that Thai academics commonly make concerning the transcriptions of Phra Ariyanuwat and Pricha Phinthaung. Similar to traditional transcribers of the literature, both tended to improve upon a work during the transcription. As both were skilled at composition, they tended to make considerable changes. As we have seen, improvements in transcription were considered commendable in the Lao literary tradition because they helped a story to better fulfill its social function as a source of education and entertainment. However Thai academics have a very different idea of what is acceptable in transcription. Although the Lao concept of literature was traditionally a flexible one, in the eyes of contemporary literary scholars, to alter a text in transcription is to diminish its authenticity and thereby reduce its value as a subject of study. Rather than appreciating the difference in their perspectives and therefore methods of transcription, several Thai literary scholars have contemptuously viewed the alterations made by these transcribers as the sign of their low education and lack of scholarly standards.[9] This attitude at some point was conveyed to both of the transcribers. Accepting the criticism and the modern standards that it implies, Phra Ariyanuwat and Pricha Phinthaung grew increasingly reluctant to reveal the manuscripts from which they made their transcriptions or admit that they were guilty of following traditional practices. True to their tradition, however, in practice they continued to make use of their artistic abilities to enhance existing stories.

THE INVENTION OF TRADITIONAL LAO LITERATURE AS A SUBJECT OF STUDY: THE WORK OF SILA VIRAVONG

SILA Viravong was the earliest and most influential modern scholar of Lao literature. From the 1930s through the early 1970s, he published a wide range of scholarly works on Lao literature, language, history, and religious practices, thereby reinventing traditional culture as an academic subject of study. In making the Lao people aware of their own historical and cultural heritage, Sila was instrumental in dictating how the past is to be given shape in the present. The contemporary relevance that Sila attributed to his literary studies (and cultural studies in general) is summarized in the introduction to his work *Panyot Khaung Vannakhadi* (The Benefits of Literature): "In the present day, literature is of considerable importance because it is where the national culture resides, and is a symbol of the ຄວາມຈະເລີນ 'khwam chaleun' (advanced state) of the nation" (1996: 2). In a work on versification composed during the French colonial period, he wrote further: "If literature is an indicator of the 'khwam chaleun' of humanity, then . . . Vientiane, when still independent, was a place that possessed 'khwam chaleun' in no lesser degree than any other city during the same period" (Sila Viravong 1993: ງ).[10] To place Sila's literary research into proper perspective, therefore, literature needs to be understood in relationship to its role as a representation of the *khwam chaleun* of the Lao nation.[11]

THE STUDY OF TRADITIONAL LAO LITERATURE AND LAO-THAI CULTURAL POLITICS

A fundamental if unstated objective of scholarship on traditional Lao literature in Laos and Thailand in the twentieth century, as illustrated in the pioneering work of Sila, is the defining of cultural and historical boundaries between the Lao and the Thai. As a result, an underlying theme of Lao and Thai academic studies from the 1930s through to the present is the struggle to assert ownership of symbols that can be used to manipulate modern conceptions of the past. It is in this context that one can appreciate the emphasis in Sila's statement above that the Vientiane Lao in the past not only possessed the quality of *khwam chaleun* but that the degree in which it was possessed was no less than other cities during the same period. Regardless of contemporary discrepancies in the size and power of the two nations, in the past they were on equal footing. As the creation of a Lao identity was fundamental to the establishment of a modern Lao nation, we have seen that the denial of a Lao identity was similarly integral to the creation of the modern Thai state. The invention of Lao literature as an academic subject of study can be seen, therefore, as part of a larger struggle to legitimize the existence of a Lao identity distinct from that of the Thai. Whereas Lao literature in scholarship that is produced in Laos serves as a symbol of the *khwam chaleun* that "adorns the Lao nation," in Thailand the identical tradition was initially suppressed in fear that it would foster an independent Lao identity and was ultimately coopted as an expression of the multi-faceted culture of the Thai.[12] According to the Lao, the proper name for the literature is "Lao literature," or "the Lao literary heritage," or "Lao literature produced during the period of Lane Xang," whereas it is referred to in Thai studies as the literature of "northeast Thailand," "the banks of the Mekong river," or "Isan–Lane Xang."[13] The script that is the precursor of modern Lao, in which much of the literature is recorded, is known as the Lao script in scholarship that is produced in Laos, whereas the identical alphabet is labeled as Thai Nauy (Little Thai) in studies of Thai origin.[14] According to the Lao, the Thai alphabet of King Ramkhamhaeng of Sukhothai was based upon the "Lao" script, whereas in Thai studies, the "Little Thai" script evolved from the alphabet of the Thai.[15] In scholarly works produced by the Lao, the literary tradition is described as testimony to the genius of the ancient Lao nation, with little or no acknowledgment of foreign influence on its origin or content, whereas to the Thai it was borrowed, with insignificant changes, from the literature of Chiang Mai.[16]

THE LIFE AND CAREER OF SILA VIRAVONG

A study of the life of Sila, with its many conflicts and contradictions, illustrates the fact that in attempting to sever the Thai and Lao into two separate national identities, it is not always possible to make a clean cut. For a man who is revered by people in contemporary Laos as a Lao nationalist, it is noteworthy that Sila was born and raised in northeast Thailand, where he received a religious education and was patronized by Phra Maha Somdet Wiravong (no relation), the administrative head of Isan monks, who through his role in introducing standardized Thai education in northeast Thailand played a major role in the integration of the region into the Thai state.[17] In an official posthumous biography published in Laos in 1990, the description of Sila's early years in Thailand is used to create his Lao nationalist credentials. He is portrayed in the following manner: as a man who "loved the Lao blood (that flowed through his veins)" (Outhin et al. 1990: 39–40). From an early age, he admired the Lao historical figure Chao Anou, a king who unsuccessfully fought to free Vientiane and neighboring regions from Thai control in the early nineteenth century. An advocate of the secession of Isan from the Thai state, his resentment of the Thai grew during his years as a monk in Bangkok, where he experienced the discrimination of the Lao of Isan at the hands of the people of central Thailand.[18] However, despite the extent to which the biographer emphasizes Sila's identification as a Lao and his anti-Thai sentiment, what becomes apparent from the work is the extent to which he maintained close connections with Thailand throughout his life. In the years that followed his initial move to Vientiane, he ran for political office (unsuccessfully) in both countries,[19] and entertained members of the Thai parliament from Isan when they visited Vientiane. When French authorities in Laos sought him for his political activities, he simply fled to Thailand, where he worked in the "Isan Literature" section of the Thai National Library until Laos achieved its independence. Much of his literary research was conducted and published in Thailand. Whereas the subjects that he studied were labeled as "Lao" when his work was published in Laos, in Thailand he wrote about the literature of "the Thai people of Isan" and the versification of "the Thai people of Vientiane."[20] It is not surprising that when selections of his Thai publications were reprinted in his biography, Sila's original use of the word "Thai" for the people of Isan and Laos was, in at least one instance, "corrected" to "Lao."[21]

One of the milestones in twentieth century Lao literary scholarship was Sila's "discovery" of one of the masterpieces of Lao literature, *Thaw Hung Thaw Cheuang*. The significance of the discovery is described in an introduction to Sila's biography:

> (Maha Sila) announced to the world the greatness (of the literary work *Thaw Hung Thaw Cheuang*). And what is of the utmost importance is his (further) announcement that the epic was created by a Lao composer in the kingdom of Lan Xang, which means that (Maha Sila's statement) is the historic declaration of the Lao people's ownership of this great work of literature. (Outhin, et al. 1990: 17)

Lao "ownership" of *Thaw Hung Thaw Cheuang* takes on added significance in light of the fact that the masterpiece was "discovered" in the Isan section of the Thai National Library in Bangkok. The location of the discovery is of particular importance symbolically, as the manuscript collection in which it is stored is believed by the Lao to consist of works that were taken when the Thai army razed Vientiane in the early nineteenth century.

Shortly after his arrival in Vientiane, Sila became the personal secretary of Phetsarath Rattanavongsa, a prince who was to become a leading figure in the Lao movement for independence. Prince Phetsarath played a prominent role in the creation of a Lao national identity through the revival of interest in Lao history and culture in the 1930s. Much of Sila's research and collection of manuscripts in Laos was carried out during this period under the prince's auspices. However, despite the patronage of Prince Phetsarath, Sila did not fit effortlessly into the Lao society of Vientiane. As an ardent proponent and creator of Lao nationalism, a major frustration in his career was his lack of influence and decision-making power in the various Lao literary committees on which he served. Regardless his knowledge of Lao culture, as a northeastern Thai of common origin, his words did not carry the same weight as did French-educated members of the Lao elite.

Perhaps the greatest irony in Sila's career, however, is the extent to which his Thai education and upbringing affected his scholastic work, and in so doing, shaped contemporary Lao perceptions of their literature. A major weakness of Sila's literary scholarship is his uncritical acceptance of previous Thai scholarship on Thai court poetry as a basis from which to analyze Lao literature. Sila influenced both the modern composition of traditional poetic forms and the interpretation of traditional works of poetry by his insistence that Lao literature conform to Thai standards of poetic composition, and his evaluation of their literary worth in proportion to their fulfillment of such standards.

SILA'S STUDY OF LAO VERSIFICATION

ALTHOUGH Sila produced scholarly works on a wide range of subjects, he is best known for his literary studies. Sila conducted research on Lao literature for a period of over ten years, both in Laos and at the Thai National Library in Bangkok. In the introduction to his initial study of Lao versification, Sila writes:

> I have not put together the various rules of composition included in this book without (relying upon proper) sources. I have arranged the rules based upon observations that I have made from the following books: *Baep Kap San Vilasini, Thaw Hung, Sang Sinsai, Vetsasantra Sadok, Nopasun, Kap Pramuni, Kap Thaw Saen Meuang,* and many other works . . . This is the first time that (such a study) has been written. Its existence is due solely to the interest of the one who has compiled it, without a teacher or advisor. I therefore expect for it to be filled with errors. I hope to be forgiven and to receive advice from those who are knowledgeable (1993: ꜟ).

The books from which Sila drew his observations, with one exception, are specific works of Lao literature. The exception is the first book that he has mentioned, *Baep Kap San Vilasini* (The Composition Style of Kap San Vilasini), which is a study of Pali verse forms.

Sila was the author of two major studies of Lao versification, *Baep Taeng Klaun Thaiy Viangjan Lae Baep Taeng Kap San Vilasini* (Methods of Composition of the Poetry of the Vientiane Thai and Kap San Vilasini), printed in Bangkok in 1942, and *Santhalaksana* (Versification), based upon the former work, published in Vientiane in 1961. These two studies were pioneering in that they provided a basic framework from which to understand the structure of Lao poetry. In works of traditional literature that are recorded on palm leaves, words are written together without separation. There are no divisions marking different hemistichs, lines, or verse. It was Sila who first analyzed the various types of Lao verse, set down their rules, and organized them visually according to those rules. It was Sila, for example, who first divided Lao verse on a printed page into two separate hemistichs.[22]

The major weakness in Sila's study is its lack of consideration of the medium in which Lao literature was recorded and performed, and the effect that this particular medium, with its opportunities and limitations, had on how it was organized. This weakness is noteworthy considering Sila Viravong's obvious familiarity with the medium, based upon his background and experience in the composition of Lao poetry.[23] It is in this discrepancy between Sila's familiarity with the literary tradition and his knowledge as expressed in his research that we witness his reinvention of Lao literature.

Sila's study of Lao poetry is based upon his knowledge of previous scholarship on the structure of Thai and Indian verse forms. When he wrote what are the first written rules of Lao versification, rules for the composition of Thai poetry had already been recorded in writing for several centuries. According to Prakhaung Nimmanhemin (1987), Sila's work *Santhalaksana* bears striking similarities to *Lak Phasa Thaiy* (Fundamentals of the Thai Language) by the Thai scholar Phraya Upakitsilapasan.[24]

In establishing the rules of Lao versification, Sila Viravong relied on previous scholarship of Thai verse forms to decide what is and is not worthy of being studied in the making of those rules. Though the specifics of certain Lao verse forms in his book necessarily differ from that of the Thai, the types of poetic rules under discussion are always the same. Lao poetry, for example, is examined for tone placement, rhyme within and between poetic lines, alliteration and assonance, etc., all of which one would find similarly in Thai scholarship on Thai poetry. On one level, taking Thai poetic rules as a background from which to study and make comparisons with Lao literature is perfectly natural. Laos and Thailand have related languages, cultures, and literature, and the poetic forms of the two can appropriately be examined for the same type of characteristics. It should, however, be asked whether Thai literary scholarship, as opposed to Thai poetry, is an appropriate model on which to base a study of Lao literature. Literary scholarship in Thailand studied the poetry of the royal court, a type of poetry that had a different method of transcription, a different style and location of performance, and a different intended audience than did traditional Lao literature as we know it at present. If Thai scholarship had concentrated on poetry of the common people, it would have served as a more relevant model from which to compare Lao verse.

Jit Phumisak's study on Lao poetic form shows a greater insight into the nature of Lao poetry precisely for the reason that it was written in comparison with the oral poetry of Thai villagers.[25] He describes the difference between poetry that was intended to be heard and poetry that was intended to be read:

> Poetry that is strictly composed according to a forced plan, that imposes fixed rules to control the meaning and emotion of an artist's creation, belongs to a later generation of poets . . . These poets wanted the poetry

seen, wanted a proper and orderly structure that was graceful to the eyes. They were not interested in how (the poetry) sounded, or if they were, they must have only wanted (the sound) to fit into an orderly framework, not to have small sounds popping up to trouble the ears . . . (1981: 191–2).

Thai literary scholarship focuses on the type of poetry that was "graceful to the eyes," whereas Lao poets, in their composition of literature, were more concerned with what was pleasing to the ear. The difference between the two different types of narrative is largely the difference between two mediums. In contrast to Lao literature, the composers and audiences of Thai court literature were largely restricted to an elite of nobles connected to the palace. Their level of education was higher than that of the composers of the majority of Lao literature, who came from all levels of Lao society. The transcribers of Thai literature similarly appear to have been connected with the court, and thus mistakes in the copying of texts, although existent, were likely to be less frequent than those made by the copyists of Lao works, who were commonly Buddhist novices of a young age. At the same time, performances of Thai works within the royal court did not present the same distractions, as did the large and often informal gatherings where Lao literature was read. There would therefore be less concern that the audience would not grasp the story's meaning.[26] Owing to differences in the production, preservation, and consumption of Thai and Lao literature, the form and content of the two were quite distinct. Thai court literature had less need for redundancy. It favored more esoteric writing, which displayed the education of the composer. This can be seen, for example, in the greater frequency with which Thai poets employed complex poetic forms, their use of erudite Khmer and Pali vocabulary, and their invention of literary words. At the same time, the contents of Thai court literature conformed to very different standards of acceptability than that of Lao literature. Characteristics of Lao stories such as obscene humor, the degree of playfulness in the depiction of the life of the Buddha, and the allowable mixture of non-Buddhist religious elements, such as belief in Tai spirits or deities, in religious tales would all be greatly restricted by the tastes of the Thai court.

As Thai literary works reflected the taste of the aristocracy, so did Thai literary scholarship, which was the exclusive domain of the elite. An example of this can be seen in the importance given in Thai literary scholarship to the study of Pali and Sanskrit verse forms and their relationship to Thai verse. In many cases it is in fact debatable whether such verse forms actually had Indian or Tai origins. Similar to labeling Southeast Asian folklore as Jataka tales, attributing Indian origins to Thai or Lao verse forms had the effect of raising their status (Jit 1981: 222–3).

Basing his research on Thai scholarship, Sila failed to adequately recognize the distinction between the two different types of literature. In his study, he attempted to "impose" on Lao poetry the "fixed rules" of a "proper and orderly structure" that is "graceful to the eye." In other words, what he did in effect was to force the characteristics of one type of medium onto poetry that belonged to another. In the introduction to Sila's first book on Lao versification, he wrote:

> I have the utmost belief that in the past a textbook must certainly have existed (that taught) composition rules of our poetry. Later on, however, it was lost, or has yet to be discovered (1993: ๑).

When considering the importance of tone placement in Lao poetry, however, the existence of such a textbook appears to be impossible. Most Lao people have trouble explaining the nature of tones. Similar to the use of grammar rules in English, placing tones on words is automatic rather than the result of conscious thought. Although tone markers have, in fact, existed for several centuries in the Lao language, they have only been used with any degree of consistency since the middle of this century.[27] In manuscripts of traditional Lao literature, they are found infrequently. Even in the works in which they occur, they are included only occasionally, and comparable to the scattering of Pali words in Lao prose, are added more for their decorative effect than for any other purpose. If there were no tone markers in common usage in the language, and the use of tones was intuitive rather than based on a concept of tones which at the time had yet to be standardized, how likely is one to have found ancient classes being held or textbooks being written in versification based upon the placement of words of low and falling tones?

In his book *Santhalaksana*, Sila describes the rules for composing *kaun an*, the verse form in which the majority of traditional literature is recorded:[28]

> One must compose it correctly according to (the rules governing the number of) lines and verses and the placement of tones . . . One verse of Kaun An must have four lines and each line must have seven words, excepting initial and additive phrases. Outside of that, one must place (syllables of) low and falling tone according to their correct position (1961: 20).

In reality, however, the rules of *kaun an* are much more flexible. Consider the rules that Sila states that the poetry "must" follow, weighed against the actuality of Lao literature:

1) The Length of the Verse—There is no fixed number of lines in *kaun an*. Although Sila states that *kaun an* must consist of complete, four-line stanzas, it is more frequently composed of two-line verses. Verses can also consist of one or three lines. The most frequently occurring verse consists of the third and fourth lines of Sila's verse pattern, which is continuously repeated throughout the course of a story.

2) Number of Syllables within a Poetic Line—While the majority of lines in *kaun an* verse consist of seven syllables (excluding initial and additive phrases), it is not uncommon to find a line that adds one, two, or even three extra syllables.

3) Position of Tones within a Poetic Line—While the position of tones frequently conforms to the rules that Sila states, it is also common to find lines where they do not.

In conclusion, the rules of *kaun an* that "must" be adhered to according to Sila are not nearly as definite as he would like us to believe. As observations of Lao poetry they serve best as flexible guidelines rather than rules to be enforced. Sila, widely read in Lao literature, did not fail to observe that his "rules" were not in fact rules. In the following quote, he introduces an example of *kaun an* that serves as an illustration of his concept of Lao versification. It appears in the work *Santhalaksana,* shortly after the previously quoted passage, and shows the strictness of his rules to be a result of wishful thinking rather than analysis:

> Examples of this style of poetry (can be found in) the verse of palm leaf manuscripts. But the majority of the poetry recorded on palm leaf manuscripts is composed not quite correctly according to the form. There is only one story, *Sinsai,* which is correct. Therefore, I will quote from *Sinsai* as my example (1961: 20).

When the entire corpus of Lao literature (with the single exception of *Sinsai)* is composed "not quite correctly" according to Sila's standards, one wonders whether it is a deficiency in the literature or rather, in the applicability of the standards themselves. If Sila had appreciated the medium of his subject matter, and distinguished it from the subject of Thai literary scholarship, he would have known that it was impossible to have fixed rules in composition. Composers of *kaun an*, as we have seen, traditionally did not know, on an analytical level, the rules of the verse in which they were composing. The verse form was learned not by memorizing written rules, which Sila, in several decades of research could never find, but rather by consistent lifelong exposure to oral performances. Rigid rules of composition that may appear orderly on a printed page were not necessarily practical or even effective in poetry recorded on palm leaves intended for a listening audience. In a Lao manuscript, in which there is no separation between individual words, there is no way to distinguish visually between the beginnings or ends of lines or verses. At the same time, there is no consistent use of tone markers to make clear the position of syllables of low and falling tones. Following Sila's rules, therefore, would have no visual effect of neatness on a manuscript. At the same time, it would not be easy to notice whether the work that one was transcribing was correct or incorrect according to such rules. Lao literature must be constantly recopied in order to survive. Each time that it is recopied it is changed in small details throughout the text. When a story is consistently copied and changed in detail, line by line, for hundreds of years, by transcribers who are frequently novices of under sixteen years of age, from manuscripts in which poetic form is not easily discernible, how is it possible for a text to remain consistent in the following of precise poetic rules? At the same time, what would be the benefit in keeping the poetry precise? Would the subtle difference between flexible and rigid adherence to such rules even be noticeable to a listening audience?

In analyzing Sila's study of versification, it is necessary to examine the standards that he set for Lao poetic composition and what they are based upon. In appreciating the reason that literature was obliged to conform to these standards in order to be "correct" in the eyes of Sila, we can understand why a man with such familiarity with the tradition approaches the subject as if he were an outsider. The significance that Sila placed on his ten-year search for a manual of versification is worthy of note. The explanation that he gives for his search indicates the importance that he attaches to literature in defining Lao-Thai relationships in the past and present. In *Baep Taeng Klaun Thaiy Viangjan Lae Baep Taeng Kap San Vilasini*, he writes that he conducted his search for the literary manual in order to show that Thai *khlong* verse was based upon a Lao poetic form of earlier origin (1993: ๑). On a deeper level, however, Sila's search was essential for the establishment of literature as a symbol of the *khwam chaleun* of the Lao nation. In a revealing statement concerning the objective of his literary studies, Sila equates the diminished state of contemporary Lao culture with the lack of precise poetic rules, and the *khwam chaleun* of Lao civilization at its height with the ancient text of versification that alas he could never find. On one level, Sila's standards of *khwam chaleun* and his pronouncements on the "correctness" of traditional poetry can be seen as the influence of his upbringing as a Thai. Ultimately, however, they are a reflection of the influence of the print media and nationalism on contemporary perceptions of the past. The importance of precise rules of poetic structure, and their existence in written form in defining the *khwam chaleun* of a civilization, are judgments of a society in which the medium of print has shaped conceptions of the nature of literature. In Thai literary scholarship one finds similar standards applied to the study of the origins and history of Thai poetry.[29]

Sila's insistence that traditional Lao poetry conform to standards of printed literature and assume a fixed form has created a mis-understanding on the part of the contemporary generation of Lao. His study of versification, *Santhalaksana,* composed in accordance to a directive of the Lao Ministry of Education and taught in schools throughout the country, has in effect been given the stamp of approval as the authorized rules of the composition of Lao verse.[30] Few of the people who I have talked to in Laos that were interested, or even involved in, research in Lao literature were aware of the fact that Sila's book of versification consists of his own interpretation of poetic structure rather than rules set down by ancient Lao poets. Many of the younger generation of novices and monks that I met in rural Laos were familiar with Sila's rules of Lao poetry, which they had learned from government schooling rather than their religious education. Despite the contrary evidence of years of listening to, transcribing, and performing Lao poetry, I have never heard them question the accuracy of the versification rules that they have been taught.

In its transformation of contemporary conceptions of traditional literature, the influence of Sila's work can be seen in both the "correction" of traditional stories and modern poetic composition. Before the revolution, the Lao National Library published many works of traditional Lao literature. One frequently finds discrepancies in these books due to mistakes that remain uncorrected from the original manuscripts. For example, individual sections often appear out of order, making it difficult if not impossible to follow the narrative.[31] At first glance one might assume that printed texts with this type of error are faithful transcriptions from the original. However, these books have often been touched up considerably, not to make the stories more comprehensible but rather to insure that that they meet Sila's requirements of four lines in every verse.[32] Examples of Sila's influence on modern poetry can be seen in the neat and orderly *kaun an* verse written by young Vientiane poets, displayed on the pages of the literary magazine *Vannasin,* with length of hemistichs, lines and verse, and position of tones all clearly marked.

Amin Sweeney in his book A *Full Hearing* (1987) discusses the effect that increased literacy had on Malay proverbs. The proverbs were originally a method of storing information orally by preserving it in memorable form. With the increase of literacy and the wide circulation of books, there was no longer a need for preserving information in such a manner. Ironically, however, the same medium that made such proverbs irrelevant also preserved them, as if frozen in their death. With the help of the printing press, Malay proverbs were collected alphabetically in books and taught to Malay schoolchildren throughout the country. They were thus preserved in a far more efficient form than they ever could have been before they lost their reason for existence (1987: 70–1). On one level, this can also be seen to be the case with Lao literature. It is largely the coming of the printing press that has rendered the traditional Lao style of writing obsolete. At the same time, it has greatly increased the efficiency of both its storage and the organization of its rules. Lao literature, typical of orally oriented poetry, has always been flexible and ever changing as a living tradition. With the coming of printed books, however, the literature, as if fossilized, has gained a rigid standardized form. As we have seen, earlier generations did not study Lao poetry, but rather learned it through informal exposure. The present generation of educated Lao, however, has little or no exposure to the tradition other than being forced to learn its codified rules in the classroom.[33] The analogy of modern Lao literature being "dead" as compared with "a living tradition" in the past also holds true for its circulation. The readership of contemporary Lao poetry is limited to a small, educated class. It is interesting to note that despite (or perhaps as a result of) the advantage of technology, modern Lao stories have a far smaller audience than did the traditional literature that was painstakingly transcribed by hand onto palm leaves.

THE POLITICAL USE OF TRADITIONAL LITERATURE IN THE REVOLUTIONARY MOVEMENT OF THE LAO PATRIOTIC FRONT

THE reinvention of traditional literature, as pioneered in the work of Sila Viravong, has continued in Laos through to the present. Sila once wrote of his scholarly efforts:

> Whatever (I have written) that is incorrect, (it is up to) my children
> and grandchildren to correct. Make use of whatever is correct. (Outhin et
> al. 1990: 16)

In the context of the social role of Lao literature in the twentieth century, the word "correct" in Sila's statement could appropriately be translated to mean "applicable to contemporary realities." This is illustrated in the political manipulation of traditional literature by the Lao Patriotic Front (Neo Lao Hak Sat) and subsequently the Lao government.

From the early 1950s to the communist victory in 1975, the Lao Patriotic Front made use of traditional literature and literary forms to serve a political end. The significant role that literature played during this period can be seen from the work *Vayakaun Lao,* a study of Lao grammar by the revolutionary leader Phoumi Vongvichit published in 1967 in the liberated zone. (See Enfield this volume.) According to the author, the preservation and revival of "books, spoken language, literature, and national cultural characteristics" marks one as a patriot (1967: 6). In the introduction, the history of the loss of Lao independence to the Thai, French, and Americans is described in terms of the bastardization of the Lao language as a result of the influence of foreign languages on the Lao. Ninety pages, or approximately one third of the work, are devoted to a description of Lao versification. Examples of poetry, which are composed by the author, are typically used not merely to teach rules of poetic composition, but also to make a statement on Lao politics and society.[34] Lao proverbs are interpreted as "an intellectual struggle between the oppressed and the oppressor" (1967: 285). The proverbs that have been collected appear to have been chosen for their relevance to the revolutionary cause. The following proverb, for example, could be interpreted as a warning to the Royal Lao Government:

> ຜັນວ່າປາກນົກກໍມົນ້ອຍ ຊ້າງປ່າຢຸບລ້ຽງນົກກຫລາຍເບີ
>
> Elephants do not step on the birds even if you see that their mouth are small
>
> ບາດນົກໂຮມແຮງກັນ ຊົືຄອດໃຕຊ້າງຕາຍ ຕັ້ນແລ້ວ
>
> When the birds gather together and collect their strength, they will peck you to death (1967: 284)

In their use of traditional literary conventions to expound their cause, the Lao Patriotic Front also made use of the traditional religious beliefs and worldview of the Lao, as illustrated in the following poem:

> ນະໂຍບາຍສອດຄ່ອງ ມັນມິ້ແຈ້ງໃສ
>
> The appropriate policies with each passing day become clearer
>
> ຂະຫຍາຍຫມົດຈິດໃຈ ກອງປະຊຸມສຸດຍອດ
>
> Expanding the essence of the most extraordinary meeting (of the Party)
>
> ແຮງມັນບໍມິ່ບວັນ ເຂັ້ມແຂງແຫນັບແໜັນ
>
> (Our) strength with each passing day grows stronger and increasingly tight

ຄືສີລາກ້າແໜ້ນ   ເອົາພະສຸເມນ
Similar to the great and firm stone of Mount Meru. (Lao Hak Sat
1973: 7)

In traditional poetic phrasing, the strength of the Lao Patriotic Front is
compared to that of the stone that comprises the center of the universe
according to Lao Theravadin Buddhist cosmology. Note that ກອງປະຊຸມ
"(Party) Meeting," a phrase that occurs consistently throughout communist
documents and speeches, fills a sequence of the poem where in traditional
Lao poetry the name of the Buddha or the Buddhist religion would have
typically been placed.

THE OFFICIAL ROLE OF TRADITIONAL LITERATURE IN THE LAO PEOPLE'S DEMOCRATIC REPUBLIC FROM 1975 TO THE PRESENT

FROM the communist victory onwards, the Lao government has made use
of traditional literature and literary symbolism in its construction of the Lao
past and present. Traditional literature serves as a useful building block in
the creation of national identity and pride and is used to show the
government's role in preserving the country's cultural independence.[35] The
prominence of traditional literature in twentieth century rural Lao society is
cited as an important example of how the people of Laos, in comparison to
their neighbors (read Thailand), have not become overly westernized, and
continue to maintain their Buddhist heritage.

The Lao government has made frequent use of literary symbolism in the
legitimization of its rule. The following poem, composed by Sau Desa in
1976, describes a national holiday commemorating the date of the
communist victory:

ສອງທັນວາເປນວັນແສງຄືອນແກ້ວ   ມະຫາໄຊເຊັ້ງຂ່າ
The Second of December, the day of precious moonlight, the victory
of wide reknown
ທັນວາແປວ່າທນ້າ   ທະນູກ້າໃຫຍ່ຍາວ
December translates as "crossbow, great, brave, and long"[36]
ທະນູສອນກົ່ງນ້າວ   ແນບເນ່ງລັ້ງຈຸດ
(The bow) is stretched, the arrow drawn, aimed, and fired
ຍັກໃຫຍ່ຈິມຕາຍມຸດ   ມາກມາຍມາແຫລ້ວ
The "nyak" giants have died in great numbers

ทะนุสอบเป็นแกๆว   ภายเป็นวันຊาๅ
The precious arrow has been transformed into our national day (Sau 1996: 1–2)

The arrow that has been "transformed into the Lao national day (commemorating the communist victory)" is a weapon that is used by literary heroes to defeat their enemies. The "nyak" are a type of demon that one finds throughout Buddhist literature. In the stanzas that follow the above passage, the defeated demons are described as imperialists and the feudal classes.

In contemporary Lao studies, traditional literature and individual works within the tradition are defined in terms of a communist interpretation of the past.[37] Although individual literary works have been criticized as tools of the feudalists in their exploitation of the masses, Lao poetic forms have been praised as an art form of the masses (Buakaew 1972: 18–19). Literary content is frequently described as the coded expression of popular discontent by the common people of Laos (Sau 1996: 20; Khamma 1987: 85–88). Interpretations of individual stories fall into two major categories, including their analysis as a) an expression of the conflict between classes in feudal society, and b) the historical struggle of the Lao people to liberate themselves from foreign invaders. In an interpretation of the traditional folktale *Nang Marong Ba Chiang* by Phau Phuangsaba published in 1984, the lesson to be taught is stated in its title: *Kha Hak Sakdina* (The Cost of Feudal Love). Two men, Ba Chiang and Baw Pasak court Nang Marong, the beautiful young woman who is the heroine of the story. Whereas Ba Chiang is a decent man who is favored by the woman's mother, Nang Malong desires Baw Pasak because of his high-ranking feudal lineage. When the young woman's mother arranges for her marriage to Ba Chiang, she elopes with Baw Pasak. After sleeping together a single time, the ungrateful man promptly abandons her. The story is interpreted as a warning that feudal lords are a dishonest thieving lot, and as a result, together with capitalist reactionary traitors, they have been driven out of Laos (Phau et al. 1984: 38–42). In a study by Sau Desa, the poem *San Leup Phasun* is interpreted as a literary expression of defiance to Thai invaders composed by the Lao king Chao Anou in the early nineteenth century.[38] The importance of this interpretation can be seen by the fact that the work has been published four times since 1998. The identical poem has been analyzed by academics in Thailand as Buddhist philosophy and imagery from the verse adapted by Lao refugees in the United States as an ode of resistance to the communist regime.[39] In the past, *San Leup Phasun* was commonly performed by villagers in Isan and southern Laos as courtship poetry.

The Lao government does not, however, have a monopoly on the manipulation of traditional literature for its own ends. There are a number of publications by Lao refugees overseas that make use both of traditional poetic forms and literary symbolism to criticize the Lao government.[40] Phomma Phimmasaun, for example, in the publication *Duang Sata Sat Lao Jak Kham Thamnay* (The Fate of the Lao Nation according to Prophecy), published in Quebec in 1990, makes use of traditional Lao poetry and the prophecies of Nostradamus to legitimize his criticism of the communist Lao government. In the introduction to a work of traditional literature, a composer would typically belittle his own intellectual and artistic abilities and state that the value of his poem lay in its faithfulness in following the wisdom handed down by past generations. In a similar fashion, Phomma Phimasaun writes:

> If any of my writing has offended the heart of any particular person or political system, I must again make the greatest of apology. It is not my intention to teach anyone. I am simply making reference to teachings of the truth and teachings of the Buddha as a follower of the Buddhist religion. The general message of the prophecies, based upon my comparative study, is to teach people to recognize the difference between good and sinful deeds . . . Therefore, it is time for people whose actions go against the truth and are contrary to human nature to realize the sin of their ways. This is especially (true for) those who are the enemies of religion, and enemies to the peace and happiness of their own race and nation. These people, based upon a comparative study of the prophecies, are identifiable as communists, the people who are currently in power in Laos. (1990: 75)

BOOKS OF SEARCH: IN CONCLUSION

THE shift in the status of Lao literature from "books of search" to "books of research" implies a significant shift in the worldview of the people of Laos and northeast Thailand. Underlying this shift is both the rise of the ideology of nationalism and the influence of print technology. Similar to nationalists elsewhere, Sila and his followers set out to create a literary canon that was unique to their country. It is not surprising that like other modern nations they have recognized the importance of the establishment of a literary canon in the creation of a Lao state, and have actively supported the preservation, circulation, and standardization of Lao literature.[41] During the 1960s and early 1970s, the Lao National Library published many works of traditional literature with the support of the Asia Foundation. In recent years, Lao literature has been surveyed, microfilmed, transcribed, and published with foreign financial assistance from a variety of sources including the Toyota Foundation, the Shell Corporation, etc. The most ambitious project related to literature in contemporary Laos is being undertaken with the financial assistance of the German government. The project, which started in 1992, is expected to be completed within eight years, at the cost of over one million five hundred thousand German marks.[42]

Underlying the political role of literature as a symbol of the "advanced state" of the Lao nation is the concept of *khwam chaleun* as defined by a generation of Lao accustomed to narrative mass-produced on a printed page as opposed to writing that has been copied on a palm leaf. The establishment of Lao literature as a specific body of works with a fixed visual form, and the creation of the standards by which its contents are interpreted and judged, reflect the influence of the print media on modern interpretations of the past.

Yet the establishment of traditional Lao literature as a national literary canon is in many ways problematic, as can be seen in the use of the word "Lao" as a label for the literature. Whereas the word "Lao" in a contemporary political sense refers to the people who inhabit the nation of Laos (which includes various ethnic groups to which the Lao literary tradition is foreign), the literature is commonly found both in Laos and northeast Thailand. During the period of the kingdom of Lane Xang when much of the literature was created, there is some doubt as to whether the people who composed the literary works would have referred to themselves as Lao. On the other hand, the people of contemporary northern Thailand, who have also been referred to as Lao, have a distinct literary tradition of their own. To further complicate the equation, the Phuthai people of Laos and northeast Thailand also make use of a similar works of literature which appear to originate from an identical tradition. Many manuscripts of "Lao" literature contain vocabulary of Phuthai or other origin that would be unintelligible to a Lao-speaking reader in Vientiane.

Furthermore, the existence of Lao literature as a single and distinct body of works is problematic. It would appear that the assumption that Lao literature is a distinct tradition with clear boundaries to separate it from other literary traditions in the region is an idea that only came into existence with the establishment of literature as a subject of study. One must realize, however, that there are important regional variations in the literature of Laos and northeast Thailand, including a) preference of prose and poetic styles, b) styles of performance, and c) specific stories. For example, the literature of northern Laos characteristically differs from that of other regions because of the strong influence of the literary tradition of Lanna. This can be seen in a) the extent to which the language of Lanna is used in literary composition, b) the circulation of specific literary works that are commonly found in contemporary northern Thailand but not in other regions of Laos or northeast Thailand, and c) the use of poetic styles and conventions that are similar to Lanna, such as the greater prevalence of Hay poetry in literary composition than in other regions of Laos or northeast Thailand. The question that arises, therefore, is not only whether Lao literature can be properly classified as a single tradition, but also where does one literary tradition begin and another end? The difficulty in providing an answer is illustrated, for example, in the case of the story Khvai Thauraphi, which was translated into English in the book *The Ramayana in Laos: (A Study in the Gvay Dvorahbi)* by Sachchidanand Sahai (1976). According to the introduction, there are only two copies of the story in existence in Laos, both of which are stored in the palace library in Luang Prabang. One work is recorded in the Lanna script and the other manuscript, of later origin, was copied into Lao as recently as 1971 and remains identical in content to the earlier Lanna version (Sahai 1976: 2). Does a mere change in the script in which a story is recorded establish a work as Lao literature? The works that comprise traditional Lao literature are frequently adapted from stories of foreign origin, or else based upon regional folklore that is not unique to the Lao. What is the extent of transformation that is necessary to define a work as Lao?

If we are to consider Lao literature as a literary tradition (without an insistence that it is an indivisible entity with clear and definite boundaries), we can establish certain characteristics, tendencies, and preferences that separate it from the related neighboring literary traditions of the Tai Kheun, Leu, and Tai Yuan (i.e. the people of Lanna).[43] These include: a) the use of the Lao and the Tham scripts,[44] b) specific conventions in how a given work can be performed under religious and secular circumstances that differ from neighboring traditions (Koret 1996: 5–11), c) a large body of stories (and/or specific versions of stories) that are found in each of the major regions inhabited by Lao-speaking people, but not in other areas (Koret 1996: 9–11), d) preference in the use of *kaun an* verse, which is not found in other traditions,[45] and e) a tendency to emphasize entertainment and romantic content in comparison with religious teaching (Koret 1996: 11–24). Further research is needed to clarify our understanding of the Lao literary tradition in its relationship to neighboring traditions in the region, such as Lanna, Mon, Khmer, etc.

Summarizing, we have seen that as a result of the major transformation of Lao and Isan society in the twentieth century, there has been a substantial change in the role that literature has been expected to play. The very factors that have preserved and standardized the literature have, in their recreation of the tradition, brought about its inevitable transformation. As the Lao grow distant from literature in its roles, traditional literature of the past has increasingly become fixed in its modern form.

NOTES

In this study I use slightly different systems for transliterating Lao and Thai, namely: a) in Lao ຈ is represented as "ch" whereas in Thai, จ is written as "j," and b) in Lao ວ is transliterated as "v" whereas in Thai, ว is written as "w." For words in general use I follow the Lao transliteration. I have, however, retained the English spelling of common Lao place-names, such as "Vientiane" and "Lan Xang," etc.

1. Lao manuscripts inevitably include frequent mistakes and portions of narrative which are difficult to interpret as a result of the nature of the medium and the impreciseness of the traditional scripts in which they are recorded. One must therefore search, and revise text simply to maintain its meaning. On a second level, Lao literature is similar to literary traditions intended for oral audiences worldwide in that there is no concept of a fixed text. Each performer and transcriber is invited to search for a way to improve on a story's content. One searches, therefore, not in order to make a new statement, but rather to find a way in which to better communicate what has already been said. On a third level, Lao literature is believed to be religious teaching taken from the Buddhist scriptures. It makes frequent use of puzzles and parable. One must search to the best of one's ability to understand the essence of the sacred wisdom that is being communicated. A more detailed discussion is provided in Koret (1994: 64–71, 78–82).

2. The Bodhisattva, or "the one who will become the Buddha," must perfect himself through the course of many life times before he can achieve enlightenment. The Jataka tales, life stories of the Bodhisattva, appear in the Buddhist scriptures known as Tripitaka.

3. Koret (1994: 21–28). Lanna was a prominent Theravada Buddhist kingdom in the region from the mid thirteenth century until its occupation by the Burmese three centuries later. It occupied an area that is roughly equivalent to contemporary northern Thailand. The people of Lanna and Lane Xang shared a related language and culture.

4. Koret (1996: 5–11). In comparison with the *khlong* verse favored in the composition of poetic literature in Lanna, the majority of Lao literature was composed in *kaun an* verse, which had a greater simplicity of form. *Kaun an* can be composed by all levels of Lao society whereas the creation of the *khlong* verse in Lanna appears to have been restricted to a highly educated elite connected to the royal court.

5. To appreciate the "invention" of poetic rules in the twentieth century, one must realize that there is no one generally accepted definition of poetry and how it is structured. Comparative studies of poetic traditions throughout the world show that the components of poetry, and the ways in which it is distinguished from prose, vary widely in different cultures (Finnegan 1977: 24–28).

6. For a description of the development of *mau lam* from traditional literature, see Miller (1983: 25–27, 40–42), and his doctoral thesis (1977: 77–97, 103–108, 132–136).

7. Based on personal observation. Works of Thai literature, such as *Phra Aphay Mani,* were similarly transcribed onto palm leaves. Thai stories were translated into Lao

and recomposed in Lao poetic forms. I have seen palm leaf manuscripts in Laos in which the composer states that the source of his work is a printed publication in Thailand. Dr. Anatole Peltier has also confirmed the popularity of the practice of copying printed material onto palm leaves.

8. Privately owned manuscript in Vientiane.

9. An interesting exception to this attitude can be seen in the article *Wanna Lila Khaung Phra Ariyanuwat* by Jaruwan (1995: 105–13), in which the author praises the poetic skills of Phra Ariyanuwat as illustrated by his transcription work.

10. In *Santhalaksana* (1961: ๒–ด) he further writes: "In the present day, nations all over the world believe that the subject of poetic composition is of considerable importance . . . All of the world's advanced nations therefore include it in their academic curriculums . . . The Lao in the past were an advanced nation. Among the Lao of the past were people of great knowledge and people skilled in the composition of verse.

11. Although this study is devoted exclusively to Sila's use of traditional literature in the creation of Laos as a modern nation, one could similarly study his scholarship of Lao history and culture for the same objective. For example, Sila's reinvention of the Lao calendar is worthy of note in comparison with his literary studies. In 1933, Sila was asked by Prince Phetsarath of Laos to study an ancient Lao astrological text entitled "Suriyakhat." The importance of the text to Prince Phetsarath is stated in Maha Sila's official Lao biography: "For a long period of time, dating from when the Lao lost their independence and became a tributary state of the Thai feudalists, followed by French colonization," the Lao neglected to make use of their ancient scientific knowledge in the creation of an official Lao calendar. Sila therefore studied the manuscript and "revised and added the work to" in order to "make it easily comprehensible." He discovered that "in comparison with (the calendars of) the Khmer and Thai, the Lao calendar showed 'a reasonable amount of science and logic.'" In 1934, combining the Lao calendar from *Suriyakhat* together with the twelve months of the western calendar, Sila created a modern Lao calendar that was immediately taught to monks at the newly opened Buddhist Institute in Vientiane and distributed to temples throughout the country. When his calculations for an eclipse based on the calendar proved accurate, "Maha Sila's name became well-known all over Laos." "From that time onwards, the nation of Laos has calculated and printed its own calendars." (Outhin et al. 1990: 50).

12. Samnak Ngan Khana Kammakan Watthanatham Haeng Chat (1989: 3–4, 214). Note that this book consists of speeches and papers from a conference entitled "Local Cultures: The Case of Isan," which was held at the Teacher's College in the Isan province of Ubon Ratchathani in 1989, sponsored by the National Cultural Commission. The opening ceremony was led by the Thai princess Sirindhorn.

13. The literature is labeled as "Lao" in works of Lao origin such as a) *Vannakhadi Udom Neung* by Kasuang Seuksa (1987), a textbook produced by the Lao Ministry of Education, b) *The Nidan Khun Burom: Annotated Translation and Analysis,* a doctoral thesis by the Lao student Souneth Phothisane (1996), and c) *Vannakhadi Lao* by Bausaeng Kham Vongdala et al. (1987), the major official study of traditional and modern Lao literature. In the latter work, the literary tradition is also referred to as 'The National Literary Heritage of our Lao Nation" (190). Thai labels for the literature can be seen in the title of books devoted to the topic, for example: *Wannakam Isan* (Isan Literature) by Thawat Punnothok (1979), *Khaung Di Isan* (Treasures of Isan) by

Jarubut Reuangsuwan (1977), and *Wannakam Thaung Thin Karani Isan Lane Sang* (Regional Literature: The Case of Isan-Lane Xang) by Jaruwan Thammawat (1996).

14. In all of the examples cited in the previous footnote of Lao origin, the script is referred to as Lao. In the Thai books that discuss the use of literary scripts, such as *Wannakam Isan* by Thawat Punnothok (1979) and *Laksana Wannakam Isan* by Jaruwan Thammawat (1979), the alphabet is referred to as Thai Nauy (Little Thai).

15. In the Lao study by Bausaeng Kham Vongdala et al. (1987), for example, the script of King Ramkhamhaeng of Sukhothai is stated to be a combination of both the Khaum (ancient Khmer) and Lao scripts. The author acknowledges that "both Thai and some western scholars" are of the mistaken opinion that the Lao script is based on the alphabet of King Ramkhamhaeng (182–183). In the doctoral thesis by Phothisane (1996: 5), the author writes that "most western and Thai scholars believe that Lao was derived from the Sukhothai script, while Dham script was derived from Yuan (i.e. the script of Lanna), but this is disputed by Lao researchers." In Thai scholarship, the development of "Little Thai" from the script of Sukhothai is described, for example, in Thawat (1979: 112–116).

16. The Lao attitude can be seen, for example, in the section on literary history in the Lao study by Bausaeng Kham Vongdala et al. (1987: 174–182, 189–199), which includes no mention of the influence of Chiang Mai. The opposite extreme can be seen in Thai works such as by Thawat, in which the height of Lao culture is summarized as: "[After Lanna fell to the Burmese] Tai Yuan [i.e. Lanna] art, culture, and literature continued to flourish in the Mekong valley [i.e. contemporary Laos and Isan]." (1979: 35).

17. For a brief biography of Phra Maha Somdet Wiravong, see Krom Sinlapakaun (1990: 45–49).

18. In one biographical episode, an Isan monk declines a challenge to debate with a monk from central Thailand at a funeral in Bangkok. He fears that as a Lao from Isan, his intellectual abilities would be no match for a "Thai." Sila, only a novice at the time, rose to the challenge, and with a wit reminiscent of the hero of the popular Lao trickster tales known as *Siang Miang,* soundly defeated his opponent. The question posed by the monk was: "Where do we go when we die?" to which Sila gave the answer: "We lie in a coffin." When the infuriated monk asked further: "Where does our soul go at death?", Sila replied: "I do not know because I have never died. Have you?" (Outhin et al. 1990: 38).

19. He campaigned for a seat in the Thai parliament as a representative of the Isan province of Khon Khaen in 1947, and for a seat in the Lao parliament as a representative of Vientiane in 1954.

20. For example, Maha Sila's earliest book on versification, published in Bangkok in 1942, is titled *Baep Taeng Klaun Thaiy Viangjan Lae Baep Taeng Kap San Vilasini* (Methods of Composition of the Poetry of the Vientiane Thai and Kap San Vilasini). He writes in this study about the "Thai people of Isan" (1–2), and hopes that his research will "help to further (the knowledge of) a branch of the literature and culture of the Thai" ("จ"). According to the *Thai-English Dictionary* by Wit Thiangburanathum printed in Bangkok, the word ไทย (Thai) Thai can mean a) any ethnic group that speaks a language within the Tai family, or b) any person regardless of nationality. To call the people of Vientiane Thai rather than Lao is thus not inaccurate (at least not in countries that print Thai dictionaries), but it denies them any status other than that of being Thai. (Note the difference between the above-mentioned word ไทย (Thaiy),

which is commonly used specifically to refer to the people of the nation of Thailand, and ไท (Thai) which is used among the Lao to mean people in general, regardless of nationality.)

21. Sila's phrase "the Thai people of Isan and Thai people on both banks of the Mekong river" in his Thai work *Baep Taeng Klaun Thay Viangjan Lae Taeng Kap Vilasini* ("ๆ") is altered to "the Lao people of Isan and Lao people on both banks of the Mekong river" when it appears in his biography (Outhin et al. 1990: 126). Note also that when Sila's original phrasing is retained in Lao reprintings, the word "Thai" as it is spelled in Lao (ไท "Thai") is less objectionable to the Lao than Sila's spelling (ไทย "Thaiy") in the earlier Thai publications. See the previous footnote for an explanation.

22. For a detailed description of versification rules as described by Sila Viravong, see Koret (1994: 95–99).

23. Sila's earliest published works, in the 1920s and 1930s, consist largely of the transcription and composition of traditional Lao poetry. Sila's biography also gives various examples of his skill at composing verse as a young man. (Outhin et al. 1990: 32, 38).

24. Similarities include the following: Sila's book on versification, *Santhalaksana*, was published as one of four books in a series on Lao grammar, each of which bears an identical title to a section devoted to a similar topic in the book by the Thai scholar. Several explanations in Sila's work are identically worded to similar sections in the same study. The names of the specific poetic lines were also apparently taken from this study rather than being indigenous to the Lao literary tradition. Most importantly, the division of Lao verse into various complex types such as Vissumali, Mahasinthumali, and Khlong Ha were influenced to no small degree by the division of Thai poetry into similar verse forms in the same book. Prakhaung (1987: 202–205).

25. The chapter "*Laksana Khaung Kap Klaun Haeng Chon Chat Thaiy Law*" (Characteristics of the Poetry of the Thai-Lao People), in Jit Phumisak (1981: 161–209) is an exception to most Thai scholarship in the perspective it brings to the study of Lao poetry. In writing his section on the characteristics of Lao poetry, Jit acknowledges Sila Viravong as a major influence on his work. (Sila is mentioned several times and quoted in reference to his transcription of the poetic work Thaw *Hung Thaw Cheuang*.) He also makes several references to a Lao poetic textbook that appears to be *Baep Taeng Klaun Thaiy Viangjan Lae Baep Taeng Kap San Vilasini* by Sila. Jit Phumisak was interested in the poetry of the common people. Much of his book is an attack on what he calls the "narrow scope" of Thai literary scholarship, which focuses on poetic forms of the elite while ignoring and belittling poetry not connected with the palace (158–160). It is precisely for this reason that his study shows insight into the literature. For the same reason it is also not surprising that his study was written while he was serving time in jail. The book was written in 1962, many years before other Thai scholars became interested in traditional Lao poetry and its relationship to Thai verse forms. However, it was not published until 1981 and has only influenced Thai scholarship on the subject in recent years.

26. Descriptions of the nature of the composers, transcribers, performance, and audience of Thai court literature are taken from a) Duangmon Jitjamnong (1997: 20–27), and b) personal conversation with Dr. Manas Chitakasem, professor of Thai language and literature at the School of Oriental and African Studies in London.

27. Although a Christian Bible written in Lao at the beginning of the century makes

consistent use of tone markers, the use of tone markers is erratic in Lao books through the 1930s.

28. Whereas the name *"kaun an"* (literally "verse to be read") was not invented by Maha Sila, he appears to be the first person to use the word to label a specific type of verse according to its poetic form.

29. This can be seen, for example, in the ongoing debate in Thai literary scholarship as to whether the primary characteristic of the poetic form of *khlong* (of which *kaun an* is a type) was originally rhyme or the placement of tone. According to Jit Phumisak, tone placement was the defining feature of *kaun an* (*"klaun an"* in Thai) and early *khlong* in general. Jit believed that early forms of *khlong* were similar to *kaun an* in their lack of strict organizational rules. In his chapter on Thai-Lao verse in *Ongkan Chaeng Nam Lao Khau Khit Mai Nai Prawatsat Thaiy Lum Mae Nam Jao Phraya* he attempts to show how *khlong* developed from a flexible poetic form based upon rules of placement of tones to a highly rigid form with strict rules of rhyme and length of line and verse. The majority of Thai scholars, however, have believed that rhyme was the fundamental characteristic of early *khlong verse*. Thanit Yupho, for example, writes: *"Khlong* composition in ancient times is not likely to have fixed placement of low and falling tones, but rather focused on rhyme. However, later on, . . . Thai pronunciation favored the use of tones. In the north, and even in other regions, although in writing there were no low and rising tones (i.e. tone markers), the pronunciation (of the regional languages) was almost as if they had low and rising tones. When the use of tone markers became established, the position of low and falling tones in *khlong* was fixed in the period following" (Prakhaung 1987: 230). How can it be, as he states, that the ancient language was pronounced "almost as if" it had low and falling tones? Did the delineation of tones in spoken language become fixed and real only after they were written down, or were they, in fact, written down in accordance with the way in which they were spoken? To say that tone rules were established only after literary symbols for the tones had been invented is to say in effect that the placement of tones is primarily a visually-oriented phenomenon and that the effect of its sound is of secondary importance.

30. *Santhalaksana* (1961) first page (not numbered). Although Sila's study *Santhalaksana* has not been continuously used as the sole textbook with which to teach literature in Lao schools, subsequent books on versification are based on this study.

31. See, for example, *Vannapham* (Lao) Hau Samut Haeng Sat (1970: 21–24) and try to make sense out of it.

32. Printed versions of Lao poetry appear to have a greater tendency to follow rules of tone placement and to consist of complete four-line stanzas than do the older versions recorded on palm leaves. This observation is based upon comparisons of several sections of the works *Thaw Kam Ka Dam, Thaw Kampha Kai Kaew,* and other stories. Even the printed versions, however, are far from being consistent in their conformity.

33. The same situation also applies to northeastern Thailand. At present "Isan literature" is taught at the college level.

34. For example, the verse condemns the interference of the United States in Lao affairs and the materialist values of the Lao elite in Vientiane. Poetry is also used to praise the progressive state of Lao society in the liberated zones and teach proper behavior for revolutionary youth.

35. See, for example, Bausaeng KhamVongdala et al. (1987: 1, 6–7), and Kasuang Thalaeng Khaw Lae Vatthanatham (1992: 4, 6).

36. The Lao word for December, "Thanva," is taken from the word for "archery."

37. This can be seen, for example, in a description of literature by Kaysone Phomvihane, whom at the time was the secretary general of the Lao People's Revolutionary Party. He writes: "Through diligent labor and intelligence . . . the Lao people had the ability to create . . . a literature . . . with a content (that is) brave . . . and uncompromising, telling of their love for the fatherland of the proletariat" (Bausaeng Kham Vongdala et al. 1987: 3–4).

38. S. Desa's interpretation appears to be based on an earlier study by Sila Viravong. In Sila Viravong's work *Panyot Khaung Vannakhadi* (Lao), published in 1960, one finds a similar analysis (pp. 242–244). According to his biography, Sila originally transcribed the work in 1942 while working at the Thai National Library. (Outhin et al. 1990: 234.)

39. An interpretation of *San Leup Phasun* can be found in the work *Khaung Di Isan* by the Thai scholar Jarubut Reuangsuwan (1977: 136–7). A tape of *mau lam* with the title *Siang Jak Pasa San Leup Hay Sun* (Voice of the People: San Leup Hay Sun) was composed by Phomma Somsuthi and produced by Freedom Security in Sacramento, California.

40. See, for example, *Meuang Lao Maen Khaung Law* (Laos belongs to the Lao) by Chan Kanya (n.d.), published in Rochester, New York, and *Kavi Law Phat Thin, 12 Thanva 1975–1985, Sip Pi Khaung Kan Phan Sat* (Lao Poet Separated from His Land, December 12, 1975–1985, Ten Years of Life) by Kongkham Pravongviangkham (1985), printed in Paris.

41. Financial support of cultural projects has also proved a useful way in which foreign countries can contribute aid of a "non-political" nature to Laos and in so doing, establish and strengthen their ties with the Lao government.

42. The German Manuscript Preservation Project has received prominent coverage in the Lao media. Major goals include: a) a survey of manuscripts in temples throughout Laos, b) education of Lao people as to the value of traditional manuscripts and methods by which they can most efficiently be preserved, c) the establishment of provincial manuscript centers in designated temples to serve as resource centers and continue the work of preservation after the project has been completed, d) the microfilming of important manuscripts throughout the country, and e) the eventual transcription and publication of selected works.

43. The literary traditions of the Tai Kheun, Leu, and Lao were all greatly influenced by the literature of Lanna.

44. Note, however, that both of these scripts are very similar to scripts that are used in Lanna.

45. *Klaun an*, however, is a form of *khlong* verse which shares similarities with the *khlong* verse of Lanna (particularly the earliest known works).

LAO AS A NATIONAL LANGUAGE   12

N. J. ENFIELD

A recurring theme in discussion amongst Lao scholars as to the right path for standardization of the Lao language is the equation of a unified standard national language with a unified national heritage, and contemporary national and socio-political integrity. In such contexts, the following proverb is often quoted: ພາສາບອກຊາດ ມາລະຍາດບອກຕະກູນ; (Language reveals one's nationhood, manners reveal one's lineage). The fact that the Lao language does not have a well-applied and codified standard is therefore telling. As a nation, Laos has experienced long years of difficulty along the road to unification. Many of the political divisions that can be traced across the history of the nation are also reflected in the current inconsistencies of the language as it is used, and in the decades-old arguments about the Lao language and its proper form. The pressures on Lao as a language are many of the same pressures as those on Laos as a nation. There is a tension between the older, ornate traditions associated with Buddhism and aristocracy on the one hand, and the more recent, austere rationalist traditions associated with socialism and the culture of modern technology on the other. In addition, the Lao are keenly aware of the need to maintain and delineate their nationhood in the face of pressures from outside, most notably those from Thailand. It is these two main themes which persist throughout the discussion below.

LAO LANGUAGE—VARIATION AND STANDARDIZATION

The national language of the Lao People's Democratic Republic, as declared on the establishment of the first government on 2 December 1975, is Lao

(Tay 1995: 169).[1] As a Southwestern Tai language, Lao is closely related to Thai (Li 1960). Lao and Thai share extensive vocabulary, and have very similar phonological and grammatical systems. Because of the mostly one-directional flow of cultural exposure, however, Central Thai is well understood by the Lao, while many speakers of Central Thai would have real difficulty understanding Lao, due essentially to lack of exposure to the language. It is important to understand for much of the discussion below that Lao and Thai are for all intents and purposes (i.e. in descriptive/ structural linguistic terms) dialects of a single "language" (but it is especially important not to interpret this as meaning that "Thai is a dialect of Lao," or vice versa). This is not meant to downplay in any way the differences between them. For a number of reasons, they *should* be treated as different languages, that is, as languages each on their own merits. This avoids serving the political purposes of either Thai or Lao nationalism. It is usually the case that Lao is treated by outsiders in terms of how it differs from Thai, and not the other way around, since outsiders are more often familiar with Thai first.

While there are many fascinating differences and similarities between Lao and Thai, the substantive issues related to the establishment of Lao as a national language almost exclusively concern orthography (very often with reference to the orthography of Thai).[2] It is thus necessary to begin with a brief digression, and sketch a few points about Lao and Thai orthography which will be relevant to the discussion below. The two languages use scripts which are quite similar, and which both derive ultimately (but indirectly) from Indic scripts. There is a robust folk (mis)understanding that the languages "come from" Pali and/or Sanskrit, including the notion that Lao and Thai incorporate higher proportions of Pali, and Sanskrit, respectively.[3] The Thai and Lao languages *do not* "come from" Pali and/or Sanskrit, in any sense of genetic continuity. They have heavily borrowed vocabulary from those languages, especially during this century. Pali and/or Sanskrit have provided for a range of neologisms required in a rapidly changing political and social world, in a similar way that Greek and/or Latin have been used creatively in stocking the modern vocabularies of European languages. Pali in particular is important in religion and religious studies in Laos and Thailand.

Modern Thai orthography includes the full range of Pali and Sanskrit characters, while Lao does not. (Lao monasteries use *nangsŭu thám* (ໜັງສື ທຳ), the "dharmic script," not known by those without religious education.) This full complement of Indic characters in Thai originated in the fourteenth century or earlier, and was "patterned closely on Khmer, not directly inherited from Indic in India" (Anthony Diller, personal correspondence; cf. Diller 1988a). Throughout the following centuries, there were considerable inconsistencies in the spelling of Indic words due to a range of factors, including the deliberate re-spelling of native words in fancy "etymological style," and the mixing up of Pali and Sanskrit spellings of common roots. In the middle of the nineteenth century, Rama IV (Mongkut) became concerned about the "flux and caprice in Thai spelling" (Anthony Diller, personal correspondence), and launched an interest in standardizing the Thai language in a "proper etymological" way, which eventually resulted in the deliberate adoption during the 1950s of full and regular Sanskrit spelling of Indic borrowings in Thai. The historical development of Lao orthography is much less clear. Today it remains the case that while Pali and Sanskrit can be transcribed literally to the letter in regular everyday Thai script, the "limited" inventory of twenty-seven Modern Lao consonants (including the letter "r"; see below), cannot handle this task.

Thus, from the naive point of view, it looks as if Lao is less complete than Thai, and if one believes that Lao really does "come from" Pali (as many apparently do), then one is led to conclude that something must have happened along the way to those "missing" characters. When people argue on this basis for a "return to tradition" through incorporation of the remaining characters, they are in fact not arguing for *restoration*, but for the modern, and in many cases novel, fixture of orthographical devices in the language. The deeper historical questions regarding developments of "native" Lao/Thai orthography are complex ones, which I cannot pursue here. But it is important to understand in the present context that the standardized etymological basis of Thai orthography in its present form, being literally designed to handle faithful transcription of Pali and especially Sanskrit, does *not* represent something that Lao once had or, in particular, could ever "go back to."

Spoken Lao, in its numerous regional forms, shows considerable variation. Not only do speakers from different regions have markedly different "accents," but they also display significant differences in regular vocabulary, as well as subtle grammatical and idiomatic differences. These differences may identify a Lao person's background, and thereby indicate much about their likely history and, probably, their position in society. Each regional variety of Lao has one or two salient diagnostic indicators (among many actual distinctions), which are strongly symbolic of that variety, and generally known in Vientiane by all speakers of Lao in the community. For example, the Southernmost varieties of Lao have a characteristic falling pronunciation (typically with glottal constriction of the vowel) of the tone inherent in "live" syllables with "low" consonant initials

(such as *láw* (ລາວ) 'Lao', *máa* (ມາ) 'come', *khúu* (ຄູ) 'teacher').⁴ This
pronunciation is immediately diagnostic of a speaker's southern origin, and
is fabled to be a "loud," "heavy," or "rough" style. On the other hand, the
variety of Lao spoken in Luang Prabang includes a distinctive high falling-
rising tone in "live" syllables with "high" consonant initials (such as *hǐn*
(ຫິນ) 'stone', *mǎa* (ໝາ) 'dog', *mǔu* (ໝູ) 'pig'). This pronunciation is
considered typical of the "softness" or "lightness" of that variety. There are
also some lexical stereotypes which are diagnostic of regional varieties, such
as Phou-Thai *kilâə* (ກິເລີ) 'where' (cf. Vientiane *sǎj* ໃສ), or Luang Prabang
'eew (ເອວ) 'play, pass time' (cf. Vientiane *lin* ຫຼິ້ນ). These examples show
features which have achieved privileged status as folk diagnostics of
speakers' regional origin. Each variety, of course, has many other distinctive
features, but these have not achieved the same diagnostic status, and are not
consciously recognized, nor publicly symbolic in the same way as those
other more stigmatized features.

While speakers' regional origin may be easily identified by accent, it has
been claimed that this has no negative consequences in Laos. Regarding the
situation in 1974, Chamberlain had this to say: "Laotians working together
accept these regional dialects with little notice. This would seem to be a
highly desirable situation, as it eliminates social prejudice . . ." (Chamberlain 1978: 267). But while aspects of regional "accents" associated with
different tone systems are indeed considered basically innocuous (sometimes
even quaint), there do seem to be more negatively stigmatized regional
"mispronunciations." Consider the perceived inability of speakers from
Savannakhet (including many Phou-Thai from that area) to produce the
labio-dental fricative /f-/, instead producing an aspirated bilabial stop
/pʰ-/ for words which in other dialects have /f-/, and which are spelt with
"f" (ຝ/ຟ) in Lao. (In other words, the distinction between /f/ and /pʰ/
collapses in favor of /pʰ/.) The stock example is /pháj-phâa/ 'electricity',
corresponding to Vientiane /fáj-fâa/ (written as ໄຟຟ້າ). While people in the
Vientiane speech community are aware of this diagnostic feature of
Savannakhet speech, many are not aware of other diagnostics, such as the
lack of diphthongs in the Phou-Thai varieties of Lao (spoken in the eastern
part of Savannakhet province), whereby /ia, ʉa, ua/ correspond to simple
long vowels /ee, əə, oo/ (such that 'wife', 'salt', and 'bridge', written as ເມຍ,
ເກືອ and ຂວ are pronounced /mée/, /kǝ̌ə/, /khoǒ,/, while in Vientiane they are
/mía/, /kʉ̀ə, /khʉ̌a/).

Another example of regional variation perceived as "mispronunciation" is
the neutralization in some Southern varieties of the phonemes /l/ and /d/. It
is an oft-related anecdote that where a Vientiane speaker says /khwáaj dǎm
khwáaj dɔɔn/ for 'dark buffalo, pale buffalo' (ຄວາຍດຳຄວາຍດອນ), the Southern

speaker says /khwáaj lǎm khwáaj lɔɔn/. This is in fact a naive perception of the Southern "accent." Rather than literally "mixing up" /l/ and /d/, these varieties instead neutralize this distinction, producing a single phoneme, usually realized as a lateral tap (which, incidentally, would seem to be the phonetically closest thing to the trill [r] found in dialects of Lao; see below). This is heard by speakers of other varieties of Lao as sometimes /d/, sometimes /l/. The stigma of such regional "mispronunciations" means that they are likely to be consciously phased out of the speech of newcomers to Vientiane, where possible.

It is of course natural to find extensive dialect variation in any region (Chambers 1995: 229ff), and out of this arises the political, cultural, and practical necessity for establishing and properly codifying an official standard language. The standard is a vehicle for leveling regional variation in administration, education, and the media, as well as providing a benchmark of prestige and "correctness," regardless of what variety of the language is spoken in an individual's own region or own home. Establishment of a standard requires an effective level of codification (i.e. the official certification in grammar books and dictionaries of what exactly the grammar, particularly the pronunciation and spelling, of the standard language is).

If it were possible at all to identify a *spoken* standard for Lao, it would have to be the Vientiane variety. Vientiane is at the geographical and political center of the country. While "Vientiane Lao" could be defined as either "the variety of Lao spoken in Vientiane," or "the variety of Lao spoken by those who have grown up in Vientiane (or whose families have been in Vientiane for *x* (number of) generations)," the former definition would allow no generalization about the form of the language itself, since a huge proportion of the population of the capital are speakers of regional varieties, born and raised in the provinces. Thongphet Kingsada, director of the Language Section of the Institute for Cultural Research (ICR) in Vientiane, evidently goes by the latter definition. He commented in an interview that it was "a shame" that "Vientiane Lao" is used less and less in Vientiane these days. Thongphet's impression is that the dialects of greatest influence in Vientiane now are the Southern varieties, especially those of Savannakhet and Champassak provinces. (The sociolinguistic implications of the large flow of immigrants into the capital over recent years are worthy of extensive research.)

An important measure of "standard" pronunciation is the language used in national television and radio programming (e.g. news), which indeed tends to follow the phonology of native Vientiane speakers, and tends not to include regional vocabulary. But actually pinpointing the distinctive features of this "standard" is complicated by the fact that the target is constantly shifting. The pronunciation of "Vientiane Lao" is nowhere codified, and its form has surely been shaped in different ways over the decades through major demographic changes, with an influx of wartime refugees during the 1960s and early 1970s, incoming revolutionaries taking power in 1975 with the accompanying flow of population into the capital which followed, and the wave of economic migrants during the 1990s, encouraged by increasing urban development and eased travel restrictions. The outpouring of post-1975 refugees must also have had some effect.

Thus, while there is no official standardization of the spoken form of Lao, and while it is perhaps even impossible to say exactly what constitutes the Vientiane variety, there is no doubt an implicit *concept* of some neutral, central style. There is at the very least a notion of "toning down" one's native (regional) speech when in the capital, or indeed when dealing with speakers from outside one's own area, particularly when in some official setting. People are quite willing, and quite able, to curtail the most representative features of their own "non-neutral" regional variety. There is thus a natural tendency to neutralize differences, at least for the pragmatic purpose of facilitating communication. Thus, if a "standard" or "central" spoken Lao can be characterized at all, it is to be characterized partly as "central" in the geographical sense (spoken by natives of the geographical and political "center"), and partly in Diller's (1991: 110) third sense of "central" language: "the intermediate or shared variety, similar to a *lingua franca* or *koine*," that is, one in which the most salient regional stereotype features are bleached away.

Spoken Lao rates pretty poorly in terms of Diller's (1991: 99–100) checklist of "national language functions." If we take the Vientiane variety as our spoken standard, then it probably passes the criteria of (a) being understood by a majority of national residents, and (b) being used in electronic media for the majority of official or national level programming. As a national standard for pronunciation, Vientiane Lao probably fails to pass other of Diller's "national language" criteria, namely (a) being the national medium of instruction; (b) being the sole language of official government business; (c) being the "prestige dialect" for social mobility; (d) being used for religious purposes; (e) being enforced institutionally; and (f) being the norm for impersonal announcements. There is no pressure on regional speakers to *pronounce* Lao as it is pronounced by natives of Vientiane. (Consider one Vientiane speaker's reported amusement upon hearing an announcement in strong regional accent over the public address system at Louang Prabang airport.)

Where Lao does have a stronger sense of standardization is in its written form, where much greater concern has been focused throughout the history of Lao as a national language. Today's *written* (i.e. orthographic) conventions of Lao do pass the "standard" criteria of being used as the national medium of instruction, the language of official business, and the object of institutional maintenance.[5] But the nature of the written language is such that it may be pronounced in a broadly varying range of regional accents. Most of the discussion below concentrates on a range of issues surrounding the history and development of the standardization of Lao as a written language, since it is this issue which has been the native preoccupation.[6]

The area of strongest standardization of Lao can be witnessed in the Lao print media. Publication of any printed material is subject to official approval by the Lao government, who since 1975 has done well in seeing that the standard writing system (according to Phoumi's (1967) grammar; see below) is adhered to. However, while it is often observed that print media can be one of the strongest forces of language standardization (cf. Ivarsson, this volume), this is compromised in Laos by the fact that Lao language newspapers have extremely limited readership. The two main Vientiane dailies *Vientiane Mai* (New Vientiane) and *Pasason* (The People) are distributed to government offices, hotels, other workplaces and some private homes, but no newsagents or magazine stands as such exist. In general, Lao people do not avidly read Lao language materials (but they are beginning to avidly read Thai language materials; see below). So, the fact of a fairly well-standardized orthography in the Lao press does not have the significant consequences for the standardization of the language that one might expect.

Radio programming across the country tends to have strong regional orientation, with local dialects being used in a large percentage of local programming. Rural areas are, however, exposed to a certain degree of "central Lao" via national news reports produced in Vientiane. As already mentioned, *spoken* Lao has been much less effectively standardized, and this is reflected in, and partly because of, the less unified spoken conventions in regional radio programming. (For further comments on radio programming, see below.)

During this century, a number of government bodies have been set up to take responsibility for the tasks of language standardization, which have included production of Lao language educational materials; research on Lao grammar, language, and literature; authorization of neologisms, borrowings, and revisions in the language; and work on an official dictionary. In the 1930s, the Buddhist Academic Council (ຜຸທະບັນດິດຕະສະພາ), presided over by Prince Phetsarath, was responsible for various recommendations regarding Lao orthography, including the attempted addition (attributed to Sila Viravong) to the Lao alphabet of fourteen supplementary consonants, making up the full complement of orthographic distinctions required for transcribing Pali (Bizot 1996). The early 1940s saw developments in language standardization associated with the *Lao Nhay* (ລາວໃຫຍ່) movement, in which the "simple etymological spelling" associated with P. S. Nginn took hold. Again the Buddhist Academic Council was involved in this process, along with the École Française d'Extrême-Orient. (See Ivarsson, this volume, for detailed discussion.) In August 1948, the Committee for Compiling and Authorizing the Spelling of Lao Words (ຄະນະກຳມະການ ຣຽບຣຽງແລະບັນຍັດການຂຽນຄຳລາວ) was set up (by Royal Decree no. 67, August 1948), and this was soon followed by the establishment of the long-standing Comité Littéraire (ກອງວັນນະຄະດີ), under the Ministry of Education (by Prime Minister's Decree no. 407, 27 August 1951). The Comité was to contain twenty-four members, and the founding five were Kou Aphay, P. S. Nginn, Phuy Panya, Sila Viravong, and Bong Souvannavong. (Sila left the Comité at the end of 1963.) In 1970, the Comité became the Lao Royal Academic Council (ລາຄະບັນດິດຕະສະພາລາວ), by Royal Ordinance no. 72, 23 February 1970. It was to last five years until the demise of the Royal Lao Government in 1975.

The reforms introduced by the post-1975 government were implemented quite effectively without the need for a distinct official regulatory body, presumably because the policy was so clear (as defined in Phoumi 1967), and also because little or no debate was entered into. The reforms adopted had already been well established for at least twenty years in the Liberated Zone. In 1999, there remains no official body specifically entrusted with regulation of the Lao language.

On 8–10 October 1990, a major conference "The Round Table on Lao Language Policy" was held in Vientiane, organized by the Institute for Cultural Research under the Ministry of Information and Culture. A number of the papers presented were collected and published as a volume (ICR 1995), in which is found a representative array of current attitudes about Lao language and culture (see below for further discussion). One of the most common demands made was the need for an institute or academy to oversee and authorize decisions about the language, particularly concerning the incorporation of neologisms, and decisions about what orthographical conventions should be adopted. Indeed, it was an official recommendation at the conclusion of the meeting that an official body be set up to work at least on problems of standardizing orthography (Houmphanh 1995: 5). But nearly a decade later, nothing has come of that recommendation. In 1999, a proposal for a Linguistic Institute was before the minister of information and culture.

Lao linguistic scholarship has of course been closely involved with the various institutions concerned with regulation and standardization of the language. The three figures of greatest importance are P. S. Nginn, Sila Viravong, and Phoumi Vongvichit, noted by Khamphao (1995: 15) as synonymous with the three most important views of the last seventy years regarding how Lao language should be written.

Sila Viravong, the most prominent figure of traditional (i.e. pre-revolutionary) Lao scholarship, produced a range of works on aspects of Lao culture, and today there is a rather romanticized notion of his scholarship (cf. Outhin et al. 1990). Sila instigated an early (unsuccessful) attempt to incorporate the full complement of Indic characters (following Pali) into Lao orthography, so that Indic etymology could be reproduced letter for letter in the everyday spelling system (cf. Bizot 1996, Ivarsson (this volume), Sila 1996 [1938]). This attempt is to be found in Sila's grammar, published in 1935 by the then recently established Chantabouri Buddhist Academic Council. One of Sila's primary concerns was to promote religious studies, and the move to make Pali accessible to anyone who knew Lao was seen as a crucial step in doing this (Sila 1935: x (cited in Thongphet 1995: 103)). This project ran into problems due especially to the Lao nationalist desire for the language to be clearly distinct from Thai, which was already well on the way to having standardized its full complement of Indic characters. Sila's approach was taken by many to be dangerously close to aping developments in Thai orthography at the time (see Diller 1991, Ivarsson (this volume)). Much later, Sila's proposals for Lao orthography were also seen as less practical and more elitist, in opposition to fundamental principles of Phoumi's "revolutionary" grammar (see below).

Pierre Somchin Nginn was head of the long-standing Comité Littéraire for over fifteen years, becoming president of the Lao Royal Academic Council, and presiding over the publication of the Royal Lao Government official Lao grammar, published in 1972 (RLG 1972). Nginn's view of Lao grammar and orthography was more progressive, whereby he partly followed a principle of simplicity and "phonetic" spelling, while allowing for Indic etymology to be reflected in the spelling of borrowings, at least to the extent that existing Lao characters could facilitate this.

Most recently, Phoumi Vongvichit has had the most direct hand in determining the current state of Lao grammar, as well as being a leading political figure throughout the history of the revolutionary struggle in Laos. The "cultural tsar" of the Lao revolution (Stuart-Fox 1997: 5), Phoumi was a "revolutionary activist member . . . of the traditional Lao elite," who was named interior minister of the Pathet Lao resistance government when it was endorsed in 1950 (Stuart-Fox 1997: 78), later becoming minister of education, culture, and information and a member of the inner cabinet and the political bureau of the government of the Lao PDR (Stuart-Fox 1997). Phoumi published his *Lao Grammar* in the heartland of the revolutionary struggle in 1967. The book was widely distributed after the revolution in 1975, and has come to assume as much significance in Laos as a historical and culturally symbolic document, as it has as an academic contribution to either linguistic description or language standardization. In the last ten years, and especially since his death in 1994, Phoumi has come to receive mixed respect within the academic community in Laos. Compare, for example, the strong support from younger scholars seen in Thongphet (1995) and Khamhoung (1995), in contrast to Thongkham and Souvan's (1997: ii) tepid, and essentially quite negative, mention of Phoumi's role in the context of Sila's much earlier traditionalist work.

"Grammar" for the Lao is essentially prescriptive, properly consisting of a set of rules which define and thereby prescribe what is correct and proscribe what is incorrect in the language. Further, the focus of "grammar" is almost exclusively on orthographic convention, i.e. correct spelling, leaving much about the overall grammar (or morphosyntax) of the language undescribed and unexplored by Lao scholars. Work that has been done on morphology and syntax is explicitly, and in many cases, inappropriately, modeled on traditional European grammar (cf. Diller 1988b, 1993 on a similar situation in Thai). Similarly, much of the descriptive linguistic work done by foreign researchers is less than comprehensive and not always reliable. No Lao "reference grammar," in the descriptive linguist's sense, has so far been produced.

With the establishment of the Lao PDR, the politically motivated reforms embodied in Phoumi's *Lao Grammar* were officially adopted, and remain officially in place today. The positions of Phoumi on the one hand, and of Nginn and Sila, on the other, have polarized, symbolizing the forces of "old" versus "new," pre-revolutionary versus revolutionary, traditional versus progressive. When Phoumi's grammar became the national standard, the people accepted and adopted the reforms in accordance with this. Clearly, it was not felt that criticism or debate regarding government policy was appropriate at the time. However, since the "perestroika" of the late 1980s, many aspects of culture and society associated with socialist ideology have decreased in popularity (especially in Vientiane), and have been somewhat "toned down," now tolerated rather than actively supported. Since then, and particularly since Phoumi's death in 1994 (cf. Sisaveuy 1996), the general feeling in Vientiane has been that Phoumi's reforms are now out of date, having already "served their purpose" in contributing to a certain phase of the revolution (Houmphanh 1996[1990]: 167). In a rather different tone, Thongkham and Souvan (1997: ii) imply that Phoumi's grammar crowned a long history of steady deterioration of the ideal embodied in Sila's four-volume grammar of more than three decades earlier (Sila 1935). It is clear that at least some of Phoumi's reforms are ready to be phased out, by popular choice. But while commentators are almost unanimous that the reforms are inappropriate for contemporary Lao, there remains the problem of determining what the new alternatives are. Let us first look briefly at the debate which occurred in the decade or so before liberation.

Lao was first officially adopted as the language of education in (Royal Lao Government–controlled) Laos in 1962, under the National Educational Reform Act (RLG 1962, cited in Chamberlain 1978: 267). While the diversity of pronunciation in various dialects of Lao was apparently considered quite tolerable ("most Lao scholars agree . . . that promoting a standard pronunciation is neither feasible nor necessarily desirable," according to Chamberlain 1978: 267), the issue that generated lively debate was orthographic standardization (Chamberlain 1978; Houmphanh 1996[1990]). The situation at the time is nicely summed up by Allan Kerr in the preface to his 1972 *Lao-English Dictionary*:

> A major difficulty which confronted the compiler was the fact that the spelling of Lao words has not been standardised; this is particularly true in the case of words of Pali and Sanskrit origin. The chief guide for correct spelling is a special directive sent by the King of Laos to the *Comité Littéraire*, which states as a general principle that all words are to be spelled exactly as they are pronounced. However, this has thus far been an ideal rather than an accomplished fact . . . In determining which of a series of [variant spellings] should be treated as a main entry the compiler has had the temerity to make decisions in doubtful cases . . . His decisions represent a compromise between the attitude of the traditionalists who oppose change of any kind and that of the modernists who are eager to change everything (ix).

Clearly, the debate was highly politicized. The original directive (Royal Ordinance no. 10, 27 January 1949, for which consult Khamphao 1995, RLG 1972), was interpreted in different ways (or to different degrees of "strictness") by different political factions of the various coalition governments. Article 2 reads:

> The orthography of Lao words, and of words borrowed into Lao from foreign languages, follows pronunciation used in Laos.

The "traditionalists" wanted aspects of original Pali/Sanskrit spelling retained in loanwords from those languages, creating apparently arbitrary complexity for those unfamiliar with Indic etymology. These spellings would have to be learnt by memory, rather than directly reflecting pronunciation in predictable fashion. Houmphanh (1996[1990]: 163; cf.

ICR 1995) mentions the added issue of foreign borrowings and neologisms, with regard to which there were many different opinions, and no unified resolutions.

Chamberlain (1978: 269) reports that at the time the Lao Patriotic Front "followed a stricter interpretation of the Royal Ordinance." Thus, not only would they dispose of spellings which used final consonants alien to Lao phonology, they would also overtly write in the epenthetic vowels which are automatically inserted by the phonological rules of Lao between consonants in erstwhile clusters.

Etymological	Phonetic	Pronunciation	Meaning
ຣັຖບາລ	ລັດຖະບານ	*lātthabǎn*	government
ສມັຍ	ສະໄໝ	*samǎj*	era
ວິຣະວົງສ໌	ວິລະວົງ	*víilavóng*	(surname)
ສນາມ	ສະໝາມ	*sanǎam*	(sports) field

While the various interpretations were subject to debate in the Royal Lao Government–occupied areas of lowland Laos, there was no such discussion in the Liberated Zone, where this stricter interpretation (which would eventually prevail) had been accepted and applied by revolutionary forces since at least the early 1950s.[7] Thus, a symbolic struggle between "grammars" directly reflected the political struggle between the communist forces in the Liberated Zone, and the royalist forces in the lowlands. The competing interpretations carried potent symbolism, throughout the embattled period up to 1975, and well beyond.[8]

PHOUMI VONGVICHIT'S REFORMS

Phoumi's *Lao Grammar* was published by the Lao Patriotic Front at Sam Neua in 1967. Its wider distribution a decade later had far-reaching effect (Houmphanh 1996: 164), setting in place as a national standard the revolutionary forces' strict interpretation of the 1949 Royal Ordinance, which had already been the norm in the Liberated Zone for at least twenty years. Phoumi takes a strongly political stance in his introduction, stressing the nation-unifying function of a "scientific" grammar, an urgent requirement at that time of struggle to unite the nation under socialism. He commits to words the principles of language reform in Laos which were established and carried through until his death. Let me quote him at length:

> Every country in the world has its own principles of speech and writing,

its own linguistic principles which may demonstrate the style and the honour of the nation, and demonstrate the cultural independence of the nation, along with independence in political, economic and other arenas.

Laos has gone back and forth as a colonised state of various foreign nations for many centuries. Those countries that have colonised us have brought their languages to be used here and mixed with Lao, causing Lao to lose its original former content, bit by bit. Most importantly, this has been the case during the time that Laos has been an "old-style" colony of the French colonialists, and a "new-style" colony of the American imperialists. They have tried to incite and force Lao people to popularise speaking and studying their languages, and so then to abandon and forget our own Lao language, little by little. Furthermore, activities along the borders adjoining various neighbouring countries have led a certain number of Lao people, who do not remember their Lao well, to introduce those foreign languages and mix them with Lao, causing their already degraded Lao to further depart from the original principles, on a daily basis. The result of this situation is that Lao people speak and write Lao without unity, where those who live close to the border with whichever country it may be, or who have studied the language of that country, write and speak according to the style and the accent of that country.

Since Lao does not yet have unified principles of writing and speech, we Lao neither like to nor dare to write books or translate books into Lao, which means the cultural struggle of our Lao nation is not as strong as other areas of the struggle. This has considerable negative consequences for our struggle to seize control of the nation and fight American imperialism.

The preservation and renovation of the nation's orthography, idiom, literature and cultural principles demonstrates the patriotic spirit, the fine tradition and heritage of bravery which was passed down to us from our forebears . . .

The leading idea in my research and writing of this book "Lao Grammar" is for the grammar of Lao to belong to the nation, and to the people, and for it to be progressive, modern, and scientific . . . Every principle and every term used herein is intended to be simple, so that the general populace, of high or low education, may easily understand . . . My greatest concern in writing this book is to have people understand and utilise the principles and the various terms in the easiest possible way (Phoumi 1967: 5-8).

Thus, two crucial principles guided Phoumi's reforms—first, to preserve the language as uniquely Lao and free of unwelcome foreign (especially Thai) influence, and second, to facilitate the greatest access to literacy for the population as a whole, not just the well educated and/or privileged.

Adult education was an important focus of educational policy in the new government, and much of this was aimed at non-Lao speaking minorities (Stuart-Fox 1986: 147–8).

It is interesting to consider why it is that while in the passage quoted above, Phoumi named the French and the Americans, he didn't explicitly name the Thai, even though he was so obviously referring to them. The passage about "neighbouring countries" could only be referring to Thailand, particularly obvious given the distribution of political control during the time the book was written. Thai influence was also already a topic of scholarly debate in Royal Lao Government areas of lowland Laos when Phoumi's grammar was published. Apparently, Thai was then noticeably influencing not only Lao orthography, but also Lao pronunciation, in daily life, as well as in the mass media. For example, it was claimed (Xao n.d: 5) that Lao *háw* (ເຮົາ) 'I/we' and *hóong-héem* (ໂຮງແຮມ) 'hotel' were being written/pronounced in the Thai manner (i.e. as ເຣົາ *láw* and ໂຣງແຣມ *lóongléem* in Lao). In these pre-1975 lowland debates, Thailand was also often euphemistically referred to, as in Xao (n.d), where most references are to *pháasǎa fāng khǔa* (ພາສາຝັ່ງຂວາ) 'the language of the right bank (of the Mekong),' and even *pháasǎa khǎw* (ພາສາເຂົາ) '*their* language.' This sensitivity is apparently less operative today, as evinced by Sisaveuy's recent open reference to the influence of Thai words bringing about the "death" of Lao words (Sisaveuy 1996: 99).

Phoumi's changes to the orthography fully reflected the Lao Patriotic Front's "stricter interpretation" of the royal directive to spell words according to their pronunciation. This especially concerned the spelling of Indic loanwords whose original pronunciation (and thus spelling) included a far greater range of syllable-final consonants than were phonologically possible in spoken Lao. Bounthan (1995: 52) and Chamberlain (1978: 269) separately discuss the example of the syllable /kaan/ which formerly could be spelt variously as ກາລ *kaal,* ກາຣ *kaar,* or ການ *kǎan* (where ລ "l" and ຣ "r" in final position are regularly pronounced as /-n/, as in Thai today). While the "purists" had hoped to preserve etymology (at the expense of ease of learning and predictability of pronunciation, according to some), the "strict" reformers at the other end of the scale now had their way, and such distinctions neutralized in speech would now also be neutralized in writing. Thus, the three syllables pronounced /kaan/ are all today standardly spelled ການ.

The most famous and most potent symbol of Phoumi's reforms was the removal from the Lao alphabet of the letter ຣ "r," theoretically representing the alveolar trill [r] (for impassioned discussions, see Bounleuth 1995: 37–39, Sisaveuy 1996: 98–99). This had already been long in place in revolutionary writing in the Liberated Zone. For example, in a Neo Lao

Issara information sheet, dated 1955, the Lao letter "r" does not appear
once; examples of ລ "l" for ຣ "r" in that document include *ǎaméelikǎa*
(ອາເມລິກາ) 'America', *falāng* (ຝະລັ່ງ) 'France', *lâatsa'ǎanáacák* (ລາດຊະອານາຈັກ)
'kingdom', and *lātthabǎan* (ລັດຖະບານ) 'government'.) Whereas Central (i.e.
the normative standard) Thai, for example, has a spoken contrast between
/l/ and /r/, there is no such contrast in spoken Lao, and /r/ is not part of the
sound system.[9] As Thongphet puts it, "no linguist, phonetician or
phonologist would ever say that the Lao language had the sound [r]"
(Thongphet 1995: 104). He goes on to quote Reinhorn (1970: x), for
whom "r" exists in Lao language "purely in theory."

If a word beginning with /r/ in Central Thai is also found in Lao, the
Thai /r/ will correspond in spoken Lao to either /l/ or /h/:

Thai		*Lao*		*meaning*
รำ	*ram*	ຮ້ຳ	*hám*	bran
รำ	*ram*	ລ້ຳ	*lám*	kind of dance
ลำ	*lam*	ລ້ຳ	*lám*	classifier for boats, and other large tubular things
รด	*rót*	ຮົດ	*hōt*	to pour (water)
รถ	*rót*	ລົດ	*lōt*	vehicle
ลด	*lót*	ລົດ	*lōt*	to reduce

Given Phoumi's premises, his reasoning for removing the symbol "r" was
perfectly rational. Why should the language retain an orthographic
distinction (i.e. "l" vs. "r") which reflects no spoken distinction, and thus
must be remembered either arbitrarily (thus harder to learn), or with
explicit reference to a distinction made in a foreign language? The removal
of "r" nicely served both of Phoumi's aims in linguistic reform—to exclude
"non-Lao" elements, and to make the system simpler, and thus easier to
learn for those with lower level of education (i.e. by not having to
remember by rote, or by knowledge of Thai, which Lao words pronounced
with /l/ are spelt with "r" and which are spelt with "l").[10]

There is an increasing popular preference in recent years to tend towards
the preservation of etymology in loanwords where possible. While
traditional etymological spellings are less likely to be seen in official
publications, they are now often seen where privately produced, as for
instance in the spelling of shop names. This is perhaps felt to be eye-
catching, for example in the case of the flamboyant etymological spelling
ສີລປ໌, in place of the "correct" spelling ສິນ, for the syllable pronounced *sǐn*.
One place where etymological spelling has recently become notably popular
is in the romanization of Lao names, virtually all of which are of Indic

origin. While many feel that they cannot write their name with its etymological spelling in *Lao*, there is a growing tendency for people to *romanize* their name according etymology rather than pronunciation. This is very common in Thailand, where the etymologically-motivated English spellings of many Thai proper names result in Anglo pronunciations often very different from the Thai—cf. Dejphol, Poolsub, for example.

Consider the following Lao examples. The name of the present vice minister of information and culture appeared romanized in the 1980s as *Bouabane Volakhoun* (Stuart-Fox 1986: 155), but now as *Bouabane Vorakhoun* (Bouabane 1996a) reflecting an etymological "r" in English, while the Lao spelling ວໍລະຄຸນ retains "l" (e.g. as in Bouabane 1996b). The pronunciation remains /vɔ́ɔlakhŭn/. Similarly, the founding head of the ICR Houmphanh Rattanavong uses the etymological "r" in the romanization of his family name, while still using "l" in Lao (i.e. ລັດຕະນະວົງ, as in Houmphanh 1996[1990]). The pronunciation remains /lāttanavóng/. The novelist whose name is pronounced /bŭnthanɔ́ɔng sŏmsájphón/ now romanizes his family name as *Xomxayphol*, using the "x" of former French transliteration (for /s/), and reflecting the final "l" of the word's Sanskrit root (pronounced as /n/ in Lao). The name of the former minister for public health was pronounced /vánnalêet lâatphóol/, and yet was romanized as *Vannareth Rajpho* (*Vientiane Times*, vol. 4.1, 1–3 Jan 1997), again reflecting etymology at the expense of correct pronunciation by the Anglo reader.[11]

How do younger Lao know what these etymological spellings should correctly be, since they have been largely erased from Lao orthography for now over twenty years? Since few Lao study enough Pali (let alone Sanskrit) to really be closely familiar with the sources of many Lao loanwords, it seems clear that they would have to rely for this on their self-taught knowledge of Thai (see below), whose orthography has long been designed to reflect etymology. The problem is not a new one, and has often been raised in debate on Lao orthography, in which there has been an ongoing tension between the desire on the one hand to maintain (or invent) "tradition" by asserting the religious and scholarly importance of having a "Pali-based" language, and, on the other hand, to adhere to the nationalist requirement for Lao and Thai to be clearly distinguished (cf. Ivarsson this volume). Interestingly, Thai is considered by some Lao to be "more correct," and even "superior" for this reason. Thai is often authoritative where there are discrepancies between the spelling systems. This is presumably a combination of, firstly, the known high level of official codification and standardization in Thai; secondly, the more "difficult" and thus "higher" (i.e. more "learned") form that Thai orthography takes; and, thirdly, the excessive humility Lao people are sometimes known to display.

There is a running joke in Vientiane about the brand name *bɨa láaw* (ເບຍລາວ 'Lao Beer': due to the similar shape of Lao ບ "b" and Thai ข "kh," in addition to a vowel symbol combination ເ-ບ which is read in Lao as /ia/, but in Thai as / əəj /, a Thai is likely to read the label of a Lao Beer bottle not as *bɨa láaw* 'Lao Beer', but as *khɔ̌əj láaw* 'Lao (son)-in-law' (or, more generally, Lao man who has married into one's family). I have heard educated Lao remark in seriousness that the Thai reading is in fact "correct" (although this is by no means the majority view).

Moving away from the issue of spelling, there are other aspects of the language which have been similarly subject to politically motivated reforms, although it seems these were not overtly published and distributed in the same way. Many changes were brought in either explicitly, or by example, during the nationwide "massive increase" in education immediately after 1975 (Stuart-Fox 1986: 145), of which a major proportion was ideological and political in nature (cf. also Stuart-Fox 1997: ch. 6).

Prior to the change of government, the particle *dòoj* (ໂດຍ) was a standard polite/deferential affirmative marker in Lao, with similar uses to Thai *khráp/khâ* (ครับ/ค่ะ; cf. *yes, sir/ma'am*), usually associated with the use of the self-deprecating pronoun *khanɔ̌ɔj* (ຂະນ້ອຍ) 'I' (literally 'little slave'). Apparently, this was regarded by the new regime as symbolic of an overly hierarchical pre-revolutionary society, asserting and perpetuating values which were to be abolished. The use of *dòoj* was immediately associated with this social arrangement, and was banned. This ban was apparently not effected by any official public decree. Rather, the changes were brought in at ground level through the education system, and in the frenzy of public "seminars" held in schools, temples, and other public places in the early years of the Lao PDR (Stuart-Fox 1986: 156).

Dòoj was deliberately replaced by another word *câw* (ເຈົ້າ). Many Lao report that the initial period of transition was a very difficult and uncomfortable one, in which ordinary people had to drop a well-established habitual politeness marker overnight, replacing it with something unfamiliar. People report having felt embarrassed in doing so, and conscious of being "rude." One must wonder how long it took for the new usage to become normal, or even if for some people it remains uncomfortable to this day.

In recent years, *dòoj* has made a comeback. Its usage began to slowly re-emerge in the early 1990s, and is now once again quite widespread, particularly by children speaking to teachers and elders, as well as by adults addressing traditionally respected people—e.g. monks, one's own elders, and so on. Many Vientiane children are now openly urged to "*dòoj*" their superiors (in the same way many English-speaking children are urged to "please" and "thank you" theirs). Som (1996: 146–7) argues in favor of this return to traditional etiquette, beginning with the question "Is *dǒoj* a word for slaves?" (clearly referring to the original revolutionary reasoning behind the word's prohibition). Interestingly, he never explicitly mentions the post-1975 ban on *dǒoj*, but in arguing that the etiquette does *not* symbolize self-deprecation, he remains out of danger of challenging the revolutionary motivation for the original ban (i.e. he simply challenges one of the argument's premises).

Complementing proscriptive reforms like the banning of *dǒoj*, there were also a number of *pre*scriptive reforms under the new regime. Consider the introduction of *sahǎaj* (ສະຫາຍ) 'comrade' as a standard "leveling" term of address (in accordance with global socialist practice). In Lao, kinship terms and other terms of address (such as occupational terms like *'ǎacǎan* (ອາຈານ) 'teacher') are used as pronouns, and *sahǎaj* was no exception. Up until the early 1990s, the term *sahǎaj* could be heard in many official transactions, meaning 'you,' 's/he,' or even 'I,' depending on the circumstances. As Lao society has begun to loosen up over recent years, and proscribed elements like *dǒoj* are returning, the use of prescribed elements like *sahǎaj* has begun to recede, correspondingly. The usage of *sahǎaj* has become a loaded indicator of socialist conservatism, and thus, in today's social climate, considerable social distance. In Vientiane today, this is often not appropriate (although there remain contexts in which this kind of talk is expected).

Other terms have taken on a stigma of association with socialist conservatism, in particular many of the expressions prevalent in the numerous propaganda slogans which Lao people have had to learn by rote (especially until the late 1980s). One example is the term *sǎamākkhíi* (ສາມັກຄີ) 'solidarity, friendship,' used most notably in the political slogans referring to "special relationships" of political nature (e.g. between Laos, Vietnam, and Cambodia). Until more recently, this term would often be used informally with regard to collective activities. I recently used the term with reference to an invitation to dine amongst friends who hadn't met for some time, but was advised that it was inappropriate (unless ironic in tone) for a casual and intimate engagement such as it was. Many other terms from socialist propaganda (often calqued from universal socialist political slogans) are now falling out of favor in Vientiane, due to their association with a conservative socialist stance. Such expressions are, however, still noticeable in more isolated rural centers.

Another interesting and perhaps more subtle area of prescriptive reform in Lao concerns the choice of certain official terminology. Prior to 1975, many standard terms were common to Lao and Thai, especially those based on Pali or Sanskrit borrowings. A number of such terms were changed in Laos, arguably based on Phoumi's two major principles of reform—to make the terms uniquely Lao, and to make them as easy as possible to teach and understand. For example, the former term for 'mathematics' *khanītsàat* (ຄະນິດສາດ; from Sanskrit *gaṇita-śāstra* 'the science of computation'), was substituted by *lêek* (ເລກ), literally 'number(s).' While *lêek* is in fact a loan from Pali, it is nevertheless a simple term in daily use, unlike the more technical term *khanītsàat*. Twenty years later, the Ministry of Education has now dropped that reform, publishing its high school mathematics textbooks once again using the former "high" term *khanītsàat*. Why the reversion? In direct contrast to the original principles behind the reform, people I have interviewed on the matter favor the adoption of the former term, partly because of its more "learned" flavor, and partly because it unified the terminology of Lao and Thai. This latter point is especially significant for the many students who utilize the considerably greater volume and range of instructional and educational materials available in Thai (see below). Here we see a direct conflict of interest between the highly practical benefit of Thai/Lao orthographic/terminological consistency, and the long entrenched nationalist opposition to the very idea.

A final example concerns the reformed terms for the Ministry of Defense and the Ministry of Interior. In the Royal Lao Government, these two Lao ministries had the same Pali-derived titles as in Thai, *Kasúang kaláahŏom* (ກະຊວງກະລາໂຮມ) and *Kasúang mahàattháj* (ກະຊວງມະຫາດໄທ), respectively. These were changed to *Kasúang pɔ̀ɔng kǎn pathêet* (ກະຊວງປ້ອງກັນປະເທດ; literally 'ministry (to) protect (the) country') and *Kasúang pháaj-náj* (ກະຊວງພາຍໃນ; literally 'ministry (of the) inner part'). The adoption of these new terms again nicely satisfied Phoumi's policy of firstly maintaining Lao uniqueness (i.e. while many ministries remained named as in Thai, these two powerful ministries were perhaps the most symbolic choices), and secondly bringing the terminology "down to earth," away from "big words" which the average peasant (or speaker of Lao as a second language) would be unlikely to use.

CONTEMPORARY DEBATE

Within current debate among today's community of Lao concerned with the state of the language, we can discern a number of divisions, related in general to the partition of "new" versus "old." But since there are three main movements in the standardization of Lao, as discussed above, the line may be drawn in different places. The extremes are the (post-) Phoumi position (e.g. Thongphet 1995) on the one hand, and the Sila position (e.g. Thongkham and Souvan 1997), on the other. The Nginn approach is progressive and rationalist from the Sila point of view, but conservative and traditional from the Phoumi point of view. From the perspective of modern socialist principles, and a concern for the integrity of the present government's cultural policies, only the Phoumi position is politically correct. But for those with the more general nationalist concern that the Lao language be kept safely distinct from Thai, only Sila's approach looks problematic. For those who are particularly concerned that Buddhism be better served in education and in public life, neither the Nginn nor Phoumi approach offer the promise of what Sila had planned. These oppositions of rationalist versus traditional, progressive versus conservative, emblems versus principles, all overlap to various extents. While I cannot attempt here to unravel this complex intellectual weaving, let me try to bring out a few of the issues which emerged in the recent conference on Lao language policy (published in ICR 1995), and which remain the main topics of contemporary debate.

One issue concerns the general choice between taking Lao as "Lao," or trying to see it from the view of how it fits in to the greater world which presses in upon it. This may concern contemporary global social and political forces such as the spread of the culture of science and technology, or it may involve historical encrustations, such as those traceable to the Indic sources of religious culture in Laos. A common theme in arguing for increasing the complexity of the Lao writing system is that foreign words, especially proper names and technical terms, must be faithfully transcribed. Bounyok (1995: 100) claims that a simplified Lao orthography (i.e. without the letter "r") prevents us from effectively transcribing foreign terms, with the result that "people of the world will figure that we [Lao] are ignorant, and have nothing good in our country." In contrast, Thongphet (1995: 103) praises Phoumi's "daring" in "serving the people" by cutting out "r," among other simplifying reforms.

This is typical of a strong theme of Lao "local pride" throughout Thongphet's work, nowhere more apparent than in his discussion of the removal of the letter "r," in which he pointedly argues that "those who are most offended are those who have previously used the letter 'r' and have held an attitude of worship towards Pali and Sanskrit, that these languages are superior to Lao, their own mother tongue" (Thongphet 1995: 110). Consider Douangdeuan (1995) and Outhin (1995), who share a view of rather extreme normative conservatism, opposing linguistic change, and even revealing a lack of confidence in the integrity and/or expressive capacity of the basic resources of the Lao language (as opposed in particular to Pali and Sanskrit). Outhin (1995: 125–6), for example, argues that a range of cases of rather ingenious folk reanalysis of expressions originally from Pali are actually "negative developments" in Lao which should be rectified. In a similar vein, Douangdeuan (1995: 133), making a case in favor of the need for Lao people to learn Pali and Sanskrit, gives a set of Pali words for 'beautiful,' arguing that they attest to the "clearer" expressiveness of Pali over Lao.[12] Scholars such as these (and many other contributions to ICR 1995) are now arguing for greater attention to Pali and Sanskrit in basic Lao language education, often (whether intentionally or not) playing on the vagueness of the Lao term *khâw* (ຂື້າ) 'source, root, basis' which is typically used to describe the status of Pali/Sanskrit with respect to Lao. Younger scholars such as Thongphet (1995) and Khamhoung (1995) point out the misleading effect of this usage, and find it necessary to stress that Pali is not "the source" of Lao language at all.

Many commentators show primary concern for issues which are essentially emblematic in nature, rather than being concerned with the application of general principles. This may be illustrated once again with respect to the tireless letter "r." Two important arguments for reinstatement of "r" are (a) that it is required for representation of the "rolled-tongue" sound [r] found in many minority languages of Laos, and (b) that it is required for representation of (at least) proper names and technical terms from European languages. In such discussions, it is often as if the presence or absence of "r" *alone* will make or break the ability of the Lao language to cope with these tasks (Souvanthone (1995: 117) is a typical example). But according to Thongphet's rationalist view, if one is really concerned with the *principles*, then there are many equally deserving candidates in the inventory of sounds required to faithfully transcribe minority languages, and to transcribe foreign technical terms and proper names. The point here is that throughout the years, the debate has revolved around the stock examples, and *not* on general principles. These examples become potent symbols, and quickly eclipse rationalist issues of principle. However, those who try to argue this line often do not acknowledge that such an emblem has a greater meaning than its face value would suggest. By orthographic convention, "r" signifies an alveolar trill, a convention Phoumi's view deems unnecessary and inappropriate for Lao. But by historical fact, the letter "r" has come to import with it the signification of pre-revolutionary Laos, a society and culture personally lived by many, and yet collectively denied in recent times. It now signifies what is missing. The removal of "r" from the language came with the removal of much more significant things in the culture and society of lowland Lao people. Thus, while Thongphet's arguments regarding the letter "r" may be more rational and consistent, many of them are likely to fall on deaf ears in a circle fixated upon such salient and historically (not to mention personally) loaded emblems.

There are many more issues which could be discussed in this context, but these should suffice to invoke the aroma of the current array of intellectual standpoints in Vientiane. On the one hand, rationalist scholars like

Thongphet harshly criticize simplistic and/or unprincipled arguments put forward by those who "understand nothing at all about the basic and unique features of the Lao language" (Thongphet 1995: 111). His aim is to retain and promote the principled rationalization of the language which began with Nginn and was taken much further by Phoumi. Others argue for the very opposite, such as Khamphan (1995: 57), for example, who demands a two-stage renovation of the Lao language, first reinstating the Nginn system (RLG 1972), as a prelude to adopting Sila's proposed Pali-fied system (Sila 1935). Such a course would precisely reverse the direction in historical trend of the last seventy years.

THAI INFLUENCE

WE may now turn to the Thai language, and consider its constant presence in the development of Lao as a language, and as a national language. In Phoumi's "Introduction," above, Thai was implicitly singled out as a language (and culture) whose influence Lao must resist.[13] It now appears that Phoumi's worst fears are turning to reality (Stuart-Fox 1997: 205), but for most modern Lao the facts are not considered quite so awful. The level of exposure to Thai in Laos has increased dramatically in recent years, and now most if not all residents of Vientiane (as well as those in many other parts of the country) have daily contact with Central Thai. In a recent survey on social makeup in urban Vientiane, over 90 percent of residents responded that they could understand Thai, while at the same time less than 30 percent said they could speak or write it (ICR 1998: 57).

By far the most pervasive and powerful medium of exposure to modern Thai culture in Laos today is television. In reporting on the reception of Thai television in Laos over ten years ago, Stuart-Fox noted that "(o)nly those [Lao provincial towns] close to the Thai frontier can receive programmes," and that in any case there were "few residents lucky enough to possess TV sets" (Stuart-Fox 1986: 155). Due to stronger broadcast signals from Thailand, or better reception equipment, or a combination of both, the reception of Thai television now goes a lot further. It has been reported, for example, that Thai programs can now be received in Attapeu, a province with no border to Thailand. Further, not even those places out of range of Thai television transmission are spared from regular exposure to Thai. Enterprising Lao are doing good business in rural areas charging for public access to video showings, whose popularity is rapidly increasing. In Sepon town, for example, a district center near the Vietnamese border in the far East of Savannakhet province, I witnessed large numbers of young men paying for entry (US$ 0.50 each) to gather around a television set and view Chinese and Thai videos, all with dialogue in Central Thai. Similarly, the advent of satellite television dishes has now well and truly taken hold, and television programming from across the world can be received virtually anywhere as long as one can afford to buy a dish (from US$ 400 to US$ 1000). Thus, fewer and fewer Lao people are isolated from exposure to the Central Thai language, and to the popular culture of mainstream Thai society.

It was noted in 1985 that the Vientiane authorities "(took) no action against those watching Thai programmes" (Stuart-Fox 1986: 155). While the official view of modern Thai culture at the time was certainly negative, the perceived "threat" of Thai TV was apparently not great, given that television sets were fairly rare. At the time, the Lao television station had only recently expanded programming from three days to five days a week (each day only a few hours in the evenings), and was about to introduce programming seven days a week. Thai programs would have often been the only choice. By the late 1990s, ownership of television sets has skyrocketed, and they are found everywhere. While there are now two Lao television stations broadcasting in Vientiane, the competition from Thailand is overwhelming, with Bangkok-based programming matching the technical level of any developed country. Thai television is loud, flashy, and technologically advanced. These are all attractive qualities to many modern residents of Vientiane. Many homes, markets, and workplaces have televisions installed to help pass the time (as is common practice in Thailand). It has been somewhat ironic to observe that even the State Bookshop has a television installed, broadcasting Thai commercial programming inside the shop throughout the day. This is the same place that ten years ago contained "nothing but Eastern bloc magazines, the works of Marx and Lenin and a few 'acceptable' novels translated into Lao" (Stuart-Fox 1986: xiv).

As in any high-consumption society, the vast proportion of television programming in Thailand is overwhelmingly consumer-oriented. The most obvious features of this are the high frequency of advertisements, and the array of consumer-oriented game shows which revolve around the accumulation of money and consumer goods. Also very popular is the plethora of implausibly dramatic soap operas, most of which are based around the lives of the wealthy and beautiful (much in the "Western" mold).

Thai radio and Thai popular music are also in high demand in lowland Laos. Ownership of radios is widespread, and it is very common for people to work outdoors (e.g. on construction sites, at marketplaces, in rice fields) to the tune of radio sets. More and more commonly, Vientiane sets are tuned to the FM stations broadcasting from nearby Nong Khai and Udon

Thani in Thailand. Vientiane residents contribute to the participating audience of the Thai stations, writing to the stations to request songs, and taking part in promotional competitions. Vientiane businesses advertise on these Thai stations. While announcers on the northeast Thai radio stations received in Vientiane speak some amount of Lao (or at least "Isan Thai," the mix of Thai and Lao spoken in northeast Thailand; cf. Preecha 1989), mostly Central Thai is used, especially in regular news bulletins and the like.

Commercial radio programming is, of course, dominated by popular music, and Thai radio is no exception. The Thai popular music industry is very advanced in terms of its levels of production quality and marketing, and among the Vientiane youth especially, the booming, heavily image-oriented Thai scene is popular. The many bars and clubs operating in Vientiane play a high proportion of Thai and "international" (i.e. Western) songs. A minimum level of "local content" is required by law (VMGO 1997, Articles 9.8 and 15) though often not followed, and is enforced by occasional monitoring (including educational "seminars") by local authorities.

Many bars and clubs in Vientiane feature live bands which play a mix of Lao, Thai, and Western music, with a few clubs playing no Lao music at all. Among the more trendy youth, Lao songs are uncool, and there are interesting ways in which language becomes a factor. For example, Thai popular songs, especially those that deal with the dominant themes of love and relationships, use the pronouns *chǎn* (ฉัน) for 'I' and *thəə* (เธอ) for 'you.' While a number of pronouns and pronominal strategies are common to Thai and Lao, these particular forms are highly marked as "very Thai," and definitely *not* Lao. Young Lao musicians who aspire to write original songs in the style of modern Thai pop are stuck. They are unable to use the Thai pronouns, since these would never pass the approval of the government, as is required for original material broadcast or published in Laos (VMGO 1997, Article 6.3). But to use Lao pronouns (*khɔɔj* (ຂ້ອຍ) 'I' and *câw* (ເຈົ້າ) 'you'; or *'âaj* (ອ້າຍ) 'older brother' and *nɔɔng* (ນ້ອງ) 'younger sister') in a song of the Thai pop style would sound embarrassing 'to a hip young Lao.[14] The result is that the Thai industry dominates the pop music market in Laos.

Print media is another major channel for Lao people's exposure to Central Thai. Lao language newspapers and magazines are somewhat limited in quantity and content, for both economic and political reasons. All Lao publications require official government approval, a fact which must, to some extent, discourage experimentation and/or enterprise in any non-established styles of publishing (for example, anything "lowbrow," satirical, critical, or politically reactionary). In this context, the sheer quantity and variety of Thai written materials attracts a lot of interest in Laos.

The Thai language written materials found now in Laos are basically of two types, the "popular," and the "practical." Thai popular written materials include novels, comics, and popular magazines (the latter often associated with promotion of Thai music or\television industries), as well as stickers, signs, and slogans advertising Thai products. These can be seen all over Vientiane, in shops and homes, in markets, and on the street. The popularity of these materials is evinced by the small shopfront or market "libraries" which can be found around Vientiane, from which one may borrow (for a price) Thai-language glossy magazines and novels. There is no such market in Vientiane for private Lao language libraries.

Thai practical written materials include educational resources, technical manuals, instructional materials, and the like. These kinds of publications are widespread and of a relatively high standard in Thailand, and many students in Vientiane now utilize the broad range of publications which provide information and resources on technical matters. There is often no alternative, since so little is available in Lao. Most of the bilingual English language teaching materials are produced in Thailand, and are on sale in most Vientiane bookshops. A number of new bookshops have opened up around Vientiane, stocking mostly Thai language titles. Thus, many Vientiane Lao are being exposed to a lot of written Central Thai out of sheer practical necessity, and much of their working technical terminology is directly borrowed from Thai. A typical example observed recently was a series of Thai health education information sheets hung on the wall of a ward in the "150-bed" Lao-Soviet Friendship Hospital in Vientiane. While it would of course be preferable for the Lao to have such materials available in Lao language, it is obviously better to have access to the information in Thai than not at all.

Thai newspapers provide elements of both the "popular" and the "practical." The nature of journalism in the Thai press is a world apart from that in Laos, and is very closely modeled on the style of developed countries. Aside from the range of human interest stories and glossy advertising, one can find critical social/political analysis, scarce in the Lao press. This in itself is engaging for Lao readers, particularly where this concerns probing of native political mechanisms, whereby readers may be privy to highly critical analysis of the activities of their national leaders, as well as no end of gossip. This for the Lao is attractive, at the very least for its novelty. (At the same time, many Lao are glad that they are not themselves governed directly by such an openly chaotic system.) It is also notable that the kinds of news people are exposed to in the Thai press (as well as electronic media) are probably slightly nerve-racking for those concerned with Lao national security, given the open political debate, criticism, and also exposure to the culture of industrial action, and so on. Recently, Lao people in Vientiane may be observed debating over morning coffee the fortunes of Thai politicians and political parties, and the dynamics of Thai politics.

Thus, with respect to mass media like television and newspapers, there is no way to state simply whether the exposure of Lao people to Thai culture in this way is "good" or "bad," "destructive" or "constructive." Like television in general, Thai television can be said to have a numbing and/or distracting effect, or it may be said to broaden horizons and promote progressive thinking by means of creating exposure to ideas from without, which can be constructively borrowed and appropriated. For better and/or worse, Lao people learn a lot from watching the Thai. And the Thai, who spend little time taking any notice of the Lao, indeed learn very little from them.

The present high level of exposure to Central Thai in Laos is having a noticeable effect on the spoken language, particularly of young people. The following chart shows a handful of the many Thai words which are coming into use among Lao in Vientiane:

Lao terms		Lao terms of recent Thai origin		meanings
ໂທລະພາບ	*thóolaphâap*	ໂທລະທັດ	*thóolathāt*	television
ເຮັດວຽກ	*hēt vîak*	ທຳງານ	*thám ngáan*	to work
ຮັ່ງມີ	*hāng-míi*	ລວຍ	*lúaj*	rich
ທຳອິດ	*thám-'ít*	ທີແລກ	*thī i-lêɛk*	at first
ຮ້ອງ	*hɔ́ɔng*	ຮ້ອງ	*lɔ́ɔng*	sing
ແກ້ວ	*kêɛw*	ຂວດ	*khùat*	bottle
ພົບ	*phōp*	ເຈິ	*cə̂'*	meet

Accent may be affected, although this is perhaps less widespread. In a number of cases, the Thai pronunciation of a Lao word may be adopted (e.g. Thai *lên* (เล่น) for Lao *lîn* ຫຼິ້ນ) 'play, pass time'). Effect on tones may be observed, where, for example, young Lao women can be heard using the (characteristically Thai) lengthened, rising tone with final glottal stop on the sentence-final perfective marker *lêɛw* (ແລ້ວ). Outhin (1995: 126–7) gives the examples of *phɔ̀ɔm* (ແພ່ມ) 'add, additional,' *lɔ̀ɔm* (ເລີ່ມ) 'begin,' *mūang* (ມ່ວງ) 'purple (color),' and *thāw* (ເທົ່າ) 'extent, amount,' which are being pronounced in Lao as *phɔ̂ɔm, lɔ̂ɔm, mûang*, and *thâw*, following the Thai tone (i.e. as if they were written in Lao as ແພ້ມ, ເລີ້ມ, ມ້ວງ, and ເທົ້າ).

There are at least two levels of usage of spoken Thai among the Lao which may be termed "flippant" versus "serious." Flippant usage of Thai is common among young people, and among those into popular culture. It involves "putting on" a Thai accent, and using Thai expressions in imitative, joking fashion (just as Australians often do with American or English accents and idioms). This conscious and deliberate usage of Thai is considered by most to be not actually "speaking Thai" in any genuine sense. Thus, someone who uses Thai expressions flippantly may still assert that their "serious" Lao does not incorporate any Thai elements at all. Nevertheless, there *is* a significant degree of "serious" usage, and this is on an apparently unconscious level, where many people would indeed deny that they do it at all. John Gumperz (1982: 75) has described this phenomenon, noting that "expressed attitudes tend to conflict with the observed facts of behaviour." Indeed, I have pointed out to Lao informants who deny seriously using any Thai, that they have in fact been recorded on tape doing just that. When the facts are attested, the result has often been considerable debate and confusion as to what is Thai and what is Lao after all. Some speakers are very clear about the distinction, others are not. The former tend to be those who oppose Thai influence, while the latter tend to see it as "no problem," since Thai and Lao are "basically the same language" anyway. This is an especially common line when defending one's use of a Thai term in Lao.

The adoption of Thai words into the Lao system has resulted in some interesting phenomena with respect to the changes in meaning that certain elements undergo. For instance, a Thai word may simply replace its Lao equivalent. An example is 'television,' *thóolaphâap* (ໂທລະພາບ) in Lao. Lao speakers have now almost unanimously adopted the same term as Thai, *thóolathāt* (ໂທລະທັດ cf. Thai โทรทัศน์). Another possibility is for a Thai *meaning* to replace the Lao meaning, where Thai and Lao had different meanings for a shared word. An example is *falāng* (ຝະລັ່ງ), which until recently meant 'French' in Lao, an abbreviation of *falāngsèet* (ຝະລັ່ງເສດ). The term *farāng* (ฝรั่ง in Thai) refers generally to 'Westerners' or 'Caucasians,' and this usage is now being adopted by children and youth in Vientiane, as well as many adults. Another example concerns the word *phɛɛ* (ແພ້), which in Lao (for older speakers) means 'to win, to defeat someone.' Interestingly, it has the very opposite meaning in Thai, i.e. 'to lose, to be defeated by someone.' With the present level of exposure to Thai, this has now become a possible source of confusion, which on occasion needs to be resolved by the question "Do you mean Lao *phɛ̂ɛ* or Thai *phɛ̂ɛ*?" (cf. English "Do you mean *funny* 'peculiar' or *funny* 'ha-ha?'"). It appears that the confusion engendered by the possibility of opposite readings for a single word is too impractical, and I have noticed that some young people in Vientiane now use *phɛ̂ɛ* almost exclusively in the Thai sense.

Where Thai and Lao have synonyms, a Thai word may be incorporated into Lao, where the meanings of the two words adjust, each taking on a separate sense. For example, the words for 'wealthy' in Lao and Thai are *hāng-míi* (ຮັ່ງມີ) and *ruaj* (รวย), respectively. The term *ruaj* (Lao *lúaj* ລວຍ) is now being used in Vientiane to refer to the kind of flashy nouveau-riche style of wealth often depicted on Thai TV, or associated with the modern new rich of Vientiane. The Lao term hāng-míi now tends to refer to more established family wealth, with inherited ownership of land and paddy, perhaps with influence because of this, and so on. Another example concerns the words for 'work,' *vǐak* (ວຽກ) and *ngaan* (งาน) in Lao and Thai, respectively. The Lao term tends now to refer to manual labor, while the Thai term is gaining currency in Vientiane for reference to white-collar work. This example is rather transparent in terms of the social levels at which Lao and Thai expressions tend to refer. David Bradley (personal communication) has suggested that these examples of former synonyms adjusting to complement each other semantically could be construed as cases where Thai actually has an enriching influence on Lao. While Lao indeed gains a semantic distinction it formerly lacked, there is a tendency, however, for the formerly neutral Lao terms to become pejorative (as in the example of Lao vs. Thai 'work,' above). This has already happened in many cases in Isan Thai.

A feature of Central Thai which modern Lao now conspicuously lacks is *lâatsasáp* (ລາຄຊະສັບ) "royal vocabulary," the special flowery terminology derived from Pali, Sanskrit, and Khmer, used for reference to activities of the royal family. Lao possessed this feature at the time Laos had a royal head of state. Tay (1995: 169) reports that upon the establishment of Lao PDR, royal vocabulary was officially banned, permitted only where appropriate or necessary in poetry and literature.[15] Today, however, the Lao in range of Thai TV are exposed daily to lengthy reports on the activities of royal family members on Thai news bulletins, and these are full of royal vocabulary. Perhaps more significantly, Lao language reportage is itself beginning to use the conventions of royal vocabulary (see front page report of Princess Sirindhorn's visit to Vientiane, *Pasason* newspaper, 20 Mar. 1998). Notably, the Thai royal family is well-liked by many Lao. Images of King Bhumibol and Princess Sirindhorn are common in shops and some private homes in Vientiane. The Krung Thai Bank distributed a 1997 calendar to shops and offices all over Vientiane featuring a large photograph of King Bhumibol of Thailand. It is amazing that in Vientiane his image is now at least as widespread as those of any of the Lao revolutionary leaders. The issue is well worth researching, but remains politically quite sensitive (cf. Evans 1998).

The bottom a line here is that while attitudes to the incursion into Lao of various elements of Thai differ considerably from individual to individual, no one denies that it is happening. And the debate goes back throughout the history of Laos as a nation-state. Adoption of Thai linguistic practices correlates with the adoption of other cultural practices, including some of the most salient symbols of the "social evils" to which the current regime's cultural policies have been so strongly opposed. Consider the following comments of a Vientiane man who spent time during the late 1970s in re-education, as a "social misfit": "They took those with long hair, they took those with platform shoes, they took those with even slightly flared pants. They'd say, 'This person is attached to social evils from the West,' like the Americans. They took out the bad people for re-education." (Enfield 1994: 189–90.) Clearly, these "social evils" were taken very seriously by the new regime. It is thus perhaps a cruel irony for some that the streets of Vientiane are once again replete with flared pants and platform shoes. And the Thai influence on Lao language that Phoumi resisted is well under way. It will thus be of great interest to monitor the progress of these influences within Laos itself over the coming decades.[16]

THE POLITICS OF LAO LANGUAGE: OUTLOOK AND CONCLUSION

Trends in linguistic and cultural policy are subject in part to fluctuating social and political attitudes. In Vientiane, particularly with the recent emergence of a consumer middle class, this correlates with the compromise of certain revolutionary ideals. But Laos remains a socialist country, and there are important signs of a continuing level of revolutionary consciousness, particularly in official contexts. For example, in a recent newspaper article on Lao language studies, Thongphet (1996) displays a similar level of political concern as Phoumi had done in his 1967 grammar. In the second part of the paper, entitled "The Viewpoint of our Party," Thongphet quotes Marx, Engels, Lenin, and Ho Chi Minh, going on to present his "Ten directions for linguistic research." The first two of these are "Research on Marx-Lenin theory," and "Research on the cultural, ethnic, and linguistic policies of the [Lao People's Revolutionary] Party." Similarly, in a classic token of political correctness, having made one of the strongest statements *against* Phoumi's revolutionary reforms in the recent "Lao Language Policy" volume (ICR 1995), Khamphan signs off "in revolutionary solidarity" (Khamphan 1995: 60). Indeed, the general trend since the early 1990s away from conservative politics in Laos was noticeably reversed in the lead-up to the general election of December 1997, during which an atmosphere of political conservatism was apparent in Vientiane and elsewhere (cf. e.g. PCPC 1997). So it is difficult to predict what the future will hold for Lao as a national language, but it is highly unlikely that the current government will officially approve restoration of conventions such as those championed by Nginn, and especially Sila, with such salient symbolic attachment to former regimes, and the foreign nations. The best that traditionalists can hope for is official restoration of the letter "r," in place already for foreign words and proper names.

In conclusion, a review of the status of Lao as a national language supports a claim that variation and change in a given language is revealing of the nature and extent of variation and change in the culture and society in which that language is spoken. The persistent disunity of grammatical convention in Laos, and the rapid change the Lao language is presently undergoing are clearly symptomatic of the sediments and fault lines across Lao social and political history, as well as the rapid and dramatic social change occurring now. The two most salient forces of change in the language today are the overall decrease in social presence of revolutionary ideals, and the active and pervasive influence (perhaps unprecedented in extent) of Thai culture, and through it, the culture of the developed world. The two are surely not unrelated, and it is impossible to give a simplistic appraisal of the value or detrimental effect of this process for Lao people. When we examine current popular debate on Lao language, we see clearly how the real issues are to a large extent not really "linguistic" (in one important sense of the term) at all. When it comes to language engineering, the pivotal arguments are often not based on theoretical principles or rational argumentation derived from linguistic science. They are based on salient emblems whose presence or absence may be exploited to achieve certain desired cultural or socio-political effects. The Lao letter "r" is a classic example. From a rationalist standpoint (e.g. from the point of view of a theoretical linguist or a Marxist-Leninist theoretician), most of the debate on "r" is appallingly simplistic, and the symbol itself, as a substantive issue, is overrated. As Thongphet has shown, by the *principles* that argue for the official reinstatement of "r" into Lao orthography, there are a number of other sounds/letters equally deserving. But they receive little or no attention in these contexts. Why? Because the stock example, "r," has achieved unique status as a potent metonymic emblem of whole cultural and social worlds denied by the movement that Phoumi Vongvichit represented, yet which remain embedded in the biographies of many Lao people. And despite the revolutionaries' principled and rational justification for the removal of "r," the symbol is a potent metonym for them, too. In language engineering driven by the social and political forces of nationalism, the "linguistic principles" at stake virtually fade into insignificance.

APPENDIX: NOTE ON LAO LANGUAGE REFERENCE
MATERIAL

The most extensive original work on Lao lexicography appears in large bilingual dictionaries compiled by American and French researchers (Kerr 1972; Reinhorn 1970), although a Lao monolingual dictionary was produced by Sila Viravong (1962, cited in Kerr 1972: xx), and some smaller bilingual dictionaries have also appeared over the years (e.g. Marcus 1970). The most extensive Lao monolingual dictionary appeared recently, largely a synthesis of these works, translated into Lao (Thongkham 1992). Published materials on the grammar of Lao (ranging from excellent to unreliable) include a small range of pedagogical and descriptive materials produced in foreign languages (e.g. Hoshino 1973; Hoshino and Marcus 1981; Morev et al. 1972; Ngaosyvath and Ngaosyvath 1984; Reinhorn 1980; Roffe and Roffe 1958; Werner 1992; Wright 1994; Yates and Sayasithsena 1970). For Lao language materials, see the three Lao grammars: Phoumi 1967, RLG 1972, Sila 1935.

NOTES

Some field support for this research has come from Australian Research Council Grant A59601467 "Thai-Lao Linguistic Interaction," for which I am very grateful. I owe much to Tony Diller for his generous and ongoing support. Grant Evans's assistance, consultation, and encouragement in Laos is also gratefully acknowledged. His direct input has made a significant contribution to the present shape of this essay. Thanks also to Marian Ravenscroft for her help in Vientiane. This essay has also benefited from comments and discussion with David Bradley, Adam Chapman, Tony Diller, Chris Flint, Joost Foppes, Søren Ivarsson, Anthony Jukes, Syban Khoukham, Craig Reynolds, Martin Stuart-Fox, and Kathryn Sweet. Usual disclaimers apply. My transcription of Lao is based on International Phonetic Association convention, except glottal stop /'/, palatal and velar nasals /ñ, ng/, low central vowel /a/, and high back unrounded vowel /ɯ/. Tones are (approximately): high level (/44/) / ˉ/; low falling (/21/) / ˋ/; high falling (/51/) / ˆ/; low rising (/213/) / ˇ/; high rising (/34/) /ˊ/. Note that "j" is pronounced like English "y" in *you* or *boy*; "c" is pronounced approximately like English "j" in *Jill*. All quotes from Lao language sources are my translation.

1. There are of course many languages spoken in Laos which are not dialects of Lao, including the languages of the Hmong-Mien group (e.g. Hmong), the Tibeto-Burman group (e.g. Lahu), and the Mon-Khmer group (e.g. Khmu). The current status, and future of these languages is of urgent concern in the present climate of rapid change and development in Laos. However, these matters are beyond the scope of this essay. Note also that in the interest of keeping the subject matter manageable, the present exposition is necessarily biased towards the situation of Lao language in urban Vientiane.

2. As Kathryn Sweet (personal communication) has pointed out, this concern with written language means that the issue of language standardization has little or no effect on the large number of people who are not literate. The level of literacy in Laos would have been especially low earlier this century.

3. Sanskrit and Pali are Indo-Aryan languages, both no longer natively spoken. Sanskrit has a specific script (the Devanagari script used in modern Hindi), and is associated mostly with Hindu writings. While Sanskrit remained very conservative due to emphasis on retaining the integrity of its original written form, Pali developed out of a spoken descendent of Sanskrit, which was used in the dissemination and subsequent spread of Buddhism. Pali does not have its own specific script (many different scripts are used for writing Pali), but does require essentially the same range of characters as the Devanagari script, with some minor differences.

4. Traditional description of the tone system of Lao (as well as Thai) makes reference to three parameters: status of syllables as "live" (i.e. with vocalic or sonorant final) or "dead" (i.e. with stop final); membership of the initial consonant in one of the three classes ("high," "middle," and "low"); and vowel-length ("long" vs. "short"; cf. Phoumi 1967: ch. 1; Preecha 1989: introduction).

5. This, however, does not mean that the standards of the language are faithfully adhered to. There remains a certain margin for slippage in the writing of Lao, as persistent variation in spelling of many words will attest.

6. For example, in ICR 1995, an important recent volume on "Lao language policy," almost no one among over twenty-five contributors identifies regional pronunciation as an issue. Bounyok (1995: 98) is one exception.

7. It must be acknowledged that those who were producing Lao language documents in the Liberated Zone constituted a small community in comparison to those in Royal Lao Government areas at the time.

8. Many overseas communities of Lao who fled Laos under the revolutionary government continue to publish their community materials using orthographic conventions based on the more traditional interpretation of the 1949 Royal Ordinance.

9. As Grant Evans (personal communication) has pointed out, there are cases where "r" *is* pronounced by Lao people. Note, however, that these are without exception *marked* usages, licensed either by the particular cultural context (e.g. religious formality or marking of class distinction), or the markedness of particular words being pronounced (e.g. foreign names). Contrary to folk belief in Vientiane, it is not the case that Lao people are "unable to roll their r's." But it remains the case that there is no *unmarked* spoken usage of an alveolar trill [r] corresponding to written s in Lao.

10. Diller (1991) reports similar issues in Thailand, where the orthographic "r" vs. "l" distinction is not colloquially pronounced by most Thai. He writes, "Occasionally higher government units take direct linguistic action. On 12 January 1988 the Prime Minister's Office issued a proclamation warning the bureaucracy to pronounce /r-/ and /l-/ distinctly . . ." (Diller 1991: 112).

11. Note that there are exceptions (and the situation is quickly changing): Lao "r" appears on the cover of the 1995 *Road Regulations Manual* in the spelling of the author's name Sisouphan Urai (ສີສຸພັນອຸໄຣ), and also in the spelling of Sila Viravong's name in various reissued publications (e.g. Sila 1996 [1938]). The abbreviation of "doctor" has always used Lao "r" (ດຣ.), following English/French "Dr."

12. Thongphet's comments seem pertinent here, given Douangdeuan's high praise of the shades of meaning Pali provides, despite the extraordinarily rich expressive power

of "native" spoken Lao. One of the special features of Lao is its category of expressives (cf. Chapman 1996), a grammatical system providing abundant and subtle distinctions across a range of semantic fields. The Pali terms Douangdeuan recommends are expressive only to the extent that semantic distinctions from a classical language can be re-created and/or contrived and deliberately imported into Lao linguistic culture. Native expressive distinctions are arguably of much greater value to the cultural integrity of Lao language, since they are already established among Lao fashions of speaking, and are naturally inculcated through existing native channels of social transmission.

13. Indeed, the influence of Thai on Lao has been a concern in Laos ever since Lao nationalism began, and is certainly not a preoccupation exclusive to the revolutionary movement. Ivarsson (this volume) discusses the long-standing nationalist issues surrounding Laos's need to distinguish itself from Siam and Thailand, and how this is manifest in the need to distinguish the languages of the two nations.

14. Compare the similar virtual prohibition on Australian popular musicians singing in an Australian accent, instead using American, or occasionally English, style. Exceptions to this tendency may be found in "country" and/or "folk" genres (both in Australia and Laos).

15. Souksavang (1995: 84) has challenged the premise that royal vocabulary is "class-ist" in the same way that Som (1996) argued against the persecution of *dǒoj* ໂດຍ, arguing that as part of the language, it is "the common property of the whole society, and of all people."

16. Consider the possibility in years to come of a conscious return to "uniquely Lao" culture, a people's reclamation of all things "truly Lao." Would the rediscovered "Lao language" and "Lao culture" have to be invented, pieced together from clues and fond memories, while accommodating the new cultural requirements of the modern society? This process of "revival" of culture has been witnessed in many parts of the world, none closer to Laos than Isan (northeast Thailand), where the people have been actively "rediscovering" (mostly reinventing) their "Lao" roots. Much of what is now emerging as "Isan" culture is in fact new, but importantly, "uniquely Isan," and also putatively "Lao." And ironically, this "Lao" style is being adopted as a hip "alternative" by some young residents of Vientiane. It would not be at all surprising to see this same process take hold in lowland Laos in a decade or two, as a backlash against the process of intense cultural change we are witnessing now.

LITERATURE CITED

ENGLISH AND FRENCH

ABOU, Selim. 1980. *L'identité culturelle, relations inter-ethniques et problèmes d'acculturation.* Paris: Anthropos.

ADB. 1995. *Subregional infrastructure projects in Indochina and the Greater Mekong Area.* Tokyo: Asian Development Bank.

ALEXANDER, Jennifer. 1987. *Trade, traders and trading in rural Java.* Singapore: Oxford University Press.

ALVAREZ, Robert R., and George A. Collier. 1994. The long haul in Mexican trucking: Traversing the borderlands of the north and the south. *American Ethnologist* 21 (3).

ANDERSON, Ben. 1983. *Imagined communities: An essay on nationalism.* London: Verso.

———. 1991. *Imagined communities. Reflections on the origin and spread of nationalism.* Revised ed. London: Verso.

ANDERSON, Benedict R. O'G. 1987. Introduction. In *Southeast Asian tribal groups and ethnic minorities: Prospects for the eighties and beyond.* Cambridge, Mass.: Cultural Survival Report 22.

ARCHAIMBAULT, Charles. 1959. The sacrifice of the buffalo at Vat Ph'u. In *The kingdom of Laos*, edited by René de Berval. Saigon: France-Asie.

———. 1971. *The new year ceremony at Basak (South Laos).* Data paper no. 78, Southeast Asia Program. Ithaca, N.Y.: Cornell University.

———. 1972. *La course de Pirogues au Laos: Un complexe culturel.* Ascona: Artibus Asiae Supplement 29.

———. 1973. *Structures religeuses Lao (Rites et mythes).* Vientiane: Vithagna.

ASIA WATCH. 1993. *A modern form of slavery: Trafficking of Burmese women and girls into brothels in Thailand.* New York: Human Rights Watch.

BALLARD, W. L. 1981. Aspects of the Linguistic History of South China. *Asian Perspectives* 24 (2).

BARMÉ, Scot. 1993. *Luang Wichit Wathakan and the creation of a Thai identity.* Singapore: Institute of Southeast Asian Studies.

BARTHES, Roland. 1972. *Mythologies.* New York: Hill and Wang.

BATESON, Gregory. 1958. *Naven.* 2nd ed. Stanford: Stanford University Press.

BATSON, Wendy. 1992. After the revolution: Ethnic minorities and the new Lao state. In *Laos: Beyond the revolution,* edited by J. Zasloff and L. Unger. London: Macmillan.

BERESFORD, Melanie, and Bruce McFarlane. 1995. Regional inequality and regionalism in Vietnam and China. *Journal of Contemporary Asia* 25 (1).

BERNARD, F. 1937. *La sécurité de l'Indochine et l'imperialisme Siamois.* Paris: Ed. Union Coloniale Française.

BERTHELEU, Hélène. 1994. *Organisation collective et ethnicité, minorités lao à Rennes, Grenoble et Montréal.* Thèse de doctorat en sociologie, Université de Haute-Bretagne-Rennes 2.

BONIFACY, Lieutenant-Colonel. 1919. *Cours d'ethnographie indochinoise.* Hanoi-Haiphong: Imprimerie d'Extréme-Orient.

BOUDOUBOU, Mohamed. 1980. *Les travailleurs immigrés marocains en France et les perspectives de retour: aspirations-projets.* Thèse de doctorat de sociologie, EHESS, Paris.

BOURDET, Yves. 1996. *Laos 1995—Labour market adjustment and human resource mobilization.* Macroeconomic Report 1996:3. Stockholm: SIDA.

BOURDIEU, Pierre. 1989. *La noblesse d'Etat.* Paris: Editions de Minuit.

———. 1990. *The logic of practice.* Cambridge: Polity Press.

BOURDIEU, Pierre, and Loic J. D. Wacquant. 1992. *An invitation to reflexive sociology.* Chicago: University of Chicago Press.

BOWIE, Katherine A. 1992. Unravelling the myth of the subsistence economy: Textile production in nineteenth-century northern Thailand. *Journal of Asian Studies* 51 (4).

BRIGGS, Lawrence Palmer. 1949. The appearance and historical usage of the terms Tai, Thai, Siamese and Lao. *Journal of the American Oriental Society* 69 (April–June).

BROMLEY, Yu. 1974. The term *ethnos* and its definition. In *Soviet Ethnology and Anthropology Today,* edited by Yu. Bromley. The Hague: Mouton.

BROWN, MacAlister, and Joseph J. Zasloff. 1986. *Apprentice revolutionaries: The communist movement in Laos, 1930–1985.* Stanford, Calif.: Stanford University Press.

BUNYARAKS Ninsananda, Kasem Snidvongse, Sumet Tantivejkul, Phayap Phayomyond, Santi Bang-Or, and Kitti Itiwitya. 1977. *Thai-Laos economic relations: A new perspective.* Bangkok.

CAMILLERI, Carmel. 1979. *Quelques facteurs psychologiques de la représentation du retour dans le pays d'origine chez les jeunes migrants maghrébins de la seconde génération.* Paris: Université de Paris V sur la demande de la direction de la population et des migrations.

CHAMBERLAIN, J. R. 1975. A new look at the history and the classification of the Thai languages. In *Studies in Tai linguistics in honour of W. J. Gedney,* edited by J. G. Harris and J. R. Chamberlain. Bangkok: Centre of English Language, Office of State Universities.

————. 1978. Language standardisation in Laos. In *Papers from the conference on the standardisation of Asian languages. Manila, Philippines, December 16–21, 1974,* edited by A. Q. Perez, A. O. Santiago, and Nguyen Dang Liem. Pacific Linguistics, Series C—no. 47. Canberra: Research School of Pacific Studies, Australian National University.

CHAMBERLAIN, James R., Charles Alton, and Arthur G. Crisfield. 1995. *Indigenous peoples profile: LPDR,* CARE International, Vientiane, December 15. Prepared for the World Bank.

CHAMBERS, J. K. 1995. *Sociolinguistic theory: Linguistic variation and its social significance.* Oxford: Blackwell.

CHANDLER, Glen. 1984. *Market trade in rural Java.* Monash Papers on Southeast Asia, no 11. Melbourne: Centre of Southeast Asian Studies, Monash University.

CHAPMAN, Adam. 1996. *The syntax of Lao expressives.* Honours Thesis, Southeast Asia Centre, Faculty of Asian Studies, Australian National University.

CHATTHIP Nartsupha. 1996. On the study of Tai cultural history, *Thai-Yunnan Project Newsletter* 32 (June).

CHAZÉE, Laurent. 1995 *Atlas des ethnies et des sous-ethnies du Laos.* Bangkok (privately printed).

CHI Do Pham. 1994. Economic reforms in Laos: an unforgettable experience in a "forgotten" land. In *Economic development in Lao PDR,* edited by Chi Do Pham. Vientiane: Horizon 2000.

CHOLTIRA Satyawadhna. 1997. Ethic inter-relationships in the history of Lanna: Reconsidering the Lwa role in the Lanna scenario. *Tai Culture* 2 (2).

CHORON-BAIX. 1990. *Les Lao, gestion communautaire et individualisme.* Paris: Revue du Groupement pour les Droits des Minorités.

CHU Thai Son. 1991. *Vietnam: A multicultural mosaic.* Hanoi: Vietnam Foreign Languages Publishing House.

CLUTTERBUCK, Martin. 1993. Writers in Laos—Indochina war is one of the few themes approved by government. *Far Eastern Economic Review,* February 11.

CŒDâS, George. 1959. An introduction to the history of Laos. In *Kingdom of Laos,* edited by Ren? de Berval. Saigon: France-Asie.

CŒDâS, Georges and Charles Archaimbault. 1973. *Les trois mondes. Cosmogonie Siamoise.* Paris: Publications de l'École Française d'Extrême-Orient.

COHEN, Colleen, Richard Wilk, and Beverly Stoeltje, 1996. Introduction to *Beauty queens on the global stage: Gender, contests, and power.* London and New York: Routledge.

COLSON, Elizabeth. 1968. Contemporary tribes and the development of nationalism. *Essays on the problem of the tribe,* edited by June Helm, American Ethnological Society. Seattle and London: University of Washington Press.

COMPTON, Carol. 1979. *Courting poetry in Laos: A textual and linguistic analysis.* Center of Southeast Asian Studies. Dekalb: Northern Illinois University.

CONDOMINAS, Georges. 1968. Notes sur le Bouddhisme populaire en milieu rural Lao. *Archives de Sociologie des Religions* 13 (25–26).

————. 1970. The Lao. In *Laos: War and revolution,* edited by Nina S. Adams and Alfred W. McCoy. New York: Harper and Row.

————. 1980. *L'espace social a propos de l'Asie du sud-est.* Paris: Flammarion.

————. 1990. *From Lawa to Mon from Saa' to Thai: Historical and anthropological aspects of Southeast Asian social spaces.* An Occasional Paper of the Department of Anthropology, RSPS. Canberra: Australian National University.

CONNERTON, Paul. 1989. *How societies remember*. Cambridge: Cambridge University Press.

CONNOR, Walker. 1984. *The national question in Marxist-Leninist theory and strategy*. Princeton: Princeton University Press.

CORDEIRO, A., and J. L. Guffond. 1979. *Les Algériens de France, ceux qui partent et ceux qui restent*. Grenoble: Université des Sciences Sociales de Grenoble, Institut de Recherche Economique et de Planification.

CORT, John. 1996. Art, religion, and material culture: Some reflections on method. *Journal of the American Academy of Religion* 64 (3).

CRONE, Patricia. 1986 The tribe and the state. In *States in history*, edited by John A. Hall. London: Blackwell.

CUAZ, J. 1903. *Essai de dictionnaire Français-Siamois*. Bangkok: Imprimerie de la Mission Catholique.

———. 1904. *Lexique Français-Laocien*. Hongkong: Imprimerie de la Société des Missions Étrangères.

DAMRONG Tayanin. 1994. *Being Kammu: My village, my life*. Ithaca, N.Y.: Cornell University, Southeast Asia Program.

DANG Nghiem Van. 1971. An outline of the Thai in Vietnam. *Vietnamese Studies* (32).

———. 1973. The Khmu in Vietnam. *Vietnamese Studies* (36).

———. 1991. About the ethnonyms of ethnicities and local groups in Vietnam. *Vietnam Social Sciences* (2, 3).

DANG Nghiem Van et al. 1984. *The ethnic minorities in Vietnam*. Hanoi: Foreign Languages Publishing House.

DASSÉ, Martial. 1976. *Montagnards revoltes et guerres revolutionnaires en Asie du Sud-Est continentale*. Bangkok: D.K. Books.

DE BERVAL, René. 1959. *Kingdom of Laos. The land of the million elephants and of the white parasol*. Saigon: France-Asie; Limoges: A. Bontemps, Co., Ltd.

DE RUDDER, V., and I. Taboada-Leonetti, F. Vourc'h. 1990. *Immigrés et Français, stratégie d'insertion, représentation et attitudes*. Paris: CNRS, IRESCO.

DE YOUNG, John E. 1966. *Village life in modern Thailand*. Berkeley: University of California Press.

DECOUX, Jean. 1949. *À la barre de l'Indochine. Histoire de mon gouvernement général. 1940–1945*. Paris: Librairie Plon.

DEUVE, Jean. 1985. *Le royaume du Laos 1949–1965*. Paris: École Française d'Extrême Orient. Publications Hors Série.

———. 1992. *Le Laos 1945–1949. Contribution à l'historie de mouvement Lao Issala*. Montpellier: Universite Paul Valery.

DEWEY, Alice G. 1962. *Peasant marketing in Java*. Glencoe, Ill.: Free Press.

DICK, Howard, and Dean Forbes. 1992. Transport and communications: a quiet revolution. In *The oil boom and after: Indonesian economic policy and performance in the Soeharto era*, edited by Anne Booth. Singapore: Oxford University Press.

DILLER, Anthony. 1988. Thai syntax and "national grammar."*Language Sciences* 10 (2).

———. 1988a. Tai scripts and proto-Tai. In *Proceedings of the international symposium on language and linguistics, Thammasat University, August 1988*, edited by Cholticha Bamroongraks et al. Bangkok: Thammasat University Press, 228-248.

————. 1991. What makes Central Thai a national language. In *National identity and its defenders*, edited by Craig J. Reynolds. Chiang Mai: Silkworm Books.

————. 1993. Diglossic grammaticality in Thai. In *The role of theory in language description*, edited by William A. Foley. Berlin: Mouton de Gruyter, 393–420.

DIXON, R. M. W. 1997 *The rise and fall of languages*. Cambridge: Cambridge University Press.

DOMMEN, Arthur J. 1985. *Laos: Keystone of Indochina*. Boulder, Colo.: Westview Press.

————. 1994. Laos: Consolidating the economy. In *Southeast Asian Affairs 1994*. Singapore: Institute of Southeast Asian Studies.

DORÉ, Amphay. 1980. *Le partage du Mekong*. Paris: Encre Editions.

————. 1987. *Aux sources de la civilisation lao: Contribution de la ethno-historique à la connaissance de la culture louang-phrabanaise*. Metz: Cercle de culture et de recherche laotiennes.

DORÉ, Pierre S. (Amphay). 1987. *Contribution ethno-historique à la connaissance de la culture louang- phrabanaise*. Doctorat d'Etat. Paris: Universite Paris V Rene Descartes.

DORÉ, Pierre-Sylvain. 1972. *La divination dans l'État de Lane Xang hom khao*. Doctorat de Troisième Cycle, Paris.

DRAGADZE, T. 1980. The place of "ethnos" in Soviet anthropology. In *Soviet and Western Anthropology*, edited by Ernest Gellner. London: Gerald Duckworth.

DUARA, Prasenjit. 1995. *Rescuing history from the nation: Questioning narratives of modern China*. Chicago: University of Chicago Press.

ECONOMIST. 1993. Laos plots its paths to riches. 6 November.

ELFIMOV, Alexei. 1997. The state of the discipline in Russia: Interviews with Russian anthropologists. *American Anthropologist* 99 (4).

ENFIELD, Nick. 1994. *Aspects of Lao syntax: Theory, function, and cognition*. Unpublished Honours Thesis, Southeast Asia Centre, Australian National University, Canberra.

————. *A grammar of Lao*. (In preparation.) Department of Linguistics and Applied Linguistics, University of Melbourne.

ENFIELD, N. J. and Grant Evans. (forthcoming). Transcription as standardisation: the poblem of Tai languages. In *First International Conference on Tai Studies*, Mahidol University, 1998, Proceedings.

ERRINGTON, Shelly. 1989. *Meaning and power in the Southeast Asian realm*. Princeton: Princeton University Press.

ESCOBAR, Arturo. 1995. *Encountering development: The making and unmaking of the Third World*. Princeton: Princeton University Press.

ESTRADE. 1895. *Dictionnaire et guide Franco-Laotiens* . Toulouse: Imprimerie G. Berthoumien.

EVANS, Grant. 1982 *The yellow rainmakers*. London: Verso.

————. 1985 Vietnamese communist anthropology. *Canberra Anthropology* 8 (1, 2).

————. 1988. *Agrarian change in communist Laos*. Occasional Paper no. 85. Singapore: Institute of Southeast Asian Studies.

————. 1990. *Lao peasants under socialism*. New Haven: Yale University Press.

————. 1991. Reform or revolution in heaven? Funerals among upland Tai. *Australian Journal of Anthropology* (formerly *Mankind*) 2 (1).

————. 1992. Internal colonialism in the southern highlands of Vietnam. *Sojourn* 7 (2).

————. 1993a. Buddhism and economic action in socialist Laos. In *Socialism: Ideals, ideologies, and local practice*, edited by C. M. Hann. London: Routledge.

————. 1993b. Hierarchy and dominance: Class, status, and caste. In *Asia's cultural mosaic: An anthropological introduction*, edited by Grant Evans. Singapore and New York: Prentice Hall.

————. 1995. *Lao peasants under socialism and post-socialism*, Chiang Mai: Silkworm Books.

————. 1997. The Sinicised Tai: Is anyone Tai *roi* percent? *Tai Culture* 2 (1).

————. 1998a *The politics of ritual and remembrance: Laos since 1975*. Chiang Mai: Silkworm Books; Honolulu: University of Hawaii Press.

————. 1998b. Political cults in East and Southeast Asia. In *Facets of power and its limitations: Political culture in Southeast Asia*, edited by I-B Trankell and L. Summers. Uppsala: Uppsala Studies in Cultural Anthropology 24.

EVANS, Grant, and Kelvin Rowley. 1983. *Red brotherhood at war: Indochina since 1975*. London: Verso.

————. 1990. *Red brotherhood at war: Vietnam, Cambodia and Laos since 1975*. Revised ed. London: Verso.

EVANS, Grant, and Rattana Boonmattaya. 1991. *Possibilities for community participation in forest areas selected for conservation in Laos*. Report to the World Wildlife Fund and the World Bank.

EVANS, Grant, ed. 1993. *Asia's cultural mosaic: An anthropological introduction*. Singapore: Prentice Hall.

FALL, Bernard. 1962. Problèmes politiques des etats poly-ethniques en Indochina. *France-Asie* 18 (172).

————. 1979. *Anatomy of a crisis: The Laotian crisis of 1960–1961*. Garden City, N.Y.: Doubleday.

FAR EASTERN ECONOMIC REVIEW. 1977. *Asia yearbook.* Hong Kong.

————. 1996. *Asia yearbook.* Hong Kong.

FAURE, Bernard. 1995. The symbolism of the *kasaya* in Soto Zen. *Cahiers d'Extreme-Asia*, 8:335–369.

FENTRESS, James, and Chris Wickham. 1992. *Social memory: New perspectives on the past*. Oxford: Blackwell.

FFORDE, Adam, and Steve Sénèque. 1995. The economy and the countryside: The relevance of rural development policies. In *Vietnam's rural transformation*, edited by Benedict J. Tria Kerkvliet and Doug J. Porter. Boulder, Colo.: Westview; Singapore: Institute of Southeast Asian Studies.

FINNEGAN, Ruth. 1977. *Oral poetry: Its nature, significance and social content* Cambridge: Cambridge University Press.

FINOT, Louis. 1917. Recherches sur la Littérature Laotienne. *Bulletin de l'École Française d'Éxtrême-Orient* 7 (5).

FIRTH, Raymond. 1966. *Malay fishermen: Their peasant economy*. London: Routledge and Kegan Paul.

FOLEY, William A. 1997. *Anthropological linguistics: An introduction*. London: Blackwell.

FORMOSO, Bernard. 1990. From the human body to the humaized space: The system of reference and representation of space in two villages of northeast Thailand. *Journal of the Siam Society* 78 (1).

FOURNIER J. B., J. Ivanoff, and P. Leroux. 1989. *Les réfugiés d'Asie du Sud-Est et leur insertion en France.* Paris: Actes du colloque SERIA-INALCO, février 1989, PSU-ECASE, Carnet du S?ria 2.

FREEMAN, Nick. 1996. Fighting the "non-attributable war" in Laos: A review article. *Contemporary Southeast Asia* 17 (4).

FRIED, Morton H. 1975. *The notion of tribe.* Menlo Park, California: Cummings Publishing Company.

GASPARD, Françoise. 1992. Assimilation, insertion, intégration: Les mots pour devenir Français. *Hommes et migrations.* n°1154, mai.

GEERTZ, Clifford. 1963. *Peddlers and princes: Social change and economic modernization in two Indonesian towns.* Chicago: University of Chicago Press.

———. 1973. *The interpretation of cultures.* New York: Basic Books.

GELLNER, Ernest. 1983. *Nations and nationalism.* Oxford: Blackwell.

———, ed. 1980. *Soviet and western anthropology.* London: Gerald Duckworth.

GESICK, Lorraine M. 1995. *In the land of Lady White Blood: Southern Thailand and the meaning of history.* Ithaca, N.Y.: SEAP, Cornell University.

GITTINGER, Mattiebelle, and H. Leedom Lefferts Jr. 1992. *Textiles and the Tai experience in Southeast Asia.* Washington, D.C.: The Textile Museum.

GOODY, Jack. 1993. Culture and its boundaries: A European view. *Social Anthropology* 1 (1).

GOSCHA, Christopher. 1995a. *Vietnam or Indochina: Contesting concepts of space in Vietnamese nationalism, 1887–1954.* Copenhagen: Nordic Institute of Asian Studies, NIAS Report no. 28.

———. 1995b. L'Indochine repensée par les "Indochinois": Pham Qùynh et les deux débats de 1931 sur l'immigration, le fédéralisme et la réalité de l'Indochine *Revue Française d'Historie d'Outre-Mer* 82:309.

———. 1996. Annam and Vietnam in the New Indochinese Space, 1887–1945. In *Asian forms of the nation,* edited by Stein Tønnesson and Hans Antlöv. London: Curzon.

GRABOWSKY, Volker. 1995. The Isan up to its integration into the Siamese state. In *Regions and national integration in Thailand 1892–1992,* edited by Volker Grabowsky. Wiesbaden: Harrassowitz Verlag.

GUIGNARD, Théodore. 1912. *Dictionnaire Laotien-Français.* Hong Kong: Imprimerie de Nazareth.

GULDIN, Greg. 1992. Anthropology by other names: The impact of Sino-Soviet friendship on the anthropological sciences. *Australian Journal of Chinese Affairs* 27 (January).

———. 1994. *The saga of anthropology in China: From Malinowski to Moscow to Mao.* Armonk, N.Y.: M. E. Sharpe.

GUMPERZ, John J. 1982. *Discourse strategies.* Studies in interactional sociolinguistics 1. Cambridge: Cambridge University Press.

GUMPERZ, John J., and Stephen C. Levinson. 1991. Rethinking linguistic relativity. *Current Anthropology* 32 (5).

———. 1996 *Rethinking linguistic relativity.* Cambridge: Cambridge University Press.

GUNN, Geoffrey C. 1988. *Political struggles in Laos. 1930–1954: Vietnamese communist power and the Lao struggle for national independence.* Bangkok: Editions Duang Kamol.

HÅKANGÅRD, Agneta. 1992. *Road 13: A socio-economic study of villagers, transport and use of Road 13 S. Lao P.D.R.* Stockholm: Stockholm University, Department of Social Anthropology, Development Studies Unit.

HALL, Edward T. 1959. *The silent language.* New York: Anchor.

———. 1982. *The hidden dimension.* New York: Anchor.

———. 1983. *The dance of life.* New York: Anchor.

HALPERN, Joel. 1961. *The role of the Chinese in Lao society.* Laos project paper no. 1. Los Angeles: Department of Anthropology, University of California.

———. 1963. *Government, politics and social structure in Laos, a study of tradition and innovation.* New Haven: Yale University Press.

———. 1964. *Economy and society of Laos: a brief survey.* New Haven: Southeast Asia Studies, Yale University Press.

HARLIG, Jeffrey. 1995. Socialism and sociolinguistics in the eastern bloc. In *When East meets West: Sociolinguistics in the former socialist bloc,* edited by Jeffrey Harlig and Csaba Pléh. Berlin: Mouton de Gruyter.

HELM, June, ed. 1968. *Essays on the problem of the tribe.* American Ethnological Society. Seattle and London: University of Washington Press.

HENDRY, Joy. 1993. *Wrapping culture.* Oxford: Oxford University Press.

HENLEY, David E. F. 1995. Ethnographic integration and exclusion in anticolonial nationalism: Indonesia and Indochina. *Comparative Studies in Society and History* 37 (2).

HICKEY, Gerald C. 1982. *Sons of the mountains: Ethnohistory of the Vietnamese central highlands, 1954–1976.* New Haven: Yale University Press.

———. 1982. *Free in the forest: Ethnohistory of the Vietnamese central highlands, 1954–1976.* New Haven: Yale University Press.

HIRSCH, Philip. 1995. Thailand and the new geopolitics of Southeast Asia: Resource and environmental issues. In *Counting the costs: Economic growth and environmental change in Thailand,* edited by Jonathan Rigg. Singapore: Institute of Southeast Asian Studies.

HOANG Thi Thanh Nhan. 1995. Poverty and social polarization in Vietnam: Reality and solution. *Vietnam Economic Review* 2 (28).

HOBSBAWM, E. J. 1990. *Nations and nationalism since 1780: Programmme, myth, reality.* Cambridge: Cambridge University Press.

———. 1992. *Nations and nationalism since 1780: Programme, myth, reality.* 2nd ed. Cambridge: Cambridge University Press.

———. 1983. Introduction: Inventing traditions. In *The invention of tradition,* edited by Eric Hobsbawm and Terence Ranger. Cambridge: Cambridge University Press.

HOSHINO, T. 1973. *Basic Lao.* Siam Communications.

HOSHINO, T, and R. Marcus. 1981. *Lao for beginners: An introduction to the spoken and written language of Laos.* Rutland and Tokyo: Tuttle.

HOUMPHANH Rattanavong. 1990. Regarding what one calls the "Thai." *Proceedings of the fourth International Conference on Thai Studies,* 11–13 May 1990, Kunming, Yunnan, vol. 2.

———. 1995. The rapid Siamisation of Lao culture today: A serious cause for concern to the Lao people. In *Culture, development and globalisation,* Proceedings of a series of symposia held at Nong Khai, Hanoi, and Tokyo. Tokyo: The Toyota Foundation.

———. 1997. *On the way to the Lolopho land*. Vientiane: Institute for Cultural Research.

HSIEH Shih-chung. 1989. Ethno-political adaptation and ethnic changes in Sipsong Panna Dai: An ethnohistorical analysis. Ph.D. diss., University of Washington.

HUTHEESING, Otome Klein. 1990. How does a "Tai" spirit come to be on a Lisu home altar? A note on the merger of lowland and highland cosmologies. In *Proceedings of the fourth International Conference on Thai Studies*, 11–13 May, Institute of Southeast Asian Studies, Kunming, Yunnan.

HUTTON, Christopher M. 1998. *Linguistics and the Third Reich: Mother-tongue fascism, race and the science of language*. London: Routledge.

———. 1998. From pre-modern to modern: Ethnic classification by language and the case of the Ngai/Nung of Vietnam. *Language and Communication* (forthcoming).

HYMES, Dell. 1968. Linguistic problems in defining the concept of "tribe." In *Essays on the problem of the tribe*, edited by June Helm, American Ethnological Society. Seattle and London: University of Washington Press.

ICR (Institute for Cultural Research) 1995. Survey of Social Change in Vientiane Municipality.

IRESON, Carol J. 1992. Changes in field, forest, and family: Rural women's work and status in post-revolutionary Laos. *Bulletin of Concerned Asian Scholars* 24 (4).

———. 1996. Field, *Forrest and Family: Women's Work and Power in Rural Laos*, Colorado: Westview Press.

IRESON, Carol J., and W. Randall Ireson. 1991. Ethnicity and development in Laos. *Asian Survey* 31 (10).

IYENGAR, K. R. Srinivasa. 1994. *Asian variations in Ramayana*. New Delhi: Sahitya Akademi.

IZIKOWITZ, Karl Gustav. 1951. *Lamet: Hill peasants in French Indochina*. Göteborg.

———. 1969. Neighbours in Laos. In *Ethnic groups and boundaries*, edited by Fredrik Barth. Boston: Little Brown and Company.

———. 1979. *Lamet: Hill Peasants in French Indochina*. Republication. New York: AMS Press.

KATAY Don Sasorith. 1943. *Alphabet et ecriture Lao*. Vientiane: ?ditions du "Pathet Lao."

———. 1948. *Contribution a l'histoire du movement d'independence nationale Lao*. Editions Lao Issara.

———. 1953. *Le Laos: Son évolution politique. Sa place dans l'Union français*. Paris: Éditions Berger-Leverault.

KAYSONE Phomvihane. 1981. *Revolution in Laos: Practice and prospects*. Moscow: Progress Publishers.

KERKVLIET, Benedict J. Tria, and Doug J. Porter. 1995. Rural Vietnam in rural Asia. In *Vietnam's rural transformation,* edited by Benedict J. Tria Kerkvliet and Doug J. Porter. Boulder, Colo.: Westview; Singapore: Institute of Southeast Asian Studies.

KERR, Allan D. 1972. *Lao-English dictionary*. 2 vols. Washington, D.C.: Catholic University of America Press.

KEYES, Charles F. 1967. *Isan: Regionalism in northeastern Thailand.* Cornell Thailand Project, Interim Reports Series, no.10.

―――. 1984. Mother or mistress but never a monk: Buddhist notions of female gender in rural Thailand. *American Ethnologist* 11 (2).

―――. 1986. Ambiguous gender: Male initiation in a northern Thai Buddhist society. In *Gender and religion: On the complexity of symbols*, edited by C. W. Bynum, S. Harrell, and P. Richman. Boston: Beacon.

KIBRIA, Nazli. 1993. *Family tightrope: The changing lives of Vietnamese Americans.* Princeton: Princeton University Press.

KIRSCH, A. Thomas. 1982. Buddhism, sex-roles, and the Thai economy. In *Women in Southeast Asia*, edited by P. Van Esterik. Occasional Paper no. 9. DeKalb: Northern Illinois University Press.

―――. 1985. Text and context: Buddhist sex roles/culture of gender revisited. *American Ethnologist* 12 (2).

KONINCK, Rodolphe de. 1994. *L'Asie Du Sud-Est.* Paris: Masson.

KORET, Peter. 1994. Lao literature. In *Traveller's literary companion to Southeast Asia.* Brighton: in press.

―――. 1994. *Whispered so softly it resounds through the forest, spoken so loudly it can hardly be heard: The art of parallelism in traditional Lao literature.* Ph.D. diss., School of Oriental and African Studies, London.

―――. 1996. Understanding the history and social use of Lao traditional literature in relationship to the literary tradition of the Tai Yuan. In *Proceedings of the Sixth International Conference on Thai Studies.* Chiang Mai: Chiang Mai University.

―――. 1997. Contemporary Lao literature. In *Contemporary Southeast Asian Short Stories.* Honolulu: University of Hawaii.

KOSSIKOV, I. and O. Egorunin. 1993. National policy in modern Laos. Paper presented at the Thai Studies Conference, SOAS, London.

KUNSTADTER, Peter. 1979. Ethnic group, category, and identity: Karen in northern Thailand. In *Ethnic adaptation and identity: The Karen on the Thai frontier with Burma*, edited by Charles F. Keyes. Philadelphia: ISHI.

KUPER, Adam. 1992. Introduction. In *Conceptualizing society*, edited by Adam Kuper. London and New York: Routledge.

LAFONT, Bernard. 1955. Notes sur les familles patronymiques Thai noires de Son-la et de Nghia-lo. *Anthropos* 50.

LAFONT, P. B. 1989. Laos. In *Southeast Asia: Languages and literatures: A select guide*, edited by Patricia Herbert and Anthony Milner. Arran, Scotland: Kiscadale Publications.

LANGER, Paul F., and Joseph J. Zasloff. 1970. *North Vietnam and the Pathet Lao. Partners in the struggle for Laos.* Cambridge: Harvard University Press.

LAO PDR. 1989. *Report on the economic and social situation, development strategy, and assistance needs of the Lao PDR.* Vol. 1. Geneva: Lao PDR.

―――. 1994. *Socio-economic development strategies.* (Prepared for the 5th Round Table Meeting in Geneva, 21 June 1994). Vientiane.

LATEGUY, Jean. 1967. *The bronze drums.* London: Mayflower Paperbacks.

LAUFER, Berthold. 1917. Totemic traces among the Indo-Chinese. *Journal of American Folk-Lore* 30 (118).

LE BAR, Frank M., and Addrienne Suddard. 1960. *Laos: Its people, its society, its culture.* New Haven: Human Relations Area File Press.

LE BAR, Frank M., Gerald C. Hickey, and John K. Musgrave. 1964. *Ethnic groups of mainland Southeat Asia.* New Haven: Human Relations Area Files Press.

LE BAR, Frank. 1967. Observations on the movement of Khmu into north Thailand. *Journal of the Siam Society* 55, part 1.

LE Van Hao. 1972. Ethnological studies and researches in north Viet Nam. *Vietnamese Studies* 32.

LEACH, Edmund. 1960. The frontiers of "Burma." *Comparative Studies in Society and History* 3.

———. 1970 [1954]. *Political systems of highland Burma: A study of kachin social structure*. London: University of London, the Athlone Press. Original ed. London: G. Bell, 1954.

———. 1990. Aryan invasions over four millennia. In *Culture through time: Anthropological approaches*, edited by Emiko Ohnuki-Tierney. Stanford, Calif.: Stanford University Press.

LEE, Yong Leng. 1980. *Southeast Asia and the law of the sea*. Singapore: Singapore University Press.

LEFFERTS, H. Leedom Jr. 1992a. Contexts and meanings in Tai textiles. In *Textiles and the Tai experience in Southeast Asia*, edited by Gittinger M. and Lefferts H. L. Washington D.C.: The Textile Museum.

———. 1992b. Textiles in the service of Tai Buddhism. In *Textiles and the Tai experience in Southeast Asia*, edited by Gittinger M. and Lefferts H. L. Washington D.C.: The Textile Museum.

———. 1992c. Cut and sewn: The textiles of social organization in Thailand. In *Dress and gender in cultural contexts*, edited by R. Barnes and J. B. Eicher. New York: Berg.

———. 1994. Clothing the serpent: Transformations of the *naak* in Thai-Lao Theravada Buddhism. In *The transformative power of cloth in Southeast Asia*, edited by L. Milgram and P. Van Esterik. Toronto: The Museum for Textiles.

———. 1996. The ritual importance of the mundane: White cloth among the Tai of Southeast Asia. *Expedition* 38 (1).

LEHMAN, F. K. 1979. Who are the Karen, and if so, why? Karen ethnohistory and a formal theory of ethnicity. In *Ethnic adaptation and identity: The Karen on the Thai frontier with Burma*, edited by Charles F. Keyes. Philadelphia: ISHI.

———. 1989. Internal inflationary pressures in the prestige economy of the feast of merit complex: The Chin and Kachin cases from upper Burma. In *Ritual, power and economy: Upland-lowland contrasts in mainland Southeast Asia*, edited by Susan D. Russell. Dekalb: Northern Illinois University, Center for Southeast Asian Studies.

LÉVY, Paul. 1959. The sacrifice of the buffalo and the forecast of the weather in Vientiane. In *The kingdom of Laos*, edited by René de Berval. Saigon: France-Asie.

———. 1968. *Buddhism: A "mystery religion"?* New York: Schocken Books.

LI, Fang-Kuei. 1960. A tentative classification of Tai dialects. In *Culture in history: Essays in honour of Paul Radin*, edited by S. Diamond. New York: Columbia University Press.

LIND, Elisabet, and Götz Hagmüller. 1991. *The Royal Palace Museum of Luang Prabang. General condition, conservation and restoration needs 1991*. Copenhagen: Nordic Institute of Asian Studies.

LINTNER, Bertil. 1984. The Shans and the Shan State of Burma. *Contemporary Southeast Asia* 5 (4).

————. 1994. Add water: Laos' hydroelectric plans seem overambitious. *Far Eastern Economic Review*, 13 October, 70.

————. 1995. Laos at the crossroads—Ties that bind. *Far Eastern Economic Review*, 9 February, 18–19.

————. 1996a. Change of face—Reform gets an authoritarian overlay. *Far Eastern Economic Review*, 18 April, 22.

————. 1996b. One of us: How to foster nationalism in a poor, diverse country?" *Far Eastern Economic Review*, 11 January: 26.

————. 1997a. Collateral damage: Laos's dependence on Thailand becomes a liability. *Far Eastern Economic Review*, 28 August, 60.

————. 1997b. Two steps back: Election slate portends a slowdown in reform. *Far Eastern Economic Review*, 18 December, 32.

LORD, Albert Bates. 1960. *The singer of tales.* Cambridge: Harvard University Press.

LUTHER, Hans U. 1982. The Laotian way to socialism—Two steps forward, one step backwards. *AMPO/Japan-Asia Quarterly Review* (Tokyo: Pacific-Asia Resource Center) 14: 1.

MARCH, Kathryn. 1983. Weaving, writing, and gender. Paper presented at Wenner-Gren Symposium, Cloth and the organization of human experience.

MARCUS, Russell. 1970. *English-Lao Lao-English dictionary.* Rutland and Tokyo: Tuttle.

MASPERO, H. 1911. Contribution a l'Étude du système phonétique des langues Thai. *Bulletin de l'École Française d'Extrême-Orient,* Tome 11 (1-2).

MASPERO, Henri. 1981. *Taoism and Chinese religion.* Amherst: University of Massachusetts Press.

MAUSS, Marcel. 1954. *The gift.* Translated by I. Cunnison. New York: W. W. Norton.

MAYOURY, Ngaosyvathn. 1993. *Lao women.* Vientiane: Lao State Publishing Enterprise.

McALISTER, John T. Jr. 1967. Mountain minorities and the Vietminh: A key to the Indochina War. In *Southeast Asian tribes, minorities, and nations,* edited by P. Kunstadter. Princeton: Princeton University Press.

McCOY, Alfred W. 1970. French colonialism in Laos, 1893–1945. In *Laos: War and revolution,* edited by Nina S. Adams and Alfred W. McCoy. New York: Harper and Row.

MEYER, Roland. 1930 *Indochine Francais: Le Laos.* Exposition Coloniale Internationale, Paris 1931, Hanoi: Imprimerie D'Extr?me-Orient.

MILLER, Terry. 1977. *"Kaen" playing and "mawlum" singing in northeast Thailand.* Ph.D. diss., Indiana University.

————. 1985. *Traditional music of the Lao.* Westport, Conn.: Greenwood Press.

MILLS, Mary Beth. 1990. Moving between modernity and tradition: The dilemma of village daughters and their families. Paper presented at Thailand Development Research Institute, Bangkok, 15 November.

————. 1995. Attack of the widow ghosts: Gender, death, and modernity in Northeast Thailand. In *Bewitching women, pious men: Gender and body politics in Southeast Asia,* edited by A. Ong and M. G. Peletz. Berkeley: University of California Press.

————. (n.d.). Between the bright city lights and the family hearth: The dilemma of village daughters working in Bangkok. *Being in Bangkok,* edited by H. Phillips. (Forthcoming).

MINTZ, Sydney W. 1995. Enduring substances, trying theories: The Caribbean region as *Oikoumene*. *Journal of the Royal Anthropological Institute* 2.

MOERMAN, Michael. 1965. Ethnic identification in a complex civilization: Who are the Lue? *American Anthropologist* 67: 1215–1230.

———. 1966. Ban Ping's temple: The center of a "loosely structured" society. In *Anthropological Studies of Theravada Buddhism*, edited by M. Nash. Yale University Southeast Asian Studies Series, no.13.

———. 1969. Western culture and the Thai way of life. In *Man, state and society in contemporary Southeast Asia*, edited by Robert O. Tilman. New York: Praeger Publishers.

MOREV, Lev N., Aleksej A. Moskalev, and Yuri Ya Plam. 1972. *The Lao language.* (Glavnaja Redakcija Vostochnoj Literatury, in Russian). Moscow: Nanka.

MUECKE, Marjorie A. 1984. Make money not babies: Changing status markers of northern Thai women. *Asian Survey* 24 (4).

MULDER, Niels. 1990. *Inside Thai society.* Bangkok: Editions Duang Kamol.

NATIONAL COMMITTEE OF PLAN (LAOS). 1986. *Population Census of 1985.* Vientiane: mimeo.

NEHER, Clark D. 1991. *Southeast Asia in the new international era.* Boulder, Colo.: Westview Press.

NEHER, Clark D., and Ross Marlay. 1995. *Democracy and development in Southeast Asia.* Boulder, Colo.: Westview Press.

NG, Shui Meng. 1991. Social development in the Lao People's Democratic Republic: Problems and prospects. In *Laos: Beyond the revolution*, edited by J. J. Zasloff and L. Unger. Basingstoke: Macmillan.

NGAOSYVATHN, Mayoury. 1990. Individual soul, national identity: The Baçi-sou khwan of the Lao. *Sojourn* 5 (2).

NGAOSYVATHN, P., and M. Ngaosyvathn. 1984. *Conversation Francais-Laotien.* Paris: Institut de l'Asie du Sud-Est.

NIELSEN, Preben. 1994. Transportation network: Current status and future plans. In *Economic development in Lao PDR, horizon 2000*, edited by Chi Do Pham. Vientiane.

NSC. 1995. *Expenditure and consumption survey and social indicator survey. 1992–1993.* Vientiane: Committee for Planning and Cooperation, National Statistical Centre.

O'HARROW, Stephen. 1995. Vietnamese women and Confucianism: Creating spaces from patriarchy. In *"Male" and "female" in developing Southeast Asia*, edited by W. J. Karim, Oxford: Berg Publishers.

ONG, Aihwa, and Michael G Peletz. 1995. Introduction in *Bewitching women, pious men: Gender and body politics in Southeast Asia*, edited by A. Ong and M. G. Peletz. Berkeley: University of California Press.

PALLEGOIX, J. B. 1854. *Dictionarium Lingua Thai,* Paris: Jussu Imperatoris Impressum.

PANTE, Filiologo Jr. 1994. Lao PDR and the Mekong sub-regional development project. In *Economic development in Lao PDR, horizon 2000*, edited by Chi Do Pham. Vientiane.

PARNWELL, Michael J. G., and Daniel A. Arghiros. 1996. Uneven development in Thailand. In *Thailand: Uneven development*, edited by Michael J. G. Parnwell. Aldershot: Avebury.

PASUK Phongpaichit, and Chris Baker. 1995. *Thailand: Economy and politics.* Kuala Lumpur: Oxford University Press.

PELTIER, Anatole R. 1988. *Le Roman classique Lao.* Paris: EFEO.

PENINSULE. 1988. Conventions and traites entre la France et le Siam relatifs au Laos, 1893–1947, no. 16/17.

PETERS, Heather. 1990. Buddhism and ethnicity among the Tai Lue in the Sipsongpanna. In *Proceedings of the Fourth International Conference of Thai Studies,* 11-13 May, Institute of Southeast Asian Studies, Kunming, Yunnan.

PHAM Duc Duong. 1991. The study of Southeast Asian languages: An approach. *Vietnam Social Sciences* 2.

PHILLIPS, Herbert P. 1965. *Thai peasant personality: The patterning of interpersonal behavior in the village of Bang Chan.* Berkeley: University of California Press.

PHOUMI Vongvichit. 1969. *Laos and the victorious struggle of the Lao people against U.S. neo colonialism.* Neo Lao Haksat Publications.

PIETRANTONI, Eric. 1943. *La problème politique du Laos.* Unpublished paper. Vientiane.

PINITH, S. 1987. *Contribution à l'histoire du royaume de Luang Prabang.* Paris: Publications de l'École Française d'Extrême-Orient.

POPULATION CENSUS OF LAOS. 1/3/1995.

PORTER, Gina. 1995. Mobility and inequality in rural Nigeria: The case of off-road communities. Paper presented at the Institute of British Geographers Conference, University of Northumbria at Newcastle, U.K., January.

PREECHA Kuwinpant. 1980. *Marketing in north-central Thailand: A study of socio-economic organisation in a Thai market town.* Bangkok: Social Research Institute, Chulalongkorn University.

PREECHA Phinthong. 1989. *Isan-Thai-English dictionary.* Ubol: Siritham Press (in Thai).

PROSCHAN, Frank. 1997. "We are all Kmhmu, just the same": Ethnonyms, ethnic identities, and ethnic groups. *American Ethnologist* 24 (1).

PURCELL, Victor. 1965. *The Chinese in Southeast Asia.* Oxford: Oxford University Press.

RAJA, Ananda. 1990. Orientalism, commensurability, and the construction of identity: A comment on the notion of Lao identity. *Sojourn* 5 (2).

RATNAM, Kamala. 1983. Socio-cultural and anthropological background of the Ramayana in Laos. In *Asian variations in Ramayana,* edited by S. Iyengar. Madras: Sahitya Akademi. Diocesan Press.

RATNAM, Perala. 1982. *Laos and its culture.* Bangkok: White Lotus.

REINACH, Lucien de. 1911. *Le Laos.* Paris: E. Guilmoto.

REINHORN, Marc. 1970. *Dictionaire Laotien-Francais.* Tomes 1-2. Paris: Centre Nationale de la Recherche Scientifique.

———. 1980. *Grammaire de la langue Lao.* Paris: Institute National des Langues et Civilisations Orientales, Université de la Sorbonne Nouvelle.

REVUE INDO-CHINOISE. 1899. Notice sur le Laos Français. Hanoi: F-H Schneider.

REYNOLDS, Craig. 1976. Buddhist cosmography in Thai history, with special reference to 19th century culture change. *Journal of Asian Studies* 35 (2).

REYNOLDS, Frank E., and Mani B. Reynolds. 1982. *Three worlds according to King Ruang. A Thai Buddhist cosmology.* Berkeley: Asian Humanities Press.

RIGG, Jonathan. 1995. Managing dependency in a reforming economy: The Lao PDR. *Contemporary Southeast Asia* 17 (2).

RIGG, Jonathan, and Randi Jerndal. 1996. Plenty in the context of scarcity: Forest management in Laos. In *Environmental change in South East Asia: People, politics and sustainable development*, edited by Michael J. G. Parnwell and Raymond L. Bryant. London: Routledge.

RLG (Royal Lao Government). 1962. *The national education reform act*. Vientiane: Ministry of Education.

ROBERTS, T. D., Mary Elizabeth Carroll, Irving Kaplan, Jan M Matthews, David S. McMorris, and Charles Townsend. 1967. *Area handbook for Laos*. Washington, D.C.: United States Government Printing Office.

ROCHET, Charles. 1946. *Pays Lao. Le Laos dans la tourmente 1939–1945*. Paris: Jean Vigneau.

ROFFE, G. E., and T. W. Roffe. 1958. *Spoken Lao*. New York: American Council of Learned Societies.

ROOM, Adrian. 1987. *Place names of the world*. U.K.: Angus and Robertson.

ROWLEY, C D. 1960. *The lotus and the dynamo: A traveller in changing South-east Asia*. Sydney: Angus and Robertson.

RUJAYA, Abhakorn and David K. Wyatt. 1995. Administrative reforms and national integration in northern Thailand, 1892–1932. In *Regions and national integration in Thailand 1892–1992*, edited by Volker Grabowsky. Wiesbaden: Harrassowitz Verlag.

SACHS, Wolfgang. 1992. Introduction. In *The development dictionary: A guide to knowledge as power*, edited by Wolfgang Sachs. London: Zed Books.

SAHAI, Sachchidanand. 1976. *The Ramayana in Laos (A study in the Gvay Dvorahbi.* Delhi: P. K. Publishing Corp.

SALEMINK, Oscar. 1994. The return of the python god: Multiple interpretations of a millenarian movement in colonial Vietnam. *History and Anthropology* 8 (1–4).

———. 1995. Primitive partisans: French strategy and the construction of a Montagnard ethnic identity in Indochina. In *Imperial policy and Southeast Asian nationalism 1930–1957*, edited by Hans Antöv and Stein Tønneson. London: Curzon Press.

SARRAUT, Albert. 1930. *Indochine*. Librarie de Paris: Firman-Didot et Compagnie.

SAUTMAN, Barry, ed. (c. 1995) *Racial identities in East Asia*. Hong Kong: Division of Social Science, The Hong Kong University of Science and Technology.

SAYAD, Abdelmalek. 1991. *L'immigration ou les paradoxes de l'altérité*. Paris: Editions Universitaires, Collection L'Homme Etranger.

SCHLESINGER, Arthur M. Jr. 1969. *A thousand days: John F. Kennedy in the White House*. Greenwich, Conn: Fawcett Publications.

SCHROCK, Joann L. et al. 1972. *Minority groups in North Vietnam*. Washington, D.C.: Ethnographic Studies Series, U.S. Government Printing Office.

SCOTT, James C. 1990. *Domination and the arts of resistance: Hidden transcripts*. New Haven: Yale University Press.

SESSER, Stan. 1993. *The lands of charm and cruelty: Travels in Southeast Asia*. Basingstoke: Picador.

SHANIN, Teodor. 1986. Soviet theories of ethnicity: The case of a missing term. *New Left Review*. 158 (July–August).

SILA VIRAVONG, Maha. 1964. *History of Laos*. New York: Paragon Book Reprint Corp.

SILVERMAN, Gary. 1996. Vital and vulnerable. *Far Eastern Economic Review* 23 (May), 60–66.

SIMON, Pierre-Jean. 1993. *Vocabulaire historique et critique des relations interethniques*. Paris: L'Harmattan, Pluriel Recherches, Cahier n°1, année.

SINDZINGRE, Nicole. 1992. L'identitié. *Encyclopedia universalis*. Paris.

SINGHANETRA-RENARD, A. 1981. Mobility in north Thailand: A view from within. In *Population mobility and development: Southeast Asia and the Pacific*, edited by G. W. Jones and H. V. Richter. Canberra: The Australian National University, Development Studies Centre.

SMITH, Anthony D. 1991. *National identity*. London: Penguin Books.

———. 1994. The politics of culture, ethnicity and nationalism. In *Companion encyclopedia of anthropology*, edited by Tim Ingold. London and New York: Routledge.

SOUNETH Photisane, 1996. *The Nidan Khun Burom: Annotated translation and analysis*. Ph.D. thesis, University of Queensland.

STEINBERG, David Joel et al. 1985. *In search of Southeast Asia: A modern history*. Sydney: Allen and Unwin.

STRANGE, Heather. 1981. *Rural Malay women in tradition and transition*. New York: Praeger.

STRECKFUSS, David. 1993. The mixed colonial legacy in Siam: Origins of Thai racialist thought, 1890–1910. In *Autonomous histories, particular truths*, edited by Laurie J. Sears. Madison, Wis.: University of Wisconsin, Center for Southeast Asian Studies, monograph no. 11.

STUART-FOX, Martin. 1986. *Laos—Politics, economics and society*. London: Francis Pinter.

———. 1991. Laos at the crossroads. *Indochina Issues* (March) Washington: Indochina Project.

———. 1993. On the writing of Lao history: Continuities and discontinuities. *Journal of Southeast Asian Studies* 24 (1).

———. 1995a. Laos: Towards sub-regional integration. *Southeast Asian Affairs 1995*. Singapore: Institute of Southeast Asian Studies.

———. 1995b. The French in Laos, 1887–1945. *Modern Asian Studies* 29:1.

———. 1996. *Buddhist kingdom, Marxist state: The making of modern Laos*. Bangkok: White Lotus.

———. 1997. *A history of Laos*. Cambridge: Harvard University Press.

STUART-FOX, Martin, and Mary Kooyman. 1992. *Historical dictionary of Laos*. Metuchen: The Scarecrow Press.

SWANSON, Herbert R. 1990. The historical context of William Clifton Dodd's *The Tai race*. *Thai-Yunnan Project Newsletter* 8.

SWEENEY, Amin. 1980. *Authors and audiences in traditional Malay literature*. Monograph Series no. 20, Center for Southeast Asia Studies. Berkeley: University of California.

———. 1987. *A full hearing: Orality and literacy in the Malay world*. Berkeley: University of California Press.

SZANTON, Maria Cristina Blanc. 1972. *A right to survive: Subsistence marketing in a lowland Philippine town*. University Park: Pennsylvania State University Press.

TAILLARD, Christian. 1989. *Le Laos—Stratégies d'un Etat-tampon*, Montpellier: Reclus.

TAMBIAH, Stanley J. 1970. *Buddhism and the spirit cults in north-east Thailand*. Cambridge: Cambridge University Press.

———. 1985. *Culture, thought, and social action*. Cambridge: Harvard University Press.

——— 1990. *Magic, science, religion, and the scope of rationality*. Cambridge: Cambridge University Press.

TANNENBAUM, Nicola. 1995. *Who can compete against the world? Power-protection and Buddhism in Shan worldview*. Ann Arbor, Mich.: Association for Asian Studies.

TAPP, Nicholas. 1996. The kings who could fly without their heads: "Local" culture in China and the case of the Hmong. *Unity and diversity: Local cultures and identities in China*, edited by Tao Tao Liu and David Faure. Hong Kong: Hong Kong University Press.

TAUPIN, J. 1893/1889. *Vocabulaire Franco-Laotien*. 2me édition. Hanoi-Haiphong.

THOMASON, Sarah Grey, and Terrence Kaufman. 1988. *Language contact, creolisation, and genetic linguistics*. Berkeley and Los Angeles: University of California Press.

THONGCHAI Winichakul. 1994. *Siam mapped: A history of the geo-body of a nation*. Chiang Mai: Silkworm Books; Honolulu: University of Hawaii Press.

TOOKER, Deborah E. 1996. Putting the mandala in its place: A practice-based approach to the spatialization of power on the Southeast Asian "periphery"—The case of the Akha. *Journal of Asian Studies* 55 (2).

TOSSA, Wajuppa. 1990. *Phadaeng nang ai*. Lewisburg, Pa.: Bucknell University Press.

TOYE, Hugh. 1968. *Laos—Buffer state or battleground*. London: Oxford University Press.

TRANKELL, Ing-Britt. 1993. *On the road in Laos: An anthropological study of road construction and rural communities*. Uppsala: Uppsala Research Reports in Cultural Anthropology 12, Uppsala University.

———. 1998. "The minor part of the nation": Politics of ethnicity in Laos. In *Facets of power and its limitations: Political culture in Southeast Asia*, edited by Ing-Britt Trankell and Laura Summers. Uppsala: Uppsala Studies in Cultural Anthropology 24.

TRIBALAT, Michèle. 1996. *De l'immigration à l'assimilation, enquête sur les populations d'origine étrangère en France*. La D?couverte: INED.

TURNER, Terrence. 1980. The social skin. In *Not work alone: A cross-cultural view of activities superfluous to survival*, edited by Jeremy Cherfas. Beverly Hills, Calif.: Sage.

VAJIRANANAVARORASA, Somdet Phra Maha Samana Chao Krom Phraya (2512). *The entrance to the vinaya (Vinayamukha)*. Vols. 1 and 2. Bangkok: King Maha Makuta's Academy.

VIET Chung. 1968. National minorities and nationality policy in the D.R.V. *Vietnamese Studies* 15.

VOTH, David E. 1971. Southeast Asian archives. *Southeast Asia* 1 (4).

WALKER, Andrew. 1995. Borderline sex. Paper read at Conference on Gender and Sexuality in Thailand, July 1995.

————. 1996. Borders, frontier communities and the state: Cross-river boat operators in Chiang Khong, Thailand. *Canberra Anthropology* 19 (2).

————. 1997. *The legend of the golden boat: Regulation, transport and trade in northwestern Laos.* Ph.D. thesis, Department of Anthropology, Research School of Pacific and Asian Studies, Australian National University, Canberra.

WEINER, Annette. 1992. *Inalienable possessions.* Berkeley: University of California Press.

WERNER, Klaus. 1992. *Learning Lao for everybody.* Vientiane: Peter Rump.

WHITAKER, Donald P., Helen A. Barth, Sylvan M. Berman, Judith M. Heimann, John E. MacDonald, Kenneth W. Martindale and Rinn-Sup Shinn. 1972. *Area handbook for Laos, foreign area studies.* Washington, D.C.: American University.

WIJEYEWARDENE, Gehan. 1986. *Place and emotion in northern Thai ritual behaviour.* Bangkok: Pandora.

WOLF, Eric. 1988. Inventing society. *American Ethnologist* 15 (4).

WOLTERS, O. W. 1982. *History, culture, and region in Southeast Asian perspectives.* Singapore: ISEAS.

WOODSIDE, Alexander. 1971. *Vietnam and the Chinese model.* Cambridge: Harvard University Press.

WRIGHT, P. S. 1994. A Lao grammar for language learners. Special edition of *Journal of Language and Linguistics* 13. Bangkok: Thammasat University.

WRIGHT, Pamela. 1995. The timely significance of supernatural mothers or exemplary daughters: The metonymy of identity in history. In *Articulating hidden histories. Exploring the influence of Eric R. Wolf,* edited by Jane Schneider and Rayna Rapp. Berkeley: University of California Press.

WRIGHT, Susan. 1998. The politicization of "culture." *Anthropology Today* 14 (1).

YANG Dao. 1972. Les difficultés du développement Économique et social des populations Hmong du Laos.Thèse de Doctorat de 3e Cycle, Université de Paris.

YANRAKKHIT, Phra. 1900/01. Report of Phra Yanrakkhit, Provincial Education Director, on khana, religion, and education in the northeast monthon. Thai National Archives, Fifth Reign, Ministry for Public Instruction, Series 12/18, folder 2.

YATES, W. G. and S. Sayasithsena. 1970. *Lao basic course.* 2 vols. Washington, D.C.: Foreign Service Institute.

ZASLOFF, Joseph J. 1988. Vietnam and Laos: Master and apprentice. In *Postwar Indochina: Old enemies and new allies,* edited by Joseph J. Zasloff. Washington, D.C.: Foreign Services Institute, US Department of State.

ZASLOFF, Joseph J., and MacAlister Brown. 1991. Laos 1990: Socialism postponed but leadership intact. *Southeast Asian Affairs 1991.* (Singapore: Institute of Southeast Asian Studies.)

LAO

BAUSAENG Kham Vongdala, Buakaew Chaleunlangsi et al., 1987. *Lao Literature,*
Vientiane: Social Science Research Institute. ບໍ່ແສງຄຳ ວົງດາລາ, ບົວແກ້ວ ຈະເລີນລັງສີ,
ວັນນະຄະດີລາວ, ອງງຈັບ: ສະຖາບັນຄົ້ນຄ້ວາວິທະຍາສາດສັງຄົມ.

BOUABANE Vorakhoun (1996b). "Introduction", *Lanxang Heritage Journal,* No.
1:5–6. ບົວບານ ວໍລະຂຸນ, ຄຳນຳ, ມໍລະດົກລ້ານຊ້າງ, ປີທີ 1, ສະບັບທີ 1.

BOUABANE, Vorakhoun (1996a). "The Status of Preservation and Promotion of the
Cultures of Ethnic Minorities in the Lao People's Democratic Republic." Paper
presented at the International Expert Meeting for the Safeguarding and Promotion
of the Intangible Cultural Heritage of the Minority Groups of the Lao People's
Democratic Republic, Vientiane, Lao PDR, 7–11 October 1996.

BOUNLEUTH Sengsoulin. 1995. Opinion. In ICR 1995, 24-44. ບຸນເລີດ ແສງສຸລິນ,
ບົດປະກອບຄຳເຫັນຜາສາລາວ, ໃນ ສ.ຄ.ວ., 1995.

BOUNTHAN Phimmasone. 1995. Opinions on the topic of Lao language policy. In
ICR 1995, 45–55. ບຸນທັນ ຜິມມະສອນ, ບົດປະກອບຄຳເຫັນກ່ຽວກັບນະໂຍບາຍວ່າດ້ວຍ ຜາສາລາວ, ໃນ
ສ.ຄ.ວ., 1995.

BOUNYOK Sensounthone. 1995. A minor opinion. In ICR 1995, 98–100. ບຸນຍົກ ແສນ-
ສຸນທອນ, ຄຳເຫັນເລັກນ້ອຍ, ໃນ ສ.ຄ.ວ., 1995.

BUAKAEW Chaleunlangsi, 1993. *The Lao revolution and Revolutionary Literature,*
Vientiane: Education Publisher (originally printed in Sam Neua, 1972). ບົວແກ້ວ
ຈະເລີນລັງສີ, *ການປະຕິວັດລາວແລະວັນນະຄະຕິປະຕິວັດ,* ອງງຈັບ: ໂຮງພິມສຶກສາ.

CHAN Kanya, (undated) *Laos is for the Lao,* Rochester, New York: Free Lao Publisher.
ຈັນກັນຍາ, *ເມືອງລາວແມ່ນຂອງລາວ,* ສຳນັກພິມເສຣິຊົນ.

DAEN Jaleunsuk, 1993. Some problems about the naming of ethnicities in the LPDR
in the present, *Aloun Mai,* 9–10. ແດນຈະເລີນສຸກ, 1993, ບາງບັນຫາກ່ຽວກັບ ຊື່ຮຽກຂອງເຜົ່າ
ຕ່າງໆໃນ ສ.ປ.ປ. ລາວ ປັດຈຸບັນ, ອາລຸນໃໝ່, 9-10.

DOUANGDEUAN Bounyavong. 1995. Proposal. In ICR 1995, 129–135. ບົດສະເໜີ, ໃນ
ສ.ຄ.ວ., 1995.

Ekasaan, 1997. *General Theoretical and Political Documents,* Propaganda Section of the
central Committee, State Publishing House. *ເອກະສານ ທົດສະດີ-ການເມືອງ ທົ່ວໄປ,*
ຄະນະໂຄສະນາອົບຮົມສູນກາງພັກ, ໂຮງພິມແຫ່ງວັດ.

HAU Samut Haeng Sat, 1970. *Vannapham,* Vientiane. ຫໍສະໝຸດແຫ່ງຊາດ, ວັນນະພາມ, ອງງຈັບ.

HOUMPHANH Rattanavong. (1996 [1990]). "Paper for Round Table for Lao
Language Policy", *Lanxang Heritage Journal,* No. 1. (October 1990), Vientiane.
ຫຸມພັນ ລັດຕະນະວົງ, ບົດລາຍງານວ່າດ້ວຍນະໂຍບາຍຜາສາລາວ, ວາລະສານມໍລະດົກລ້ານຊ້າງ.

ICR (Institute for Cultural Research) 1995. Round Table on Lao Language Policy.
Vientiane: Institute for Cultural Research, Ministry of Information and Culture.
ກອງປະຊຸມໂຕະມົນວິທະຍາສາດກ່ຽວກັບຜາສາລາວ, ອງງຈັບ, ສະຖາບັນຄົ້ນຄ້ວາວັດທະນະທຳ,
ກະຊວງຖະແຫງຂ່າວ ແລະວັດທະນະທຳ.

JALEUN Yiabaoleu, 1995. *Kaysone Phomvihane Concerning the Party's Policies on Ethnic
Groups.* Praka Printers, Vientiane. ຈະເລີນ ເຢຍປາວເຣ, ທ່ານປະທານ ໄກສອນ ພົມວິຫານ ກ່ຽວ
ກັບນະໂຍບາຍຊົນເຜົ່າ ຂອງພັກ, ໂຮງພິມປຣະຊາ(ອງງຈັບ)1995.

KASUANG Seuksa, 1987. *Literature – Udom (level one) First Year,* Vientiane: Joint
Educational Publishing and Distribution. ກະຊວງສຶກສາ, ວັນນະຄະດີ ອຸດົມພີ່ງ, ອງງຈັບ:
ວິສາຫະກິດ ພິມຈຳໜ່າຍສຶກສາ.

KASUANG Thalaeng Khaw Lae Vatthanatham, 1992. *Project to Propose 'The
Preservation of Lao palm Leaf Manuscripts',* (unpublished document), Vientiane.

ກະຊວງກະແຫລງຢ່າງ ແລະວັດທະນະທຳ, ໂຄງການບຳສະເພີປິກປັກຮັກສາຫົວສີໃບລາບລາວ ຕໍ່ລັດກະບານ
ສາທາລະນະລັດ ສະຫະພັນເຢຍລະມັນ, (ບໍ່ໄດ້ຫິຫີນ).

KAYSONE Phomvihane. 1982. Reinforce and expand the basic trust and solidarity
between various ethnic groups in the Lao national family, and strengthen unity.
Resolutely uphold and strengthen the country and build socialism to its
completion. National Printery, Vientiane. ໄກສອນ ພົມວິຫານ, ເສີມຂະຫຍາຍມູນເຊື້ອແຫ່ງ
ຄວາມສາມັກຄີ ລະຫວ່າງເຜົ່າຕ່າງໆ ໃນວົງຄະນາຍາດແຫ່ງຊາດລາວ ທີ່ເປັນເອກະພາບ, ຕັດດຳຮວປິກປັກ
ຮັກສາປະເທດຊາດໄວ້ໃຫ້ໝັ້ນຄົງ ແລະກໍ່ສ້າງສັງຄົມນິຍົມໃຫ້ສຳເລັດຫີນ, ໂຮງພິມແຫ່ງຊາດ 1982.

KHAMDAENG Khommadam and Khamphaeng Thipmountali, *Tourist of Ethnic
Groups in Laos*, Social Sciences Committee, Vientiane. ຄຳແດງ ກົມມະດຳ ແລະ ຄຳແພງ
ທິບມຸນຕຣີ, (1992) ທ່ອງທ່ຽວບັນດາເຜົ່າຢູ່ລາວ, *Tourist of Ethnic Groups in Laos*, ຄະນະ
ກຳມະການວິທະຍາສາດສັງຄົມ, ວຽງຈັນ.

KHAMHOUNG Senmani. 1995. Opinions for the conference on Lao language. In ICR
1995, 162–166. ຄຳຮຸ່ງ ແສນມະນີ, ປະກອບຄຳເຫັນຕໍ່ກອງປະຊຸມສຳມະນາກ່ຽວກັບພາສາລາວ, ໃນ
ສ.ຄ.ວ. 1995.

KHAMMA Phonkaung, 1987. *History and Culture,* Vientiane: State Book Publishing
and Distribution House. ຄຳມາ ພົມກອງ, ປະຫວັດສາດແລະວັດທະນະທຳ, ວຽງຈັນ: ສຳນັກພິມ ແລະ
ຈຳໜ່າຍປຶ້ມແຫ່ງລັດ.

KHAMPHAN Virachith. 1995. Opinion. In ICR 1995, 56–60. ຄຳພັນ ວິລະຈິດ,
ບົດປະກອບຄຳເຫັນ, ໃນ ສ.ຄ.ວ. 1995.

KHAMPHAO Phonekeo. 1995. Contribution. (No title.) In ICR 1995, 14–23. ຄຳເຜົາ
ພອນແກ້ວ, (ບົດປະກອບຄຳເຫັນ), ໃນ ສ.ຄ.ວ.1995.

KONGKHAM Pravongviangkham, 1985. *A Lao Poet Separated From His Homeland:
The Second of December 1975–85, Ten Years of Life's Passage,* Paris: Association for
the Study of Lao Culture and Tradition. ກົງຄຳ ປະວົງວຽງຄຳ, ກະວີລາວພັດກີ່ນ: ສອງທັນວາ
1975-1985 ສິບປີຂອງການຜ່ານຊາດ. Paris: ສະໂມສອນວັດທະນະທຳແລະຄື້ນຄ້າວປະເພນີລາວ.

LAO Hak Sat, 1973. *Kaun Lam Verse Selected From Competition, Fifth collection
(volumes one and two)* Samneua: Lao Patriotic Front Publishing and Distribution
House. ລາວຮັກຊາດ, ກອນລຳກວດສອບຊຸດທີ່ຫ້າ(ເຫລັ້ມໜຶ່ງກັບສອງ), ຊຳເໜືອ: ສຳນັກພິມຈຳໜ່າຍລາວ
ຮັກຊາດ.

LÊ-DUY-LUONG and Blanchard de la Brosse, S. (1926*). Histoire du Laos, Cours
Élémentaire*, Vientiane:Imprimerie Gouvernmentale. ພົງສາວະດານລາວ ຊັ້ນອະອະສານ
ມູນລະສຶກສາ

MAGNIONT, M. (1932). *Manuel de Lecture*, (Cours enfantin), Vientiane: Imprimerie
Gouvernmentale. ແບບສອນອ່ານ, ຊັ້ນຕຶ່ງມສຶກສາພາສາລາວ.

OUTHIN Bounyavong, 1995. Negative developments in Lao language. In ICR 1995,
125–128. ອຸທິນ ບຸນຍາວົງ, ການປ່ຽນແປງໃນທາງລົບຂອງພາສາລາວ, ໃນ ສ.ຄ.ວ., 1995.

OUTHIN Bounyavong, Suban Luangrat, Othong Khaminsou, Duangdeuan
Bounyavong (eds). (1990) The Life and Work of Maha Sila Viravong. Vientiane:
Committee for Social Sciences. ອຸທິນ ບຸນຍາວົງ, ສຸບັນ ຫວງລາດ, ໂຫທອງ ຄຳອິນຊູ, ດວງເດືອນ
ບຸນຍາວົງ, ມະຫາສິລາ ວິຣະວົງ: ຊີວິດແລະຜົນງານ, ວຽງຈັນ.

PCPC (Party Central Propaganda Committee) 1997. *Documents in general political
theory*. Vientiane: Party Central Propaganda Committee. ຄະນະກຳມະການກາງໂຄສະນາ
ສູບກາງພັກ, ເອກະສານ ທິດສະດີການເມືອງທົ່ວໄປ, ວຽງຈັນ: ຄະນະກຳມະການກາງໂຄສະນາສູບກາງພັກ.

PHAU Phuangsaba , et al. 1984 *Hom Kawi Sut Haum Kin Champa*, Samnak Phim Lae
Chamnay Peum, SPPL. ພ. ພວງສະບາ, ໂຮມກະວີຊຸດຫອມກິ່ບຈຳປາ, ສຳນັກພິມແລະຈຳໜ່າຍປຶ້ມ,
ສ.ປ.ປ.ລ.

PHOMMA Phimmasone, 1990. *The fate of the Lao Nation According to Prophecy,* Quebec: Les Presses De Champa Muong Lao. ພິມມະ ພິມມະສອນ, ຄວງຊາຕາຊາດລາວ ຈາກຄຳທຳນາຍ.

PHOUMI Vongvichit (1967). *Lao Grammar.* Sam Neua: Central Education Department. (2nd edition, 1991) ໄວຍາກອນລາວ, ຟູມີ ພົມໝື່ອ: ກົມການສຶກສາສູນກາງ.

RLG (Royal Lao Government) 1972. *Lao Grammar.* (4 vols) Vientiane: Lao Royal Academy, Ministry of Education. ໄວຍາກອນລາວ, (4 ຫຼຸ້ມ), ອຈຈັບ: ລາຊະບັນດິຕະສະພາ, ກະຊວງສຶກສາທິການ.

SAU Desa, 1993. *Revealing (the meaning of) 'San Leup Bau Sun',* Vientiane: State Publishing and Distribution House. ສ. ເດຊາ, ເຜີຍສາບລັບບໍ່ສູນ, ອຈຈັບ: ສຳນັກພິມແລະ ຈຳໜ່າຍປື້ມແຫ່ງລັດ.

SAU Desa, 1996. *To Turn Over the Earth and Rotate the Sky,* Vientiane: State Publishing and Distribution House. ສ. ເດຊາ, ພິກແຜ່ນປື້ມແຜ່ນຟ້າ, ອຈຈັບ: ສຳນັກພິມ ແລະຈຳໜ່າຍປື້ມແຫ່ງລັດ.

SILA Viravong, (1935). *Grammaire Laotien,* Vientiane. ສິລາ ວິຣະວົງ, ໄວຍາກອນລາວ, ອຈຈັບ.

SILA Viravong, (1962). *Lao Language Dictionary,* Laos: Comité Littéraire. _. ສິລາ ວິຣະວົງ, ວັດຈະນາບຸກິມພາສາລາວ, ອຈຈັບ: ກອງວັນນະຄະດີ.

SILA Viravong, 1961. *Lao Grammar,* Part Four: Versification, Vientiane: Literature Committee. ສິລາ ວິຣະວົງ, ໄວຍາກອນລາວ, ພາກສີ່: ສັບທະລັກສະນະ, ອຈຈັບ: ຄະນະກຳມະການ ວັນນະຄະດີ.

SILA Viravong, 1993. *Methods of Composition of the Poetry of the Vientiane Thai and Kap San Vilasini,* Vientiane: Phai Nam (originally published in Bangkok in 1942). ສິລາ ວິຣະວົງ, ແບບ ແຕ່ງກອນໄທວຽງຈັບແລະແຕ່ງກາບວິລາສີນີ, ອຈຈັບ: ໄຜ່ໜາມ.

SILA Viravong, 1996. *The Benefit of Literature,* Vientiane: Phai Nam (originally published in 1960). ສິລາ ວິຣະວົງ, ປະໂຫຍດຂອງວັນນະຄະດີ, ອຈຈັບ: ໄຜ່ໜາມ.

SILA VIRAVONG, 1996 [1938]. *Pali Grammar: Orthography.* Vientiane: Lao Ministry of Information and Culture/ French Ministry of Foreign Affairs. ສິລາ ວິຣະວົງ, ບາລີ ໄວຍາກອນ: ອັກຂລະວິທີ, ອຈຈັບ: ກະຊວງຖະແຫຼງຂ່າວ ແລະວັດທະນະທຳ.

SILA VIRAVONG, (1996). *Viceroy Phetsarath,* Vientiane: Phainam Publisher. ສິລາ ວິຣະວົງ, ເຈົ້າມະຫາອຸປະຮາດ ເພັດຊະຮາດ, ອຈຈັບ: ໄຜ່ໜາມການພິມ.

SISAVEUY Suvanny. 1996. Linguistic Problems. In *Lanxang Heritage Journal.* No. 1, 1996, 85–101. ສີສະເຫວີຍ ສຸວັນນີ, ບັນຫາກ່ຽວກັບພາສາສາດ, ວາລະສານມໍລະດົກລ້ານຊ້າງ.

SOM Phraxaignamongkun, 1996. Some Lao "savoir vivre". In *Lanxang Heritage Journal.* No. 1, 1996, 144–152. ໂສມ ພະໄຊຍະມຸງຄຸນ, ມາລະຍາດພື້ນຖານບາງຢ່າງຂອງຄົນລາວ, ວາລະສາບມໍລະດົກລ້ານຊ້າງ.

SOUKSAVANG Simana 1995. Lao language and orthography, and their connection with the languages and cultures of various minorities. In ICR 1995, 83–89. ສຸກສະຫວ່າງ ສິມະນະ, ພາສາລາວແລະຕົວອັກສອນລາວຕໍ່ກັບພາສາແລະວັດທະນະທຳຂອງຊົນເຜົ່າຕ່າງໆ, ໃນ ສ.ຄ.ວ., 1995.

SOUVANTHONE Bouphanuvong. 1995. What is language? In ICR 1995, 117–118. ສຸວັນທອນ ບຸພານຸວົງ, ພາສາແມ່ນຫຍັງ? ໃນ ສ.ຄ.ວ., 1995.

TAY Keoluangkhot. 1995. Proposal. In ICR 1995, 167–170. ໄຕ ແກ້ວຫຼວງໂຄດ, ຄຳສະເໜີ, ໃນ ສ.ຄ.ວ., 1995.

THONGKHAM Onmanisone & Souvan Thilavong. 1997. *Lao language: words and their meanings.* Vientiane: Department of Literature and Culture. ທອງຄຳ ອ່ອນມະ-ນີສອນ, ວັດຈະນາບຸກິມ ພາສາລາວ, ອຈຈັບ: ມູນນິທິໂຕໂຍຕາ.

THONGKHAM Onmanisone (1992). *Lao Language Dictionary,* Vientiane: Toyota Foundation. ທອງຄຳ ອ່ອນມະນີສອນ, ວັດຈະນາບຸກິມ ພາສາລາວ, ອຈຈັບ: ມູນນິທິໂຕໂຍຕາ.

THONGKHIEN Khamtakoun and Boualy Manithip (1990). "Historical and cultural relations between the Zhuang ethnic group and the Lao and Thai people, according to the spoken language", ທອງຂຽນ ຄຳຕະກຸນ ແລະ ບົວລີ ມະນິທິບ, ຈາກພາສາຄວາມ ເວົ້າມາພິສູດ ເຖິງຄວາມສັມພັນ ທາງດ້ານປວັດສາດວັທນະທັມ ລະຫວ່າງເຜົ່າ ຈວງ ຂອງ ກ/ອງສີ ກັບ ຊົນຊາດລາວແລະຊົນຊາດໄທ, *Peninsule*, Numero 21.

THONGPHET Kingsada (1996). "How should we research and utilise the Lao language?" *Vientiane Mai*, Vientiane, 17–19 June. ທອງເພັດ ກິ່ງສະດາ, ຄັນຄ້ວາແລະບຳໃຊ້ ພາສາລາວແນວໃດ?, ວຽງຈັນໃໝ່.

THONGPHET Kingsada. 1995. The problem of the letter "r" in Lao. In ICR 1995, 103–116. ທອງເພັດ ກິ່ງສະດາ, ບັນຫາຕົວ "ຣ" ໃນພາສາລາວ, ໃນ ສ.ຄ.ວ., 1995.

VMGO (Vientiane Municipality Governor's Office) 1997. Agreements of the Vientiane Municipality Governor, No. 1270/VMG, 19 December 1997; Concerning the administration and monitoring of cultural activities in the Vientiane municipality.) Vientiane: Vientiane Municipality Governor's Office. ຂໍ້ຕົກລົງຂອງເຈົ້າຄອງກຳແພງນະຄອນວຽງຈັນ, ເລກທີ 1270/ ຈນ.ກພ, 19.12.97, ວ່າດ້ວຍການຄຸ້ມຄອງ ແລະກວດກາ ການເຄື່ອນໄຫວວັທນະບະທຳ ໃນກຳແພງ ນະຄອນວຽງຈັນ.

VIETNAMESE

Lê Cu' Nâm, (1990) Dôi nét vê cu' dân và su' phân bô dân tôc hiên nay ô Công hoà Dân chu Nhân dân Lào, *Tap chí Dân tôc hoc*, No. 1. (Some features about the location and division of ethnic groups in the People's Democratic Republic of Laos at present).

Nguyên Duy Thiêu (1996) *Cáu Trúc Tôc Nguòi O' Lào, Ethnic Structure of Laos*, Nhà Xuât Khoa Hoc Xã Hôi.

Nguyên Hõai Nguyên (1970). *Survey of ethnic minorities in northern provinces of Lao: Phongsaly, Luang Namtha and Oudomxay*. (Roneo in Vietnamese). Diêu tra các dân tôc o' các tính phía bac Lào: Phông Saly, Luang Nam Tha vã Udomxay. (Ban Viêt Tay).

THAI

DUANGMON Jitjamnong, 1997. *The value and Significant Characteristics of Thai Literature in the early Rattanokosin Period (Khun Kha Lae Laksana Den Khaung Wannakhadi Thaiy Samay Rattanakosin Taun Ton)*, Bangkok: Samnak Phim Mahawithayalay Thammasat. ดวงมน จิตรจำนงค์, คุณคาและลักษณะเด่นของ วรรณคดีไทยสมัยรัตนโกสินทร์ตอนต้น, กรุงเทพ: สำนักพิมพ์มหาวิทยาลัยธรรมศาสตร์.

JARUBUT Reuangsuwan, 1977. *Treasures of Isan (Khaung Di Isan)*, Bangkok: Rong Phim Kan Sasana 1977. จารุบุตร เรืองสุวรรณ, ของดีอิสาน, กรุงเทพ: โรงพิมพ์การศาสนา, 1977.

JARUWAN Thammawat, 1979. *The Characteristics of Isan Literature (Laksana Wannakam Isan)*, Bangkok: Jintaphan Kan Phim 1979. จารุวรรณ ธรรมวัฒน์, ลักษณะวรรณกรรมอิสาน, กรุงเทพ: จินตพรรณการพิมพ์, 1979.

JARUWAN Thammawat, 1996. *Regional Literature: The Case of Isan-Lan Xang* (*Wannakam Thaung Thin Karani Isan Lan Sang)*, Maha Sarakham: Mahawithayalay Maha Sarakham 1996. จารุวรรณ ธรรมวัฒน์, *วรรณกรรมท้องถิ่น-อิสานลานซ้าง*, มหาสารคาม: มหาวิทยาลัยมหาสารคาม, 1996.

JIT Phumisak, 1981. *Ongkan Chaeng Nam and New Thoughts Concerning the History of the Thai of the Jao Phraya River Basin, (Ongkan Chaeng Nam Lae Khau Khit Mai Nai Prawatsat Thaiy Lum Mae Nam Jaw Phraya)*, Bangkok: Duang Kamon 1981. จิตร ภูมิศักดิ์, *โองการแช่งน้ำและข้อคิดใหม่ในประวัติศาสตร์ไทยลุ่มน้ำเจ้าพระยา*, กรุงเทพ: ดวงกมล, 1981.

KROM Silapakaun, 1989. *The City of Ubon Ratchathani (Meuang Ubon Ratchathani)*, Bangkok: Baurisat Aumarin Printing Group Jamkat 1989.

PHAU Phuangsaba, 1984. *Hom Kawi Sut Haum Kin Champa*, Samnak Phim Lae Chamnay Peum, SPPL.

PRAKHAUNG Nimmanhemin, 1987. *The Epic Thaw Ba Jeuang (Mahakap Thaw Ba Jeuang)*, Bankok: Khana Asksaunsat Chulalongkorn Mahawithayalay (doctoral dissertation) 1987. ประคอง นิมมานเหมินทร์, *มหากาพย์ท้าวบาเจื่อง*, กรุงเทพ: คณะอักษรศาสตร์ จุฬาลงกรณ์มหาวิทยาลัย, 1987. กรมศิลปากร, *เมืองอุบลราชธานี*, กรุงเทพ: บริษัทอมรินทร์พริ้นติ้งกรุพ จำกัด, 1989.

SAMNAK Ngan Khana Kammakan Wattanatham Haeng Chat, 1989. *Local Culture: The Case of Isan (Wattanatham Pheun Ban: Karani Isan)*, Bangkok: Borisat Amarin Printing Group Jamkat 1989. สำนักงานคณะกรรมการวัฒนธรรมแห่งชาติ, *วัฒนธรรมพื้นบ้าน: กรณีอีสาน*, กรุงเทพ: บริษัทอมรินทร์พริ้นติ้งกรุพ จำกัด, 1989.

THAWAT Punnothok, 1979. *Isan Literature (Wannakam Isan)*, Bangkok: Odian Store 1979. ธวัช ปุณโณทก, *วรรณกรรมอิสาน*, กรุงเทพ: โอเดียนสโตร์, 1979.

WIT Thiangburanathum, 1984. *Thai-English Dictionary (Phojananukrom Thaiy – Angrit)*, Bangkok: Baurisat Ruam San Jamkat 1984. วิทย์ เที่ยงบูรณธรรม, *พจนานุกรมไทย-อังกฤษ*, กรุงเทพ: บริษัทรวมสาสน จำกัด, 1984.